THE ABSURD AND THE BRAVE

CORB — The true account of the British Government's World War II evacuation of children overseas.

THE ABSURD AND THE BRAVE

*CORB — The true
account of the British Government's
World War II evacuation
of children overseas.*

Michael Fethney

The Book Guild Ltd
Sussex, England

To kind and brave folk who care for children.

The Book Guild Ltd.
25 High Street,
Lewes, Sussex

First published 1990
© Michael Fethney 1990
New edition 2000

Set in Baskerville
Typesetting by Hawks Phototypesetters Ltd.,
Copthorne, West Sussex.
Printed in Great Britain by
Antony Rowe Ltd.,
Chippenham, Wiltshire.

British Library Cataloguing in Publication Data
Fethney, Michael
    The absurd and the brave : CORB — the true account of the government's World War II evacuation of children overseas.
    1. Great Britain. Children. Evacuation, 1939–1945
    I. Title
    940.53'161'0941

ISBN 1 85776 556 7

CONTENTS

LIST OF ILLUSTRATIONS

FOREWORD

The wartime initials CORB have not passed down into the history books like ENSA or UNRRA, other wartime initials that have. Behind CORB, however, is a fascinating story that Michael Fethney, a CORB boy himself, memorably narrated in *The Absurd and the Brave*.

The Children's Overseas Reception Board, devised in the early summer of 1940 by Sir Geoffrey Shakespeare, Parliamentary Under Secretary to the Dominions, was controversial at the start. And its subsequent history had many controversial features too. It raised more issues than the evacuation of children inside Britain which has been well covered by historians.

The Absurd and the Brave is not an autobiography, which the author might well have written. Instead, it is a rounded social history, capturing individual experiences, but at the same time providing general perspectives. It is the kind of history that should appeal to a wide audience of readers, including those for whom it will be distant history. The social history of the Second World War has recently received as much attention as the military and the political. From it we can learn much both about ourselves and, more particularly, about how we have seen and still see ourselves. This highly readable study of CORB is central to any such understanding, and I am glad to know that it is being reprinted in time for the Diamond (and final) Reunion of the South African CORB children together with others taking place in other parts of the world this year.

Asa Briggs
February 2000

ACKNOWLEDGEMENTS

My thanks must go to the late Sir Geoffrey Shakespeare, and to his secretary, Kitty O'Shea, for their help in the earliest stages of my research into the CORB story; as also to Sir Leonard Allinson, then Permanent Secretary to the Foreign Office, and Ms Ann Morton, then Assistant Keeper in the Search Department at the Public Record Office, Kew, who both steered me towards relevant documents, particularly the Dominions Office 'CORB files' when they first went to Kew in January, 1981; and to ex-CORB evacuee Mrs Pat Weekley, who put me in touch with my first big 'catch' of other former evacuees.

I have to thank many people associated with CORB in various ways: former evacuees, their hosts abroad, their escorts, their parents, whose names are listed under Other Sources at the end of the book. But I mention here my special thanks to several people who have not only answered my questions, but also extended generous hospitality to me: Mr and Mrs Bob Bullard, who kindly gave me a copy of the book *Prison Life on a Pacific Raider*, long out of print, as well as entertaining me in their Ashford home; Mrs Margaret Cross, who showed my wife Bath and had us both to stay with her, whilst I perused the private papers of her sister, a former CORB escort who was sunk by Pacific Raiders, the late Eleanor Pearson; Mrs Elspeth Davies, CORB's Welfare Director throughout the operation of the scheme, who gave me invaluable information and opinions, as well as lunch, whilst we talked about CORB for several hours in her London apartment; Mrs G E E Porteus, of St Jude's Vicarage, Hampstead-on-the-Hill, who led me to the 'City of Benares' mural in St Jude's Church, and provided tea before I rejoined the A1, northbound; and Mr Marian Slabosz, former Assistant Purser aboard *MS Batory*, and his wife Nessie, who entertained me and my son Jeremy, for a whole day, treating the antics of our tape-recorder with great good humour.

I am also grateful to the following for particularly kind help: Miss Kyrsty Page, CORB's liaison officer in New Zealand, who stayed with us, and talked to me about CORB, during a hectic UK visit she made from New Zealand in 1982; Mrs Ada Lowes and Mrs Gwen Staynes who spent a whole day with me in 1983, talking about evacuee life in New Zealand, whilst Mrs Staynes was making a lightning visit to the UK owing to the illness of a relative; Mrs Maureen Jepson for bringing her late husband's CORB papers relating to his evacuation to South Africa all the way from Portsmouth to Harrogate; Mr G A Coombes of the Records Department at the Boy Scout Association Head-quarters, and Miss Cynthia Forbes, Archivist to the Girl Guides' Association; the Rev O R Fulljames, former Chaplain, 9th Destroyer Flotilla; my former schoolmaster colleague, Lt Cdr John Sherwood, RNR, for his meticulous chart work when I was researching CORB ships in convoys; and the many Newspaper Editors in Britain, Australia, Canada, South Africa and New Zealand, who gave space to my appeals for information, and to Mr E Darbyshire, of Victoria, who contacted several Australian newspapers for me. My thanks to Copyprint, Harrogate, for much help at typescript stage, and to Wrightson's Photographers, Knaresborough.

I am greatly indebted, too, to Mrs Kath Roberts, my indefatigable secretary whilst I was Head at Abbey Grange C of E High School, Leeds, for her enthusiastic and practical help with correspondence, and in organizing a filing system for me during the early stages of my research; to my older daughter Joanna and my niece Ann for their work in completing my compilation of the full list of CORB escorts and the CORB children from PRO records.

I record gratefully that Crown-copyright material in the Public Record Office is reproduced by permission of the Controller of Her Majesty's Stationery Office, as also is material from RM Titmuss's *Problems of Social Policy* and T O'Brien's *Civil Defence* in Professor Hancock's *History of the Second World War*, and the facsimiles of government-issued documents supplied to me by former evacuees, their parents and their overseas hosts.

In addition, I am grateful to the following for their kind permission to include copyright material:

Faber and Faber, from *America: Lost and Found*, by Anthony Bailey; Hamish Hamilton Ltd., *1940: The World in Flames*, by R Collier; Cassell, *The Second World War, Volume II: Their Finest Hour* by W S Churchill; Mrs Elspeth Huxley, author of *Atlantic Ordeal*, published by Chatto and Windus; Methuen, *The Cambridge Evacuation Survey*, edited by Susan Isaacs; Pennyfarthing Publications and Mr D E Johnson, author of *Exodus of Children*; Century Hutchinson, *Pilgrim Children*, by Jean Lorimer, originally published by Frederick Muller Ltd; Routledge, *Evacuation Survey*, by Padley and Cole, originally published by Routledge, Kegan and Paul; Macdonald and Co, *Let Candles be brought in*, by Geoffrey Shakespeare; John Murray, *Borrowed Children*, by Mrs St Leo Strachey; Weidenfeld and Nicolson, *Children of the Empire*, by Gillian Wagner; Hodder and Stoughton, *Prison Life on a Pacific Raider*, by Geraldine Edge and Betsy Sandbach; A K Muggenthaler, author of *German Raiders of World War II*, published by Robert Hale, Ltd; the Editors of '*The Times*', '*The Guardian*', '*The Yorkshire Evening Post*', the Bradford '*Telegraph and Argus*' and '*Yorkshire Observer*', the South Shields '*Northern Press*', *Times of Ceylon*, the '*Sydney Morning Herald*', the *Australian Government Publishing Service*, and '*The New Zealand Herald*'.

I am also very indebted to the following for kindly supplying illustrative material in their possession:

Betty Atkins; Colin Crafer; Barbara Fethney; John Fethney; Joan Flewers; Dennis Furnish; Joyce Hazeldon; Margaret Heald; Rita Jackson; Barbara Morley; Ruth Morton; Bet Osbaldiston; Edith Penwarden; Mary Smith; and to the following for their assistance in my search — not always successful — for holders of copyright: The Australian Attorney-General's Department; Chatto and Windus and the Hogarth Press; Robert Hale Ltd; Hodder and Stoughton Ltd; the US Embassy in London; Victor Gollancz Ltd.; the

US Copyright Office and the Library of Congress, Washington.

If I have incorrectly acknowledged or breached anyone's copyright, despite my efforts to get things right, I apologize to the holder, and will take steps to rectify the error in any subsequent edition of this book.

To Margaret, my wife, I give special thanks for her patient encouragement since I began the project in 1979 — not least when I fretted whilst illness kept me away from working at it; and, more recently, for reading the entire text, making many valuable suggestions, as well as helping with numerous mundane, time-consuming tasks on the manuscript. My thanks to her again, and to our children, Joanna, Jeremy, and especially Jackie, for accepting my need for 'time off' in order to research, to ponder and to write.

Lastly, my thanks, too, to The Book Guild staff, particularly Carol Biss and Douglas Quiggan, for their help in preparing both text and illustrations for publication, and, not least, in performing wonders by reproducing from faded photocopies of fading documents, newspaper clippings and snap-shots — (including those taken by my brother John with his box camera bought for 2s/6d in 1939) — results which could never hope to be 'perfect', but which surpass my most optimistic expectations.

INTRODUCTION
Making the CORB Story

This book is about the work of the Children's Overseas Reception Board, whose organizers deliberately chose a title that would shorten to one convenient word. Hence, 'Corb' to start with, soon written as 'CORB'.

The British Government set up CORB in June, 1940, to plan the evacuation of children abroad, 'Seavacuees', as they were briefly known. Bits of that story have been told here and there. But, despite references to CORB in a few recent works about evacuation generally, the best account to date is still the summary given by Sir Geoffrey Shakespeare in one chapter of his memoirs, *Let Candles be Brought in*, published in 1949. However, his account is not only short, it is also one-sided in its appraisal of the scheme. He was, after all, Parliamentary Under-Secretary to the Dominions in 1940, and planner and first Chairman of CORB. The scheme was his baby.

So, this book attempts to tell the 'whole' story; that is, not only to ask what happened, but why; and to investigate some long term effects the CORB scheme has had on people originally involved in it. Thus, the personal recollections and observations of former evacuees, their parents, their overseas hosts, their adult escorts, and others who helped administer the scheme, play as important a part in this book as the documentary sources.

Whether one sees CORB as an absurd scheme, hopelessly confused in its intention; or as a ridiculously ambitious plan aimed at denuding Britain of vast numbers of her children; or, as some did see it, merely as a political sop to the British working class; or, as others insisted on seeing it, as an important aspect of Civil Defence policy when Britain stood alone against the threat of Nazi invasion; or as part of British policy to woo the USA to fight against Nazism; or, as it was to most of the CORB children themselves at the time, simply a rather unusual if, at times, frightening adventure — the story of CORB is still worth telling.

As with the scheme itself, the picture that emerges of the knock-on effects is very varied. For some families, the effects are scarcely noticeable: the CORB years were a phase soon over in terms of an average life-time. For others, the CORB years were also an interlude, but produced effects that have been beneficial in the long term for some, and painfully bad for others. There are some, parents as well as ex-evacuees, who regard the CORB years as the most significant years in their lives, though for totally different reasons. For some, they were idyllic years, providing the springboard for happy, successful lives in the ensuing years. For others, they were utterly miserable years, bringing permanent estrangement, divided loyalties and, let us not forget, for some families, the death of children who might well have lived to old age had they remained at home, for all the threat of blitz and invasion.

In this connection, although I name at the end of my book those who kindly provided me with a wealth of information, opinions, and feelings about CORB, I must pay special tribute to them, here and now, at the beginning. Many suffered pain simply in contacting me, and even more in answering my questionnaires. Just a few excerpts from letters sent to me with answered questionnaires illustrate the mixed feelings still felt by former CORB children, not to mention their parents.

'Your questionnaire,' writes one, 'certainly stirred up a number of memories, many of which, I suspect, had been intentionally buried, and dealing with your questions helped put a better perspective on them. As a mother myself, I'm humbled by the sacrifices made by our parents, in order that our lives should be made safe . . . Our mother missed vital years and was unable to even be our friend for a long time after our return.'

Another admitted, 'It has taken me three months to finish answering your questions. I am in tears again as I dredge my memory.' And another, 'I have mixed feelings about the publishing of your results. I don't tell many people I was an evacuee. You can change my name if you wish.'

An appreciable minority of those who contacted me requested anonymity only to avoid any hurt to parents or hosts. Like the one who says, 'Do write to my aunt; but PLEASE don't mention I was unhappy or unduly homesick. It would be hurtful now, and I have much more understanding of her difficulties now.'

One torpedoed on the way to 'safety' hints at much, long-term distress. 'I have a problem with loss of voice. No physical cause; it is primarily due to stress . . . and it has occurred again this week.' She had just completed my questionnaire on CORB.

But there were those who wrote with enthusiasm, too, like the one who said, 'It was a wonderful time of my life. I really grew up out there and would have stayed if anything had happened to my parents.'

There simply was not room in one book to include all the material sent to me. But, I thank all for their response, especially where it brought back painful memories, or reminded them of constant ill effects. And my thanks to them all, as well, for the reminder they give throughout this story that it is not just a strange slice of social history, with rather quirky political undertones and overtones, but a story about real people, most of them very sensitive human beings, whose lives have been touched by CORB, for better or worse.

The fact that my brother and I were CORB boys in Australia is irrelevant to this book, apart from keeping alive my long-held intention to write the whole story one day. More relevant, or perhaps more significant, is the fact that my sister opted not to avail herself of the CORB scheme and risked losing two brothers, and that my mother answered the first sheet of my questionnaire for CORB parents, and felt she could tackle no more.

But, I have not aimed to write an autobiography. Where my CORB past affects my opinions of events and people I make no apology. I would still hold the basic view, even if I had not been a CORB boy, that the enterprise was a typical example of our British talent for behaving very absurdly, yet being very brave, at one and the same time. And this is why folk all over the world can laugh at us, but envy us and love us, all at the same time.

In a letter written in August, 1980, the late Sir Geoffrey Shakespeare, planner and first Chairman of CORB, told me: 'I am so glad you intend to write the romantic story of the CORB scheme . . . When you have finished I will write a short preface for you, if you desire it.' Alas, he died the following week. Whether he would still have wished to introduce my book, had he lived, I am not sure, because this book does not tell so much a romantic story as a story of sorrow, human error, and absurdity — though also of inspiration, dedication, bravery and great human kindness. But, I should have been proud for Sir Geoffrey, a man of integrity and deep humanity, to have written his piece had he still been willing. In the event, I am equally proud and grateful that Lord Briggs, historian, and Provost of the College where my love of history was much enhanced, has kindly undertaken the Foreword.

I

SEEDS

A former CORB evacuee, looking back on the CORB scheme after more than forty years, says this: 'I don't think we could have parted with our own daughter to go so far away from home. My parents must have been less selfish, and worried about the future in Britain, and hoped to give us a better chance in Australia.'

Another, evacuated by CORB to New Zealand when a girl of twelve, states: 'My main memory is that I had no love after I said goodbye to my parents in Edinburgh, as no-one really loves you, only your parents and relatives.'

What did drive parents to part with their children? Britain was not occupied by the Nazis like the rest of Western Europe, and not yet even subject to large-scale bombing, when CORB started. How could parents let children face the perils of an ocean voyage in wartime in seeking safety overseas? What about the inherent risks they took of causing permanent psychological damage to their children, and the lottery of trusting them to the care of total strangers or, quite often, of half-willing relatives and acquaintances?

Perhaps more difficult: why was the British Government prepared to plan and run such a hazardous undertaking?

Lots of questions. Yet, these are not the only ones that need to be asked. Before the answers to these questions become clear, it will be necessary to examine two others: First, what led Britain to accept the need for large-scale evacuation of civilians on the outbreak of war? Second, how, if at all, did the notion of overseas evacuation fit into the scheme of things?

Now for some answers.

Heavy emphasis on civilian evacuation was an integral part of British Government defence policy for many years before the outbreak of the Second World War; and such a policy, steered by the Imperial Defence Committee from 1921 onwards, was thrust at the British public throughout the 1930s.

The reasons for this were simple: from the moment the First World War ended, the Imperial Defence Committee assumed that any future war with Germany would produce air-raids on an horrific scale. Each year, the Committee produced up-dated estimates of the tonnage of bombs that would fall on British cities within twenty four hours of a war starting. These estimates escalated alarmingly — even absurdly — as the carrying capacity and range of bomber planes increased. Thus, as early as 1924, the Government appointed a special defence sub-committee to investigate ways of evacuating densely populated parts of the country in the event of war.[1]

Later, during the 1930s, ordinary British citizens read for themselves in newspapers, and heard on the wireless, about the devastating damage and human suffering caused by bomber raids. A succession of wars in Manchuria, China, Abyssinia and Spain, demonstrated that modern war tactics relied heavily on the use of bomber planes against 'open' cities, with large civilian casualties as a result.

During these same years, a handful of British politicians warned that long-range bombers would place Britain's civilians in the front line in any future war. Therefore, the need to plan for the evacuation of large numbers of civilians became a major priority. Not only that, successive governments assumed that civil evacuation was an essential, unavoidable part of defence policy. Without it, they believed, refugees would constitute such a huge problem that the defence of Britain might well prove totally impossible.

Hence, for example, in the autumn of 1934, Winston Churchill warned in the House of Commons that 'under the pressure of continuous air attack on London, at least three

---

[1] This, and all subsequent notes, appear on pp (270-280).

or four million people would be driven out into the open country'.[2] So, common sense seemed to dictate the need to plan orderly evacuation of large sections of the population to avoid having refugees to contend with.

Then, in May, 1938, Sir John Anderson, already a distinguished civil servant, was appointed by the Home Office to chair the evacuation planning sub-committee of the Imperial Defence Committee. Shortly afterwards, he became a Cabinet member as Lord Privy Seal, the first 'modern' civil servant to receive such a distinction. This move indicated the Government's view of the seriousness of mass evacuation in future defence planning; and it also gave Sir John the opportunity to keep evacuation matters to the fore in top level Cabinet discussions about future war.

During the weeks ahead, with the co-operation of most Local Authorities throughout the land, Sir John's evacuation sub-committee planned for the mass evacuation of all civilians not involved in essential war work in Britain's major cities. His now famous report of July, 1938, warned that the efficiency of Britain's civil evacuation could well be the most crucial issue to the outcome of any future war.

This explains why, on the 1 September, 1939, when war with Germany looked imminent, a mass civilian evacuation began. Much has been written about this evacuation. Suffice to point out here, therefore, that in three days a million and a half civilians were moved by local authorities from densely populated areas of Britain, and over two million other people arranged private evacuation in the two months before Neville Chamberlain declared war.[3]

These figures show how successfully Government propaganda indoctrinated the British public into accepting the need for evacuation. Many families clearly considered that separation was preferable to allowing their children to experience the horrors of heavy bombing which, they had been educated to believe, would shortly pour from the skies.

Nevertheless, acceptance of the need for mass evacuation and a commitment to that policy, by no means explain the emergence of a Government-sponsored overseas evacuation scheme. Moreover, in all the official preparations for evacuation in the event of war, whether at national or local level, there is no mention at all of a possible overseas evacuation scheme.

As far as officialdom is concerned, the impression given is that, even when war did at last break out, the idea of sending children to safety abroad had yet to be born. Even the official documents revealing how CORB came into being in June, 1940, add to this impression, for they contain no reference to any earlier thoughts about the possibility of overseas evacuation.

And yet, although hitherto unpublished, there had been some thought on the subject. In fact, the rather scatty notion of a children's overseas evacuation scheme goes back to the beginning of 1939. In January, Miss Evelyn Mitchell, a resident of Southern Rhodesia and daughter of a former Premier of the colony, wrote to the Governor outlining a plan to evacuate two hundred children from danger zones in England to safety in Southern Rhodesia. Her aim was to place these children on farms in the country, and she had already contacted two hundred families willing to take part in such a venture.[4]

The Governor wrote that he thought the plan 'very good, if it should prove feasible'. Thus encouraged, Miss Mitchell wrote in February to the British Prime Minister, Neville Chamberlain, describing her plan in some detail.

Her letter quickly went to Mr W C Hankinson in the Migration Section of the Dominions Office. He had serious doubts about such a plan 'being in any way practicable', and wrote that 'it would clearly be impossible to hope to move children simply on the threat of war.' Worse still, he thought that to move them just as a war was starting, 'apart from the difficulties of arranging transport at such a time, would expose them to other risks on the seas.'

When Mr Hankinson consulted colleagues in the Ministry of Health, they agreed with his misgivings. As a result, Miss Mitchell's file was marked 'Idea good-hearted, but impracticable.' Mr Chamberlain's Secretary wrote politely to Miss Mitchell saying that the practical difficulties made the scheme impossible.

Impracticable or not, just over twelve months later these same two government departments, the Dominions Office and the Ministry of Health, took the lead in the planning of the CORB scheme, and proved that the strange dream of a colonial lady was possible after all. And, perhaps it is to hide embarrassment that the remaining CORB records include no mention of Miss Mitchell's original overseas plan, nor of other suggestions made well before the establishment of CORB in June, 1940. For whilst Miss Mitchell was the very first to float the idea, there were other noises being made on the subject before the outbreak of war.

For instance, in mid-July, 1939, Mr Chamberlain received a letter drawing his attention to the possibilities of overseas evacuation from Mrs Marjorie Brightman, wife of an English Congregational Minister. She enclosed press cuttings from Canada suggesting that other Canadian provinces would probably follow the example of the Ontario Government and offer homes to children from Britain in the event of war. The Ontario authorities, said Mrs Brightman, were prepared to find homes for children and give support to host families, as 'an aid to Britain's home defence problem.'[5]

Mrs Brightman's letter travelled the same route through Whitehall, and received virtually the same reply from Mr Syers, the Prime Minister's Secretary, as Miss Mitchell's had done.

But, at the same time as the Dominions Office was dismissing Mrs Brightman's suggestion, Miss Grace Ord wrote from Toronto to Mr Malcolm MacDonald, the Colonial Secretary, acquainting him with the work of the Voluntary Register of Canadian Women, of which she was the National Secretary. She explained that one of its main objectives was to tabulate those Canadian homes that would be available 'to take in the British population under sixteen and over sixty' if war were to break out in Britain. She claimed that the British authorities were well aware that their chances of protecting London in the event of war were 'very slight', whereas effective and large-scale overseas evacuation could be organized using the same ships that would have to supply Britain with North American troops, food and equipment. Furthermore, she argued, those people evacuated would relieve the strain on food supplies, reduce the danger of malnutrition, and be safe from the psychological strain of war.[6]

Whilst Miss Ord's strongly argued proposals made the usual rounds among civil servants, her ideas were receiving supportive publicity in the Canadian press. There was mention of the 'duty' Canadians owed to British children. There were reminders, too, that Canadians were only being asked to do for Britain what the British had been generously doing for Spanish refugees ever since the outbreak of their Civil War in 1936.

Interest grew rapidly on both sides of the Atlantic, and several London Sunday papers gave generous space to the subject. On the 1 August, 1939, there were questions in the House of Commons seeking to know the British Government's attitude; and, for a brief period, it seemed possible that evacuation to Canada might become part of official Government policy, perhaps even be part of the scheme scheduled to begin as soon as the outbreak of war was certain.

However, this was not to be. The antagonism aroused by the confrontation tactics of the Voluntary Register of Canadian Women militated against the evacuation proposals receiving official acceptance. Most important of all, Miss Ord's aggression had made her an enemy of Mr MacKenzie King, the Canadian Prime Minister. Hence, when the British Secretary of State for the Dominions answered the questions about an overseas scheme in the House of Commons on the 1 August, he said that 'the difficulties would be insuperable.' And, next day, the Canadian Prime Minister quoted him with relief.[7]

Apart from the obvious problems of planning such a scheme, an overseas evacuation on the large scale proposed in Canada could have appeared an over-nervous reaction to Hitler's threats against Poland, and even seem defeatist just when the Government was urging the British public to brace itself for the onset of war. But, the fact remains, many British parents now had the possibility of overseas evacuation planted in their minds by the publicity given to Miss Ord and the proposals from Ontario; and several thousand British families did evacuate their children privately overseas, mainly to Canada, during the next three months.

Within two months of war actually breaking out, three more suggested overseas schemes cropped up, although they received little publicity compared with the Canadian idea.[8] The three concerned Australia, Eire and New Zealand; and the New Zealand proposal gave rise to some important thinking on the concept of overseas schemes.

The proposal came to the Dominions Office via the UK High Commissioner in New Zealand, and was unique in suggesting that 'the children of "well-to-do" parents might be sent.' When Mr R A Wiseman of the Dominions Office wrote back to the High Commissioner in December, 1939, he took the opportunity of summarizing present British policy towards the whole subject of evacuation, both at home and overseas.[9] Having pointed out that neither the Canadian Federal nor Provincial Governments 'were giving such a scheme any consideration', he mentioned the more recent rejection of an Australian proposal concerning orphans, and a general scheme from Eire. Both had foundered, he explained, because parents in Britain were already reacting strongly against the mass evacuation that had taken place within Britain the previous September.

Mr Wiseman went on to conclude that the fundamental reason for rejecting any overseas evacuation scheme was that 'the question of evacuation is not really a pressing one here at the moment. In fact,' he ended, 'the position is very much the reverse. I do not imagine, therefore that any suggestion is likely to be put forward at present by New Zealand.'[10]

There is no doubt whatsoever that Mr Wiseman was correct in declaring evacuation unfashionable in December, 1939. The drift of evacuees homewards from the reception areas all over Britain during October had become a steady flood by November. And there were enough horror stories circulating about under-organized reception, vindictive hosts, badly behaved and dirty evacuees, and aggressive parents, to fill many large volumes.

However, one significant group could have disagreed with Mr Wiseman's conclusions. This was the sizeable section of middle class parents who were sufficiently well off to make private arrangement for members of their families to leave Britain for safer places abroad. Writing after the war, Professor R M Titmuss calculated that the number of children evacuated overseas privately in 1939-40 was probably between 11,000 and 13,500.[11]

But, for the majority of parents Mr Wiseman's assessment of the lack of interest is wholly apt. Yet, as we have seen, the concept of internal evacuation had not only been popular as war approached, it was also regarded as essential. And we have also seen that this attitude stemmed from deliberate Government policy adopted since the end of the First World War.

So, we still have to tackle the questions: how could British parents come to part with their children, and ask for them to be sent abroad with all the physical and psychological risks involved? Why, too, was the British Government to plan such a scheme?

In addition, we have now to discover why, having lost all interest in any form of evacuation by the end of 1939, did parents adopt the CORB project the following summer? And why, having resisted and shelved every suggestion of an overseas scheme, did the Government itself swing round to plan one?

2

BIRTH

'If I could, I would not have any of my children taken away until I found out exactly where they were going and who was taking them ... I think in some cases evacuation was not carried out properly. When I learned the truth about all that happened to my children in Canada, I vowed evacuation would never happen to any members of my family.'

So writes a Durham mother, widowed in 1934, who decided to send her two sons and daughter abroad on the CORB scheme. True, she writes after more than forty years' hindsight. True, also, parents of other CORB evacuees can write in happier terms about their experience. But, in trying to analyse why parents supported the CORB scheme, and how they managed to part with their children, we need to bear in mind that, potentially, all parents who applied to CORB could have ended up with the same sad conclusion that it was a terrible mistake.

The change of attitude in the public and the Government hangs entirely on two factors: the rapid and unnerving changes in the war situation after April 1940, and the mounting hostility towards the continuing, private middle class overseas evacuation, seen increasingly as an undesirable privilege. The strength of feeling against this privileged action is illustrated by the Countess of Bessborough offering her resignation from CORB's Advisory Council, of which she was a founder member, because she was conscious of the antagonism caused by her arranging the private evacuation of her child overseas. Other members of the Council dissuaded her from leaving, on the grounds that at least she had not accompanied the child, whereas many well off mothers were accompanying theirs.[1]

The drift overseas also underlined the urgency of the war situation in some minds. As one CORB mother says: 'Only having one child I was very concerned for her safety, and when I read in the paper that quite a number of prominent people wanted their children overseas, I thought it must be very serious.' She applied for her seven year old daughter to go to Australia with CORB.

With the occupation of Denmark, Norway, Belgium and Holland, and the collapse of France imminent, the so-called 'Phoney War' was decidedly over. To add to the mounting apprehension in Britain, newspapers described through April and May how Nazi bombers were attacking civilian refugees as they sought to leave the war zones.

On the British side of the Channel and North Sea, the Government suddenly recognized that some supposedly 'safe' reception areas in East Anglia, Kent and Sussex for evacuees from urban areas were now part of the front line, both for aerial attack and the feared invasion from France and Belgium. And the fear of bombing and invasion was not confined to the Government, as a look at Mass Observation reports, contemporary newspapers, and personal diaries confirm.

Thus, from mid-May to the end of July, the Ministry of Health ran a second phase evacuation of about 213,000 children, unaccompanied by their parents, to safer regions of the British Isles.

Amidst this anxious atmosphere, many families in Britain received pressing invitations from friends and relatives overseas to join them. Certainly, fear of the immediate future led some to think more earnestly about the possibility of overseas evacuation. As one fourteen year old Edinburgh boy says, 'My parents discussed it and felt it was a good opportunity for one of the family to get away from a Britain threatened by invasion.' So, some families, if they could afford it, made hasty, private arrangements to send their children abroad, sometimes accompanied by their mothers. The most popular destinations were Canada and the USA simply because they were relatively nearer, served by more frequent shipping, and cheaper to reach than anywhere else that was deemed safe.

But, very rapidly, the whole issue took on an 'official' complexion. On the 29 May, the Secretary of State for Dominion Affairs, Lord Inskip, was asked in Parliament 'whether he would approach the Canadian Government and other Dominion governments to see whether children and others willing to go could be evacuated to places of safety.' Next day, Mr Robert Gilson, MP, noted his intention to ask the Under-Secretary of State for Dominion Affairs, Mr Geoffrey Shakespeare, MP, 'what steps he had taken with regard to evacuating children from the United Kingdom to Canada and Australia.'

Two days elapsed. Then, on the 1 June, the British press first announced that official invitations had now come from four Dominion Governments to send evacuees from Britain. *The Times* report stressed that, as heavy bombing would be a likely prospect before very long, it was desirable that full advantage be taken of 'the generous offers of hospitality.'

The Times account stated that Senator H S Foll, Australian Federal Minister for the Interior, was volunteering Australia's help in caring for British children 'for the duration of the war.' Also raising the question of receiving war orphans from Britain, Holland and Belgium, he acknowledged that shipping 'would constitute the main problem', but claimed that, if the scheme could develop, it would be recognized by the world as 'one of the most humanitarian ever undertaken.' Australia hoped that 'many thousands of British and refugee children would be able to avail themselves of the opportunity.' Finally, Senator Foll revealed that he was prepared to open his home 'for two boys.'[2]

So, be it noted, the concept of a large scale scheme was again in evidence as it was in Miss Ord's suggestions just before war broke out.

The story from Canada was very similar to the Australian version. Mr Crerar, the Federal Minister for Mines and Resources, and also responsible for immigration, said that most of the Provincial Governments had already supported the idea of 'offering sanctuary to European refugees on a generous scale', and the Provincial Government in Quebec had taken the first practical steps already, by offering to

Fig 1.
*Children in
air-raid shelter
during air-raid
in 1940 — one
reason for the
CORB scheme.*

Australian Government
Publishing Service

take immediately one thousand French and Belgian refugee
children.

The Mayor of Napier in New Zealand, supported by
thirty other compatriot mayors, was urging the New
Zealand Government to offer hospitality and, 'if necessary,
permanent adoption' in private homes to twenty-five
thousand British children. Such a large figure added, once
again, to the rapidly growing illusion that there could be a
speedy mass exodus of children from Britain.

There were two cautionary slants in the South African
report, namely, the view that an evacuation scheme would
'present racial difficulties', and — an intriguing suggestion
— 'the question of potential spies had to be considered.'
But, in spite of these reservations in official South African
circles, many families in the Dominion were ready to
'adopt' British children for the duration of the war.[3]

It fell to Mr Geoffrey Shakespeare, the Dominions Under-Secretary in Mr Churchill's newly re-shuffled Government, to answer MPs who asked what British policy would be towards these offers. From that point onwards, Geoffrey Shakespeare became the key figure in the establishment of CORB and its subsequent operations.

Now aged forty-six Mr Shakespeare was the son of a noted Baptist minister in Norwich, the city he represented in Parliament from 1929 to 1945. He had stronger gifts than he would have cared to acknowledge. A former President of the Cambridge Union, he was basically a kind, sensitive, and modest man, thoroughly conscientious and enthusiastic about anything he undertook. He had genuine sympathies for the under-privileged; and was a patriot and keen supporter of the British Empire in the paternalist tradition.

Like many gifted men, he probably chose the wrong career. In retirement, he mused with typical good humour on whether he should have been a journalist, or should possibly have emigrated to Rhodesia or South Africa 'where enterprise and industry are more regarded and rewarded.'[4]

Be that as it may, it was Geoffrey Shakespeare's lot to answer questions in the Commons, and make the first authoritative statement on the Government's policy towards evacuation of children to the Dominions since the war began.

At first, he admits himself, he was against the idea, and questioned 'the morality of dispensing greater safety to a selected few', or the wisdom of 'pandering to the weaker elements in the community'. He thought the Government 'should not encourage people to run away from the gathering dangers. Nor should it lead the rout by fostering evacuation.'

Moreover, he was also worried about the possible psychological and emotional harm that could come to families if separated to the degree that an overseas evacuation scheme was bound to entail. He even argued that the evacuation scheme within Britain had 'already gone to the limits of prudence' in the extent to which it had disrupted family life.[5] This last objection shows that Mr Shakespeare held similar views to those expressed in Evacuation Surveys already emerging in 1940. These

Surveys listed the serious ill effects, both to children and their parents, that had resulted from the evacuation scheme carried out in September, 1939.

In other words, Mr Shakespeare was clearly aware of the strong case against promoting an overseas evacuation scheme. Nevertheless, despite the strength of his own arguments against such a scheme, Geoffrey Shakespeare hastily and totally revised his opinions.

Amazingly, less than two weeks after changing his mind he was presenting to the War Cabinet detailed plans for a Government-sponsored overseas evacuation scheme for children. And henceforth, he never deviated from the rightness of his decision. Had he retained any doubts at all, it is certain that the CORB scheme would never have got off the ground, so much did it owe to his personal and unswerving zeal.

Mr Shakespeare later revealed that his astonishing change of mind was influenced by Mr Alec Beechman, a fellow Liberal-National MP, who was his Parliamentary Secretary. Discussing the matter together, the two men concluded that, as England 'was rapidly coming under siege' it was sensible 'to get rid of the weaker members of the fortress — the old and the young.' Mr Shakespeare admitted that his long-standing interest in migration and 'the redistribution of population within the Empire' made him look on a possible overseas evacuation scheme 'as a twin blessing.'[6] His confusion of evacuation with emigration continued, but his own civil servants and full-time CORB workers avoided the same trap, insisting always, that CORB was about evacuation alone.[7]

Following the official offers of hospitality from the four Dominions on the 31 May, it became urgent for the British Government to act, and to be seen to act. The result was that Lord Inskip, Secretary of State for the Dominions, and Mr Malcolm MacDonald, now Minister of Health, together asked Mr Shakespeare immediately to convene and chair a Government Committee 'to inquire into the feasibility of the scheme.'[8] With Mr Shakespeare now so strongly supporting the idea, and the Dominions Governments pressing for such a scheme to start on a grand scale, the question of 'feasibility' was a foregone conclusion.

Invitations went at once to twelve different Government departments to appoint representatives to this Committee, an action showing great foresight on Geoffrey Shakespeare's part. If an overseas evacuation scheme were to succeed, it would require the expertise and co-operation of many different sections of government.

This Inter-departmental Committee first assembled on the 7 June, 1940, in the Conference Room at the Dominions Office. It consisted of the Parliamentary Secretaries to the Ministry of Health and the Board of Education, and seventeen civil servants representing the twelve invited Departments.[9] A notable, and eventually disastrous omission, was the Admiralty.

The Committee members were deeply conscious that their existence as a Committee could be construed, in the eyes of the public, as panic action on the part of the Government. They agreed, therefore, that they must avoid giving the impression that Britain was so afraid and so defenceless that she was 'prepared to ship off her children to the Dominions.' Such an impression, they recorded, could have 'grave effects on the rest of the world,' and damage British hopes of continuing the war against the Nazis.

The Committee also dreaded the response that might come from an anxious general public to any overseas evacuation scheme they produced. Events proved they were right to be apprehensive: the clamorous welcome their plan actually did receive illustrates that. But, no-one foresaw just how dangerously popular the scheme would rapidly become, nor the political storms it would generate.

Meantime, Mr George Kimber of the Dominions Office, whom Mr Shakespeare appointed Committee Secretary, was lucky to start his new duties on time. A week before the Committee first met, he had asked for leave of absence 'for urgent private business.' Next weekend, he sailed his yacht to Dunkirk and back, together with thousands of other amateur sailors, helping to rescue men of the British Expeditionary Force from the beaches — a relevant reminder to his fellow Committee members of the background to their work.

In his opening remarks at the first meeting of the Inter-departmental Committee, Mr Shakespeare made clear that their brief was limited to making recommendations about the offers from overseas 'to house and care for children, whether accompanied or unaccompanied, from the European war zone residing in Britain, including children orphaned by the war.'

The Committee set to work with tremendous zest, showing extraordinary talent, both for planning in depth and in detail. Indeed, their achievements were nothing short of spectacular. Following their initial meeting on the 7 June, they met again in full Committee six times in the next ten days, and the last two of these meetings took place after the detailed CORB plan had already been put to the War Cabinet. Sittings were sometimes so lengthy that they virtually ran into the next session, from one day to the next. Yet, the plans were so thorough that they became, almost wholesale, the final shape of the CORB operation, both at home and abroad.[10]

Writing after the war, Geoffrey Shakespeare claimed[11] that his Committee achieved more in less than two weeks than a similar committee might have managed in three months in peace time: possibly a very modest appraisal. By the 15 June, only eight days after the Committee first met, Mr Kimber already had a full report prepared for the Cabinet members to peruse.

Just two days later, when the War Cabinet met to discuss the report,[12] there was a large attendance, including the Prime Minister, the First Lord of the Admiralty, and the Chief of the Imperial General Staff. Mr Shakespeare was in attendance by invitation to deal with any points of detail. The Home Secretary, Sir John Anderson, went straight to the point. If the Cabinet approved the scheme detailed in the report, he said, then he proposed that the plan 'be brought into operation forthwith.'[13]

Nevertheless, there was quite considerable discussion. Mr Arthur Greenwood, Minister without Portfolio, for instance, said it would be 'repugnant' to many people to think of families being so drastically split up; but, he went on, if Britain were 'to become "an island fortress" it would be desirable to have fewer mouths to feed.'[14] This image of a 'beleaguered Britain', and the attraction of reducing food problems by overseas evacuation, had captured the imagin-

INTER-DEPARTMENTAL COMMITTEE

ON THE

RECEPTION OF CHILDREN
OVERSEAS

REPORT

*Presented by the Secretary of State for Dominion Affairs, and the
Minister of Health, to Parliament by Command of His Majesty
June, 1940*

LONDON
PRINTED AND PUBLISHED BY HIS MAJESTY'S STATIONERY OFFICE
To be purchased directly from H.M. STATIONERY OFFICE at the following addresses:
York House, Kingsway, London, W.C.2; 120 George Street, Edinburgh 2;
26 York Street, Manchester 1; 1 St. Andrew's Crescent, Cardiff;
80 Chichester Street, Belfast;
or through any bookseller

1940
Price   net

Cmd.

FIG 1a: — *Facsimile of Cmd 6213. The British Government's Inter-departmental
Committee condensed three months' work into one week. Its Report formed the basis of
CORB.*

ation of the press, and continued to do so for about another month. Winston Churchill detested the notion, but he did not take the opportunity to refute Mr Greenwood's statements. In fact, it seems likely that he was paying very little attention to the discussion at all, in view of statements he was to make later about the events of that morning.

Just before 1 pm, very abruptly, discussion about overseas evacuation ceased. A messenger dashed into the Cabinet room with a note for the Prime Minister. Moments later, Mr Churchill solemnly announced to his colleagues the gravest news: the French Army had ceased fire at 12.40 pm. Requested to give any additional detail he could, the messenger paraphrased Marshal Pétain's speech broadcast on the wireless a few minutes earlier. He concluded with the Marshal's own words: 'It is with a heavy heart that I tell you today that fighting must cease.'

Obviously, discussion about overseas evacuation had to move aside at once. As Geoffrey Shakespeare wrote later: 'All interest in the evacuation of children was eclipsed by the stark magnitude of this momentous event.'[15] Britain was now in the last ditch.

Immediately and tactfully, Mr Shakespeare withdrew from the Cabinet, leaving his senior colleagues to concentrate on more urgent matters of war strategy. He describes the scene as he left: 'Winston Churchill was now only present in the sense that his body was sunk in the Prime Minister's chair. His spirit was far away — soaring over the battlefields of France . . .'[16]

Having left the meeting in this way, Mr Shakespeare felt considerable doubts about the Prime Minister's commitment to the plan. Had the Cabinet pursued the matter as far as it wished? Had there been any decision, tacit or otherwise, to proceed with the plan? He was almost certain the answer to both questions was 'No'.

However, next day, having consulted the Cabinet minutes, Mr Shakespeare discovered that the Cabinet's approval of the scheme had indeed been minuted. The records show these entries for the 17 June, 1940:

'(a) approved the recommendations of the Inter-departmental Committee as set out in the report circulated . . .'

'(b) agreed the scheme be announced in answer to a

Parliamentary question the following Wednesday; after that, the Committee report be published . . .'[17]

But, the Cabinet records then proceed to minute that it was only and precisely *after* these two decisions were taken that the Prime Minister received the message about the French cease-fire, thus ending consideration of the CORB scheme. Yet, this clearly could not possibly have been the order of events. If it were, why ever should Geoffrey Shakespeare have left the meeting wondering about the fate of the CORB plan? He records himself that he was still present when the news about France was announced in Cabinet, but left in grave doubts about the future of the scheme.[18]

Obviously, the decision to go ahead with the CORB scheme must have rested with the Cabinet Secretary, rather than on a Cabinet vote. This means that CORB and the Government's overseas evacuation scheme owed its existence to the personal initiative of a senior civil servant who boldly, for better or worse, minuted a decision that had not actually been made and which Winston Churchill was soon to make clear he deplored.[19]

As far as Geoffrey Shakespeare was concerned, the Cabinet minute was sufficient approval. He set to work with instant gusto to implement the full recommendations of the Inter-departmental report.

And, on Wednesday, 19 June, as 'agreed' in Cabinet, Mr Clement Attlee, Lord President of the Council, put the Shakespeare report to the House of Commons, informing MPs that the Government had already accepted the report's recommendations, and that CORB was therefore to be set up at once, with Geoffrey Shakespeare as its first chairman.

The favourable response that greeted Mr Attlee's announcement in the Commons was nothing compared with the rapturous reception given to it by the press and public at large. Of course, the decision came as no surprise to anyone. Since the first mention of the Dominions' offers to care for large numbers of evacuees, hardly a day passed without speculation about a possible Government scheme to take up the offers, and the newspapers regularly reported increases in the numbers of families overseas offering places.[20]

These press reports kept the overseas evacuation issue alive. They appeared alongside the daily progress reports on the evacuation of the British Expeditionary Force, stories of fifth columnist arrests, the imminence of a Nazi blitz on British cities, and the likelihood of a Nazi invasion involving parachute troops and landings of Nazi forces on British beaches. These pressures created their own political impetus. By the time Mr Attlee put the CORB plan to the House, there was such a mood of expectancy about an overseas evacuation scheme, as an escape route for the defenceless, that it would have been very difficult to hedge the issue.

The hope that a scheme would emerge, added to the insistence and generosity of the Dominions' invitations, and also the anxiety and downright fear caused by the deteriorating war situation, all explain why the British Government felt constrained to go ahead with such a potentially dangerous scheme. The same mixture of enthusiasm, hope and anxiety explains why ordinary British parents were prepared in their thousands to part with their children.

Thus, in very short time, the British Government and people, together with the four Dominion Governments and their people, were to turn a 'good-hearted, but impracticable'[21] concept into a hazardous reality. But the going was to be far from smooth.

3

CORB OPENS FOR BUSINESS

It was well into the early hours of Thursday, 20 June, before final preparations for opening the CORB scheme ended at the newly acquired CORB Headquarters. Geoffrey Shakespeare records that he 'went to bed at last, exhausted.'[1]

During the previous three days, he had worked almost without ceasing, only snatching the odd hour's sleep before starting work each morning. There had been Circular 1515 to compose, sent off in the greatest secrecy on the 17 June to all Education Authorities and independent school governing bodies in Britain, giving them contingency guidelines for a possible Government overseas evacuation scheme.[2] A 'possible' scheme, because this was the very day when the Shakespeare Committee report was on the Agenda for the War Cabinet, and it might just have come to nought.

Also on that day, Mr Shakespeare held a long meeting with all four Dominion High Commissioners.[3] He eventually let them depart when he was sure that they would give the scheme high priority, get the full assistance of their staff to draw up more detailed contingency plans, and appoint a panel of Dominion doctors who would standardize medical tests for intending evacuees.

By the next day, Tuesday, 18 June, Mr Shakespeare had successfully appointed the nucleus of his Children's Overseas Reception Board, a mixture of civil servants and people of note and experience in public life, 'all possessing considerable administrative experience.'[4] During that same afternoon, Mr Shakespeare sent out urgent messages to thirty voluntary societies 'with interests in migration or children's welfare' to send representatives to a meeting to be held at 10 am next day in the Conference Room at the Dominions Office.

Lord Snell agreed to chair this meeting, whose main purpose was to form a CORB Advisory Council to oversee and support the executive work of the Reception Board. Lord Snell, like the other senior appointments to CORB, was to prove an excellent choice.[5]

Next morning, which was the day on which Clement Attlee would present the CORB plan to Parliament, there was almost total representation of the thirty societies Mr Shakespeare had contacted, with thirty two people attending the inaugural meeting of the Advisory Council. Almost all of them remained to give many months' valuable service to the CORB scheme, quite voluntarily, of course, and in no way put off by Geoffrey Shakespeare's warning that they 'would have to be available day and night' in the early stages of CORB's work.

Striking whilst the iron was hot, Lord Snell asked at this inaugural meeting for the immediate formation of two sub-committees, one to consider all matters relating to the transportation of children, embarkation on ships, and the selection of children's escorts and medical staff for CORB ships; the other to investigate financial aspects of the scheme, liaison between the British and Dominion Governments, and the reception and care arrangements after arrival of evacuees in the Dominions.

In the meantime, Mr Shakespeare had left Lord Snell to run the new Council, and hurried to CORB Headquarters in the former Thomas Cook's premises at 45, Berkeley Street, W1.

That these premises were available testifies to Geoffrey Shakespeare's determination to get the CORB venture off the ground. One day, shortly after forming his Inter-departmental Committee, he ran into Mr Stanley Adams, Chairman of Thomas Cook's. Mr Adams asked Mr Shakespeare if he knew of a government department that might make use of the building that Cook's were vacating on the corner of Berkeley and Stratton Streets. Mr Shakespeare said 'Yes', but added that he could not divulge which department it would be.

So, late to bed or not, it was barely 8 o'clock on the opening morning, the 20 June, 1940, when Geoffrey Shakespeare arrived at CORB's offices in Berkeley Street, the rest of the staff having instructions to arrive at 9 am. He noted with satisfaction, en route, that the intended announcements about the establishment of CORB were in the morning papers. Because those parents whose children attended independent schools had to make direct enquiries at CORB Headquarters, Mr Shakespeare had arranged for a group of women, led by Mrs Thelma Cazalet MP, and including Mrs Vera Brittain, a writer and Mr Shakespeare's cousin, to interview these parents at Berkeley Street and provide any information about the scheme they might require.

By 9 am, opening time, pandemonium reigned. Fortunately, the telephones in the building were still cut off. This meant that the CORB staff only had to contend with enquiries made in person, and could not be distracted by telephone calls. Even so, they were overwhelmed and shocked by the astonishing flood of personal enquiries.

By 10 am there was a crowd estimated at three thousand people waiting in a queue several hundred yards long. Once the doors opened for business, every single bit of space inside was packed with parents and other relatives, all anxiously seeking further information about the scheme, or waiting to be interviewed, and some of them clamoured about the delay in being attended to.

Just before 10 o'clock, the members of the newly appointed CORB Advisory Council began to arrive for their first 'official' meeting, in order to hear reports from two overnight sub-committees.[6] They had to resort to elbowing their way through the crowd, receiving abuse from those in the queue who thought they were jumping ahead of their turn. The members of the Overseas Reception Board, who had also intended holding their first full meeting in Headquarters that morning, admitted defeat and adjourned their meeting, in order to help with interviews and distribute information amongst the surging mass of clients.[7]

From its inception, Mr Shakespeare's Inter-departmental

Committee had feared the public reaction that an overseas evacuation plan might cause. Now their fears were realized. No-one had dreamt of the deep anxiety, the near panic response that would greet the CORB staff on that opening day. After all, the people queuing at Headquarters represented only a tiny proportion of British families, namely, those who could afford private education for their children. The rest, as informed by the morning's newspapers, had to apply to CORB through their Local Education Authorities or maintained school Head Teachers.

Faced by this alarming pressure, the Headquarters staff nevertheless stood their ground. 'Out of chaos grew, not order, but less chaos,' wrote Geoffrey Shakespeare. 'The machine creaked, groaned, spluttered and almost stopped — but, somehow, went on revolving.'[8]

During that incredible day, the queue continued to lengthen outside. Police had to marshal the crowd down Berkeley Street. At times, members of the queue became impatient, and even antagonistic; whilst inside, Board members, volunteer helpers, and clerks alike battled bravely against the tidal wave of enquirers, working non-stop until well into the evening. Not until 8 pm did the administration begin to assume some shape. But, unfortunately, by this time the day's mail also began to arrive like a torrent, in specially despatched mail vans. At once, there were many thousands more applications and enquiries to see to.

Miss Marjorie Maxse, CORB's first Director, described the applications received that first day as 'an avalanche impossible to keep pace with and beyond even a large staff to cope with.'[9]

Although it took only three days to sort out the overall administration at Headquarters — a magnificent achievement after such an unnerving and panicky start — the backlog of mail remained a major problem for several more weeks. This was despite having a night shift operative, and despite the fact that CORB's clerical staff expanded drastically from thirty on the opening day to a phenomenal total of six hundred and twenty men and women less than a month later.

By that time, the first CORB party had set sail for Canada. Indeed, the time taken from the day the Dominion

Governments invited Britain to send children overseas, up to the departure of the first CORB sailing from Liverpool, was exactly six weeks. A remarkable achievement by a country standing alone, and trying desperately to rally its resources to continue resistance against the enemy.

CORB's course was to get rougher during the month ahead.

4

SUCCESS — OR 'DEFEATISM'?

'I am perturbed at these most recent developments.' The War Cabinet listened as Mr Churchill growled his misgivings about CORB.

It was Friday, 21 June. CORB had only been open for business for twenty four hours. The public's response smacked of panic, and it angered the Prime Minister. 'It is one thing to allow a limited number of children to be sent to North America,' he continued, reprovingly, 'but the idea of a large-scale evacuation stands on a different footing.'[1]

Without doubt, the unforeseen extent of popularity for the overseas evacuation organized by central government was threatening to swamp CORB's hastily assembled resources. Much more serious, however, was that the fervour of the response horrified members of the Government, and most of all the Prime Minister himself.

Warned by 'a high Treasury authority'[2] that senior Cabinet colleagues were wary of the overseas evacuation concept, and that he must tread very delicately when the scheme opened, Geoffrey Shakespeare had made a full statement to the press on CORB's opening day, and spoken against the notion of a large-scale overseas evacuation scheme. 'Any idea of mass migration is absolutely contrary to the wishes of the Governments concerned,' he said. 'For scores of thousands of children to be transferred in a few weeks, as suggested in some quarters, is outside the bounds of any practical scheme and would be an extremely dangerous process.'[3]

Treading equally delicately, Mr Shakespeare did not remind the public of recent press reports announcing that the Dominions were ready to offer homes to scores of thousands of children, and it was only three weeks since the first official offers reached Britain. Neither did he — nor anyone else, for that matter, at this early stage — say exactly what the point of the Government scheme was, if it was not to be available to large numbers of children.

Bemused and confused for their part, the War Cabinet decided, just the day after CORB opened, to adopt a cooling policy aimed at 'damping down' the hysterical response to the scheme. Thus, the Cabinet asked the Minister for Information, Mr Duff Cooper, to prepare an appropriate statement indicating that the Government did not seek to obstruct the scheme, but felt obliged to underline the risks involved, the transport difficulties, and the need to accept that only small numbers of children could ever hope to join the scheme.[4]

In fact, Mr Shakespeare found himself having to compile the damping down speech, and arranged with the BBC to broadcast it on radio the following Sunday, keeping to a limit of five hundred words set by the BBC.

During his speech, broadcast at 1 pm on Sunday, 23 June, Mr Shakespeare tried to balance the attractions of the CORB scheme with his orders to allay the threatened stampede by the public. But, even as he warned of the huge risks involved, he allowed hints of adventure, excitement and challenge to creep into his message.[5]

True, having rebuked those people who were talking of sending 'hundreds of thousands of children overseas in the space of a few weeks', describing such speculation as 'both dangerous and stupid', he warned his listeners: 'This is not a mass migration, but a plan to send overseas as many children as we can, subject to the limitations of shipping and offers made by each Dominion.'

Then, Mr Shakespeare's intense enthusiasm for the scheme broke through. 'It is surely inspiring,' he claimed, 'that lovers of freedom, far removed from the war zone, are so concerned about the safety of our children. Many parents will want to send their children to homes overseas . . . and this will be made possible under our scheme.'

Trying to be fair, Mr Shakespeare insisted that parents alone could decide the right action for their own children, and stressed the dangers that would face the children at sea, whether from aircraft, submarine, or mine. Parents had to weigh these hazards against the hazards of remaining in Britain and being exposed to invasion and air-raids, he said.

But, Mr Shakespeare ended his supposed 'damping down' speech with what could be interpreted as a defiant touch, telling parents, perhaps, to ignore the risks and the anxiety of separation. 'If you decide to take advantage of the benefits of this scheme,' he said earnestly, 'I know there will be much burning of heart at the thought of parting, but parents will not allow themselves to be influenced by these considerations where the safety of their children is concerned. You will ask me, how long will the parting be? The answer is: our children will come back to us when we have secured the final victory, as inevitably we shall.'

Brave words. So, it is hardly surprising that Geoffrey Shakespeare's broadcast did nothing to reduce the overseas evacuation fever amongst parents. CORB Headquarters staff, together with the Local Education Authorities, continued to be inundated with floods of applications from anxious parents, impatient to get their children to safety abroad.

Meanwhile, predictably, the Prime Minister's unhappiness grew deeper. Ten days after CORB started business, Mr Churchill complained to the War Cabinet that he was very disturbed indeed to realize that many people were still expecting the scheme to develop 'on a considerable scale.' He was aghast and opposed to everything this attitude stood for. 'A large movement of this kind,' he urged, 'encourages a defeatist spirit . . . entirely contrary to the true facts of the position, and it should be sternly discouraged.'[6] Most Cabinet Ministers present seemed to accept their leader's view that 'public opinion had got out of hand' — which, of course, it had.

At this same meeting, the Cabinet also discussed the growing demand from public (ie., independent) schools to be 'adopted' by CORB. At this stage, both the Government and the public assumed that CORB would take over the supervision of all evacuation plans for sending minors abroad, whether at Government or private expense. But, this was soon to prove an impossible task. Meanwhile, the

Cabinet was unanimous in feeling that public schools should not plan any corporate overseas evacuation arrangements.

In reaching this cautious decision, the Cabinet members were probably influenced by the opinion of Mr Spencer Leeson, Headmaster of Winchester and also Chairman of the Headmasters' Conference — as well as by the Prime Minister's castigation of the 'defeatist spirit'. *The Times* had printed a letter from Spencer Leeson just before the Cabinet met.[7] The writer considered that youngsters under the age of sixteen should not be forced by their parents to 'seek refuge' in the Dominions, and reminded them that the public schools stood for training in leadership and the service of others. As there was going to be a tough time ahead for Britain, these privileged young people should be allowed to stay and assist the nation, rather than encouraged to put their own security first. What is more, he argued, producing his trump card, 'Those who have left their elementary schools at an earlier age will not be going!'

Cabinet not only agreed to discourage schools from going overseas but also, at the same meeting, on the 1 July, took the more fundamental step of deciding that CORB should close its application lists to the public — at least for the time being. CORB had only been operating for ten days. But, in addition to Mr Churchill's fears about the panic, poor morale and defeatism represented in the vast number of applications CORB had received, the Cabinet also expressed alarm on hearing that CORB's staff had already risen to three hundred and fifty — ten times larger than it was ten days before — and was still rapidly rising. Was it sensible to encourage this degree of expansion, Cabinet members questioned, when the scheme was not intended to be large-scale, and could never hope to be so, in view of the 'considerable practical difficulties' it faced?[8]

During this same, lengthy CORB discussion by the Cabinet, the First Lord of the Admiralty, Mr A V Alexander, summarized the most serious practical difficulties facing the CORB scheme. He said these were: the provision of suitable shipping for large groups of children; the increasing problem of finding sufficient naval escorts for convoys; and the more urgent need to apportion shipping space for large consignments of enemy aliens awaiting transfer to Canada.[9]

On hearing the First Lord's report, the Cabinet felt even more justified in deciding to call a halt to the overseas evacuation scheme and, 'without killing it', to make sure that if and when it ever started up again, it would aim to move only small numbers of children. Thus, Geoffrey Shakespeare was directed to give another summary of CORB's position to the House of Commons in a Debate scheduled for the next day, the 2 July.

With CORB banned from receiving more applications, halted without being 'killed', with ships not available, and more crucially, insufficient warships to protect the evacuee ships, CORB's prospects of starting to operate seemed well nigh doomed. This Cabinet meeting could well have signalled the end of the CORB scheme altogether. Obviously the Prime Minister and most of his senior colleagues in the Government would have been happy for the scheme to die; and, although it would have caused some consternation to announce the end of the scheme before it had even started sending children abroad, the First Lord of the Admiralty had given enough justification for doing so.

On the grounds of unreasonable danger to CORB children whilst at sea, the Government could have disbanded CORB without losing a great deal of face; and, with hindsight, that is really what should have happened. But, there were those who felt strongly otherwise, as we shall see later; and, without doubt, the longer the Government delayed an end to the whole scheme, the more pressure would rise and insistence that the scheme should operate — partly in order to appease the Dominions, and partly to compensate for the privileged, private evacuation that had continued quietly, steadily and unabated.

So, instead of disbanding CORB at that crucial Cabinet meeting on the 1 July, the members contented themselves with a 'halt'. And, just before they left the Cabinet room, they listened to another searing attack by the Prime Minister on the mentality underlying the CORB scheme. He scorned the popular idea that with Britain becoming 'an island fortress' it would be 'desirable to have fewer mouths to feed.' The argument that the overseas evacuation scheme 'would reduce the number of "bouches inutiles" was simply not sound,' he complained, and, he asserted, the CORB scheme could only hope to reduce the amount of food required in Britain 'by a negligible amount.'[10]

If it had not been clear hitherto, it was now demonstrably obvious that the whole issue of overseas evacuation, and the attempts to justify it in terms of strategic need, incensed the Prime Minister. And he ended this particular tirade by directing memos be sent forthwith to all Government Heads of Departments instructing them to 'take drastic steps to put a stop to defeatist talk!'[11] Very shortly afterwards, defeatist talk became a criminal offence punishable with imprisonment. No wonder that Mr Shakespeare received an urgent phone call from a harassed Prime Minister's wife one day, asking him to do what he could immediately to get a young relative ashore: the little girl concerned, completely without Winston Churchill's knowledge, was about to set off for America on a ship carrying privately evacuated children. Mrs Churchill was worried about the effects on morale if news of the child's departure spread; and, in recounting this story,[12] Geoffrey Shakespeare mused on what 'the unscrupulous mouth of Lord Haw Haw' might have made of it.

Obeying the instructions of his Cabinet colleagues, Mr Shakespeare spoke about CORB in the debate scheduled for the 2 July in the House of Commons. He summarized events to date, covering CORB's organization, the sterling work of the Local Education Authorities, and the total of applications so far. He said that CORB had received forty thousand in the ten days the scheme had been open; but this is almost certainly an under-statement, as the total stood at well over two hundred thousand only four days later. He also revealed that by the next day, the 3 July, 'some parents will have been notified that their children have been provisionally accepted.'[13] Thus, no-one could doubt the speed and efficiency with which CORB staff and the LEA's had worked since opening day on the 20 June.

Then, in an attempt to reduce enthusiasm, Mr Shakespeare dutifully turned to some bad news for parents. Re-emphasizing the terrible risks involved, and that only parents could weigh up these risks, he stressed that the Dominions and the USA could only take 'a very small proportion of our child population.' As for the public schools, said Mr Shakespeare, CORB would not be assisting any of these to evacuate their pupils corporately to Canada because 'the essence of the CORB scheme is that there must be no discrimination or special treatment of a privileged few.'

But, the one glaring and mystifying omission in his speech was that he made no mention of the worst news of all, namely, Cabinet's decision to close CORB's application lists. Perhaps further discussions in private after the Cabinet adjourned led some ministers to conclude that too sudden a closing of the applications could cause even worse panic than seemed to exist already. The fact remains, for whatever reason, Geoffrey Shakespeare merely delivered a speech damping down public reaction to the scheme and scotching the idea of a massive exodus from Britain. He ended his speech with brief praise for the proposed scheme, mentioning with gratitude that Dominions Armed Forces were now arriving to help defend the United Kingdom, and how fitting it was that Britain should export in return to the Dominions 'the best of our children. For this double blessing the Mother Country will be forever in the debt of our daughter Dominions,' he said.

Mr Shakespeare's speech received a very mixed reception in the House, and the ensuing debate grew acrimonious. There were justifiable complaints that it was difficult to know 'what the Government really meant by the scheme.' Its policy was 'not properly thought out.'

Colonel Wedgwood, Labour MP for Newcastle-on-Tyne, attacked the scheme as 'trivial, valueless, and disappointing.' On the other hand, Mr Woolley, MP for Spen Valley, disapproved of the accusation that the scheme was 'defeatist'. He felt the term was unjust because the scheme could 'make a direct and useful contribution to the general war effort,' thus expressing the widely accepted, orthodox, pre-war view of the strategic value of civilian evacuation — whether overseas or not.

Statements made during this debate illustrated not only the width of differing opinions held about the scheme, but also a disturbing amount of confusion about its aims. For instance, Mr Shakespeare had just made a cautious speech, stressing that only small numbers of children could be sent abroad. Mr Chuter Ede, on the other hand, Secretary to the Board of Education and a member of Mr Shakespeare's Inter-departmental Committee, said the Government 'aimed to make the scheme as large as Dominion and US opportunities would allow.'

Ending the debate, Mr Attlee introduced a fresh angle altogether, reminding the House that there was still a lot to be said for evacuation within the United Kingdom. It was 'wrong to suggest there is no safety for children here,' he urged, 'and in any case,' he claimed, amidst the cheers of his fellow MPs, 'we are going to defeat the Invasion!' What was more, he went on, 'The Government and the country are not facing the situation in any panic sense.'

But, perhaps he was wrong to speak of both Government and people in the same sentence. The public's response to the CORB scheme looked very much indeed like panic; and it is questionable whether many parents of young children shared his optimism at that point in Britain's history.

5

ON OR OFF? CHAOS REIGNS

The rousing reaction to Mr Attlee's defiant words at the end of a Parliamentary debate sounded reassuring enough in the security of the House of Commons. But was he right to say there was no sense of panic?

He had just put his finger on the most worrying feature of life in Britain at the time, 'the Invasion'. True, he said that Britain would defeat it. But he assumed that the invasion was going to happen. Secretly, so did the Joint Chiefs of Staff, who warned the Cabinet two days after France capitulated: 'We must regard the threat of invasion as imminent. We must not overlook the fact that a major air offensive against this country will almost certainly take place as well, (taxing) our air defences and the morale of our people to the full.'[1]

Naturally, this top secret assessment was not even available to the bulk of MPs, let alone the general public. But, common sense, based on the fate of all the other countries that had opposed Hitler, indicated that Britain's turn to be invaded was imminent. This inevitability produced a vacillating public mood: fear and doom on the one hand, and an absurdly defiant optimism on the other.

King George VI, in his annual Empire Day speech, (25 May), epitomized this mixed mood with words of courage and depressing solemnity: 'Let no-one think my confidence is dimmed,' he said, 'when I tell you how perilous is the ordeal which we are facing.'[2] Again, US Ambassador Joseph Kennedy struck the same mixture when commenting on the King's speech: 'To suppose the Allies have much to fight with except courage is fallacious,' he said.[3] And the sight of Anthony Eden's new Local Defence Volunteers drilling with broomsticks and scythes in towns and villages throughout the land, whilst amusing on the one hand, gave chilling proof of the nation's predicament on the other.

It is no wonder that the Mass Observation Units testing the opinions of 'the man in the street' for the Ministry of Information, discovered that only half the population expected Britain would fight alone once France surrendered, and that 'everyone is going around looking as if they want to put their heads in a gas oven!'[4] In some instances, they found that good morale had ceased to exist altogether.

In view of this atmosphere, it should be no surprise — nor cause for shame — that British parents were nearly panicking to get large numbers of children overseas. And the numbers were very large indeed. CORB received applications on behalf of exactly 211,448 children in Britain. What is more, that staggering pile of applications reached CORB in the space of a mere two weeks.

Equally staggering, and just as indicative of the depressed state of adult morale, is the fact that a CORB staff member, working at the request of the CORB Advisory Council and using the 1931 Census as a guide, calculated that the 211,000 applications made in those two weeks represented nearly half the children eligible to join the scheme.[5] This suggests that, if the scheme had remained open much longer, it is probable that a majority of parents would have sought the CORB escape route for their children.

On the 6 July, 1940, the War Cabinet, still alarmed at the over-popularity of the CORB scheme and the 'defeatist' attitude it represented, reaffirmed the decision made a few days earlier to suspend the overseas evacuation. Then, three days later, Sir John Anderson presented to the Cabinet a memo from Geoffrey Shakespeare giving further strong support to the suspension party. The memo reported that representatives of the Admiralty, the Ministry of Shipping and CORB had just examined the drastic effects on Britain's strength caused by the French capitulation. The results of this on the Royal Navy were such that it was 'no longer possible to provide adequate naval protection' for ships carrying evacuees. The naval forces available 'must be used for more vital purposes than escorting ships carrying children overseas.'[6]

The War Cabinet had to accept that CORB's future was most unpromising. Doubtless, the Prime Minister and his senior colleagues felt privately relieved.

But, aware that an indefinite suspension of the scheme, when announced, would create 'widespread disappointment' in the Dominions and possible distress to anxious parents at home, Cabinet members felt that they should not delay the painful news of their decision any longer than necessary, and instructed Mr Shakespeare to prepare a statement immediately for Parliament's consideration.[7]

In the event, they delayed for nearly a week, with the deliberate intention of letting the Dominion Governments know the news first. This led to some confusion, following announcements in the British press that the Dominion High Commissioners in London had notified the Dominions Office of their respective governments' 'bitter disappointment' about the suspension of the scheme by the British Government.

This meant that Mr Attlee faced some dismayed MPs on 16 July, when he tried to explain to the House of Commons the Cabinet's action, and smooth over the fact that the British Parliament had been kept in the dark. Quoting the sinking of the liner *Arandora Star* as proof that even a fast ship could not always rely on speed alone for its safety when sailing unescorted, he stressed that the Cabinet had suspended the CORB scheme on safety grounds.[8]

Though many MPs would have already seen in the press that the *Arandora Star* had been torpedoed en route for Canada, few of them knew before Mr Attlee revealed it, that she had sailed with 734 'Fascist Italians' and 579 'Category "A" Germans' on board, and there had been colossal loss of life.[9] Mr Attlee emphasized that the fate of the ship, and of the passengers, made it essential for any evacuee-carrying ships to sail in escorted convoys. But, he pointed out, as the Admiralty could not guarantee 'adequate protection' for shiploads of evacuees in convoys, then clearly no CORB children could be allowed to set sail.

Immediately, there was some cynical questioning of Mr Attlee, notably from Mr Ammon MP for Camberwell North, who had hitherto been a firm supporter of the

CORB scheme. He claimed that the whole thing was 'merely a camouflage', a feeble gesture to working class families; and that the Government had never had any real intentions of seeing the overseas evacuation through. Mr Attlee contested this view, insisting that the reasons he gave for the suspension were perfectly genuine, and he concluded by saying, 'It is hoped to renew the scheme as soon as the military situation allows.'[10]

Next day, however, the House of Commons was still seething and this time Mr Shakespeare had to endure even more flak than Mr Attlee had suffered. There were accusations that the Government had been far too slow in taking action, with the result that many children from privileged homes had been safely evacuated overseas by private means already. This, MPs claimed, was producing divisive effects on Britain at a time when unity was essential, and reducing the morale of lower income families, who felt let down and frustrated. Other criticism repeated the accusation that the Government was confused in its basic aims for the CORB scheme.[11]

In reply, Mr Shakespeare defended those parents who arranged private evacuation for their children, and stressed that the Government scheme was deliberately set up to restore the balance by providing 'the same facility for the working class children who formed the majority of CORB's responsibility.' As to recent accusations that the scheme was 'defeatist', he refuted them, partly on the rather slender grounds that many soldiers he had spoken to wanted their children to go to safe homes overseas. He even reiterated the traditional view about evacuation being a contribution to Britain's defence programme — albeit, he added, 'a very limited one, as we cannot get rid of all our non-combatants.'

Next day, the 18 July, for the third day running, CORB was the burning issue in the House of Commons, and the suspension was again the subject for debate. This time, Mr Cocks, Labour MP for Broxtowe, asked the Prime Minister himself: 'Whether in view of the fact that the large-scale evacuation of children overseas was an important factor in the military defence of Britain, he would reconsider the decision to postpone the scheme, bearing in mind that children could be evacuated in ships already being convoyed.'[12]

No straight-man ever fed his lines better than Mr Cocks did on this occasion.

In reply, Mr Churchill, with apparent glee, expounded a mixture of his own personal views about overseas evacuation, together with a version of the reasons for the scheme's suspension prepared for him by Ministers.

'It is most undesirable,' he growled, 'that anything in the nature of a large-scale exodus from this country should take place, and I do not believe that the military situation requires or justifies such a proceeding, having regard to the relative dangers of going or staying . . .' He assured the House that if there were an opportunity to re-open the scheme, then it would be carefully regulated 'with a view to restoring the balance between classes, and not in pursuance of any policy of reducing the number of persons in this well-defended island.' Even if the scheme re-opened, he continued, it was bound to be on a small scale, and the availability of 'naval facilities' would always remain the crucial factor.

Lastly, Mr Churchill hinted at the strange background to the Cabinet's authorizing of the scheme on the day France capitulated. 'The full bearing of this question was not appreciated by His Majesty's Government at the time it was first raised,' he confessed. Nor had the Government foreseen that, 'by giving mild countenance' to the CORB scheme, there would follow 'a movement of such dimensions and a crop of alarmist and depressing rumours . . . detrimental to the interests of national defence.'[13]

Nobly, if a bit vaguely, Mr Churchill said he accepted 'full responsibility for the steps that were originally taken.' But he hoped that the House would 'be indulgent' and bear in mind that the Prime Minister and the Government had had weighty matters to consider 'on account of the many difficulties through which we have been passing.'

Whilst Mr Churchill probably squeezed a little sympathy from MPs, it is unlikely that they left the Chamber any less confused about the Government's aims concerning overseas evacuation. A scheme that had originated as the Government's response to Dominion generosity, with hopes of a large-scale exodus of children to safety, was beginning to sound like a misguided and embarrassing indiscretion committed by the War Cabinet. Or, no better, it seemed that the scheme had received the go-ahead so long as it remained small scale, and no more than a half-hearted attempt to give poorer families a political sop, compensating them for previously having to watch, helplessly, whilst the children of richer parents departed overseas. Was this the 'mild countenance' about which the Prime Minister spoke?

However, embarrassment, indiscretion, political manoeuvres were not the whole story; nor was this hard-hitting day to prove the finish of CORB. Suspended or not, CORB continued to select evacuees to go overseas, and escorts to accompany them on their ocean voyages. Much more significant than that: on this very same day the first party of CORB children was actually assembling in hostels in Liverpool prior to embarking for Canada. What is more — adding to the confusion — it seems clear that Mr Churchill knew they were assembling.

The indication that he knew lies in a peremptory note he wrote to Sir John Anderson, in response to an invitation to send greetings to the Canadian Premier, via the oldest evacuee in this first CORB group to set sail. 'I certainly do not propose to send a message by the senior child to Mr McKenzie King, or by the junior child either. If I sent any message by anyone, it would be that I entirely deprecate any stampede from this country at the present time!'[4] The note was dated 18 July: the day on which Churchill lambasted overseas evacuation in the House of Commons, and justified the suspension of CORB on the grounds that 'naval facilities' were not available to protect evacuee ships.

What is even more intriguing than the fact that the group was meeting in Liverpool, or even that the Prime Minister might have known about it, is the fact that suspension of the scheme had been questioned by MPs on three consecutive days, and each day the justification for the suspension was that safety could not at present be guaranteed.

If the Admiralty could not hope to provide the protection which it insisted was required, why ever was the scheme going ahead at all? The question becomes more puzzling when account is taken of the fact that the First Lord of the

Admiralty did not know that CORB was about to start sending children overseas.[15] If he had, he would presumably have insisted that the suspension agreed by Cabinet should be observed.

This all adds to the atmosphere of chaos and confusion. Possibly Geoffrey Shakespeare and a small group of senior members of CORB were deliberately taking a gamble,[16] and going ahead with the scheme, fearful of the recriminations, both from MPs and parents, if British parents were kept indefinitely frustrated in their attempts to send their children to safety abroad, to say nothing of a growing pique in the four Dominions which had extended their warm and massive offers of hospitality.[17] For, at home and abroad, despite the obvious risks inherent in the CORB scheme, there was enormous support for it.

This theory, that Geoffrey Shakespeare and a few others in leading positions at CORB felt they should go ahead despite all the risks, is supported by some significant words Mr Shakespeare used in his report to the eighth Meeting of the Advisory Council, held on the 23 July — just two days after the first batch of evacuees set sail. Having confided that 'some members' of the War Cabinet 'interpreted the magnitude of parents' response to the scheme as an indication of panic', he said he disagreed. His reason was that 'if anything, the proposed scheme would improve the morale of the nation, because the ability to send children to safety overseas would bring relief from anxiety.'[18]

Whether he was right or not, on Sunday, 21 July, the first batch of CORB children had sailed from Liverpool for Canada.[19] Admiralty records show that there was no difference at all in the naval protection afforded the convoy in which this evacuee ship sailed.[20] And, as a reminder of the gigantic risks CORB was taking, at lunch-time on the 27 July, a sunny, summer's day, U-boats were able to torpedo and sink four ships in the convoy. The meagre Royal Navy escort made no 'contacts' whatsoever.[21]

6

'YOUR CHILD HAS BEEN SELECTED'

Probably about half the CORB evacuees went abroad without any sort of consultation by their parents. However, some who were not consulted rightly point out that, as children, they did not expect to be included in the discussions in those days. Furthermore, they were not particularly unhappy to have the news sprung on them that their parents had applied.

As one former Canadian evacuee reports: 'My brother and I were told we had been accepted for evacuation to Canada, and what a wonderful experience it would be!' Another, also evacuated to Canada as a boy of thirteen, writes: 'We were not consulted at all, really. We were told we were going, and were probably checked for "adverse reactions".'

For some, this lack of prior consultation led to some difficult experiences, as ex-CORB girl Mary McKeon writes: 'My first memory of the CORB scheme is of sitting at the top of the stairs and hearing my mother telling a friend that my brother and I were going to Canada the following day. I was very upset.' Mary, ten years old at the time, was back home two weeks later. Her Canada-bound ship had been torpedoed; she and her brother were lucky to have survived.

Some parents seem to have delayed telling their children that CORB had selected them, or delayed telling them any details about departure, because CORB's letter notifying them of acceptance laid down the need for as much secrecy about the impending departure as possible. Londoner Gerald Budgern, aged eleven, whose parents had told him

SDL/18   CHILDREN'S OVERSEAS RECEPTION BOARD,
                                45, Berkeley Street,
                                       W.1.

Telephone:
Mayfair 8400

CONFIDENTIAL

Dear Sir (or Madam),

        I am writing this personal letter on the instruc-
tions of Mr. Geoffrey Shakespeare who is the Minister
responsible for the administration of the Children's
Overseas Reception Scheme. Mr. Shakespeare is sure
that you will appreciate its reassuring nature.

        You may have heard over the wireless, or have
read in the Press, that the Government cannot take responsibility
for sending children overseas under the scheme without adequate
naval protection.

        In the accompanying letter you are notified

        ~~You have already been notified~~

that your child (or children) has (or have) been accepted
for evacuation overseas. You can rest assured that arrangements
will be made for naval convoy. You can also rest assured that
we shall not let your child (or children) go overseas if
at the last moment we find that the situation has changed
and that no convoy can be provided.

        In the interest of the safety of your child (or
children), and others who will accompany them, we ask you to
regard this information as confidential - that is to say,
you should not discuss the matter even with your neighbours,
and you should ask your child (or children) also not to talk
about it. We know we can rely upon you in this matter.

                        Yours faithfully,

FIG 2: *CORB's letter to parents accepting a child for evacuation overseas, and*
attempting to reassure them about naval protection.   *Crown Copyright*

he was going, but stressed the need for secrecy about it,
recalls: 'I remember being called out of class one morning,
and put into a waiting ambulance, where I said goodbye to

my parents, and was then taken to a railway station. From there I went by train to Liverpool.'

There were parents who, although they might not have consulted their children before applying, prepared the way for their possible selection. Thus, Barbara Turner, aged fifteen, remembers: 'I was told on the walk home from school one day that my parents had decided that I would go to South Africa. The attraction for me was freedom, new places, new experiences.'

By contrast, there were families where the children first mooted the matter of applying to go overseas. Their reasons for wanting to go were very varied, and usually had nothing at all to do with the war. 'I was the one who wanted to go,' writes Joyce Briant, 'so I applied for the forms and filled them in for my parents.' The writer was aged fourteen and went to Australia simply because, she says, 'I had always wanted to travel and this seemed a good opportunity.'

'I believe I chose to go,' writes Nora Lupton, then aged nine, 'and I helped convince my parents, having enjoyed meeting a great uncle whilst he was visiting Darlington during a trip from Melbourne. He told such wonderful tales of Australia and really captured my imagination.'

Similarly, fifteen year old Yorkshire girl, Gwen Laycock, remembers: 'I took the CORB forms home from school. I had always been keen to travel and persuaded my parents to arrange for me to go to an uncle and aunt in New Zealand.' In many cases, the possibility of seeing relatives was part of the attraction of going overseas. As Freda Stout, who went from York to Australia, aged thirteen wrote: 'I wanted to visit the "Fairyland" — and also to meet my cousins.'

A few CORB children felt forced to go for a younger child's benefit, with varying reactions. A fifteen year old Kent girl states: 'I only knew I had to go to Australia in order to look after my young brother. He wanted to go!' She goes on to admit that she did not want to go at all, and deeply resented being forced to do so — a fact that has added to emotional problems in adult life.

On the other hand, Ron Smith, a twelve year old from Middlesborough, Yorkshire recalls: 'My parents asked if I would like to go to Canada and if I would take care of my seven year old brother. I was excited: the whole idea was that of an adventure in a strange new land. The last thought was of getting away from the war.'

One of the more unusual reasons for someone to go abroad with CORB — though it might have loomed large with families able to afford private evacuation — was a health problem. Alec Hedgecock explains that he was evacuated to South Africa because 'as a chronic asthmatic I was treated at the Royal Chest Hospital, and sometimes used as a student doctors' live sample. It was through the efforts of the specialist that my parents were induced to have me evacuated to South Africa when the opportunity presented itself.' This instance is unusual because the stringent medical tests applied to CORB children would normally have led to Alec's automatic exclusion. Obviously, the specialist played a key role here.

A few children saw the scheme as a possible chance of escape, not from the dangers of war, so much as from their domestic circumstances. Ten year old orphan Evelyn, living with a great aunt in County Durham says: 'I heard the radio broadcast and suggested going myself.' In due course, CORB sent Evelyn to Australia. Edna, another orphaned girl, a ten year old from Middlesex, writes: 'I really do believe it was basically my idea. I have always said, tongue in cheek, that I wanted to go because I saw New Zealand as a way of escape from the stern Aunt with whom I was living. But, perhaps, that really was true!'

There are far stranger reasons for children being caught up in the scheme. Thirteen year old Betty, from Edinburgh, had a younger sister who suffered from bronchial asthma. The parents, who had lived in New Zealand in earlier days, hoped that one day the whole family would return there. Meanwhile, if they could arrange for their older daughter to be evacuated to that country, they believed they would stand a better chance of getting permits for themselves and their asthmatic younger daughter. Optimistically, they thought they might get these permits within six months.

In the event, CORB did accept Betty, and she duly arrived in New Zealand. Alas, not until 1946 did mother arrive out there with Betty's younger sister, and two more years elapsed before her father was able to join them.

Extract from Circular of Children's Overseas Reception Board, dated 23rd July, 1940.

"The parents should be warned that no child who has been in recent contact with infection should be sent to the port of embarkation. I am also to request that parents may be informed that in order to avoid waste each child should carry only a sufficient supply of food and thirst quenching fruit to last twelve hours (instead of twenty-four hours previously indicated in correspondence with them from this Board); that no bottles should be carried but that it is very desirable that each child should take a carton (half pint) filled with either milk or water; that no chocolate should be included. They should also be asked to arrange that nothing which the child may require for two or three nights (e.g. identity and ration cards, sleeping clothes, soap, towel, tooth brush and tooth-paste) shall be packed in the child's suitcase but carried in a separate haversack or attache case."

Fig 3: *CORB's circular to parents sent immediately before a child departed for embarkation port. It is dated two days after the first batch set sail.*   Crown Copyright

Throughout her evacuation, Betty felt isolated from her family and lived on hope. 'For the whole six years,' she says, 'I expected to get word at any moment that they were on their way.' Hardly surprisingly, Betty was desperately unhappy for most of those years.

Another strange background to a child's introduction to the CORB scheme involved Dorothy Graham, a thirteen year old from Newcastle-on-Tyne. Dorothy's mother, when a child of twelve herself, had had an opportunity to travel to China. But, as she was the oldest child in a large family she was dissuaded from going because she was far too useful in looking after the young ones. 'She always said she would never stand in my way if a child of hers had the chance to travel,' says Dorothy, 'and I often wonder whether one of my reasons for going to Australia was to assuage my mother's disappointment in her childhood.'

When CORB notified parents of a child's inclusion in a batch about to sail overseas, they also included detailed instructions about clothing, food for the train journey to the embarkation port, and a warning not to send children if they had been in contact recently with an infectious disease. Children had to travel with their overnight clothes in a haversack, and the rest of their kit in 'one manageable suitcase.'

The required kit list[1] was drawn up by Health Ministry officials, and contained slight variations depending on whether the child was sailing to Canada or one of the three other Dominions, which would involve spending time in the tropics. Both lists reveal a fascinating bureaucratic view of adequate clothing for 'ordinary' children about to embark on a lengthy ocean voyage in war time. The omission of underpants for boys travelling through the tropics is an interesting social insight, and now seems rather dated.

Included with CORB's instructions and the clothing list was a cold legal document which both parents had to sign and return forthwith to CORB Headquarters. In signing, parents absolved CORB, the Government and 'any carrier providing the means of transport from any liability in respect of injury, including fatal injury, to the child.' Such chilling words cannot have made it easier for parents to proceed with their agonizing decision to send their sons and daughters overseas.[2]

But, the parents' accounts of their reasons for applying help to explain how they were able to steel themselves. 'Convinced after Dunkirk that England would be invaded,' writes one whose only child went to Australia, 'I grabbed the opportunity to get her out of danger.'

Again, another parent explains: 'At that time we lived very near Rosyth Naval Base and considered this to be a danger zone. We hoped to secure the children's physical safety, and freedom from the fear engendered by frequent air-raid warnings.'

Yet another illustrates how the majority of these anxious parents weighed the odds: 'She was only eleven years of age. Her two brothers were nearing active service age so, of course, they had to stay in this country. We had long consultations with her. She was an intelligent and talented child, and she was very sure in her own mind that she wanted to go to Australia. At that time, most of us in this country thought invasion was inevitable. So, we decided to give our consent when she was selected. Looking back to 1940, it was a very hard decision we had to make, and heart-breaking for us.'

That parent must speak the mind and heart of the vast majority whose children sailed in CORB ships.

7

'AS YOU WAVE ME GOODBYE!'

'The arrangements were shrouded in the greatest secrecy,' writes former New Zealand CORB girl Geraldine Robb, eleven years old at the time of departure. 'We were forbidden to discuss anything outside our home. Everything was labelled in one suitcase lying on the sitting room floor, ready for departure at a few hours' notice. All of this was arranged calmly by my parents, not involving me. The day came. A taxi collected me, as arranged, from a crossroads near my home. The taxi, already containing one small girl, duly arrived. I felt no emotion. My mother was very upset. She gave me a last minute opportunity to change my mind. The taxi took the other girl and me to a railway station in Manchester to join the train which already contained other children, also labelled, gasmasks dangling . . .'

Usually at three or four days' notice, small groups of CORB children gathered at local main railway stations or, less often, at bus termini. There they met their train or bus escort, appointed by the Local Education Authority, and said goodbye to their families. CORB forbade parents to accompany children to their ports of embarkation. Parting would be difficult enough nearer home.

For the parents, without exception, parting must have been a harrowing business. The children differed enormously, some of them admitting, well over forty years after the event, that they were not really aware of what was going on, other than setting off for some sort of 'holiday'. But, for many of the children, it was grim.

Rita Patterson, eight years old when she left Blyth, Northumberland for Australia, remembers departure morn-

Fig 4: *CORB girl Rita Patterson, aged 8, says goodbye to her brother Derek, aged 4, on the day she left Blyth for Liverpool and Australia.* *South Shields "Northern Press".*

ing with outstanding clarity. 'We were walking through the deserted streets, early morning, my suitcase on baby brother's pram. As instructed, my parents had not told the neighbours because of war-time secrecy. I remember the local news photographer taking a photograph of me kissing my little brother, and there were seven of us left in charge of the school welfare officer — the old "School Board Man". As the train left, I think I first realized I was leaving my parents and family, and cried all the way to Liverpool.'

Betty Hooper, thirteen years old on leaving Edinburgh, writes about her parting: 'My only memory was waiting and waiting, and then my father dropping onto his knees in front of me, and crying as he hugged me. I was not crying, then, and just felt very embarrassed. Then I remember the bus pulling away, and I suddenly didn't want to go as I realized I might never see them again. I had a terrible sinking feeling somewhere around my chest, as though I had done some terrible thing, and didn't know what it was — a feeling I was to have many times over the next few years.'

Eight year old Rose Burder, leaving for New Zealand, recalls: 'I was very excited about the trip ahead as we had never left our home before. I could not realize that we were going to be travelling so far away, and I was upset to see my father with tears in his eyes as we left.' Sadly, her father died the following year.

For some, the experience left permanent, discernible marks, as a former South African evacuee says: 'Our parting was tearful and upsetting. I still cannot bear "goodbyes".' And, similarly, John Hillier, twelve years old when setting off for Australia, remembers that, as he and the other CORB children left their borough for a London train terminus in a coach, 'we were all singing *Wish me luck as you wave me goodbye*. Whenever I hear this song, it brings back that memory and a lump in my throat.' That is after more than forty years.

There were the inevitable attempts to be brave. John Hare, who was only seven on being evacuated to Australia, writes: 'My mother and my three sisters who left with me were very tearful. Dad was visibly upset, but joked about the "holiday".' And an eight year old recalls: 'We parted at a local school in Tottenham. I left in an ambulance with two boys and another girl, and I can just remember my father saying, "Keep your chins up, kids," and giving Churchill's famous "V" sign.'

Stoicism again: Freda Stout, a thirteen year old York girl, having said 'Goodbye' to her grandmother and widowed mother, 'who were weeping copiously' on the railway platform, says, 'I stayed in the corridor gazing out of the window until the lump in my throat had vanished. I didn't want to upset the other York evacuees who were all younger than me.'

Another thirteen year old departing for Australia with her nine year old brother recalls the emphasis on keeping the 'stiff upper lip'. 'We parted outside the library in Sutton,' she writes. 'I think there were about eight children and we were put into two cars. My parents, an aunt and a cousin were there when we left, and I can remember my father saying to me that, if I was going to cry, not to do so until we had left, so that my mother could not see that I was upset. I didn't cry.'

However, some evacuee memories of the parting are very matter of fact indeed. Alec Hedgecock, a ten year old from North London, says: 'I walked from Bowes Road School to the station, carrying my own baggage. I had a great feeling of excitement at going to South Africa. No regret!' Again, seven year old Catherine Webster, leaving Bradford for Australia: 'It was a cheerful parting on my part. At seven years of age, the fact that I might not see my parents for several years made no real impact, and it was as if I was going to stay with a relative for a few weeks — the only difference being that it was an uncle and aunt in Australia.' Equally undaunted was Keith Austin, only six years old as he left his home in Kent for Canada. 'My parents were upset,' he recalls, 'my two brothers and sisters less so! I had a pile of *Beano* comics, and my prime interest was reading the latest until the train moved off. I did manage to wave goodbye!'

For some families, there were complications over and above the wretched 'goodbyes'. 'It was a disastrous morning,' says Edna Chase, former New Zealand evacuee, who left Staines, Middlesex, aged ten. 'There was an air-raid just as we were to leave for Surbiton station. All the buses stopped. By the time we finally arrived, the others we were to meet had gone; but an aunt who was waiting had instructions for us about the London main line station we were to get to, and we arrived there with about fifteen minutes to spare. I remember being hastily whisked onto the train, then, to my consternation, being whisked off again into another carriage. The floodgates opened, and I honestly don't know whether the tears as the train pulled out were for the parting with parents or because I had been moved!'

An emotional complication for some evacuees was the knowledge that they were leaving homes where strained relationships existed between their parents. The extra stress this provoked is remembered with poignancy by two sisters evacuated from East Anglia to Canada. The younger one, aged eleven, recalls her mother warning her: 'Your father won't come to see you off — he doesn't care.' But, her mother was wrong. 'He arrived dressed in his best suit, (he was a railway plate-layer), a short time before the train left. I was sure he would come. He loved us. But, we never saw he (sic) again.' (And, is it significant that, as she recalls that parting, she slips into her old East Anglian dialect again, even though she has lived in Canada since 1940?)

Her sister, aged twelve, describes the parting with equal feeling: 'My sisters and I were on the train. I remember looking back at my parents as the train began to move slowly away. They were standing together, with my father slightly behind my mother. They waved to us and I waved back. Perhaps my sisters waved too — I don't know. I never saw my father again.'

Naturally, some CORB youngsters found the parting easier to cope with than others; and it is not easy to know why. But, perhaps, those with the least conscious memories of all are the ones who suffered most. A former Canadian evacuee, a London girl of seven when she left home, says: 'I can't remember the parting, nor the name of the embarkation port, nor any events in it.' She is by no means alone in this. What is more, the age of the individual concerned does not seem to be significant. Thus, a girl from Kent, aged fifteen when she set off for Australia, and very angry that her parents were forcing her to go, writes: 'I do

not remember where we parted. I was angry at being sent
— and being forced to wear a hat I hated. I threw it away.
Otherwise, no memory of any of it. I seem to forget things I
don't like, or can't bear to remember. My younger brother
remembers all of it. Interesting isn't it?' she concludes.

Several former evacuees comment about the strange
snippets of memory that linger in the mind. One of these is
Nora Lupton, who went from Darlington to Australia, aged
nine. She describes waiting to leave her family at
Darlington railway station. 'Initially I was thrilled and
excited, as if leaving for a day at the seaside. Gradually, I
became aware of the awful implications, but not until it was
too late to voice any doubts. Although very young, I was
quite disgusted because one girl in our party simply refused
to answer her mother's questions, or even talk to her, but
kept banging her on the head with a rolled up comic —
funny what sticks in one's mind!'

Some children, as we have seen, realized that their
parents were in torment as their children left. In fact, they
must have suffered more heartache than the majority of the
children. After all, they had had to agonize, already, about
the final decision to let their children travel overseas. They
would also be more aware, not only of the dangers, but also
of the fact that their separation could be for a very long
time.

Mary Webster, a Bradford mother whose son Derric,
nine, and daughter Catherine, seven, went to Australia says
that she and her husband decided she should say goodbye
at home, in order to avoid taking their third child, a little
boy of three, to the station. 'I cannot describe my feelings,'
she admits. 'A traumatic experience of that nature must be
put into the background. Purposely, *I did not think!*'

Heather Johnston went to New Zealand aged six. Her
mother writes about the departure: 'It was at a school in
Greenford — I can't remember which. She left in a coach
and, although my heart was breaking, I tried to get them
all to sing *Wish me luck as you wave me goodbye!*'

The train and coach escorts appointed by the Education
Authorities had to witness these farewells. Writing a little
later in the war, Miss Meta Maclean, a ship escort to
Australian evacuees, commented that she and her sea-going

colleagues felt that the train escorts had a far worse task than those on board the ships, simply because they had to be present at the final moments of parting.[1]

Miss Ella Appleby, a school teacher in Northumberland, was train escort to a party of four boys and a little girl of five who were travelling from Newcastle-on-Tyne to Liverpool to await their ship overseas. She writes: 'The parents of the boys quickly effaced themselves after handing over my charges. The girl arrived with her parents and paternal grandparents. All, except the mother, wished the child to be evacuated. But, the mother was against it. In a rather distressing final scene, the child had to be taken forcefully from the mother and handed over to me.' Who can blame the mother?

For many who managed to wear brave faces in front of the children, no doubt there came delayed shock at the feeling of separation. Mrs Florence Spence, whose daughter Barbara left York for Canada at the age of ten, recalls this: 'I was quite calm when the train left. But, when we got home, it was so quiet and tidy — it really hit me then.' And the Scottish mother of two boys, aged twelve and six, who departed for New Zealand, says: 'We parted at the local school. How I remember the subsequent anguish, the fear and the doubts about our decision to send them abroad.'

Londoner, Mrs Grace Hedgecock is very direct about it all. Her son Alec, asthma sufferer, walked from Bowes Road School, carrying his own baggage to the station, an excited ten year old, without a care in the world.[2] But he left his mother in a totally different frame of mind. After more than forty years, the enormity of that day returns all too vividly. 'It's a curious, disturbing feeling — reliving the past,' she writes. 'We parted in Bowes Road, Southgate. It was outside a tobacconist's shop a few yards from my home. Only a few children went. I can't remember who took them, or by what means of transport. I can only remember thinking: "I must be raving mad!" And now, I know I was!'

Perhaps she sums up, not only the feeling of most CORB parents about a terrible day in their lives, but also the concept of the whole CORB venture.

8

'A PORT SOMEWHERE . . .'

'I remember only images of that train journey,' writes an ex-CORB girl, eight years old as she left Wallington, Surrey, for a 'port somewhere in Britain' in order to embark for Canada. Small snatches of memory enter her mind: 'Sitting on the seat with my feet not touching the carriage floor; the gas mask box; the CORB labels.'

Fig 5: *One suitcase only, 'about 26" x 18" ', was allowed each CORB evacuee. The suitcase had to be correctly labelled.*   *Crown Copyright*

Angus MacLeod, a fourteen year old leaving Edinburgh for New Zealand, recalls the atmosphere of uncertainty on the train journey to the port. 'All the station signs had been removed, so we had no idea where we were going until we arrived at 6 pm in Liverpool, on the 14 August, 1940. We were then taken to the Fazakerley Homes.'

For many, there is a mixture of clearly detailed memory, small, personal snatches, confusion, blurring, and blanks. A former Australian evacuee, thirteen when she left London, writes: 'I left Wimbledon Station bewildered and excited. I was a little unsure, but found the situation of being with others challenging, especially in such a novel setting. I wondered whether I would ever see my parents again. I was shocked at the thought. I will always remember their brave smiles as they looked through the carriage window. Then all was blotted out by dismay once the train moved from the platform. It was dark when we left the train, and we were taken to a High School where we slept on palliasses on the floor.'

Derric Webster is one of several who remembers the emphasis on security. 'My memory is pretty hazy,' he admits about the journey from Bradford, 'but we changed trains somewhere — possibly Brighouse — and I remember seeing our luggage with "Liverpool" written on it. At this I exclaimed: "We're going to Liverpool!" in a loud voice; and was promptly told to "hush". It was all very secret.'

The strongest memory for some of these ex-CORB children is the seemingly endless time it took to get to their embarkation port. A thirteen year old girl says the journey from Sheffield to Glasgow was 'an exciting adventure to begin with. But, the further from home, the more morose we became, and quite miserable and tired. It was a very long journey, first on the train to Glasgow, and then by bus to a school.'

Her younger sister, aged nine, gives more details, but also emphasizes the length of the journey. 'I was apprehensive and resentful with four of us leaving and three left behind — Mum, Dad and baby sister. There was a lot of hustle and bustle and kissing. But I did not kiss my father — I blamed him for getting rid of us, and then regretted it as I knew I might never see him, or my mother or little sister again. The train journey was very, very long and very, very tiring . . .' Perhaps it was fortunate that the sisters' ship was one that did not sail. Just over a week later they were home again, and the younger girl was able to make peace with her father.

The bus and train escort aspects of the CORB operation went very smoothly. From the earliest planning days, through Circular 1515 sent from the Board of Education in Whitehall to all the Local Education Authorities, CORB had asked for local provision of escorts to the ports of embarkation. The advantage of this was that, quite often, the evacuees knew the person in charge of them during the first few hours of separation. Even for those in a group who did not know the escort previously, it helped preserve a link with the home town to know that they were with a local person.

Freda Stout recalls that 'our escort from York just happened to be my beloved Mrs Nightingale who had taught me in Standard 7 and in whose class I had won my scholarship to Mill Mount, so we talked . . . It was all excitement.'

Twelve year old Margaret Jones was another who knew her train escort very well. 'There were six children in the care of Miss Redfern who happened also to be my own class teacher at Cromwell Road School in Manchester.' But, in Margaret's case, even the welcome presence of the familiar face did little to assuage her disturbed feelings. She continues: 'My parents tried to be very brave, but as the train pulled out I saw them break down through my own tears, and I thought my heart would break. On the train to Liverpool, my young sister was happy and excited, bouncing up and down on the seat. But I cried bitterly all the way, and Miss Redfern tried everything to comfort me without success. On our arrival at Holly Lodge School in Liverpool, I was given a large dose of castor oil which was supposed to make me better. This still puzzles me!'

CORB arranged with the Directors of Education in Glasgow and Liverpool, the two embarkation ports for Atlantic convoys, to plan hostel arrangements and the bussing of evacuees from their hostels to the docks to join their ships. Schools formed the obvious choice for hostels, although none of those used was particularly suitable. But, the advantages of schools were that they were directly under the control of the Local Education Office, had at least some basic feeding facilities and, during the height of the CORB operation, (ie., the month of August), they were closed to their own pupils for the summer holidays.

Those evacuees who stayed in the Fazakerley Cottage Homes were the most fortunate. This was a Barnardo's institution in Liverpool, and had the bonus of reasonable boarding accommodation for children. In the local authority schools, never intended to accommodate overnight boarders, conditions were frugal at best. Most ex-CORB children who remember anything at all about the strange, limbo existence prior to embarkation, speak of the spartan conditions, especially the straw mattresses on the school room floors, where they slept with 'hairy grey blankets' for warmth, and a bundle of their clothes sometimes sufficing for a pillow. Throughout, there was only ever cold water available for washing in the pupils' wash basins, and there were no facilities for baths.

In Glasgow, the conditions at Albert Road School, used by CORB for boys, were the worst of all. By early September, CORB Headquarters in London had received so many adverse reports from CORB chief escorts about the Albert Road premises that it requested the Glasgow authorities to discontinue using this school, and they duly agreed.[1]

However, shortly afterwards, Mr Roland Cartwright, a South Yorkshire Headmaster who was the chief escort to a batch of children intended for South Africa, sent a detailed list to London of the inadequacies of the Balgrave Road School premises.[2] The catalogue was so familiar to Miss Maxse, CORB's London Director, that she guessed the school was actually Albert Road under another name.

To be fair to all concerned, it had not helped Mr Cartwright nor the Glasgow Education Office billeting officials, that his CORB boys had first been accommodated in Liverpool for a few days, and then rushed to Glasgow for a re-scheduled embarkation. The party had then to stay in the Glasgow school for ten more days and nights, during which one hundred and forty boys shared only two lavatories, both of them situated across an uncovered yard, and it rained for a whole week of their stay. Adding to the problem of maintaining morale, there were no laundering facilities, no playing fields, nor did the Scottish Division of CORB take kindly to any adverse criticism emanating from

English sources, whether London Headquarters or escorts.

In the event, the CORB operation was suspended before Miss Maxse was able to take Glasgow authorities to task about Balgrave Road and, ironically, Mr Cartwright's party had to disembark from the *Llandaff Castle* just before she set sail for Cape Town.

One of many generous gestures CORB received during these hectic days of summer, 1940, came from Mr Simon Marks of *Marks and Spencers*.[3] He phoned Geoffrey Shakespeare early in July and offered to put a stockpile of £7,000 worth of children's clothing in both Liverpool and Glasgow for issue to CORB children by the WVS. The proportion who really needed this help once movement to the ports began was surprisingly small. Major Violet Chalmers, a Salvation Army escort to CORB children who sailed to Canada aboard the *Duchess of York*, recalls: 'They were dressed very well indeed, and every mother had done her best for her child or children.'

This opinion is echoed by other escorts, including Miss Nora Belgrove, escort to another Canadian group aboard the *Oronsay*, who reports: 'They were quite presentable, and parents had obviously equipped them with care.' Miss Ruth Morton, escort to the second Australian batch, who sailed aboard the *Nestor* reported: 'Most children were adequately dressed, but a few from poor homes had no really warm clothes . . . The WVS outfitted those children . . .'

An illustration of the efforts parents made to comply with CORB's suggested kit list appears in some correspondence later between Miss Maxse and the mother of two children involved in the *City of Benares* disaster. She wrote that she had fitted out her two sons (one of whom, sadly, was lost at sea), 'with all new clothing to last about a year.' The average cost per child for such provision in 1940 was about £12, a considerable sum for a working class family.

During their stay in Liverpool or Glasgow, the CORB children underwent quite rigorous medical checks, the doctors who carried out the examinations being appointed by the various Dominion High Commissions. As agreed between the Dominions Office and the High Commissioners, the standard of checks had to be sufficiently high to avoid any child being returned to the UK on arrival in any particular Dominion.

The proportion of children sent home from the two ports was eleven per cent. This percentage, amounting to a total of about three hundred and thirty children, might seem rather high in view of the medical standards laid down by CORB, with the advice of Ministry of Health experts, for the Schools' Medical Officers to impose in each area when examining potential overseas evacuees. The requirements stipulated that no children should be accepted for the CORB scheme if they 'had the slightest degree of mental defect or feeble mindedness . . . nor if they were epileptic, blind, partially blind, or severely deaf . . . and every endeavour should be made to exclude enuretics.'[4]

The regulations gave a long list of complaints that must automatically exclude an applicant, ranging from congenital syphilis to ringworm and TB 'in any form'. Also, presumably a reminder of the South African wish that no Jews should be included, Medical Officers had to give details if 'the child is not of pure European extract.'

The rejection of the eleven per cent at the ports, Miss Maxse later claimed, was because of the tremendous speed at which selection had to proceed.[5] As a result, the Medical Officers could not be as thorough in every case as they should have been, leading, in turn, to a few cases of petit mal and TB even going abroad, as well as numerous cases of enuresis — although, to be fair to the MOs, many enuretics were not habitually such at the time of their examinations.

Some former evacuees recall having wet the bed in their hostels without any undue fuss being made, and their condition, as might be expected, soon righted itself. But, in addition to suspected enuretics, a tiny number of children was sent home because they were homesick to such a degree that they were considered likely to become ill on the voyage. One former CORB girl who remembers requesting to be allowed to go home is Gwen Laycock, fifteen years old when evacuated from Wakefield, Yorkshire, to New Zealand. 'The shock of what was really happening to me came to me on the way to the station,' she writes. 'My father sat next to me on the bus and said, "If we all get killed, you must return to care for your sisters." ' Gwen had two sisters, one not medically fit for the CORB scheme, and the other not old enough. 'By the time I reached Liverpool,' she continues, 'I was very unhappy and asked to be returned home. . . . But, it was too late: I just had "to grin and bear it".' On reaching New Zealand six weeks later, Gwen was surprised to receive a silver pencil from her chief escort because, she was told, 'You have been homesick.'

It is possible that a tiny proportion of those sent home from the ports on medical grounds actually involved 'social' grounds. If this is so, then doctors were contravening, in a serious way, the philosophy underlying CORB's selection procedures. These intended that ninety per cent of CORB children would be from families who could never have afforded to send them overseas privately.[6] This percentage roughly represented the proportion of British children in non-fee paying schools.

A case remembered by Miss G B Finlayson is worth mentioning. She was a Glasgow special school teacher who worked on secondment at the Albert Road School whilst it was in use as a CORB hostel.[7] One day, Miss Finlayson observed a doctor examining a boy aged about ten and his sister aged five. 'They were poorly clad,' she states. 'Their possessions were in one small attaché case and a brown paper parcel. They were from a slum area of Glasgow and, of course, they spoke the "Glesca" lingo. The boy managed to tackle the doctor's questions not too badly. But the five year old girl had not a clue what he was saying. I could not interfere. She was so shy, timid and pathetic. And, of course, she was rejected out of hand. That meant the brother, too, was not accepted.'

Miss Finlayson had the unenviable task of taking 'the two wee souls' on a tram to their home, where their parents were surprised to discover they were not already half way to their destination. 'It was one of the most dreadful experiences of my life,' says Miss Finlayson, whose entire teaching life was spent in the city.[8]

Apart from the palliasses, the 'hairy grey blankets', and the mixture of excitement, homesickness, and bewilderment, the memory most frequently recalled by ex-CORB evacuees is the air-raid alerts. Some, of course, had already experienced quite heavy air-raids on their own cities; a tiny

12, august/40
6th July TUESDAY   Edinburgh

DEAR MAMMY & DAD

            I HOPE YOUR ARE HAPPY
and well. THE ESCORTS are keeping us in
safety. We are quite well and happy. I am
sleeping in the hall of Holt High school. We
sleep on sacks filled with straw. and have
two blankets. I expect to be going on
the boat in the next day or two. We are at
LIVER POOL and there are many barrage
balloons around here; THere are about 300
children going To Canada about 150 boys are
staying and about 150 girls 4 miles away.
Each morning we have a good wash
and clean our teeth and every evening we
have a warm shower bath.. Today a lot
of soldiers with big guns on therr lorries
passed by also some aaroplanes & From
A Merica without wings and windows

                From your loving
                son Douglas

Mrs C Edith Penwarden

Fig 6: *Letter to parents in Darlington from CORB boy Douglas Penwarden aged 8, in embarkation hostel prior to departure for Canada. Adult escorts ensured that all evacuees wrote before sailing, but the letters were delayed for security reasons.*

handful had even been bombed out of their homes. But, the majority found the raids on Glasgow and Liverpool a new experience, and quite a number of these, ironically, came from towns that never would endure any air-raid throughout the war.

Very few recollect any fear. More often it is the weariness of it all, the disturbed sleep, and the discomfort and cold of the shelters. 'We had to stand in concrete, above-ground shelters. It was chilly and bleak,' recalls eleven year old Evelyn Kershaw from Darlington. And Margaret Jones remembers: 'As I had to care for my younger sister who was a heavy sleeper, we were the last out of the school to the shelters — by which time everyone had gone, and we were out in complete darkness in a field where we sat out the raids. Never once did I manage to reach the shelters!'

Another who remembers the burden of responsibility is Betty Hooper, thirteen years old when waiting to board her ship for New Zealand. 'There were raids every night,' she recalls, 'and every night one very small girl next to us was forgotten. I used to stagger across the playground carrying her, and refused to give her up to a warden because he kept forgetting her.'

A few evacuees had somewhat unusual experiences in those hostel days. Geraldine Robb, an eleven year old waiting to join the *Rangitata* for New Zealand, writes: 'I became the centre of a "mini-drama". My parents had not packed my ration book, identity card, etc, as required. Staff didn't know whether to refuse me permission to sail! Eventually, they contacted my parents who were able to forward the documents, but this meant the risk of letting outsiders know where we were.'

Eight year old Bob Bullard, destined for Australia from Wembley, says: 'I travelled with my younger brother who contracted measles at Liverpool. He was not allowed to sail and subsequently was sent home.'

Edna Chase, evacuated from Staines, has a very clear memory of one of those events that push danger and fatigue and boredom into the background. 'In our Liverpool school hostel we had a small case and our gas masks by our beds,' she writes, 'and when the sirens went, we took these and ourselves to the shelter. Sometimes, we only just got back to bed and the sirens would go again. I remember one night flopping down exhausted on to a bed which collapsed under me, only to be told, "You're on my bed!" So, I happily moved off to my own, knowing that someone was going to be rather uncomfortable!'

Maurice Pike, a fourteen year old from Essex, waiting to embark for South Africa, recollects: 'At Albert Road School, there were high iron railings all round, behind which we were kept for several days. We used to cling to the railings saying "Good morning" and "Good afternoon" to the people walking past outside. The meals ladies warned us repeatedly to have no truck with one named "Mimi" who was on the outside — and SMOKED!'

The attempts to put a shroud of secrecy around those few children waiting to sail from ports which were actually their home cities, gave a tragi-comic atmosphere to some CORB children's experiences. For instance, nine year old Jean Cheyne of Glasgow recalls: 'On leaving our parents, we were put aboard a bus and blinds were drawn. We were driven about for at least three-quarters of an hour. On arrival at a school, we found all names and signs had been removed. But, my brother recognized pictures of the "school champion" on a wall as he was a neighbour. My brother climbed down a drainpipe that night and went home, just to let them know where we were. We were only about a ten to fifteen minute journey from home and from where we'd boarded the bus. It must have zig-zagged all over town. . . . One boy outside the school recognized my brother and told his mother, who told my mother. She got word that we were going to the park and spent the whole day in the nearby Botanical Gardens; but we were taken to the other side of town to Queen's Park. It made it much harder for her. But, she did bring along some doll's clothes she had been knitting . . .'

It was in these embarkation hostels that the CORB children first met their sea-going escorts, who took over from the LEA appointed bus and train escorts. On meeting their groups in Liverpool and Glasgow, the ship escorts were struck by the appearance and bearing of the children. Miss Diana Close, for instance, an escort with the batch due to sail to Canada on the ill-fated *Volendam*, recalls:

'Their morale was high. It was a big adventure. The youngest boys in my group were with older family members, and I don't remember any distress beyond what could be expected.' Similarly, Mr Bill Oats, deputy chief escort to the first Australian batch: 'The children's health was generally good; and their morale was admirable considering the circumstances.'

John Doughty, aged fifteen at the time, and therefore in CORB's top age-group, looks at the other side of the coin, and registers appreciation of the escorts. 'I can remember no worries about luggage or anything else,' he comments, 'which must indicate some degree of organization by the adult escorting staff.'

Indeed, these escorts were mostly a remarkable set of people. About eighty five per cent were women, many of them in their twenties. Most volunteered for a taste of adventure, as well as hoping to make a humane contribution to the war effort. In almost every case, they received only about forty eight hours notice to be at their port of embarkation and, usually, they had only heard two weeks earlier, at the most, that they were now on the CORB 'accepted for service' list.

The escorts certainly did not volunteer for the money. For the entire voyage, the Treasury paid them £5 if they went to Canada, £12 if they went to South Africa, and £20 if they went to Australia or New Zealand, whilst the chief escort received the handsome responsibility payment of twenty five per cent more. Their instructions, invariably, were to take the first available ship from their Dominion back to Britain. Whilst waiting for a passage home, they could expect 6/3 a day, (approximately 31p) for 'out of pocket expenses'.[9] They just had to be a dedicated bunch of people.

9

'HEARTS OF OAK'

Embarkation day came as a relief from the depressing, limbo life in the hostels.

But, amidst the relief, there was often shock, too, at the suddenness of the order to embark. Norman Standage, evacuated to Australia, aged nine, recalls: 'After a few nights, without pre-warning we were told to pack our suitcases and get on a bus. We then moved to the Mersey and were taken out to a grey-painted ship anchored in mid-stream. There we boarded the *TSS Nestor* of the Blue Funnel Line.'

Jean Cheyne, billeted in a pre-embarkation hostel in her home city of Glasgow, writes about the unexpectedness of embarkation day: 'We were taken for outings every day in buses loaded with our luggage, and then brought back again. We eventually went out one day for a trip and ended up at Greenock, where we immediately went on board a tender which took us out to the Tail of the Bank where we climbed on board the *SS Bayano*. We left almost at once.'

There are the strangely remembered details, too. Just before embarking aboard the *Rangitata* for New Zealand, Geraldine Robb remembers, 'I was upset at having my hair combed with a special comb to see if it was clean.' And Mary England, aged ten boarding the *Nerissa* for Canada, says, 'All I can remember is having a quarrel with my sister at the dockside.'

Some CORB batches embarked at night, which cannot have been easy in the black-out. Mary McKeon records: 'I remember going to the docks in the evening. The ship seemed huge, especially as there were hardly any lights. We boarded the ship, the *SS Volendam*, and my brother and I were taken to a cabin for two. But, we were then transferred to a cabin for four — presumably so that the older children could "keep an eye on us". We went to bed. I did not hear the ship sail, but woke up next morning to find we were at sea and were part of a large convoy of ships . . .'

Not only had the escorts, the dock authorities and the ships' crews to contend with passengers embarking in the dark, but there could be complications caused by air-raids, too. An escort on the *Volendam*, Diana Close, states that Liverpool was bombed during the night that they embarked, 'and we had ring-side seats!'

Other problems the dock and shipping authorities experienced during these uncertain days are well illustrated by the embarkation plans of the first CORB batch destined for Australia. The arrangement was that they should board the P & O ship *Orion* on the 5 August. But, at the very last moment, the Nautical Surveyors reported that the *Orion* could expect a recurrence of serious engine trouble. Rather than send the four hundred and seventy seven children home — and the fact that this would only be the second CORB sailing probably affected the decision — Ministry of Shipping officials and CORB representatives in Liverpool quickly agreed that the evacuees should embark aboard the Polish ship *Batory* instead.[1]

This revised plan was so last minute that the *Batory* crew was taken utterly by surprise. 'We saw, suddenly, a crocodile of children! We knew we were to carry troops and a few private passengers. But, we were delighted to know there were now to be children as well!' recalls Mr Marian Slabosz, the assistant purser and English specialist on board. He also remembers that there was only one dissentient crew member who complained: 'Oh! Now it's the war, eh? The Germans are in Poland, eh? The Germans are in Norway and France, eh? And we are going to play with children, eh?' But, he complained only once, adds Mr Slabosz.[2]

The CORB children, with their thirty eight escorts, had all arrived in a fleet of Liverpool Corporation buses by 11 am, CORB discs around their necks, haversacks on backs, gas masks on shoulders, and the statutory suitcase in one hand. For the next four hours, they had to queue along the dockside, past the massive-looking grey liners loading with thousands of troops for the Middle and Far East, soon to be part of their convoy, whilst Marian Slabosz interpreted for his Chief Steward and Charles Kilby, the CORB chief escort, as they wrestled with the practical problems of accommodating the children.

A further reminder of the enormous adaptability that lay behind wartime embarkation, involving dockers, shipping officials, customs, crews of ships, naval representatives and, in the case of the CORB ships, the Dominion and CORB officials as well, lies in a signal presented to the First Sea Lord at the Admiralty two days after the *Batory* convoy had put to sea. The message read: '*SS Orion* with children and troops reports blow out in main steam pipe; has returned to Clyde escorted by aircraft.'[3] The chiidren, of course, never boarded that ship. But, considering the feat of getting the Australian batch afloat at all, what mattered one inaccurate signal to London?

A poignant account of a CORB embarkation day comes from a girl who sailed aboard the *Batory* aged eight. True, her batch was the only one to sail overseas aboard a troop-ship, which colours her description, but the mood she recaptures will strike a chord in many an ex-CORB evacuee's heart. 'I will never forget the day we boarded the *Batory*,' she writes; 'the Scots pipe band; the lines of soldiers on the grey, dismal quayside. Once on board, we hung out of a porthole watching them file up the ship's side. We cried to see the soldiers saying goodbye between the railings. We cried with the women reaching through the railings for that last touch. I may have been only eight years old, but the sights and sounds of that embarkation day are deeply etched on my mind.'

In her classic book on overseas evacuation, *Pilgrim Children*, published in 1942, Jean Lorimer reflected on these CORB sailings. 'Geoffrey Shakespeare and members of the Board' (usually it was Mrs Elspeth Davies who accompanied him, as CORB's Welfare Director) 'were always there to see them off; but no parents or friends were allowed. There was no waving of flags . . . no shouting. But the expectancy of high adventure hung in the air, and gallantly these children responded.'[4]

Mr Shakespeare tried to see each batch of CORB youngsters, either in their hostels or on the docks, just before they embarked. He would exhort them to remember that they were ambassadors of their country and, as such, they could not always behave as they would like. If they behaved well, he argued, 'people will say, "What splendid children these are: we must do everything we can to help their parents win the war." When things go wrong, remember you are British — grin and bear it!'[5]

Later in the war, he delighted in telling the story about an eleven year old CORB girl, newly arrived in Canada, striding up to a weeping seven year old evacuee on a Canadian rail-road station. 'Stop it at once: be British!' ordered the older girl. A nearby escort claimed that the child stopped crying immediately. But, Geoffrey Shakespeare's advice, although brave and well-meant, might well have contributed to a cause for complaint levelled at some CORB children, namely, that they tended too often to mask their true feelings. And, in some cases, taking the advice to 'grin and bear it!' too much to heart led, almost certainly, to deep and lasting ill effects on their emotional development.

A newspaper reporter set the scene for one of Mr Shakespeare's send-off appearances in these words: 'The night before sailing, they sang songs, gave interviews, and hearkened to little cheerful speeches. The Under-Secretary of State for Dominion Affairs and Chairman of the Board — who had become, quite in the BBC manner, "Uncle Geoffrey" for the occasion — made one of them from the elevation of a chair. It was a sort of prize-day speech before the holidays, with hints on how one should behave during the holidays, particularly in other people's homes. It was very kindly, with hopes for a good voyage, happy times, and a glimpse into the future, when the war is won, and, shall we say, "The 'kids' come home"?'[6]

But, there were other slants to this jolly description, as Geoffrey Shakespeare was well aware. 'It is always a thrilling if mournful experience,' he wrote after the war, 'to see hundreds of small children climbing the gangway, clutching a bundle of luggage as big as themselves. . . . We

Macdonald, Publishers

Fig 7: *Geoffrey Shakespeare, CORB's planner and first chairman, with CORB children about to leave embarkation hostel for Canada. He saw most batches before they sailed.*

were very wise to make it a rule that parents should not accompany their children to the port. There would have been unendurable scenes. ... The farewell scenes were heartrending enough for those who had never seen the children before. They nearly always sang, in the final stages, *There'll always be an England*! It has a patriotic lilt and is a catchy tune. But when it is sung by small children leaning over the rail of a great ship it has a profoundly moving effect. I could hardly ever hear them singing without a lump in my throat . . .

'Mr Graham Cunningham, who joined the (Overseas Reception) Board . . . came as a hard-headed businessman, with little respect for politicians, and with less for civil servants! . . . I thought he was devoid of feelings until, on one occasion, we stood together on a small barge to wave final farewells to a crowd of CORB children, singing, as usual, *There'll always be an England*. I turned to pass a remark to Graham Cunningham and, to my surprise, the tears were coursing down his cheeks . . .'[7]

10

'CHEERFUL AND WELL BEHAVED'

Altogether, nineteen batches[1] of CORB children set sail,
eleven to Canada, three to Australia, three to New Zealand
and two to South Africa. Sixteen of these shipments
arrived safely at their destination; some of these were very
lucky to do so, and the danger signs were evident when the
first of the batches was in the early stages of its voyage to
Canada.

'We travelled in convoy of thirty two ships,' writes former
CORB evacuee Ronald Smith, now a parson in West
Vancouver. 'I remember the day vividly, I was sitting with
my brother and one or two friends on a large box at the
stern of the ship. It was a beautiful, sunny day. We were
enjoying the sunshine and watching the other ships in the
convoy.

'Suddenly, there were loud explosions. Ships began to
blow up as torpedoes hit them. Emergency whistles blew.
The emergency alarm sounded on our ship and we had to
rush to our life-boat stations where we were issued with
life-jackets. ... The convoy scattered. We sailed on alone
...'

There were thirty nine boys and forty three girls aboard
Ronald Smith's ship, the Booth Line's *SS Anselm*, in the care
of seven escorts, a doctor and two nurses. This, the first
CORB batch to sail, had the coding 'D1'.[2] It was a modest
start to the scheme. CORB had intended a much grander
opening: five hundred aboard the *SS Britannic*. But these
plans were scrapped with the suspension of the scheme on
the 11 July.[3] As far as the British public was aware, of
course, the CORB plan was still in suspension when, on

Sunday, 21 July, 1940, the *Anselm* sailed from Liverpool with the D1 batch on board.

Chief escort to the evacuees was Miss Edith Gowans. A welfare worker serving employees' children at the Woolwich Arsenal, Miss Gowans came to CORB with strong recommendations from the WVS and her chief at Woolwich. On the 15 July, Miss Gowans received a telegram from CORB Director, Marjorie Maxse: 'Report for duty mid-day Friday. Written instructions follow.'[4] This was precisely the day on which the British press reported the Government's decision to suspend operation of the CORB scheme.

The *Anselm* joined the other ships of convoy OB187 near the Rock Light. There were thirty eight merchant ships, escorted by only two naval vessels: the destroyer *HMS Enchantress* and the corvette *HMS Clarkia*, whose task was soon to prove utterly impossible.[5] Indeed, the arguments for suspension of the overseas evacuation scheme remained very convincing as D1 set sail on the *Anselm*. The Admiralty had no chance whatsoever of giving adequate naval protection to convoys in general, let alone to convoys that included evacuee ships. And, only two days before convoy OB187 sailed, Naval Intelligence warned of the presence of three U-boats known to be within range of the convoy's scheduled course.

Nevertheless, all went well with the convoy until mid-day on the 27 July. Then, at 1.55 pm, in brilliant sunshine, about two hundred miles north-west of Ireland, the situation suddenly deteriorated. Without warning, just as Ronald Smith remembers, the leading ship in the convoy's port column blew up. This was the *SS Vinemoor*. Torpedoed near her No 4 hatch, her bulkheads rapidly caved in, and she sank.

Meanwhile, in rapid succession, three more ships were struck and crippled: the *Accra*, the *Sambre* and the *Thiara*. Within half an hour they, too, had sunk, fortunately with very few casualties. The survivors were soon aboard the *Hollanside*, a merchant ship that had remained behind to assist, and arrived safely in Liverpool on the 30 July.[6]

The rest of the convoy dispersed in obedience to the convoy Commodore's signal, whilst the *Enchantress* and the *Clarkia* hunted for the hidden attacker. But, they made no contact at all.

In his U-boat report, the Commanding Officer of the *Enchantress* complained bitterly that two escort vessels were 'a quite inadequate escort for a large convoy,' especially as the dangers were getting worse 'now that the German subs have taken new heart and are attacking our convoys with vigour.'[7] Vice-Admiral L F Crabbe, the RN Flag Officer in Liverpool, passed on his escort commander's comments verbatim to the Commander in Chief Western Approaches, adding a note that 'Three escort vessels are the absolute minimum.'

But, at that stage of the war, with the invasion of Britain apparently imminent, and submarine attacks on the increase, there was nothing the Commander in Chief could do nor, for that matter, the Admiralty itself, so stretched were British naval resources. In the long run, only four CORB ships had impressive naval escorts to their convoys. Batches D5, D7 and D8, aboard the *Antonia*, the *Duchess of York* and the *Oronsay*, and totalling 1,131 evacuees, sailed for Canada in convoy ZA with an escort of six destroyers and the battleship *HMS Revenge*.[8] Besides the CORB ships, there were only three other liners in the convoy. But, the reason for the exceptional naval protection was that these six liners had been modified to carry thousands of troops, and had been ferrying Canadian divisions to Britain since December, 1939, to assist in defence against the invasion. Loss of any of these large liners could have been crucial to the war effort.

Similarly, one other CORB ship benefited indirectly from military urgency, and had high naval protection. This was the *Batory*, which set sail in a convoy of sixteen liners, heavily laden with troop reinforcements for the Middle and Far East Land Forces. For the first three days, the convoy had the undivided attention of all eight destroyers of the 9th Destroyer Flotilla, and the cruisers *Emerald*, *Shropshire*, and *Cornwall*.[9] After those three days, the destroyers returned to base, the *Emerald* proceeded to Canada with gold bullion, whilst the convoy split into a fast and slow half, one escorted by *Shropshire*, the other by *Cornwall*.[10] Apart from these privileged CORB ships, all others that set sail had to run the risks entailed in an over-large convoy escorted by a painfully small number of naval vessels.

As far as the *Anselm* was concerned, after the U-boat attack, convoy OB187 dispersed and the *Anselm*, with its eighty two CORB evacuees, sailed westwards completely alone for eight days. At last, as Ronald Smith writes, 'It was with a feeling of relief that we pulled into Halifax Harbour.'

Out of range of U-boats, and with no accompanying ships to divert the attention of the children, life had settled down to a rather tame routine aboard the *Anselm*. A lack of foresight, (or possibly over-hasty planning, owing to D1 setting sail whilst the scheme was officially suspended), meant that the ship was carrying very little equipment suitable for children. This increased the escorts' difficulties, and led Miss Gowans to stress, in her voyage report, that future CORB sailings 'must have more cards, books, crayons and drawing books; and more wool and needles to carry out running repairs on children's clothing.'[11]

Ironically, the very next CORB batch to set sail fared even worse as far as provision for children was concerned. This was batch C1 who, because of the switch from *Orion* to *Batory* at only a few hours' notice, on the 5 August, sailed to Cape Town without any equipment at all, except the New Testaments issued to all CORB children by the Scripture Gift Mission, and five films intended for screening to the private passengers.[12] This stretched the ingenuity of the *Batory* escorts in the three weeks it took to reach Cape Town. But, to their intense relief, the South African Red Cross, Rotary and other organizations in Cape Town, hearing of their plight, sent vanloads of children's books, games and toys to help them on their way.

On the 3 August, 1940, the day the *Anselm* arrived with D1 in Halifax, the Ministry of Information allowed the British press to announce the news.[13] This was the first intimation to the British public that the Government was going ahead with its overseas evacuation scheme after all. But, by then, the next two CORB batches, D2 and C1, had already reached their hostels in Liverpool, and were about to face the dangers of the voyage ahead.

These dangers, potentially, were very real. But, the majority of memories held by former CORB evacuees and their escorts about U-boat attacks and 'U-boats tailing the convoy', are based on rumours. Sometimes, the sight of escort vessels dropping depth charges led to the assumption that the convoy was under attack. For example, ex-evacuees who sailed with D12 aboard the *Nerissa* refer to their convoy being attacked during the early period of their voyage. But, Admiralty records show that convoy OB210[14] in which the *Nerissa* sailed suffered no attack; although the Commodore's report reveals that two Anti-submarine Trawlers, part of the convoy escort, did report a possible submarine contact on the second day out from Liverpool. Both ships investigated, but inconclusively, and the *Nerissa's* convoy continued its way unmolested.[15]

Another rumour, even more convincing in its basis, lives on with former members of batch Z1 who sailed to New Zealand aboard the *Ruahine*. On the second day of their voyage, Captain Oxnard, the ship's Master, summoned all the passengers to muster stations where they heard from ship's officers that there was possibly a U-boat in the vicinity. The convoy Commodore's report makes no reference to any such alarm, however, nor to any search having to be made by his escort vessels.[16] But, clearly, Captain Oxnard was acting out of caution, and was not going to be caught unawares with his precious cargo on board. Thus, for the next few days, the CORB children had instructions to wear their day clothes, as well as keeping on their life-jackets, day and night.

Two CORB boys aboard different ships in convoy OB203 have clear memories of the kind of incident that led to long-held rumours about attacks. Alec Hedgecock, ten years old when with the three hundred and eight children of batch U1 aboard the *Llanstephan Castle*, records that the convoy was 'attacked' on the third night out from Liverpool, and he heard depth charges exploding 'like giant hammers'. Next morning, he adds, 'we were sailing alone.' And also with convoy OB203, George Eccles, heading for Australia with CORB batch C2 aboard the neighbouring ship *Nestor*, mentions a 'sub-scare — though nothing sighted.' But, the depth charges heard were dropped only as a routine measure against a possible contact. Admiral Sir Ralph Crooke, RNR, the convoy Commodore, makes no mention of any attack in his official report, noting only that he had to order the convoy 'to make emergency turns to keep clear of the escort whilst hunting.'[17]

Like most CORB ships, the Polish ship *Batory*, carrying C1 and six hundred troops, was rife with rumours, particularly in the early stages of the voyage. In view of the U-boat situation into which convoy WS2 sailed, they were very lucky not to undergo such an attack.[18] An Admiralty signal sent to the convoy Commodore during the *Batory's* first day at sea warned: 'six or seven U-boats operational in Western Approaches.'[19]

Several ex-*Batory* evacuees report seeing depth charges being dropped by escort vessels and heard explosions during the first twenty four hours. Certainly, four of the destroyer escort reported 'contacts' on the first morning at sea, dropping a depth charge apiece on each occasion; and, just over twenty four hours later, two destroyers made a 'contact' dropping another depth charge each. But, they were simply obeying the orders of the Destroyer Flotilla Commander who, at the convoy briefing, had insisted: 'No chance will be taken. Therefore a depth charge will be dropped in every case, even on suspicion.'[20] When the fast section of this convoy arrived in Freetown, Captain Hammell, aboard the cruiser *Cornwall*, reported that these 'contacts' were 'only slightly suspicious' and 'the voyage was without incident.'[21]

Nevertheless, the *Batory* story about a ship in the convoy being torpedoed and limping back to Liverpool was understandable in view of an incident that actually did take place. At 9 pm on the second night at sea, WS2 convoy escort vessels received an SOS from the torpedoed merchant ship *Mohammed Ali el Kebir* about two hundred miles astern of the convoy. Captain Hammell, as Senior Naval Officer with the convoy, sent two of the escorting destroyers at full speed to assist in the hunt for the attacking U-boat, and assist the stricken ship into port.[22]

But, the most soundly based rumour of all, was about the possibility of the *Batory* being attacked by a German raider in the Indian Ocean. Now in a tiny convoy, but still escorted by the cruiser *Cornwall*, the *Batory* sailed eastwards from Cape Town to rendezvous south-east of Madagascar with an Australian Armed Merchant Cruiser, *HMAS*

Kanimbla who would take over from the *Cornwall* on the 3 September. However, the convoy had to 'mark time' in fog awaiting the *Kanimbla* whilst she investigated the whereabouts of the German raider *Pinguin* further to the north. Just before giving up the search, *Kanimbla* found an oil slick marking the spot where the *Pinguin's* last victim had sunk, and soon afterwards joined the *Batory's* convoy.[23] Following this alarm, and in view of the close proximity of the raider ship, the convoy changed course drastically, heading back to Madagascar, then northwards off the East African coast, eventually skirting the Seychelles on the way to Bombay.[24]

Even more imminent than the *Batory's* dangers, however, were those facing the one hundred and thirteen children of batch Z2, who left Liverpool in the early hours of the 29 August, aboard the *Rangitata*, to join convoy OB205. During the following night, the alarm sounded aboard the *Rangitata*, and former evacuees retain clear memories of subsequent events. Eleven year old Colin Crafer, for instance, already interested in ships, and in later life a Royal Navy Chief Petty Officer, knew immediately that the stricken ship he saw when arriving on deck was the *SS Volendam*, another CORB ship.[25] Edna Chase, also aboard the *Rangitata*, 'simply thought the alarm had gone for a practice, but then saw the *Volendam* all lit up in the mist.' In fact, the *Volendam* was on fire, and the children with Z2 learnt later that she had just been torpedoed. But, they did not learn that two other ships in the same convoy were also torpedoed that night; and one of those could obviously have been the *Rangitata*.

The Z2 children spent the next few nights sleeping on the floor of the first-class lounge and Captain Holland, the ship's Master, forbade them to go below decks for any purpose whatsoever, even during day-time. As the weather turned very stormy and most of the children became very seasick, this, with the cold and discomfort, made life miserable and put a great deal of extra stress on chief escort Pamela Redmayne and her assistants. But, as the Rev H A Hayden, the CORB Anglican Chaplain on board wrote: 'The children behaved splendidly during this critical time. There was no sign of alarm or panic . . .'[26]

With these obvious dangers around them, and facing

difficult odds, ships' Masters and CORB escorts had to insist
on stringent attention to emergency regulations, although
there was wide variation aboard CORB ships in their
approaches to lifeboat practices and other safety matters.
Miss Nora Belgrove, an escort to batch D8 aboard the
Oronsay, recalls that she and her colleagues slept fully
clothed during the first few nights of the voyage, until the
convoy was considered beyond U-boat range.

Aboard the same ship, ex-evacuee Marion Freedman
remembers that there were daily practices at boat-stations
— required of all CORB ships whilst in the U-boat danger
zone — but also the life-boats were lowered frequently,
presumably to test that davits were in working order. Her
sister, Thelma, adds that sometimes the children were
actually lowered whilst seated in the boats; and Kathleen
Lovegrove, also aboard the *Oronsay*, writes of a day when
the children sat in the ship's life-boats for four hours 'as a
U-boat attack was expected.'

In the same convoy with batch D7 aboard the *Duchess of
York*, escort Violet Chalmers, a Salvation Army Major,
reports that the evacuees had instructions 'to wear life-
jackets day and night', whereas the usual practice in other
CORB ships was for them to be carried compulsorily
absolutely everywhere during the day, and placed at the
foot of each evacuee's bunk at night.

Inevitably, the emphasis on emergency drill, though
essential, caused anxiety to some sensitive children. One
ex-CORB boy, aged eleven at the time, admits that he
sometimes wondered how he and his companions would
negotiate the route from their cabin to the life-boat station
if the ship were torpedoed, especially if the lights failed. His
batch had been told, when they had to transfer from
Liverpool to Greenock before embarkation, that the reason
was the torpedoing of a shipload of evacuees just out of
Liverpool. Hardly surprising that he worried about his
escape route. A girl who sailed on the *Nestor*, aged eight,
simply says: 'I still remember the feeling of terror when
practising life-boat drill.'

On the other hand, not all CORB children worried.
Keith Parker, a seven year old member of D2, and now a
Professor of Canadian Studies in Florida, ·sums up his

memory of the *Hilary's* voyage succinctly: 'The journey was like a big new game — and a war game! I was oblivious of the danger and the worry it caused others.'

The worry was shouldered by the steamship companies, the ships' crews, and the CORB escorts. Rules for children whilst on board, drawn up for the guidance of CORB escorts by Mr Shinwell's Joint Committee at the Ministry of Shipping, illustrate some of the worry they had to face. For instance:

> Children must not put their heads out of port holes.
>
> Children will not be allowed on the upper deck during the hours of darkness, or when coming alongside.
>
> Children must not climb on ship's rails.

More sobering still were the notes on 'Emergency Arrangements' issued to CORB staff. 'War game' or not, many former evacuees recall with a chill the dire warnings about emergency procedures. Typical were these:

> It is vital for the safety of anyone wearing the standard life-jacket that it should be tied tightly by the strings *in front*, and this is particularly important with children.
>
> In the case of small children it may be necessary to stuff a pillow case or other convenient article between the chest and the jacket. If the strings are not tied tightly there is grave danger of the child being throttled on getting into the water, or having its neck broken if it falls into the water from any height.[27]

Two incidents remembered by escort Major Chalmers aboard the *Duchess of York* epitomize the tremendous anxiety the CORB escorts generally must have endured. She was horrified one day to see a small boy throw his life-jacket into the sea. 'He was thrilled to bits to see it floating in the water and said "Oh! Look! If I'd gone overboard, I'd've been safe!" ' And, a terrible reminder of the perpetual risks

these CORB ships were running, escort Chalmers writes:
'Just before we sailed over one stretch of water, a ship had
been sunk. We saw men in the water but, of course, were
not able to stop and pick them up because we had the
children on board.'

The competent CORB escorts who made up the large
majority kept constant watch for sinking morale. Apart from
the fear of attack, the anxiety caused by safety and
emergency regulations, and worries about younger brothers
and sisters — 'My main occupation at sea was constantly
searching for my younger sister who managed to be in six
places at once!' — it was homesickness and seasickness that
asserted themselves as the chief enemies. Many former
evacuees have vivid memories of the torture of seasickness.

One eight year old girl with D12 aboard the *Nerissa*
claims: 'Everything reduced to seasickness. I ate half an
apple in eight days! Meanwhile, my sister's freckles turned
green!' Her sister, two years older, agrees that she was 'most
miserably seasick', though she does not mention her freckles.
She remembers 'the deck going up and down; swaying from
side to side when trying to walk in narrow passages; and
trying to eat dry biscuits which were supposed to settle the
stomach.'

John Wood, aged ten aboard the *Antonia* with D5, says he
could eat nothing at all during the time he was seasick.
However, he recalls, sailors insisted he should try to eat
something, because this would 'soothe the stomach and also
feed the fish!'

Angus Macleod, a fourteen year old with Z1 aboard the
Ruahine, noted in his diary that on the fourth day out from
Liverpool well over half the eighty nine children in the
batch were suffering seasickness. There was general relief, he
noted later, when the storm-wracked ship eventually
reached the Panama Canal Zone, having taken a month to
cross the Atlantic. Peter Beams, also aboard the *Ruahine*, was
one of the many who shared in the relief. 'There were such
mountainous seas,' he recalls, 'that the escort destroyers
simply disappeared under the waves, only to reappear as
though by some miracle. . . . Most of those four weeks saw
me hanging over the side being violently ill!'

An eleven year old aboard the *Duchess of York* speaks for

many. She says, very succinctly: 'I was very seasick for the
first few days. At that time, I wanted to die.' But, for most
who suffered, it was only the first few days that were really
bad. The worst case of all was probably that of ten year old
Joan Hare with C1 on the *Batory*. She was so ill with
seasickness during the three weeks it took to reach Cape
Town that, she writes, 'My escort, Mrs Clothier, with whom
I still correspond, did think I might be taken off the ship at
Cape Town, as the medical people were afraid of
dehydration.' However, perhaps the magnificent welcome
given to the CORB children in Cape Town was sufficient
tonic; for Joan completed the voyage aboard the *Batory*, and
felt it was more and more 'like one long holiday.'

Diane Clarke, another member of the *Batory* batch says: 'I
think my younger sister Patsy and I must have been the
only two children who weren't seasick; but we were
desperately homesick.' Some suffered both; and, for some,
there were doubtless psychological links between their
seasickness and their homesickness.

Homesickness was obviously more difficult for escorts to
spot. Geoffrey Shakespeare showed understanding when he
said that this 'strange disease' can overwhelm a child
completely; yet that same child 'within an hour is laughing
and joking again, for a child's make-up is very resilient.'[28]

Many former evacuees would echo the simple statement
of Thelma Freedman aboard the *Oronsay*: 'I know I missed
my mother terribly, and I was very homesick.' And,
sometimes, the homesickness rubbed off one on to another.
'Once at boat-drill,' recollects a fifteen year old girl on the
Llanstephan Castle, 'my sister broke down and said, "I want
to go home!" ' The older girl found the effect temporarily
devastating.

The more detailed recollections of an eleven year old
Rangitata girl poignantly illustrate the difficulty for an escort
recognizing homesickness, which could manifest itself in so
many emotional 'aches'. 'I remember a great feeling of
loneliness,' she writes. 'The misery of being removed from a
concert party because I couldn't get the hang of a dance
routine to *Just like the ivy on an old garden wall*; and being
upset at the loss of special farewell gifts from relatives. I was
not particularly happy, except when I received a small

John Fethney

Fig 8: *Mrs Constance Fox, CORB escort to the West Yorkshire boys, and Cub and Scout Leader aboard the Polish ship "Batory". With several other escorts she spent over two years as a prisoner of war after her returning ship was sunk by a German raider.*

sailor doll with *Rangitata* on his cap — a share-out of toys donated by American passengers en route for the USA. By coincidence, it was the only thing I wanted above all else from the window of the ship's shop.'

However, the resilience of the children, combined with the watchful care of their CORB escorts, seem to have left most evacuees with happier memories. Aboard most CORB ships, there was a wealth of talent — both amongst the evacuees and the escorts. This ensured concerts in plenty, with solo singers, instrumentalists, conjurers, comedians, as well as choirs and instrumental ensembles. Community singing was ever popular.

Mr Charles Kilby, Headmaster of a Surrey Junior School, who was Chief escort to C1 aboard the *Batory*, reported: 'We soon found we had experts in every branch of education, and enthusiasts in every form of entertainment, organized games and pastimes.' Only batch Z2, aboard the *Rangitata*, had the full-time services of a professional entertainer, Mr E Vidal, amongst other things a gifted pianist. The evacuees appreciated his presence, finding him a sympathetic counsellor as well as a good entertainer. But, the experience of other batches showed that there was no need to hire a professional.

Invariably, singing was the most popular activity. In several CORB batches, community singing was conducted by Salvation Army Officers or professional music teachers. The C1 batch had amongst the escorts Miss Meta Maclean, well-known Australian song-writer and versatile pianist, and Miss Margaret Osborne, a competent singer. They helped the ship to earn the nickname 'The Singing Ship' from the world's press, and together these two escorts wrote a CORB song, *The Call*, which was a spirited piece about children responding to kind voices overseas.[29]

More properly, however, the *Batory* batch's song was *Rota*, a Polish national song, translated on the suggestion of Captain Deycharkoski by assistant purser Marian Slabosz:

'Never we'll leave the land we love,
Her tongue relinquish never!
Polish in nation, blood and kings,
Piast's line shall live forever . . .!'

John Fethney

Fig 9: *King's Scout Keith Langdale displays the Troop flag made by "Batory" crew members on the day Mrs Fox received it from Captain Deycharkoski.*

Most ships, and invariably those with large batches on board, had well ordered daily programmes of activities ranging from deck-game tournaments, boxing championships and talent competitions, to lectures on Shakespearean plays, birds of the Dominions, astronomy in the Southern Hemisphere, and life in the Dominion soon to be lived in. Scouts, Guides, Cubs and Brownies flourished on several ships, and especially those sailing to more distant lands. The work of Miss Eleanor Pearson for the *Batory* Guides, and of Mrs Constance Fox, another *Batory* escort who ran a Cub Pack of thirty boys and a Scout Troop of forty eight on alternate days throughout the voyage, assisted by fifteen year old King's Scout, Keith Langdale from Bradford, still arouses an enthusiastic response from ex-members after more than forty years. The ship's crew was so impressed with the Scouts that they made a Troop flag for them, and Keith Langdale had the honour of receiving it from the hands of the Captain in a special ceremony on the after deck.

There are happy memories, too, of the less formal events: the hours spent playing games with friends in cabins, or on deck, perhaps in the shade of a life-boat as the ship sailed through tropic waters. There were hours of draughts, chess, ludo, snakes and ladders, and the obsessive 'fiddlesticks', now long out of fashion. In this game, if a player moved any other stick in trying to pick one up, he forfeited a 'go'; so, arguments abounded as to whether it was the motion of the ship that was to blame.

Barbara Spence, evacuated from York aged ten, recalls the midnight parties held in the cabins of her escort group aboard the Canada-bound *Antonia*. Jean Cheyne, nine years old aboard the *Bayano* with D9 — an all-Scottish batch — remembers the constant fun with her escort Miss Ernds who was returning to Canada; the sailors giving film and variety shows; her excitement on seeing the Northern Lights; 'interesting talks about Canada'; and she adds gleefully, 'No lessons!'

John Fethney aged thirteen at the time, writes: 'My main memories are pleasant to very pleasant: Scouting, boxing, gym; our shore leaves, especially in Cape Town — so much free food and drink ashore we could hardly face meals back on board[30]; smells, poverty and beggars in Bombay; coconuts and the Zoo in Colombo . . .'

Amongst the hundreds of CORB children, there are a host of memories, many of them quite different from anyone else's. An ex-*Ruahine* girl writes: 'I remember a steward bringing us fruit from the Captain's table. One of the girls named Louise gave me a beautiful gold locket when we parted in Wellington and I still have it. I often wonder what her parents would have said if they had known she had given away such a beautiful thing . . .' Freda Stout, thirteen years old when aboard the *Batory* wrote: 'I can remember feeling intensely patriotic — idiotically patriotic! I wrote a poem in this vein for the *Albatross*, a magazine printed during the voyage, and it now makes me shudder; but I was proud of it at the time. Fresh limes at Freetown; our Polish Captain — who could forget him? The solid custard with pink sauce — gorgeous!' And ten year old Alec Hedgecock aboard the *Llanstephan Castle*, and in later life an ocean-going ship's Master, recalls: 'I had great interest in the ship. Got into trouble with escort through adventuring out of bounds! But crew members took me all over, even down to the engine room.'

And there are also innumerable snatches of memory of the brief, simple moments of excitement, or the simple, human touches: 'Trying to climb the greasy pole on the ship for biscuits as prizes.' — 'Sing-songs in the dining-room during the Captain's inspection of our cabins; Guide meetings; sitting on deck trying to knit a jumper, and making so many mistakes one of the girls wrote a poem saying I unpicked more than I knitted!' And: 'The kind words from one of the ship's officers — just a brief exchange.' And another: 'A passenger, a German Jewish lady, gave me an orange.' Whilst a nine year old who travelled aboard the *Nova Scotia* confesses: 'I do remember a feeling of satisfaction when a girl in my cabin who had bullied me since leaving the UK was afflicted with seasickness — and I wasn't.'

There seems to have been a good community spirit amongst these CORB children, however. At least two CORB ships, both with Headmasters as chief escorts, exploited the age range of the evacuees and set up a 'prefect' system. Mr Hossack aboard the *Bayano* — who usually referred to his charges as 'pupils' in his reports — involved older boys and girls in specific duties, helping younger children to wash, dress, go to bed.[31]

Aboard the *Batory* the duties were more earnest. When the six hundred troops left the ship at Singapore, Mr Kilby asked the senior boys to volunteer to undertake those sentry duties previously done by soldiers on companionways, landings and stairs that needed to be manned in case of emergency. Sufficient boys came forward to man these crucial spots from 8 am until 10 pm, after which members of the crew took over. The Scout patrol leaders in Mrs Fox's Scout Troop provided the seven 'sergeants' who commanded the companies of sentries; and guard-changing took place every two hours with proper ceremony — although occasionally mocked by irreverent little girls.

The only CORB batch to run into difficulties over discipline seems to have been C2 aboard the *Nestor*.

C2 escort Ruth Morton writes: 'We were not allowed to use corporal punishment, of course. I was a bit taken aback one day when two or three of my group came to me and said, "Miss, we think you're soft!" When I asked them why, I was told, "Because you don't smack us when we're naughty!" I just said, "Wait till next time!" A smack on the back of the legs then seemed to restore their confidence in me!'

Escort Father Ernest Ball, Church of England Chaplain to C2, and member of the Society of the Sacred Mission, an Anglican Order, writes: 'It might be thought a simple matter to manage such a small group of boys, but for me it was far from easy. . . . One was apt to cause alarm by his sudden disappearances, when searchers would eventually find him in some remote part of the ship. Another was particularly troublesome. . . . He took delight in causing annoyance, and incited the other boys to do the same, mostly at meal-times . . .'[32]

Australian Miss Rosalie Golding, a nurse with C2, recalls that eventually, the *Nestor*'s Master, Captain Power, had to insist on some better discipline from the unruly element aboard his ship. But, he was far from prejudiced against the CORB children. Quite the reverse. During the voyage, he

Ruth Morton

Fig 10: *CORB escort Ruth Morton with members of her escort group on deck aboard the "Nestor" bound for Australia.*

discovered that some private passengers were complaining about the CORB presence generally. (Similar unsympathetic grouses arose on other ships carrying small groups of private passengers). Captain Power invited these passengers and the CORB escorts to a cocktail party, Miss Golding states, 'where he told the private passengers in no uncertain terms that the children were evacuees "not refugees"; that they were his "main concern"; and that, if anyone were not satisfied, the ship was calling at Cape Town, and they knew what they could do about it!'

In fact, the behaviour and morale of most CORB children seems to have been remarkably good. Commander J S M Ritchie, RNR, the convoy Commodore to OB194, who sailed with his staff with D2 aboard the *Hilary* reported that the evacuees were 'extraordinarily cheerful and well behaved ... despite leaving their parents behind in England. No parents need have any qualms,' he added, 'in sending their children to Canada if they are looked after as well as they were on board the *Hilary*.'[33]

Similarly, most comments about CORB escorts are full of praise, too. Writing to CORB Headquarters about the thirty eight escorts under his command, C1 chief escort Charles Kilby spoke enthusiastically about the care, initiative and resourcefulness of his team, recommending several for future voyages as chief escorts. He criticized one or two for being over-fussy or seeking too much attention; and suggested that fifty should be the upper age limit, because one of his lady escorts, well over fifty, suffered a heart attack early in the voyage.

Captain Holland of the *Rangitata*, in addition to questioning why CORB hired a professional entertainer, Mr Vidal, also expressed some mixed feelings about the chief escort on his ship. He thought she had too heavy a load to carry single-handed. Yet, despite reservations, he had found her very keen, most conscientious, and a born organizer. On the one occasion when an emergency did arise, '(she) impressed me very much with her calmness and good leadership.'[34]

Adverse criticism of escorts by evacuees is rare. Perhaps the strongest complaint comes from a former *Batory* girl who reports: 'I was terrified of my escort who told us we were ungrateful to complain about the Polish food when our parents were starving like rats in the gutter!'

Far more typical are the favourable comments. Barbara Spence, implying a tribute to her escort, writes: 'I was a very shy child, yet encountered no problems whatsoever.' Brenda Standage records: 'Throughout the journey we were always treated with great care and understanding.' And Muriel Evans, ten years old when aboard the *Batory*: 'We were wonderfully cared for by both escorts and crew.' Not surprisingly, after ten and a half weeks on board another ten year old recalls: 'The *Batory* had become a second home to us kids, and there were lots of tears as we disembarked.'

Several CORB batches had to contend with high illness rates, adding to the stress imposed on escorts. Some of the *Antonia* and *Llanstephan Castle* children landed in Canada and South Africa respectively with scarlet fever. The *Nestor* had an epidemic of measles after calling at Cape Town and escorts and medical staff had to wrestle with the effects of the epidemic for the rest of the voyage.

The *Batory*, in its 20,000 mile voyage involving three

Fig 11: *(above) On the* Llanstephan Castle — *a group of CORB boys with an officer.*

Fig 12: *(below) On the* Llanstephan Castle *in the Tropics — an improvised swimming pool gives lots of fun.*

crossings of the equator, developed serious problems to be expected aboard a ship built for the short, North Atlantic crossing now spending weeks in tropical seas. Fresh water was permanently scarce; prickly heat, various rashes, a plague of boils, impetigo, and measles hit epidemic levels, the highly contagious impetigo causing considerable difficulties and necessitating the apportioning of much cabin accommodation as an isolation area.

Yet, aboard these CORB ships, there were remarkably few serious injuries to children — (apart from the terrible effects of the torpedoing of the *City of Benares*).[35] The worst injury on record involved CORB boy William Riley, eight year old son of a railway fireman from Stockton-on-Tees. Contrary to safety warnings, William had his head through a port-hole on the *Batory* as she prepared to move berths in Bombay Harbour. One of the mooring hawsers, on being released, hit William's head, inflicting a massive wound. Fortunately for the victim a cabin-mate, thirteen year old scout Maurice Taylor, a fisherman's son from Hull, immediately grabbed his legs and 'undoubtedly saved him either from a smashed skull or from drowning, or both,' wrote Mrs Fox. William required seventeen stitches in his head, and spent several days in a Bombay hospital, being deposited aboard the *Batory* from a motor launch just as she was setting sail for Colombo.

Clearly, much could be said about the educational advantages that CORB evacuees gained from their wartime voyages. Some of them consider that their experiences on board and in ports of call made an impact on their future development. Meta Maclean, escort with C1, wrote a little later[36] about the *Batory* children having their first taste of a united Empire in the remarkably warm welcome they received in Cape Town, Bombay, Colombo, Singapore, and the three Australian ports visited. But, the welcome given to the New Zealand batches at non-British ports suggests that all humane people were ready to open their hearts — and often their homes, too — when these war exiles had made their way through perilous seas to their countries.

Thus, whether it was the generous hospitality of General and Mrs Smuts at *Westbrooke*, the South African Governor-General's official residence, made available to the three

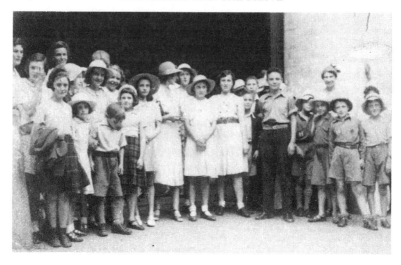

"Times of Ceylon"

Fig 13: *(above) Australia-bound CORB children (including the author, third from right) about to re-embark after a day spent in Colombo with the Forces' Welfare Committee.*

Fig 14: *(below) The news anxiously awaited from CORB Headquarters by all parents: a telegram announcing a CORB child's safe arrival overseas.*

Crown Copyright

Charges to pay
s. d.
RECEIVED

POST OFFICE
TELEGRAM

No.
OFFICE STAMP

Prefix. Time handed in. Office of Origin and Service Instructions. Words.

From

48 7.0 MAYFAIR C OHMS 11

PENWARDEN 41 PIERREMONT GARDENS DARLINGTON =

SHIP WITH CHILDREN ARRIVED SAFELY = AVONCORB +

For free repetition of doubtful words telephone "TELEGRAMS ENQUIRY" or call, with this form at office of delivery. Other enquiries should be accompanied by this form and, if possible, the envelope.

Australian and the two South African batches; or the
Women's Armed Forces Reception Committee entertaining
the C_1 children on a day's excursion in private cars in
Colombo; or the gigantic 'picnic spread for us all' provided
by the Rotary Club of Durban for batch C_2; or the
memorable reception laid on by the American Entertain-
ments Committee for Z_2 in Balbao — (again, piles of
exciting food, gallons of cool drinks, outings in private cars
through the ruins of Old Panama) — these children
amassed a lifetime's lessons about human kindness and
altruism.

It is appropriate to let a former CORB escort, himself a
distinguished educator of children, speak about the educational benefits of a CORB voyage. Mr Bill Oats, Australian
schoolmaster from the International School in Geneva, aged
only twenty eight when appointed deputy chief escort to the
Batory batch, puts it like this: 'I regard the experience of
those ten and a half weeks as a major one. I crammed more
educational raw experience into those weeks than into the
same number of years of ordinary schoolmastering.' He is in
a rare position to make such a comparison. A first class
honours graduate of Adelaide University at the time, with
two higher research degrees to his credit later, Mr Oats
spent thirty two years of his working life as a Head, most of
them at the Friends' School in Hobart.

Continuing his reflections on the impact of those weeks at
sea he says: 'In effect, we were cast adrift, escorts and
children, with a minimum of equipment, a maximum of
goodwill, perhaps; but also with many quite forbidding
difficulties. And we came through singing! Praise be! And
we landed in Australia with no one missing, despite a
couple of close calls!'[37]

Seventeen out of the twenty CORB ships to set sail
arrived safely at their intended destinations, each bursting
with a wealth of experience gained. Nevertheless, a few ex-
Canadian evacuees admit they have no memory of their
voyage across the Atlantic: not even the name of their
escort, nor of the ship on which they sailed, 'all blanked
out' as several put it. But, the majority remember the
excitement and relief as they arrived safely at last in
whatever Dominion.

One writes of arriving in Canada: 'We arrived at four minutes past two, after nine days on board. Such a beautiful place, surrounded by forest-clad hills, like a bristly door-mat at the gates of a new land.' Less poetically, perhaps, but no less aptly, Ronald Smith says: 'Seeing land and sailing into Halifax Harbour was, possibly, the happiest memory I have.'

Alec Hedgecock, arriving in Cape Town with batch U1 aboard the *Llanstephan Castle*, reminds us that there was joy and relief for others beside the children. He writes, with some amusement: 'We arrived, after sailing uneventfully from Freetown, to a tumultuous welcome in Cape Town on 3 September. Well tutored in advance, we gave a lusty rendering of *Sarie Marais* from the ship's deck for the benefit of the reception committee on the quayside. Then, as the children disembarked, the crew loudly cheered, probably,' he suggests, 'from relief!'

The unmatchable splendour of Sydney Harbour, as bay after bay came into view, was enough to silence the remnants of batch C1, more than half having already disembarked in Fremantle and Melbourne. To add to their amazement, every conceivable shape and size of small craft was there to escort the *Batory* across to Circular Quay where the first settlers landed. In the distance was the famous Harbour Bridge; and there too, adding to the thrill of their triumphal entry, was the unmistakable giant, recognizable through her grey warpaint, the Cunarder *Queen Mary*, towering above the CORB ship, but acknowledging this was the *Batory's* moment with an enormous welcoming blast on her siren.

By the end of October, 1940, the last batches of CORB children had reached their Dominions. For all its glaring faults, particularly its risking the odds in favour of a major disaster at sea, CORB's overseas evacuation operation had become an extraordinary symbol of victory over difficulty, a cause for pride, a humane peak in a war-torn world, and a captivating morale-boosting story of Allied and Commonwealth co-operation in defiance of an apparently ruthless enemy. All of this, some might have conceded if pressed, could just possibly have justified the dangerously absurd exposure to danger, and the narrowly avoided risks some of the safe arrivals had endured.

11

BEHIND THE SCENES

The efficiency of CORB's sea-going operations owed a tremendous amount to two civil servants, Mr F H Norman and the Hon J G Simon, who both represented the Ministry of Shipping on Geoffrey Shakespeare's Inter-departmental Committee in June, 1940. On their recommendation, less than a week after CORB opened for business, Sir Julian Foley, Permanent Secretary to the Ministry of Shipping, set up a special group chaired by Mr Shinwell, one of his civil servants, to thrash out urgent matters relevant to CORB's activities at sea. The group consisted of representatives of the Sea Transport and Liner Divisions of the Ministry, with Mr Hinde, an ex-Thomas Cook's Director as representative for CORB.

Quickly, Mr Shinwell's group compiled lists of all ships scheduled to sail to the Dominions in the weeks ahead; assessed which of them would be suitable for evacuees; the best ratio of escorts to children (fixed at one to fifteen); the number of children to be allocated to each ship, and to each life-boat aboard that ship; the instructions to be provided for CORB escorts on safety matters aboard ship. The committee also ensured a thorough check by the staff of the Nautical Surveyor in Glasgow or Liverpool of the efficiency of each CORB ship's life-saving apparatus, and the adaptability of living and dining accommodation for children's use.

Finally, the committee supplied Ministry of Shipping officials to accompany CORB representatives and Dominions Office immigration officers aboard each ship before it sailed, in order to observe CORB escorts undergoing safety

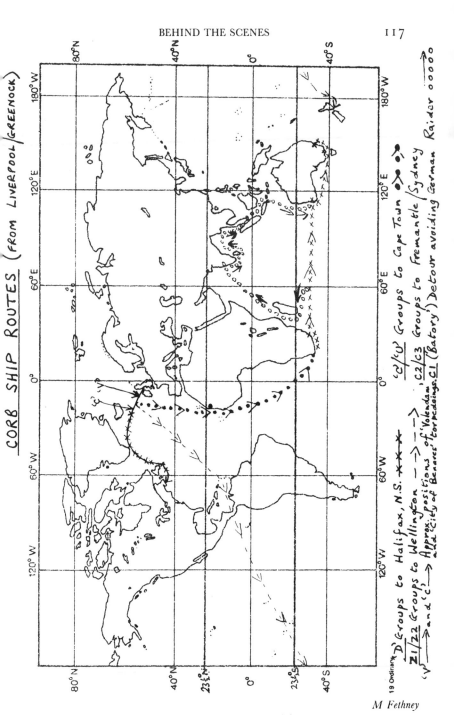

Fig 15: *Routes sailed by CORB ships to the four Dominions.*

M Fethney

instruction and to suggest improvements where necessary. Occasionally, they also suggested improvements to proposed ships' menus, as when Miss Churchard, the Ministry representative, said she thought 'a menu a yard long in French was a little superfluous' aboard the CORB ship *Oronsay*.[1]

Meanwhile, the CORB Advisory Council, chaired by Lord Snell, was giving attention to many concerns other than the evacuees' ocean voyages. It discussed the procedures for selection of both children and their escorts; allowances to be paid to escorts; the payment that parents should contribute — (6/- per week was agreed, the same amount as that paid for evacuees within Britain).

The Council argued successfully for children from vulnerable areas to get priority in the scheme; drew up details for evacuee medical inspections; the information to seek from Head Teachers about each evacuee applicant; the legalities to be signed by the parents when accepting CORB's offer of a place to a child; and laid down plans for the care of evacuees after arrival in the Dominions.[2]

In the earliest days, the CORB Council strongly encouraged the notion of evacuating European refugee children overseas together with Britons. To this end, Mrs Clifford Norton, wife of a distinguished British diplomat, who had escaped from Warsaw then Paris, joined CORB's London staff to run a specific 'Refugee Section'.[3] By the 30 July, 1940, CORB had received nearly nine thousand requests to evacuate refugee children, seven thousand of which involved Austrian and German children, with the remaining two thousand spread between French, Czech, Polish, Belgian, Dutch and Norwegian. The majority of these applications made the USA their first choice, with Canada second.

Amongst these nine thousand children were many Jewish refugees, often in dire straits, with parents in concentration camps or their whereabouts totally unknown. They were cared for by small committees in Britain, such as that organized by Mrs Lasky 'from her fastness in Claridge's'. But, by August, 1940, CORB's Advisory Council reluctantly had to recognize that it could not hope to organize overseas evacuation for foreign children, whether Jews or otherwise.

Apart from the fact that most of them wanted to go to the USA, with which CORB never did succeed in agreeing an evacuation scheme, the problem of legal guardianship proved eventually an insurmountable stumbling block.

In the long run, however, many of the Jewish refugee children probably fared better by having to stay in Britain. Some of those who successfully crossed to the USA were very badly treated: families split over wide distances; children forced to change their names and, in the case of some of the youngest, to change their identity.[4]

Only one refugee child sailed under CORB auspices. This was a Dutch boy called Marinus Verstraeten who went to South Africa with U1 aboard the *Llanstephan Castle*. His evacuation was only possible because a British naval officer had sought legal guardianship for him, after finding the lad in France where he had cycled on being orphaned and left homeless by the Nazi blitz on Rotterdam. The Netherlands Red Cross Emergency Committee in London sponsored Marinus's application to CORB.

Whilst the CORB Advisory Council thrashed out policy decisions on a host of issues, the Children's Overseas Reception Board, (ie., the 'Executive'), under Geoffrey Shakespeare's chairmanship was running the actual scheme. Always having to work in haste, the Board sifted its way through the massive backlog of applications. By the 7 July, 1940, only two and a half weeks after applications opened, CORB Director, Marjorie Maxse reported that the Board had already opened 52,400 evacuee applications complete with School Medical Officers' certificates. A further 18,000 applications had come from parents of children in independent schools.[5]

Of those applications opened by the 7 July, 7,666 children in state schools had already been provisionally accepted by CORB, and only ten in independent schools, because of delay in getting their medical details. The parents of all these children had had notification of acceptance.

Both the Board and the Advisory Council were sensitive to the need for the scheme to include at least ninety per cent state school children, in order to counter the idea that the privileged alone could send their children to safety

RECEIVED
' JUL 1940
DOMS. OFFICE.

CHILDREN'S OVERSEAS RECEPTION
BOARD,
45 Berkeley Street,
London, W. 1.

C.O.R.B. Reference No.............

SCHOOL REPORT.

Name of child...
(Block capitals - surname first)

Address..

Conduct (Give a brief note on social qualities or defects).

Ability

Remarks (If not suitable for evacuation give reason, e.g. a
"problem" child.)

Decision I consider this child (x suitable in every respect
(x not suitable
for evacuation to a private family overseas

Signed...............................Head Teacher

.....................................School

.....................................Date

x Delete where inappropriate.

N.B.   In the case of a child attending a grant-aided school
this form should be returned to C.O.R.B. by the Local
Education Authority.
In the case of a child attending a NON-grant-aided
school this form should be returned direct to C.O.R.B.
by the Head Teacher

Crown Copyright
Fig 16: *CORB's form to Head Teachers in Britain seeking information about a potential CORB evacuee.*

overseas. When CORB batches had begun to sail overseas, Geoffrey Shakespeare was upset on one occasion when he overheard 'an ill-disposed woman' watching CORB children board a ship: 'Look!' she remarked, 'there go the children of the rich!'[6]

But, in no way was CORB running a scheme for the rich. Of the 2,664 CORB children who arrived safely overseas, 2,606 were in CORB's Category A, ie., from state schools; and only fifty eight were in Category B, ie., from independent schools. In the case of fifteen of the Category B children, the parents' income was so low that they were only required to pay the basic evacuation fee of 6/- per week. A brief look at the recorded occupations of the CORB children's fathers underlines the success CORB had in selecting from 'normal' families, particularly within the 'working class'.[7]

In addition to its bias towards lower income families, CORB set itself further constraints. For example, the proportion of Roman Catholics in any one batch was not to exceed twenty five per cent of the total, and the proportion of Jews was not to exceed ten per cent. Consciousness of Welsh and Scottish national feelings led to about two fifths of the total being selected from Wales and Scotland, and the sending of entire shipments abroad made up of Scottish children, aboard the *Ruahine* to New Zealand, the *Llandaff Castle* to South Africa, and the *Bayano* and *City of Paris* to Canada.[8]

Sensibly, the most crucial selection criterion for each individual child was the vulnerability to air attack of the home town. To help assess this, the Ministry of Home Security supplied CORB with lists of 'vulnerable areas and their degree of danger', and Miss Beryl Power of the Ministry of Labour undertook the task of relating CORB selection to the vulnerability lists.[9]

By and large, the selection of overseas escorts was much easier than that of evacuees.[10] Major youth organizations such as the YMCA, the Boy Scouts' and Girl Guides' Associations, and the Boys' Brigade, recommended names to CORB or urged leaders to apply. The British Medical Association helped with the recruitment of doctors for CORB ships, and the Church authorities with nominations for ships' chaplains.

In addition, many Dominion residents who happened to be in Britain as the scheme opened were approached by representatives of their High Commissions, or sometimes went along in person to their High Commission offices on hearing about CORB, and offered to help. Again, Salvation Army Headquarters staff in London 'earmarked' several officers experienced in children's work — including a few who had worked with child migration schemes — and set up its own interviewing system, sending suitable names to the CORB selection department.

The selection of these sea-going escorts in the very earliest days was organized by Miss Thelma Cazalet, MP, assisted by Vera Brittain, the writer, who was a cousin of Mr Shakespeare, and by Elspeth Huxley, another writer. But, very soon, the flood of applications from would-be escorts was so vast that the selection passed into the hands of senior civil servant Miss Eleanor Nicholas, assisted by personnel from the Board of Education, a few HMIs, Ministry of Health staff, and members of the various High Commissions in London. Miss Nicholas was described by her wartime colleague Mrs Elspeth Davies, CORB's Director of Welfare, as 'very sweet, very gentle, and very competent'.[11] Miss Nicholas maintained that wise escort selection was crucial to the success of the entire scheme, and also to the happiness of hundreds of children. Her policy, therefore, was to look for people 'preferably with ocean experience', who were also 'young enough to be agile, and able to dash after young adventurers with intentions on the rigging!'[12]

Surgeon's wife, Mrs Ella Clothier, one of many whose local authority employers asked her to apply to CORB, and later went to Australia aboard the *Batory*, recalls: 'I presume that I was asked to volunteer for CORB because, in anticipation of war, I trained on an official course in baby and child care, completing this in 1939. Then, in September, 1939, I helped mothers with their children under five to evacuate by train to Somerset, following this by working as an assistant in an emergency residential nursery in Bedford College, Regents Park, for babies and young children en route for evacuation to the country.'

The escort selectors were wary of 'joy-riders' or people

originating from the Dominions who simply hoped to use the scheme for a cheap return passage home. Miss Rosalie Golding, one of two nurses aboard the CORB ship *Nestor*, which took the second batch to Australia, recalls her selection experience very clearly, and the stress on that last point. She writes: 'I finally came to the last interview — with a doctor, of course. "Why did you say you'd be willing to go to South Africa?" he asked. I said I wanted CORB to know that I'd be willing to go farther than Canada, but did not want to ask to go to Australia. Nor would I wish to get to New Zealand and not be able to see my parents in Australia! The doctor seemed to like this thinking: "I believe we'll be wanting you," he said.'

By the time CORB ceased sending children abroad in September, 1940, well over one thousand men and women, experienced or qualified in some form of children's work, had their names on CORB's 'stand by for duty' list. Over nineteen thousand men and women had volunteered, of whom many thousands had had interviews.

Of course, the Overseas Reception Board had far wider responsibilities than the selection of escorts and evacuees, vitally important though this work was. Within days of opening for business, CORB was already functioning in seven Divisions:[13]

> 1. **Finance**, (including rail and shipping costs); 2. **Selection**, (of escorts and evacuees); 3. **Home**, (liaison with the LEAs; forms to parents; medical examinations); 4. **Transport**, (travel to ports; accommodation in ships); 5. **Welfare**, (care of the children from the moment they arrived in embarkation ports to their arrival in Dominions; supervision of CORB liaison officers in Dominions; liaison with Dominions Governments); 6. **Dominions**, (migration details; reception arrangements in the Dominions); 7. **Foreign**, (dealt with offers of help from non-Commonwealth countries, the most pressing being from the USA and Argentina).

Despite the complexities of the overseas evacuation, and

the pressures on CORB once launched, Miss Maxse was able to report (in March, 1941):[14] 'No child got lost or sent to a wrong destination.' But, she did omit to mention that, once abroad, three CORB children managed to 'sneak' into Southern Rhodesia to pre-arranged addresses, when they should have been billeted in South Africa;[15] and that another child was 'abducted', in quite bizarre fashion, by her own mother on a Liverpool dockside.[16]

Perhaps most errant of all the 'lost' not mentioned by Miss Maxse, was the CORB doctor who caused a great commotion when, having arrived in Cape Town with batch U1 aboard the *Llanstephan Castle*, she decided to visit her boyfriend in Portuguese East Africa instead of taking the first available ship back to Britain according to CORB's standing orders. The South African Government alerted the Dominions Office, fearing that the boyfriend in Laurenço Marques was a Nazi spy. However, this wayward young doctor redeemed herself six months later. She performed heroic deeds on the sinking of her return ship, and earned high praise from the owners for her rescue work.[17]

In October, 1940, on the suspension of the overseas scheme, CORB's seven divisions rapidly and drastically shrank. By that time, the CORB staff had dealt with over a million letters since the previous June. But, by March, 1941, the 620 full-time workers had reduced to only twenty and, three months later, only eight remained to soldier on for the rest of the war.[18]

Miss Maxse continued throughout as Director, though she was steadily diverted more and more by her work as Lady Reading's lieutenant at the WVS. Increasingly, therefore, Miss Eleanor Nicholas and Mrs Elspeth Davies assumed responsibility for the running of CORB. In the middle of 1941, they moved Headquarters to five small rooms in Devonshire House, just off Piccadilly, with their tiny staff, and thereafter, with scarcely adequate resources, continued to deal with a constant flow of cables from liaison officers in the Dominions, and deal with parents back in Britain, by personal interviews, letters, phone calls and, in Mrs Davies's case as Welfare Director, by a succession of regional meetings in various Education Offices throughout the country, to which parents from a wide area received invitations. In addition, they wrestled with many legal complexities, involving escorts as well as evacuees and parents, placated the relatives of escorts — particularly those sunk on returning ships, — and those taken prisoner as a result of being sunk.

A measure of the volume of painstaking administration they accomplished during the war is the destruction, in 1957, of twenty seven sackfuls of CORB correspondence, and files. Each sackful weighed fifty five pounds.[19]

12

FALSE OPTIMISM — AND DISASTER

It was 10.10 pm on Friday, 30 August, 1940. Admiral G H Knowles, RNR, Commodore to convoy OB205, studied the Admiralty signal just handed to him by the *Volendam's* radio officer. It read: 'Enemy unit — unreliable fix in position 56°10'N, 09°30'W.' This was perilously near the scheduled course of his convoy.[1]

Dennis Furnish

Fig 17: *The Dutch ship "Volendam", torpedoed 30/8/40 with 321 CORB evacuees on board, all of whom were rescued.*

Admiral Knowles was travelling with his small staff aboard the Dutch ship *Volendam*. He had every reason to be worried. There were thirty four merchant ships in convoy OB205, and an escort of only one destroyer, *HMS Warwick*, assisted by two sloops. And, further cause for anxiety, the *Volendam* was carrying CORB batch D10, consisting of three hundred and twenty one children, twenty six escorts, two doctors and three nurses. Just visible to port, also, was the dark outline of the *SS Rangitata*, another CORB ship, carrying batch Z2, one hundred and thirteen evacuees bound for New Zealand.

Already, not far ahead of the convoy, the enemy was waiting in the shape of *U-60*, a German submarine commanded by Oberleutnant Adelbert Schnee. If patient enough, Schnee was sure to make a kill.

At 11 pm, the *Volendam* broke radio silence with the terse message: 'Torpedoed position 56°05′N, 09°50′W.'[2] The Admiralty's 'unreliable' forecast had been painfully accurate. In layman's terms, when attacked the convoy was about 200 miles west of Glasgow, and U-60 had been able to fire its torpedoes at a range of only 250 metres.

First sign of the U-boat was 'a terrific explosion' aboard the *Volendam*. Immediately, huge flames belched out on both sides of the ship near No 1 hold. The ship had actually received two torpedoes simultaneously on the starboard side about sixty feet from the bows. Fortunately, only one had exploded, but it left a massive hole fifty four feet by thirty two feet on that side of the ship. Amazingly, no-one was killed, and there were few injuries.[3]

At once, the escort vessels began their hunt for the attacker, and the *Volendam's* Master, Captain J P Webster, radioed the Admiralty for tugs. Meantime, there was order and calm aboard the ship as alarms rang, and no sign of any panic. Ten year old Mary McKeon, CORB evacuee on board, explains: 'We had had a number of practice drills. Consequently, when the alarm went in the night, no-one panicked as we thought it was just another practice, until we actually got into the life-boats and they were lowered.'

Thirteen year old CORB boy Raymond Hesling was asleep when the torpedo exploded. 'The ship gave a shudder,' he reported, 'and we could smell the explosion though we heard nothing . . . I hurried into some clothes, then, taking my life-belt, went with others to the library where everyone was assembled. Then the Captain came and told us not to worry . . .'[4]

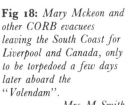

Fig 18: *Mary Mckeon and other CORB evacuees leaving the South Coast for Liverpool and Canada, only to be torpedoed a few days later aboard the "Volendam".*

Mrs M Smith

Miss Crowe, one of the CORB escorts, was writing in her cabin when the torpedo struck. 'There was no mistaking what it was,' she says. She hurried to muster her group of evacuees and, helped by stewards, had them all at their boat-stations in a very few minutes, despite having to use torches when the ship's lights failed for a time.[5]

Captain Webster delayed the order to abandon ship for a good half hour. But, by midnight, the barometer had fallen, the south-west wind had risen to force six and, with worse weather forecast, the Captain feared his ship might turn turtle. Thus, in the end, it was not the fire but the weather that forced him to order 'Abandon ship!'[6]

The *Volendam's* crew lowered the eighteen life-boats in remarkably quick time, especially considering that they had to manhandle some boats from the port to the starboard side because of the ship's list; and children loaded into the port-side life-boats had to be lifted out first — not always an easy operation.

Luckily for the survivors, three ships had opted to stay behind the scattering convoy and give assistance: the *Basset Hound* and the *Valldemosa*, both small tankers, and the *Olaf Fortensen*, a banana boat. The three ships' crews had lowered rope ladders over the side, whilst the Captain of the *Olaf Fortensen* showed particular ingenuity by ordering the huge baskets normally used for loading bananas to be roped to the ship's winches to pick up survivors from their boats.

Most of the children were so cold and numb that they could not cope with the rope ladders. Hence, the crew members of the *Basset Hound* and the *Valldemosa* had to scramble down into the life-boats to tie ropes around the waist of each child, and manhandle them aboard. The rescue was no mean feat in rough seas and rising wind, and under constant threat of a renewed submarine attack on the stationary ships. Indeed, two more ships in the dispersing convoy were torpedoed.

Yet, despite the frightening conditions, the children's voices carried through the storm as they sang their lungs out with *Roll out the barrel* and *Run, rabbit, run*. Captain Webster remarked, 'The whole operation was more like an extensive boat-drill than a reality!' As Raymond Hesling said: 'No-one seemed frightened. We rowed for about half an hour before we fell in with a freighter and were hauled aboard in a large banana basket.'[7]

Once dawn broke, the crews aboard the tiny rescue vessels tried to ensure that the children, at least, stayed below decks as they were rarely clear of the water. The *Valldemosa*, carrying two hundred and fifty survivors — she only had a dozen crew — was permanently awash amidships. Down below, in each ship, every bunk, cabin and companion-way, and all lounge space was cluttered with a mass of salt-covered humanity; and the cramped conditions got worse with widespread seasickness.

But no-one complained. And the ships' galleys cheerfully ran a non-stop service of hot drinks, huge chunks of bread and butter, and dozens upon dozens of boiled eggs.

At daylight, Captain Webster with his firefighters and repair party aboard the *Volendam* spotted HM Tug

Salvona nearby. By 7.45 am, escorted by *HMS Scimitar*, the pair left the area in tow for the Clyde at five and a half knots; and the *Volendam* was eventually beached in Kames Bay two hundred and twenty miles away.[8] Later, after repairs, she contributed again to the Free Dutch struggle against the Nazis.

Just before the stricken *Volendam* left the attack area, however, a strange parting took place. A nine year old Glasgow boy was transferred from the *Volendam* to the destroyer *Wanderer* which was on her way back to base after searching unsuccessfully for the U-boat. Amidst the confusion and the darkness following the torpedoing of the ship, Robert had been left asleep in his cabin, despite all CORB escorts reporting their groups present at muster stations.

Young Robert apparently awoke in his cabin and, finding himself alone, went on deck to find that the life-boats had already gone. Far from panicking, he calmly returned to his bunk and went to sleep. Next morning, the sound of hammering led him to the skeleton repair crew at work; and, shortly afterwards, his rescuing destroyer appeared.

Geoffrey Shakespeare had sped to Glasgow the moment he heard of the *Volendam's* plight, and visited every hostel in which CORB survivors were billeted. Then, he announced to the Press that all on board the torpedoed CORB ship were now safely ashore.[9] But, no sooner had he arrived back in Troon, where he was snatching the first break he had managed since CORB opened for business, than he received a phone message telling him about Robert's escapade. 'It was a cruel blow,' he wrote later. 'The confidence parents placed in us and our whole operation would be impaired.'[10]

He might well have feared that a lowering of confidence would have resulted from the whole *Volendam* affair anyway. But, astonishingly, this was not the case. Quite the opposite. Parents when questioned by reporters stressed that they intended to send their children again aboard the next available ship, should the opportunity be given. Typical was an interview that appeared in the *Yorkshire Evening Post*: 'I am certainly going to have another shot at Canada,' said thirteen year old Raymond Hesling. 'I think it's very unlikely that we'll be torpedoed a second time.' 'I shall certainly let him go again if he wants to,' said his mother.

And the newspaper described the lad as 'the hero of his schoolmates.'[11]

In the event, a handful of ex-*Volendam* evacuees were re-allocated, two sailing to Australia with C3 on the *Diomed*, and another, sadly, dying three weeks later when the *City of Benares* was sunk.[12] Two ex-*Volendam* escorts were also re-selected, and sailed to Canada with batch D13 aboard the *City of Paris*. Other *Volendam* escorts readily accepted CORB's invitation, if required, to help on another occasion. Miss Diana Close, one of those to re-volunteer, said over forty years later: 'I was very young. It was all a great adventure. Danger simply did not enter into it!'

In fact, danger did not seem to enter into it for anyone, whether parents, evacuees or escorts. Most serious of all, the Ministry of Information, together with the press, made fortuitous propaganda out of the affair. They treated the rescue like another Dunkirk, with all the merits of a naval triumph. They stressed that the ship had not sunk; 'the only loss of life was the purser'; the CORB children transferred to other ships 'in perfect order . . . like guardsmen on parade . . . in high spirits . . . with pride at their adventure.'[13]

Naturally, this was all good fodder for Britain's morale, especially with the blitz increasing in intensity and the Battle of Britain still precariously in the balance. And, of course, Geoffrey Shakespeare was justified when he wrote that the bravery of the *Volendam* children completely discredited the disparaging view, put forward by opponents of the scheme, 'that only children of low morale sought refuge overseas.' As he pointed out, 'their conduct that night, in small boats, tossed about in an angry sea, was worthy of the finest traditions of our race . . .'[14]

But, these were by no means the only factors that demanded consideration. This torpedoing exposed the extreme gravity of the risks that CORB was taking. It also demonstrated that, although the rescue was inspiring in its way, its success owed a great deal to pure luck. Even the presence of the three rescue ships was a matter of goodwill, and not of fixed convoy routine.[15]

Mrs Elspeth Davies, CORB's Welfare Director, recalls that there was some discussion at Headquarters about a

CHILDREN'S OVERSEAS RECEPTION BOARD.

45, BERKELEY STREET,
W.1.

C.O.R.B. Reference:

S/1942

Your Reference:

Telegrams:
Avoncorb, London.

Telephone:
MAYFAIR 8400

23rd September, 1940

Dear Miss Close,

Although your experience in going
with a party of children to Canada was
so unfortunate, I am writing to ask
whether there is any likelihood of your
being able to help us in this way on
another occasion. If so, will you
please let me know when you will be
free and which of the Dominions you
would prefer. We will then let you
know exactly what is being done with
regard to a renewed Exit Permit.

Yours sincerely,

B. S. Reehola

Miss D. A. Close,
53, Hillfield Court,
Belsize Avenue,
N.W.3.

Fig 19: *Escorts torpedoed aboard the "Volendam" received letters like Miss Close's.
Most, like her, said they were willing to serve again* (Note: *this letter was written four
days after the news broke about the "City of Benares" disaster*).

possible suspension of the scheme, but not, she thinks, in any great depth. It seemed to everyone that CORB and the Royal Navy had the power to surmount all problems, all risks, however fearful.

Worst of all was the continuing lack of liaison between the Admiralty and CORB. The stark truth is that, when the *Volendam* sailed from Liverpool, the U-boat menace was increasing perceptibly week by week, and the Admiralty was fully aware of the situation. The Western Approaches Diary, full of foreboding, summarizes the two weeks before the *Volendam* set sail as follows: '*U-boats* — Attacks on shipping continue on a large scale, and losses heavy. Most casualties at night. A few promising counter attacks, but generally U-boats escape, probably on the surface, without being sighted or contacted.'[16]

It is now impossible to say whether CORB would have discontinued the scheme's operation if the Admiralty had informed them how desperate the convoy situation really was. Quite probably, CORB would still have gone ahead, with misplaced optimism. A comment written six months after the *Volendam* affair sums up the prevailing attitude immediately after the event: 'The torpedoing of the *Volendam* . . . had not seriously discouraged those parents who wished to send their children away, nor given the authorities pause. It underlined the knowledge that risks must be run . . . but suggested . . . that a few hours in a life-boat was the worst to be feared.'[17]

However, tragedy beyond imagining had already struck the CORB scheme by the time those words were written. Just over two weeks after the *Volendam* children escaped disaster, CORB and the British public had pushed luck beyond the bitter limit.

The news broke for most parents with a candid letter from Miss Marjorie Maxse at CORB Headquarters: 'I am very distressed to inform you that, in spite of all the precautions taken, the ship carrying your child to Canada was torpedoed on Tuesday night, 17 September. I am afraid your child is not amongst those reported as rescued, and I am informed that there is no chance of there being any further list of survivors . . .'[18]

There were ninety CORB evacuees aboard the SS *City of*

Benares when she was torpedoed. Of these, seventy seven
perished. Twenty sets of parents lost more than one child.
The hardest hit, the Grimond family of South London, lost
five of their ten children in the disaster. Meanwhile, a
terribly cruel irony, the five brothers in the family who
stayed at home survived the destruction of their house in an
air-raid.[19]

The *City of Benares* had sailed from Liverpool on Friday,
13 September, in convoy OB213 — nineteen ships escorted
by the destroyer *HMS Winchelsea* and two sloops. The
convoy Commodore, Admiral E J G Mackinnon, RNR,
sailed with his staff aboard the *City of Benares*, together with
the ninety children of CORB batch D11, their eight escorts,
a doctor and a nurse.

Those superstitiously inclined made much of the sailing
date, Friday 13. But, obviously, the disaster owed far more
to the scant defences available for convoy OB213 at the
time of its departure than to any downright bad luck. The
lack of naval resources which led the Admiralty to
recommend suspension of the CORB scheme back in July,
was now reaching its lowest ebb.[20] With the threat of
German invasion imminent in the east of Britain, there was
no hope at all of providing 'adequate protection' for CORB
ships.

So short was the Commander in Chief Western Approaches of escort ships that they had to leave outward-bound
convoys no more than two hundred miles out from
Liverpool, then carry out anti-submarine patrols in the
area, whilst awaiting an incoming HX (= from Halifax)
convoy to escort into Liverpool or the Clyde. Yet, the
Commander in Chief would know only too well that, by the
end of August, 1940, U-boats were increasing their patrol
range westwards, and several merchant ships had been sunk
on the Atlantic convoy routes a good four hundred miles
beyond the turn-round point for escort vessels — ie., six
hundred miles from Liverpool.[21] So, the convoy situation
was desperate, but beyond any short-term solution.

Thus, according to the standard, risky procedure operating at the time, the escort to the *City of Benares* convoy
parted company near Longitude 16° West with orders to
pick up incoming convoy HX71.[22] The time of the escort's

departure was 1 am, on Tuesday, 17 September. And, of course, those ships were still within range of marauding U-boats for another four hundred miles westwards into the Atlantic.[23]

Just before leaving OB213, the Senior Naval Officer aboard *HMS Winchelsea* warned the convoy Commodore that a U-boat was known to be operating ahead, west of Longitude 20° West. The following afternoon, when the unescorted convoy actually reached Longitude 20° West, the Commodore received a further signal from the Admiralty warning him that the U-boat was believed to be still in the vicinity.[24]

By this time, other factors were beginning to work against convoy OB213. The ships were only making six and a half to seven and a half knots against a headwind. As darkness fell, the headwind freshened to force six; there were squalls of gale force wind, with hail showers; and the sea became 'rough and confused'.[25]

Yet, between times, visibility remained too clear for safety; helping Kapitänleutnant Heinrich Bleichrodt, commanding *U-48*, to follow the ships' progress easily through his periscope at a distance of half a mile to the south.[26] Bleichrodt knew that the leading ship in the centre column of the convoy was the *City of Benares*, a worthwhile target, though he did not know her destination nor her cargo. No doubt he was relieved, if mystified, to see no naval vessels in the vicinity: simply nineteen merchant ships in five columns, on a straight course at a slow speed, and taking no evasive anti-submarine zig-zag manoeuvres. A perfect target in perfect conditions.

At 10.05 pm, six hundred miles out in the Atlantic, Heinrich Bleichrodt struck with a 500 lb torpedo. That one launching proved enough to sink the *City of Benares*.

Chief Officer Joseph Hetherington, who was off-duty and asleep in his cabin when the torpedo struck, at once made for the bridge. There he met Captain Landles Nicholl, who told him to assess the damage as soon as possible.[27]

The alarm bells started to ring within seconds of the explosion, but not everyone on board reacted rapidly to the situation. In parts of the ship distanced from the impact, crew members and private passengers alike were quite unaware of any immediate danger. Some said later that they felt no explosion, only gradually becoming aware of an 'unusual, pungent smell and a strange blue mist.'[28]

Even though the alarm bells were sounding, passengers who mustered in the lounge immediately misinterpreted the gravity of the situation when they met fellow passengers still calmly drinking and playing cards.

Meanwhile, Chief Officer Hetherington reported back to Captain Nicholl that there was serious flooding in the engine room, and the position was rapidly worsening. At this juncture, the ship was listing to port, and visibly sinking at the stern. Captain Nicholl took the only course open to him and ordered 'Abandon ship!'

Unlike most of the private passengers, the CORB contingent was distressingly aware of the seriousness of the situation from the moment the torpedo struck. Miss Mary Cornish, forty one year old private music teacher in Baker Street, together with Miss Sybil Gilliat-Smith, a young art teacher from south-west London, had just spent an hour on deck with the CORB chief escort, Miss Marjorie Day, a fifty three year old Housemistress from Wycombe Abbey girls' public school. They had cheerfully shared their relief at the news they were 'through the "danger zone" ', and hummed folk song tunes together as they leaned on the deck rail watching the white-topped waves.[29]

Then, at 10 pm, Miss Cornish left her companions in order to check that her mixed group of Sunderland and East London girls was asleep. She had just reached the end of the companion-way on C deck leading to her group's cabins, when the torpedo exploded.

At once, she found her way forward blocked by a mass of debris. To her side, she was looking into 'a black abyss' where the bathroom had previously been. As she peered down, she realized there was a massive hole in the centre of the ship, rapidly filling with water beneath her.

Frantically, Miss Cornish cleared away rubble with her bare hands and, having made a gap wide enough, crawled through to her girls' cabins, many of which she found completely shattered. There she also found New Zealand escort Mrs Lillian Towns with a group of children she had managed to assemble with the aid of an engineer officer.

Together, they pulled the children through the gap Miss Cornish had made and hurried them to their boat-station.

The children appeared to be 'frightened, but not panicky'. One girl was so seriously injured that she kept collapsing into unconsciousness. Mrs Towns had managed to drag her from her mangled cabin by breaking down the remains of a splintered partition.

Thirty CORB evacuees were already dead, killed instantly by the force of the explosion immediately beneath the cabins where they were sleeping. Most of the CORB children who survived were so near the heart of the explosion that it threw them from their bunks. Adding to their confusion and fright, the lights temporarily failed in their part of the ship. As a result, most of them arrived at their boat-stations without managing to snatch any extra clothing to put on over their night-clothes. This proved a fatal deficiency during the long, cold hours ahead.

Hoping to keep the children calm as she and Mrs Towns steered them to the life-boats, Miss Cornish kept repeating: 'It's all right! It's only a torpedo!' She realized later what strange reassurance this was.

Up on deck, Miss Day was performing the sort of feats with the calmness her Headmistress would have expected. She had told CORB that Marjorie Day was 'the sort of person who will not lose her head in an emergency, and is usually at her best in a crisis.'

Miss Day had never faced a crisis as horrifying as this before. Even so, by the time Miss Cornish and Mrs Towns appeared with the dazed evacuees they had pulled from their wrecked cabins, Miss Day already knew which of her escorts had complete groups of children with them, and which children had not survived the explosion. She also knew that all eight CORB escorts had survived, together with the nurse and doctor. Everyone found her calm grasp and efficiency a comfort.

But, alas, much worse was now to come, and the real anguish started with the attempts to launch the life-boats. Miss Day watched helplessly as the boat containing Miss Gilliat-Smith, with her entire group of evacuees, was tipped into the water. All had survived the attack but none survived the cold of the sea.[30]

In the confusion that followed, some of the life-boats got
launched before the allotted number of survivors had
climbed aboard. As a result, some survivors had to slide
down ropes that trailed from the life-boat davits. Some fell
into the icy, choppy seas in the attempt. Others had to wait
for the ship to start settling in the water before trying to
leap into life-boats that were tossing like bits of driftwood
on towering waves.[31] Eleven year old CORB boy Howard
Clayton, on being rescued, amazed everyone with his
description of the way he jumped into a life-boat 'when the
water was level with the deck of the ship.' Some of those
waiting with him launched rafts, swimming desperately to
them, striving to escape the undertow as the ship finally
tilted her bows and sank.

Marjorie Day was the last of the CORB personnel to
enter a life-boat. Mr Hetherington helped her aboard,
together with the seriously injured CORB girl rescued from
C deck. Other CORB children in Miss Day's boat expressed
concern about the severity of the girl's wounds. Miss Day
said she found them all 'very sensible and brave.'

But then, as had happened to several others, the moment
Miss Day's life-boat hit the waves it filled with water to the
gunwales. At least the bitterly chill sea-water stopped the
wounded girl's bleeding. Then, very soon, and no doubt
mercifully, she was the first to die. Tragically, her young
sister followed quickly afterwards, 'seeming too shocked to
want to live any longer,' said Miss Day.

As that dreadful night dragged slowly on, Miss Day wrote
later, 'the little ones faded out, quite unable to stand up to
the awful conditions. . . . All we could do was to hold them
above the water till they were gone. . . . We gave them
what comfort we could.'[32]

Similarly, in her life-boat, Mrs Towns recalls, 'the
children started to go into a coma one by one. . . . We
slapped their hands and faces, and then we kept their heads
above water until we could tell it was no use.'

A few children grew a whole life-time during that terrible
night. Sometimes, it was the stoical courage of a child that
maintained morale and gave adults the resolution to
survive. In one life-boat, for instance, eleven year old
Edward Richardson cradled a dying woman's head on his

knee, stroking her hair, and talking patiently to her about rescue being on the way.

In the middle of the stormy night, the occupants of Miss Day's life-boat heard the sound of singing across the mounting waves. Eventually, in the gloom nearby they saw two CORB girls, Beth Cummings, fourteen, from Liverpool, and Liz Walder, fifteen, from Kentish Town, clinging doggedly to the upturned keel of a life-boat, and singing their hearts out as if on some sort of children's outing. Willing hands dragged the girls into Miss Day's life-boat. Both happily survived; and Liz's ten year old brother, Louis, also had the good fortune to come through the disaster, the only CORB child in his life-boat to do so.[33]

It was just over twenty hours before the tiny, half-frozen, and salt-crusted remnant of survivors in Miss Day's life-boat was picked up. They were the last people rescued by the destroyer *HMS Hurricane*. This ship was escorting convoy OB214 about two hundred and eighty miles to the east when she received an urgent signal from the Commander in Chief Western Approaches to proceed to the assistance of the *City of Benares*. It was then ten minutes past midnight, two hours after the *City of Benares* was torpedoed.[34]

But, hampered by the heavy seas and gale force wind, the *Hurricane* was unable to sail at anything like her top speed, and could only increase to a reasonable twenty seven knots at just after 8 am on the 18th. This delay inevitably increased the loss of life.

Eventually, at 2.15 pm, still fourteen miles from the position in which the *City of Benares* sank, the *Hurricane* encountered the first survivors and began the delicate picking-up operations. Continuing their search to windward, the ship's company became more and more saddened and angered by the scene. Too often, they found bodies with hands still tightly clenched, still seeming to cling·for life to a raft, a plank of wood, a float, or anything that promised buoyancy. Too often, the bodies were those of small children, faces sometimes tilted upwards, as though still hoping for rescue.

During one phase of the rescue, the *Hurricane* passed several fully occupied life-boats, each completely water-logged, with not a survivor amongst them. Then, between 4 pm and 6.40 pm they 'closed' on eleven boats and five floats spread over an area of four square miles. The rescuers' spirits rose as they saw that each contained at least some people alive.

Hurricane's Commanding Officer, Lieutenant Commander Hugh Simms, RN, performed remarkable feats of seamanship that day. He had to approach each boat, raft, float or plank of wood painstakingly slowly, and always from windward, in order to give a lee-side from which to assist the weakened survivors aboard the destroyer. Pathetically, only one life-boat had more than six survivors in it and, significantly, this was the one boat that had neither capsized nor filled with water. It held thirty one people still alive, most of them in reasonable condition considering their plight.

Though most of the hundred and five survivors were exhausted, and many were even unconscious on being rescued, they all revived except three. Those three were young CORB boys, one of whom had an older brother who did survive. Commander Simms tersely noted in his report: 'I conducted the Burial Service for three children at 2100 on the 18th and 0900 on the 19th.' They were committed to the deep with full naval honours.

Next day, as *HMS Hurricane* edged into Gladstone Dock at Liverpool after landing her survivors at Greenock, the Anglican Padre to the 9th Destroyer Flotilla, the Reverend Owen Fulljames, RN, went on board to issue replacement clothing to the ship's company, for they had parted with most of theirs for the survivors' benefit. In the Wardroom he heard very briefly and simply the story of the disaster from the Captain and his officers.

Lieutenant Commander Simms showed the padre a poem he had written in an attempt to express his pain. He vowed he would never pick up any Germans he might find sunk at sea. Mr Fulljames tried to persuade his friend to tear up the poem and rescind his vow. But, he only half relented: for the rest of the war, until he was himself killed in action, he left Germans and Italians whose ships had been sunk as long as he could in the sea before picking them up. Forty years later Mr Fulljames comments: 'It was a sad business; he was a very gallant man.'[35]

Some words in Hugh Simms' poem have poignancy and bitterness together:

'A cold grey sea and a cold grey mist
Are kissing little children that their mothers kissed
    . . .
Think on it, my England, ever shall you live,
But, never, never, never must the sea or you
    forgive.'[36]

One story[37] that particularly captured the imagination of the British public concerned the continuing experience of Miss Mary Cornish. After she had mustered the evacuees from the mangled mess of D deck, she became separated from Mrs Town who took the surviving girls from Miss Cornish's group with her into a life-boat. Obeying Miss Day's instructions, Miss Cornish then joined one of the last life-boats to be launched in which she recognized a handful of CORB boys.

This life-boat was one that tilted awkwardly on being lowered and, as it hit the waves, shipped a lot of water. As a result, the occupants suffered horribly from the cold. To make matters worse, no-one was adequately dressed; only one of the evacuees had a coat, and only two were wearing shoes. All were in their pyjamas.

There were forty six people in the boat: six CORB boys, Fr O'Sullivan, the CORB Roman Catholic Chaplain who was suffering the throes of seasickness, thirty three Indian seamen, and five British crew members. They were to travel for eight days, cramped, cold, storm-tossed, perpetually wet and hungry in what Miss Cornish described as 'thirty feet of timber, shorter than a London bus.' Mr Purvis, a ship's steward, rigged a canvas awning in the bows to shelter the CORB contingent, but they had only one blanket between them.

Gradually they drifted eastwards, all taking turns at winding the stiff propeller apparatus, hands blistered, backs bruised where the handles hit the person sitting in front. Their feet were permanently numb with the wet and cold, and constantly in need of massage. They were so hungry that a favourite game Miss Cornish played was to have the boys imagine the meal they would eat, given the chance. Fish and chips was top choice every time.

Their strangest and most testing experience occurred on their fifth day adrift. The lookout spotted smoke from a ship. Hurriedly, they ran up Mary Cornish's petticoat at the masthead, and the steamer changed course straight towards them. The CORB boys were shouting and singing excitedly in the bows.

The steamer stopped and turned broadside on to the lifeboat, as if about to attempt to pick up the survivors. But then, incredibly, she started to slew around and sailed away, giving no hint of recognition and no signal to explain her action.

Fortunately, a violent storm with cold hail quickly followed this cruel encounter. Thus, they all became preoccupied again with survival, and dismissed the affair by deciding that the ship's Captain must have feared there was a U-boat in the vicinity — although this does not explain why the ship gave no account of its action. Another possibility is that the ship was a German raider, which would have been embarrassed by the presence of a woman and children on board. But, the mystery of this strange episode has never been unravelled.

On the eighth day adrift, the boys' strength ebbing noticeably, with hunger, thirst, and the condition of their feet a constant anxiety, one of the boys spotted a Sunderland flying boat of Coastal Command. Once more, the petticoat went to the masthead. The plane flew very low over them. The reassuring waves and the huge grin of the Australian pilot left no doubts, this time, that they were in the care of friends.

Soon afterwards, a second Sunderland appeared to drop a parcel of precious food: beans in tomato sauce, cans of salmon and, most wonderful of all, peaches in cool, soothing syrup. But, Steward Purvis, careful and disciplined as ever, refused to issue any extra water ration 'just in case!'

The survivors had not long to wait before they saw the destroyer *HMS Anthony* speeding towards them. Once she was alongside, each boy was hoisted aboard by two naval ratings. A sailor told Miss Cornish kindly, 'You've handed over to the Navy now!' But, only when she knew that her

DE Johnson

Fig 20: *(above) The ill-fated "City of Benares", seventy-seven of whose CORB children perished when she was torpedoed in convoy OB213 on 17/9/40.*

Fig 21: *(below) The last "City of Benares" survivors with Mary Cornish, CORB escort, just before rescue by HMS "Anthony" on 25/9/40.*

DE Johnson

six boys were safe in officers' bunks did she agree to have
hot tea, bread and butter. And then, before she could even
eat, she collapsed.[38]

The sudden, splendid, and totally unexpected news that
six more CORB children and two of their escorts had
survived the *City of Benares* tragedy inevitably raised excited
hopes that more might still be picked up alive.[39] Alas, this
was not to be so.

A few weeks later, the press and the British public
applauded the award to Mary Cornish of the British Empire
Medal, as well as to Mr Purvis, and to Mr Cooper, the *City
of Benares* 4th Officer who, aged twenty two, was the
helmsman in their life-boat. The three attended an
investiture at Buckingham Palace, receiving their medals
from King George VI.

Another heroic part of the CORB story linked with the
City of Benares is permanently commemorated in the
beautiful mural set in St George's chapel in the Church of
St Jude-on-the-Hill, Hampstead Garden Suburb, in North
London. The mural shows CORB escort Michael Rennie,
whose father was vicar of the parish in 1940, sitting in the
bows of a *City of Benares* life-boat with a small boy on each
side of him, nestling close for warmth. With his left hand,
Mr Rennie is pointing across a wild sea to the rescuing
destroyer, *HMS Hurricane*.

Having graduated in theology at Keble College, Oxford,
in June, 1940, Mr Rennie volunteered to CORB for escort
duties, hoping to be back in time to resume his studies in
the autumn at Westcott House in Cambridge. He was just
twenty one years old. Mr Rennie was with his group of boys
the moment the torpedo struck the ship, calmly took them
all to the muster station and helped them into their life-boat
when the order came to abandon ship, then joined them.
Unfortunately, this life-boat was one that tilted so steeply
before reaching the sea, that everyone toppled out. But
Michael Rennie managed to help several boys onto a
nearby raft and climbed onto it himself.[40]

Shortly afterwards, Louis Walder, a ten year old
Londoner from Mr Rennie's group, having been picked up
from the sea by a life-boat, espied his escort and the other
boys on their raft. The helmsman in Louis' boat managed

to negotiate the waves, and pulled alongside the raft to take them off. But, not content with his own rescue, Michael Rennie insisted on diving into the rough sea to assist children who were still in the sea after being tipped out of life-boats during the launching. Other men in Michael Rennie's life-boat warned him that he would drown. He replied, 'There are children in the water. I must get them.'

Louis Walder later described how his escort 'eventually got back into the life-boat ... suffering from exposure and exhaustion.' Nevertheless, he continued to encourage people throughout the night 'with words of comfort.' His last words were: 'Here comes the destroyer. Thank God.' Then, as he stood up to attract the *Hurricane's* attention, he suddenly collapsed, fell into the water-logged boat, and died immediately.[41]

Said Louis, in a letter to Michael's father: 'I am sure he was a very brave man.' But it added to the sadness surrounding Mr Rennie's death that Louis was the only child in that life-boat to survive, despite the young escort's unstinting efforts in rescuing so many.[42]

On the day the news of the sinking of the *City of Benares* hit the press throughout the world, King George VI made a speech condemning the inhumanity of the action. In his speech, he also announced that he was instituting a new award for gallantry, to be called the 'George Medal'. In the New Year, Geoffrey Shakespeare recommended CORB escort Michael Rennie for the George Medal. Though the request was not granted it is appropriate that CORB's Chairman considered him a worthy recipient and it would have been doubly appropriate for one of the first winners of a George Medal to be linked, however tragically, with the day on which the King introduced the award.[43]

On New Year's Day, 1941, the BBC broadcast a memorial service in honour of the children lost in consequence of the torpedoing of the *City of Benares*. The closing words of the lesson, fittingly, contained the description of the New Jerusalem in Revelation 21:4 — 'There shall be no more death, neither sorrow, nor crying, neither shall there be any more pain; for the former things are passed away.'

13

QUESTIONS, COVER-UP, AND CONFUSION

Assuming that the sinking of the *City of Benares* had to happen at all, it was soon clear that it need not have been anything like the terrible shambles it became. The loss of life was inordinately high. The exploding torpedo killed two passengers, both CORB children.[1] But the final tally of dead was one hundred and thirty four passengers, (seventy seven of them CORB children), and one hundred and twenty one crew.

Put simply, the casualty figures increased more than many-fold between the order to abandon ship and the end of the *Hurricane's* rescue search.

Naturally, in view of wartime security, public discussion laid off the aspects of possible inefficiency, or the absurdly high risk involved. The Ministry of Information statement released in Britain referred to the sinking as 'a new Nazi outrage against all the rules of war.'[2] Geoffrey Shakespeare spoke of his 'horror that any German submarine captain could be found to torpedo a ship over six hundred miles from land in a tempestuous sea. . . . This deed will shock the world.'[3]

He was right about the shock. 'Murder at sea'; 'Mass Murder'; 'Dastardly act'; 'Nazi outrage'; and 'Loathsome lawlessness of German conduct in war' were amongst reactions from overseas. Some of the most emotive reactions appeared in the US press. One newspaper described Hitler as the 'mad butcher'. Another conceded that the U-boat commander probably did not know that the children were on board the ship, but added vindictively: 'There is no reason to suppose it would have made any difference to his intentions if he had ' Yet another suggested that 'Tuesday's tragedy adds nothing to our knowledge of Nazi mentality and morality . . .'[4]

Perhaps it is as well that the press on both sides of the Atlantic diverted attention away from the really painful questions that needed to be faced. And even Goebbel's Nazi Propaganda Ministry in Berlin drew public attention away from the major issues, by accusing Churchill of sending children across the Atlantic 'in armed auxiliary steamers' as a deliberate provocative act, and in a cold-blooded manner, so that he could castigate the German Navy for sinking them.[5]

But, away from the press, questions were coming thick and fast, if quietly, from survivors of the disaster. These included people with some expertise, well-travelled, and with knowledge of technical as well as maritime matters. Thus, an RNVR Lieutenant Commander called Dean, who had to watch his wife die in his life-boat, having made a highly critical report of the disaster, also wanted to know whether his life-boat filled with water immediately on entering the sea because the drain plug was not in position. The spanner-like handles for propelling the boat proved 'too stiff to operate,' he wrote, 'and were quite unusable.' He had to resort to using the one, broken oar in the life-boat to fend it from the ship's side in the rough sea.

Mr Eric Davies, a BBC technician, questioned the number of life-boats that were successfully launched, the competence of the crew, the wisdom of putting such a large number of women and children in the care of such a crew, and the fairness of each CORB escort having to look after fifteen children in an emergency.

Mr Bokdan Nagorski, Director of the Polish Gdynia-Amerika Shipping Line, (owners of the *Batory*), was on his way to fill a Diplomatic Post in Washington when he was torpedoed. He was another who expressed concern about the difficulties apparent in launching the life-boats, and the fact that no rescue ships were in evidence until many hours had elapsed.[6]

Quite a stream of letters reached MPs and Government Departments, notably the Admiralty, CORB and the Ministry of Shipping, and these, together with questions asked in the House of Commons, indicated some vital issues that had to be settled: Why was the *City of Benares* sunk at all? Why was the convoy sailing without any naval escort? Why was the CORB ship in the leading, vulnerable position, and sailing at less than half its maximum speed? Why were the nineteen ships sailing in convoy formation, but not zig-zagging as an anti U-boat measure? Why did no ships in the convoy attempt to rescue, and why did eighteen hours elapse before help was at hand?

Consequently, Mr R H Cross, the Minister for Shipping, formed a committee of shipping experts. Their findings, never hitherto made public, are far-reaching but, in certain respects, they were also inconclusive and, at times, deeply disturbing.[7]

On the more immediate and obvious weaknesses raised by survivors, the Committee's report answered as follows: The *City of Benares* was 'well found, classed A1 at Lloyd's'. Her life-boats were fully and properly equipped according to the Life Saving Rules of the Board of Trade. All the life-boats were launched and water-borne within fifteen minutes of the vessel being torpedoed. But, with the heavy sea running, and the ship sinking by the stern with a list, water entered the life-boats, some of which were swamped. Two life-boats capsized and one was drawn under the water as the ship sank. Some boats had difficulty unhooking from davits on reaching the water — 'a hazard not uncommon in bad weather.' The ship's engines being disabled by the explosion meant that the ship was unable to turn to provide shelter for the life-boats. Five members of the crew testified that the life-boats' plugs were in place in the bottom of each boat.

There was no evidence of any panic on the part of the children, or other passengers, or any of the crew. Apart from the actual torpedoing and the swamping of the life-boats, 'the lamentable loss of life was caused by eighteen hours' exposure in severe weather and, unfortunately, many of the children were inadequately clad.'

Compared with eye-witness accounts from survivors, who saw davits apparently jam, and life-boats tip up and empty occupants into the sea before reaching the water, the statements about the life-boat launching look like a white-wash.

On the even more fundamental causes of the disaster, Mr Cross's Committee disclosed some more deeply disturbing findings: The orders for convoy OB213 from the Commander in Chief Western Approaches required the escort to part company at dark on the 16 September, and to meet incoming convoy HX71. But, the OB213 orders also required the convoy to disperse at noon on the 17 September. Yet, although the escort had duly left OB213 at 1 am on the 17th, the convoy continued to sail, without dispersing, until attacked at 10.05 pm. Only at that point was the order given to disperse, ie., ten hours later than directed by the Commander in Chief.

The report said that the Committee could not establish why the Commodore decided 'to ignore his orders to disperse . . . and, as he went down with the ship, it will never be known.' Ship's officers, when questioned, 'produced no answers at all . . . (about) the Commodore's motives; nor why the convoy was not even zig-zagging at the time of the attack.'

On the question why the *City of Benares*, capable of a top speed of fourteen and a half knots, was sailing at six and a half knots in an OB convoy, (whose best speed would never be more than nine knots), it was established that her owners had requested convoy protection in preference to letting her sail alone. It adds terrible irony to the tragedy that, when torpedoed, she was travelling at less than half her possible speed. Also, of course, had she travelled alone, she would not have been allowed to have CORB children on board.

On the complaint that no other ships in the convoy gave assistance to the stricken ship, the report quoted Western Approaches standing orders in force at the time. These allowed rear ships in convoy columns to act as rescue ships 'only when a local escort is present. If such an escort is not present, a "rescue ship" should not act as such unless this can be done without undue risk.' The Committee concluded that 'it would not have been proper to depart from these orders on account of the children . . . as this would have endangered another ship.'

Some of the most crucial perplexities remained unsolved. But Mr Cross and Mr Shakespeare accepted the recommendation of the Committee not to set up a formal public inquiry, nor even to issue any formal statement to the press about the Committee's Report. After all, it was wartime, and some of the report revealed strange Admiralty orders; flouting of orders; and an element of non-cognisance of the evidence of eyewitnesses. To throw these matters open to public criticism would have done little for the war effort. Furthermore, as the report stated, 'if a public inquiry were held, so much of the evidence would have to be taken in camera to avoid helping the enemy, that the investigation could hardly be described as a "public inquiry".'

Mr Cross and Mr Shakespeare also agreed with those Ministry of Shipping officials who felt that a public inquiry 'would re-awaken public bitterness — and they might question too much.'[8]

As for the CORB scheme, it is incredible that there was still a strong lobby for its continuation. The intensity of the Battle of Britain, the desire not to offend the Dominions, and the lingering hopes of establishing an official evacuation scheme with the USA — all help to explain the reluctance to scrap the scheme immediately and permanently.[9]

Above all, the CORB scheme had strongly captured public imagination on both sides of the Atlantic to an unrealistic degree. People saw the evacuation of children to safety abroad as an act of defiance against Hitler. So, mixed with grief over the disaster, there was anger, and there was also inspiration derived from the bravery of the survivors.

As a result, the affair proved an even greater source of anti-Nazi propaganda than the torpedoing of the *Volendam*, giving rise to an even stronger resurgence of the Dunkirk mentality. One Canadian Senator averred: 'The latest sinking strengthens our determination to bring our children to safety!' A *Yorkshire Evening Post* leader typifies the mood. Praising the courage of parents who opted to send their children overseas, 'believing this course was better than continuous air-raids,' the writer states, 'there can be no reproach in their mourning.' Equally, the leader continued, there should be no reproaches aimed at CORB.[10]

For its part, CORB issued a press statement: 'The precautions taken were on the scale which has made it possible to transport overseas nearly three thousand children without, hitherto, a single casualty.'[11] Bearing in mind the woeful scale of naval protection available, the statement begs innumerable questions.

An ally in the incredible cause of keeping the scheme operative was Miss Marjorie Day, ex-chief escort aboard the *City of Benares*. On being rescued, she wrote to CORB offering any help she could possibly give 'to keep the scheme afloat.' She regretted 'that such a magnificently constructive piece of work for the Empire should receive such a setback.'[12]

For their part, however, CORB Headquarters staff felt that the scheme should stop. Mrs Elspeth Davies, the former Welfare Director, says she recalls that she and her colleagues never expected any more CORB batches to sail, despite the defiant mood outside Headquarters.[13] And Mr Shakespeare, who described meeting the main party of survivors aboard *HMS Hurricane* in Gourock as 'the most melancholy day in my life', foresaw that the War Cabinet would question the wisdom of continuing the scheme.[14] But, suspension was not going to prove the logical and straightforward move it should have been.

On the 24 September, five days after news of the sinking broke, the Prime Minister declared to the Cabinet that he was anxious for the scheme to be 'discontinued'. But, he acknowledged 'there is strong feeling against a complete discontinuation.'[15] When the First Lord of the Admiralty then announced that a CORB batch was about to sail to South Africa, the Cabinet agreed that 'all sailings should be postponed until a report was available about the future of the scheme.' They asked the Home Secretary to get Mr Shakespeare to sound out the Advisory Council for their views and report back.[16]

Mr Shakespeare informed the Home Secretary that the Overseas Reception Board 'recommended that, during the winter months, at any rate, no more children be sent overseas in slow convoy.'[17] An announcement to this effect would keep the door open for a possible resumption later on. But, much more firmly, when the Cabinet returned to the matter on the 30 September, Sir John Anderson recommended that 'no more CORB children be evacuated, either in fast or slow convoys,' and that the Government should announce that the scheme was suspended. He went straight on to raise the issue, equally in the balance, whether 'permits should continue to be given for parents to evacuate children privately.' This was still a hot political potato, a timely reminder that the CORB scheme was originally justified on the grounds that it provided for less-privileged families the means of escape for their children.[18]

Before the Cabinet could take up either of Sir John's points, however, Mr Alexander, the First Lord of the Admiralty dropped the most almighty bombshell. The Admiralty, he disclosed, 'had not been aware of the extent to which, (after the decision reached by the War Cabinet on the 12 July, that the operation of the scheme should be postponed), arrangements had continued to be made to send a number of children overseas under the scheme, except that a request had been received from the Ministry of Shipping for the provision of defensive armaments for certain specified ships.'[19a]

The Home Secretary immediately sprang to CORB's defence, pointing out that the Prime Minister, in his House of Commons speech on the 18 July, had given 'a modified version of the decision referred to by the First Lord.' Nevertheless, the First Lord's revelation of the Admiralty's ignorance of CORB activity underlined the serious lack of liaison between Admiralty, CORB and Shipping Ministry.

Bringing the discussion back to the future of overseas evacuation, the Dominions Secretary asked for suspension of the scheme but requested two days' grace before any public announcement was made, in order to give him a chance to inform the Dominion High Commissioners 'well in advance'.

This is a reminder of the political delicacy of the situation. Suspension, despite the now blatantly obvious danger to children's lives, might still create disappointment, even disenchantment with Britain and the war effort, in the Dominions. Thus, the Cabinet settled for two decisions to operate for the time being.

First, they agreed that the Government should publicly announce the *temporary* suspension of the CORB scheme two days later, conceding that a sudden, permanent suspension could be bad for morale at home and abroad. Second, they agreed that they should *not* refuse permits to parents wishing to make private evacuation arrangements. In its way, this is one of the most fascinating Cabinet decisions of the Second World War: it ignored one of the strongest arguments for the original founding of CORB, and allowed, once more, a divisive situation to exist in which money and privilege could buy safety overseas for one's children.[19b]

However, there was more behind the Cabinet's second decision than a move to placate the moneyed, influential sections in British society. Allowing private evacuation overseas to continue seems to be strongly linked with the relationship of Britain to the USA. So far, the USA had received far more privately evacuated children from Britain than had any other receiving country. Furthermore, thousands of American families still cherished the hope that the British and US Governments could resolve guardianship problems, and let CORB initiate large-scale evacuation of working class children to their country. Indeed, at the very time the *City of Benares* was sunk, Mr Eric Biddle, Director of the American Committee for the Care of European Children was in London at the insistence of Mrs Eleanor Roosevelt, wife of the American President, and herself Honorary President of Mr Biddle's Committee. Mrs Roosevelt wanted Mr Biddle to iron out the difficulties preventing CORB from sending Government-sponsored evacuees to the USA.[20]

When the *City of Benares* news came, Mr Shakespeare told Mr Biddle that he saw 'little chance of children going in British ships in view of the limited number available.' For his part, he learnt from Mr Biddle that the USA would only consider sending its own ships for evacuees as far as Ireland, and 'only then if Hitler gives a safe conduct, which is extremely unlikely.'[21] Mr Biddle was therefore reaching the reluctant conclusion that they should 'close down the American organization' speedily, 'rather than allow it to continue, and funds be raised, with all the consequent disappointment, and perhaps anger, that all their hard work had been in vain.'[22]

In detailing these American complications, Geoffrey Shakespeare intimated to Sir John Anderson that he would welcome Mr Biddle being given an 'official reply, as the nature of it may affect the whole attitude of America to our cause.' The words 'our cause' are ambiguous. Did Mr

Shakespeare mean CORB's cause, or the wider cause of the British Empire against the Nazis?

Whichever it is, it seems that the need to sustain American goodwill, just as much as the need to avoid offending the Dominions, led the War Cabinet to keep the doors open to overseas evacuation and to announce only 'a temporary suspension' of the CORB scheme on the 2 October, having secretly agreed that the scheme should end at once. Meanwhile, the decision to allow private evacuation to continue would keep US hopes alive as well.

Also meanwhile, the Home Secretary, John Anderson, in acquainting the Cabinet of Geoffrey Shakespeare's letter about Eric Biddle, recommended that Mr Biddle be told 'frankly' about the position, but also that, as far as the possible re-opening of the scheme was concerned, 'no definite statement can be made until it is seen how the war situation develops.'[23]

In view of the War Cabinet's secret determination already expressed to end the CORB scheme altogether, it seems clear that Mr Biddle and the US Care Committee were being 'used' — either in the cause of maintaining US interest in CORB or, possibly and much more vitally, of keeping alive the hope of her becoming an ally. Certainly, these delaying tactics paid no heed to Mr Biddle's local committees, hundreds of which were now wasting their time working towards the future reception of large numbers of CORB children in America.

Whilst these political games were going on, considerable confusion was affecting the lives of six hundred CORB children who were either waiting to embark as news of the *City of Benares* disaster reached Britain, or were on the way to hostels in the ports.

The day the news first broke, on the 19 September, the thirty seven children who had just boarded the *City of Simla* for South Africa at once got orders to disembark, and their passage was cancelled. This was sensible and understandable. What is more, the ship's owners, the Ellerman Line, who also owned the *City of Benares*, would be relieved at the children's removal.[24]

But, far less sensible, and understandable only on the assumption that extreme chaos prevailed, thirty three of the thirty seven children removed from the *City of Simla* were immediately reallocated and joined batch U4 in their pre-embarkation hostels. This batch had already been waiting for five days to board the *Llandaff Castle* for South Africa.[25]

To add to the confusion, the U4 batch actually proceeded to embark on the *Llandaff Castle* four days later. Maurice Pike, a fourteen year old from Rayleigh, Essex, remembers this episode in his life very vividly. Together with the three hundred children in the batch, he spent the night of the 23 September anchored half a mile off Gourock. Next morning, his group escort told Maurice that they were all being sent home 'because there were insufficient escort vessels available.' So, back the evacuees went — not straight home, however, but for two more nights in their Glasgow hostels, in which the majority had already spent ten uncomfortable and uncertain days.

Adding even more to the terrible confusion, there had not been time to prevent batch C4, consisting of one hundred and forty children, arriving in their Liverpool hostels on the 21 September. But, they were not sent home. Instead, they went ahead with embarkation plans aboard the *Largs Bay* on the 24 September — the day the U4 children *left* their ship — only to be taken off later the same day, and sent home the next.

By a sheer coincidence, for one family there began a bizarre chain of events on the dockside as the C4 batch left the *Largs Bay*. A CORB mother, whose husband had agreed to her sailing, on health grounds, to join a married daughter in Australia, saw her CORB evacuee younger daughter disembarking from the *Largs Bay* aboard which her own passage was booked. The mother managed to persuade the Shipping Company to sell her a 'half' ticket for her daughter, and also badgered Major Wheeler, the Australia House representative for CORB in Liverpool, to release the girl into her care.

Mother and daughter duly sailed together to Australia, but her father complained, with justification, that his wife had abducted his daughter and that, by aiding her, CORB was to blame. At any rate, after two years of complaint, he won his claim that he was not liable to pay his daughter's fare.[26]

The final mix-up in the days immediately after the sinking of the *City of Benares* involved batch Z3. They, too, had arrived in hostels in Liverpool just as the news broke. They, too, embarked on their ship, the *Rangitane*. But, unlike these other batches, Z3 did not disembark and actually set sail at 6.30 am on the 25 September to rendezvous with convoy OB219 — the same convoy in which the *Largs Bay* and the *Llandaff Castle* were also sailing, minus their CORB children. Some hours later, escorted by the destroyer *HMS Winchelsea*, the *Rangitane* returned to Liverpool and landed a somewhat disappointed and bewildered batch of CORB children. The ship then set sail once more, caught up convoy OB219, and arrived safely in New Zealand in November. She was just in time to enter another episode in the CORB story.[27]

One piece of good fortune emerged from these chaotic and unpredictable days. The removal of South African batch U3 from the *City of Simla* on the 19 September probably saved a needless loss of CORB children's lives. The ship was torpedoed by a U-boat at 9 am on the 21st, and sank some forty miles north-west of Malin Head.[28]

Yet one ship did set sail with 29 children on board. Despite the losses, the disembarkations and the increasing threat of U-boat attack, the *Nova Scotia* joined convoy OB217 on the 21 September bound for Canada. They were attacked by a pack of U-boats in that part of their journey beyond the 'limit of convoy' when they were temporarily unescorted. Five ships were sunk but the *Nova Scotia* sped on alone and reached Pier 21 in Halifax, Nova Scotia, in safety. This was the last CORB ship to sail.

On the 2 October, the Government at last publicly announced the suspension of the CORB scheme, at least for the coming winter,[29] having previously notified the Dominion High Commissioners of the decision. Two days earlier, in a memo to the Cabinet, the Minister of Shipping confided: 'Losses continue at a rate which is causing me profound disquiet ... Ten ships recently sunk in one convoy ... The rate of shipping lost (is) higher than Britain can hope to replace ...'[30]

14

RECEPTION OVERSEAS — THE EARLY DAYS

'We have brought you the Crown Jewels!' declared chief escort Charles Kilby when the C1 *Batory* batch reached Melbourne.

Some host families who took in CORB children might not have put it in quite the same terms. Nevertheless, many were aware of the tremendous responsibility they were undertaking, whatever reasons they had for hosting evacuees.

Patriotism loomed large. 'We considered it a patriotic duty to assist the programme,' writes Mr Robert Dickinson who, with his wife, hosted a brother and sister from Glasgow in their Ontario home.

'My husband, a First World War veteran, said it would be our contribution to the war,' says Mrs G Millin, another Canadian foster-parent, who looked after two brothers from Middlesborough, Yorkshire. 'Having no children of our own, we decided to make this a war effort,' states Mrs J R Osbaldiston of Wellington, who hosted two Aberdeen boys.

In addition to patriotism, many Dominion families offered homes because of family ties with the Mother Country. The daughter of a South African parent-host[1] writes: 'My father was asked by his brother to have the girls for the war. My father felt deep family ties with his brother, Thomas and, being of British stock, felt very patriotic.'

A former Australian foster-parent says: 'I had already written and urged my sister to consider sending Freda to me for the duration. When I heard from my sister that Freda was coming, we were all delighted.'

Other hosts, whilst not mentioning patriotism, nor ties with relatives, had varying worthy intentions. 'With no

WELLINGTON CITY "YOUNG BRITONS" COMMITTEE

Telephone: 46-010   P.O. Box 1300,

                                                        Wellington.

                                                        26th August, 1940.

Mr. J R. Osbaldiston, ...
        179 Karepa Street, Brooklyn,
              WELLINGTON SW1.

Dear Sir/Madam,-

        I have to acknowledge with many thanks the receipt
of your application for TWO.... of the children to be evacuated
from Great Britain.

        His Worship the Mayor has set up a Committee which
has undertaken the responsibility of placing the children in
suitable homes and environment.   With this end in view a
Contact Committee has been set up to interview applicants in
their homes, to establish a friendly contact between the foster
parents and the Committee and obtain what additional information
is required.

        Would you, therefore, kindly receive two members of
the Contact Committee to interview you in your home at your
convenience.   The two members detailed to visit you will ring
you to make an appointment and will carry with them a letter of
introduction.

        I trust that these arrangements will meet with your
approval.

                                Yours faithfully,

                                alfa sharles.

                                Secretary.

Mrs JR Osbaldiston

Fig 22: *This letter from the Wellington "Young Britons" Committee gives an insight
into New Zealand's careful plans for the reception of CORB evacuees.*

children of our own, we thought we should help by caring for one of the children. Being young ourselves, we wanted one young,' says Mr Roy Lucas of Cronulla, New South Wales. 'Only two Jewish children were sent to Edmonton,' writes Mrs Rose Gofsky. 'We were Jewish also. So, it was decided Bernie would come to us, and Ivan to another Jewish family.'

There were instances, also, of people seeking to repay a kindness. 'My father had been wounded during the landing at Gallipoli, on the 25 April, 1915,' states Mrs Roy Goyen, whose parents hosted an Edinburgh boy in Tasmania. 'My father convalesced in Manchester, England, where he received much kindness. We decided to take an evacuee to help repay the kindness.'

And there were those wanting to add to family dynamics: 'We had two sons and always wanted a daughter. Here was the opportunity,' recalls Mrs M Rhind of Christchurch.

Many probably responded to the scheme because of a sense of public duty. Former New Zealand hostess Mrs F Scott-Miller writes: 'The Mayor of Wellington called a meeting of a number of citizens known to have an interest in young people, particularly youth. I was invited to attend and was elected a member of the "Contact Committee" which was to ask other people to help. Naturally, I offered my own home and services.'

There was abundant goodwill in each of the Dominions as many thousands of families offered homes. But, of course, finding the right homes for 'uprooted' children required professional competence at least as much as goodwill. In the event, the level of competence varied enormously.

Awareness of the likely difficulties in finding suitable placements was evident in CORB's initial planning.[2] Lord Snell, Chairman of the CORB Advisory Council, stressed the need 'for most careful arrangements for placing and after-care ... and ensuring that children are sent to congenial homes.' The Council commissioned Mr W J Garnett, a senior civil servant in the Dominions Office, to write guidelines for CORB representatives overseas. A few weeks later, Mr Garnett himself sailed with batch C1 aboard the *Batory* in order to become CORB's first liaison officer in Australia.

The Garnett guidelines were excellent. Alas, they were too often ignored. On the vital matter of placement of evacuees, Mr Garnett emphasized the need for prior inspection of all homes. He strongly recommended that children of the same family should be kept together or, if too numerous for this to be possible, at least billeted in the same locality; and placement officials should recognize the wishes of friends to be near each other, including the case of friendships formed on board ship.

Also, he advised, children should go to homes of the same social strata and of the same religious beliefs as the homes from which they had come; and the use of 'institutions' should be avoided, except for temporary hostel accommodation on arrival in the Dominion, or for the very occasional 'problem' child.

Very significantly, in view of future developments, the Advisory Council agreed that the supervision of evacuees and their hosts would be best left to the representatives of the Local Authorities in each Dominion, and the CORB liaison officer should 'remain in the background, letting the local machinery operate.'

Once CORB children began to arrive overseas, it became apparent that both the Dominions Office and CORB were leaving far too much to local initiative. More specific guidance to the UK High Commissioners, with consistent advice on the reception and welfare provision expected in each Dominion could have helped the development of standardized methods, if only in the matter of placement policy. As it was, each Dominion differed greatly in its approach and, with the exception of New Zealand, there was much variation in local practice from one area to another within each Dominion.

The most extreme form of localization was in South Africa. Working nominally under the Union Government's Social Welfare Department, local reception committees saw not only to placement visiting, but also to continuing welfare matters throughout the war and they guarded their local autonomy with great intensity. To strengthen this local control in South Africa, the neighbourhood magistrates were designated the legal guardians of all the evacuees in their judicial area, whereas, in the other three Dominions, the overall guardian was someone designated at national level.[3]

In Canada, nationwide plans for reception developed through the specially formed Council for Overseas Children, although the Welfare Departments of the Provincial Governments accepted official responsibility for evacuee placement and after-care. However, local 'contact committees' and charitable organizations such as the Children's Aid Society continued to play a significant role in the administration of evacuee matters from early reception days throughout the war.

Only in New Zealand was placement and after-care actually organized centrally and from the top by the Welfare Division of the National Government's Education Department. Of course, New Zealand had distinct advantages in looking to the welfare of the children by being a smaller country. Even in the matter of caring for the new arrivals Canada, on the other hand, had a distance problem. With the exception of one CORB batch that disembarked in Montreal, all the others landed in Halifax in the extreme East. The majority had therefore to travel vast distances before reaching their allotted area. Partly for this reason, the Council for Overseas Children recommended all Provincial Authorities to put new arrivals into 'Distribution Centres' — in residential schools, University halls, etc., before allowing them to join their host families. Whilst in these centres, the evacuees received inoculations and vaccination against a host of possible diseases. This idea originated with the Chief Medical Officer for Ontario and proved a mixed blessing, as some children met their foster parents for the first time feeling, not only the after effects of a wartime Atlantic crossing, but also of their inoculations.

Immediate reception arrangements in the other Dominions were much simpler. All South African evacuees stayed at *Westbrooke*, the Governor General's residence at Rondesboch in Cape Town, for two or three days. There they waited for hosts to collect them, or to form groups to travel with rail escorts to areas northwards and eastwards.

Australian evacuees stayed in residential hostels for two or three nights in their port of disembarkation if awaiting for hosts to take them farther afield or, in the case of 'un-

Fig 23: *An overflow of evacuees from 'Westbrooke' sitting on the steps of the Cape Jewish Orphanage before they travelled to their foster homes.*

nominated' children, to await allocation to foster-parents. Those whose foster-parents were able to collect them on the day of disembarkation went straight to their new homes.[4]

The New Zealand Welfare Department adopted a very enlightened policy of using CORB escorts from the *Ruahine* and *Rangitata* to accompany the evacuees beyond their port of embarkation where necessary. With hindsight, it proved a better plan than placing newly arrived children in strange accommodation with unknown staff to care for them.

For some Canadian evacuees, the journey across Canada left more vivid memories than the sea voyage from Britain, suggesting that, for many, the experience was much more pleasant.

'The train journey from Halifax to Vancouver took — I think — six days,' writes Richard Harris, fifteen years old at the time, who travelled with his twin sister, Madge. 'It was interesting but exhausting. I do remember our stopping at Riviére du Loup, and being approached by French-speaking Canadians who asked us something in French which none of us could understand. Whilst at that railway station, we saw a train full of Canadian soldiers destined for England. One

Mrs B Morley

Fig 24: *CORB children recently disembarked from the "Antonia", and still wearing labels, stay at Hart House, University of Toronto, to acclimatise and receive inoculations before joining host families.*

of them took a note of my name and address so that he could write to my parents . . . Above all, I remember being astounded by the vastness of the countryside, particularly the wheatfields, stretching as far as one could see, for two days on end through Manitoba and Saskatchewan. At Edmonton, we "lost" those destined for Alberta, and this left a mere forty eight going on to British Columbia.'

The journey from Halifax to Vancouver is about the same distance as the voyage from Liverpool to Halifax. Another ex-CORB evacuee speaks with a clear memory of that trip: 'I learnt that the coaches used were called "the old colonist" coaches, and this put me in touch with a bit of Canada's history. To amuse ourselves on the way, a small group of us made hats and dolls from the paper cups supplied for drinking. We also formed a small band and sang with paper and comb instruments. At one stop we "raided" an orchard and picked up several apples each. I don't think anyone stole from a tree. We were small children and took only the windfalls. Nobody objected.'

For a few children there were health problems immediately on arrival. Several arrived in Cape Town aboard the *Llanstephan Castle* with scarlet fever and others with measles. They were taken at once to the fever hospital and missed their stay at *Westbrooke*. Two sisters and a brother evacuated to East London, Natal, from Herefordshire, aged six, eight and nine, developed measles, scarlet fever and diphtheria between them in October and November, 1940. It is a tribute to their hostess, previously unknown to the children's family, that the evacuees suffered no complications and stayed happily together in the same home for the rest of the war.

Kenneth Austin, aged six on arriving in Halifax, Nova Scotia aboard the *Duchess of York*, recalls: 'I was unwell on arrival. My condition worsened on the train journey. I lost sense of time and believed that the train had reversed! On arrival in Saskatoon, I was hospitalized with scarlet fever. I was visited by some officials and told that I could not go to my aunt and uncle for some time.'

Extending the epidemic that had struck their ship, several ex-*Batory* evacuees developed impetigo soon after reaching their foster-homes, and some of the girls were found to have lice-ridden hair. A few ex-*Nestor* evacuees went down with measles on arrival, also continuing a theme of their voyage, the disease having been widespread after contact with it in Cape Town.

Several cases of enuresis occurred in each Dominion, but most quickly adjusted, only a handful proving more than their hosts could cope with. One rather sad case who did not adjust was a boy aged nine on arrival in New Zealand. After a spell in hospital for 'persistent enuresis' a month after disembarkation, he suffered four changes of foster-home over the next two and a half years. Was the root of the disorder, perhaps, the fact that this boy was originally placed in a different foster-home from his brother? They were eventually billeted together, in May, 1942, but, after a year, he was moved again to two further foster-homes.

A disturbing illness detected during the reception period involved a six year old Glasgow girl. She had TB on arrival in Wellington, New Zealand. This ought to have been

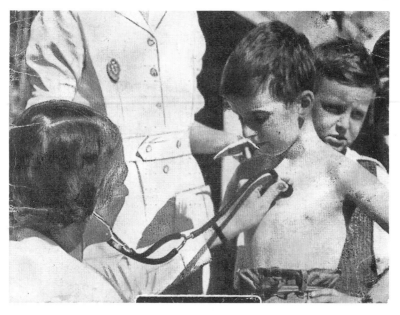

Australian Government Publishing Service

Fig 25: *CORB evacuees queue for a medical check shortly after arrival in Sydney.*

spotted sooner but, fortunately, her health improved later. Another serious discovery, concerning a South African evacuee, aged nine, from Middlesex, was that she had 'petit mal'.

Illness on arrival could be expected. Less expected was a number of complications caused soon after arrival by administrative mistakes, some of which might have been avoided. For instance, fifteen year old Gwen Staynes had been 'nominated' by her parents to live with an uncle and aunt whose home was in Christchurch in the South Island of New Zealand. About a month before Gwen arrived aboard the *Rangitata* her uncle informed the Child Welfare Authorities that he and his wife had now moved their home to Auckland in the North Island. This message was either mislaid or completely forgotten. As a result, Gwen arrived in Wellington, spent her first night in New Zealand on board ship with the South Island contingent, caught the ferry with them the following evening, and arrived in Christchurch early in the morning — only to be told that her uncle and aunt, of course, were in Auckland. She was taken with nine other evacuees to St Saviour's Orphanage where she stayed for the next two days, watching her companions dwindle as they were collected by foster-parents. Fortunately, Miss Kyrsty Page, a *Rangitata* escort, hearing of Gwen's plight and knowing her to be a shy girl, travelled with a child welfare officer to bring her back to the North Island. Eventually, six days after first arriving in New Zealand, and by now thoroughly dazed and homesick, Gwen met her uncle and aunt at Auckland.

Much more unfortunate was the experience of three 'unnominated' children, two sisters and a brother. Shortly before their arrival in Fremantle, Western Australia, they persuaded Mr Garnett, who was conducting placement interviews on board the *Batory*, that they ought to be billeted in Western Australia in order to be near evacuee friends from their home town. When the older girl heard from Mr Garnett that they had already been allocated to a Tasmanian foster-home, she was 'absolutely panic-stricken and argued forcibly against it.' As might be expected, in view of Mr Garnett's own guidelines to CORB about placements, he readily agreed that the children should not have to leave their friends behind in Western Australia, and arranged for three other children without strong feelings to replace them in Tasmania.

Thus, the children, aged nine, eleven and thirteen, disembarked in Fremantle and waited in a hostel for three days, expecting someone to come and take them to their home. But, on the third day, they were told that they were to continue their journey to Tasmania after all. The lady in Tasmania to whom they had originally been allocated had 'flatly refused' to take the three children sent instead.

So, a few days later still, they joined CORB batch C2 aboard the *Nestor*, sailed to Melbourne, and then went by ferry and train to Hobart. By now, the three children were 'determined to hate everything and everybody ... and Tasmania was landed with a little hornet's nest! We were introduced to our guardian. Poor soul! She was elderly, very severe looking, and a spinster. She said we could call her "Auntie"! Not a smile from any of us. The way I felt, I could no more unbend to call her Auntie than fly. And this was only the beginning!'

Whilst administrative slips and misjudgements about human nature were bound to occur, some of the unsuitable placements need not have happened. For example, it was obvious that it would not always be possible, nor desirable, to carry out the parents' wishes concerning nominated families, particularly when more than one or two children in a family had been evacuated together. But, it is difficult to understand why the authorities split up pairs of children, allowing one to go to the nominated host and not the other. A fifteen year old girl, who reluctantly went to Australia to look after her younger brother, was taken by the nominated family, who were business associates of her father. But her brother was billeted several minutes' walk away. Even this degree of separation devastated the girl, who could only rationalize being overseas at all if she was looking after her younger brother.

To make matters worse, in this particular case, her equilibrium was further disturbed when her new 'aunt' gave birth to a baby only a few weeks after the girl's arrival in the home. It seems clear that the sister and brother should have been placed together, from the outset, in an un-nominated home prepared to take two children from the same family, and where the foster mother was not pregnant.

Equally surprising, but more involved, was a case in Queensland. Two sisters aged eleven and fourteen were expecting to live with their mother's sister. However, their aunt had just left her husband, so the Child Welfare Department sensibly arranged for them to go to another home. But, incredibly, they sent the girls to a younger aunt who was not only on the point of getting married, but was also occupied full-time in running a guest-house. Soon after going to live with this younger aunt, the two girls were on their way to live with complete strangers. They were not all that happy there but they might just as well have been housed with strangers from the outset. And they probably would have been, had the circumstances of both aunts been properly investigated in the first place.

Occasionally, nominated hosts could not afford to look after the evacuees sent to them. For instance, three children evacuated to relations overseas found themselves living in unaccustomed, primitive conditions. The oldest child, aged fifteen, was old enough to realize the root of the problem. 'It was not simply the privy in the garden, and no running water,' she writes. 'Our relations were too poor to cope.' After a few months, welfare workers moved the three children. This time they were to live with three different families. The oldest child settled very happily. The middle child was quite happy, 'though expected to do many chores and much child care for the family.' Sadly, the youngest, an eight year old girl, developed 'emotional problems' and made three more moves before finally settling with an elderly foster-parent. In view of the generous offers of homes from many thousands of Dominion families, it seems a great pity that the placement officer for the area had not managed to put those three CORB children into another, un-nominated and financially secure home from the beginning.

The Canadian Committee for Overseas Children wisely realized that many nominated homes were unsuitable. By the time the scheme was suspended in October, 1940, the Committee was trying to persuade CORB London Head-quarters to contact parents and give them the chance of stopping their children leaving the UK if nominated homes were found wanting when visited by welfare officers. But, more stringent inspection of all placements, nominated or not, might not have avoided the sad experience of another three CORB children sent to live with an aunt. The youngest of the three writes, 'She did not want us. She separated us within days of our arrival. I have blanked out most of my year with her.'

Questionable placements arose with un-nominated and nominated homes alike. A problem for some nominated hosts was their feeling of obligation to take a relative or a friend's child they could not really cope with or did not really want to have. A problem for some un-nominated hosts was the matter of social mis-matching. For instance, the London bus-driver's son who was sent to an Australian Professor's home might possibly have settled, but he did not — and it must have seemed a gamble from the start.

Several evacuees were moved from their first foster-homes during the reception period with the brief note on their record cards: 'Home unsuitable'.[5] If a home proved 'unsuitable' in a matter of weeks, then it is likely that a little more investigation would have revealed the unsuitability before the child went there. This would have spared both evacuee and host-family the distress of an early move. As it was, between ten per cent and fifteen per cent of all CORB evacuees had a change of foster-home within the first six months after arriving in their Dominion.

A combination of distressing mix-ups over placements involved one thirteen year old CORB girl when she arrived overseas. The family her parents had nominated for her to live with, were not in evidence at her reception hostel. So, whilst at the hostel, the girl 'chose' a couple who were hoping to take an evacuee; they took her home and she settled very happily with them — for just three months. Then, the family friends originally nominated complained to the Welfare Department that they could not understand why she had not been sent to them.

The evacuee was now given the impossible choice of staying with the couple with whom she was already living very happily, or moving to the other family, which had always been part of her life in the regular, long-term correspondence between the two families. This ex-CORB girl realizes she must have hurt her first hosts terribly by deciding, after all, dutifully to leave them and go to the nominated family. But then, matters got worse: the nominated family friends discovered, after having her with them for a year, that they could no longer afford to keep her. Deeper investigation by the Welfare Department revealed that the family was truly in financial difficulties, and could not manage to feed the extra mouth.

It is easy to say, with hindsight, that welfare workers should have ignored the claims of the nominated family, especially as they had waited three months before voicing their complaint. On the other hand, placement officers in each Dominion did occasionally decide that a nominated home was unsuitable from the outset — and later got their fingers burnt for sending a child to an un-nominated home instead. One such instance involved a CORB girl who was allocated to an un-nominated foster-home in Australia, because the welfare authorities decided that the outback town where her nominated uncle lived, was not a suitable place in which to care for a teenage girl fresh from England. But, in March, 1941, after a battle lasting all the five months the girl had been in Australia, the uncle won his case and his niece went to live with him. Then, doubly unfortunate, after another five months had elapsed, the uncle requested the authorities to send her to another family, as his 'relationship with her was not a success.'

Understandably, during the early settling-in days, some evacuees showed signs of emotional disturbance. Bed-wetting manifested itself quite commonly, amongst both boys and girls. Other children developed nervous rashes, nail-biting, headaches and nervous tics. In the case of one boy in South Africa, the tic developed into St Vitus' Dance.[6]

A former Canadian evacuee remembers vomiting in the early stages, whilst living with a foster-parent who was a Christian Scientist. Her older sister at last called the doctor on her own initiative. He found the girl had psoriasis.

An ex-Australian evacuee, aged nine on arrival in Melbourne, recalls: 'I could not sleep in a room on my own. This lasted for perhaps nine months.' A girl in Canada, aged seven, says: 'My sister and I were a handful for our first hosts, an elderly couple. We used to ride the cows on their farm.' An eight year old evacuated to Australia remembers: 'I became a terrible worrier and would not let my sister or brother out of my sight day or night.'

Some of the symptoms of disturbance arose almost certainly because CORB's guidelines for placement overseas were not thoroughly enough applied, and particularly those recommending that children be placed with families who had children of a similar age, with families of similar economic background, and not with foster-parents too elderly to cope with youngsters.

An ex-Canadian evacuee, aged seven when he arrived overseas, writes: 'Although my foster-parents, an elderly couple, were generous and well-intentioned, I had trouble adjusting and developed bed-wetting problems . . . When placed with a family with children of similar age, I became completely happy.' An eleven year old girl evacuated to New Zealand recalls a more unusual aspect of difficulties with elderly foster-parents. 'I lived at first with an elderly, childless great aunt who, with other elderly relatives, was exceedingly kind,' she writes. 'But, my great aunt's husband was jealous of the attention I received. After six months, I was very suddenly handed to other foster-parents.'

Sometimes, it was the relationship between evacuees and their hosts' own children that proved the main obstacle to a happy settling-in process. A former Canadian evacuee, aged nine, recalls: 'Their daughter was a bit jealous, I think, and used to call me names and pull my hair. This upset me, but I kept it to myself.' Similarly, a thirteen year old girl in Australia records: 'In my first home I tended to quarrel with my cousin, an only child.' An eight year old recalls this sort of problem from the start: 'I met my foster-mother the first day in Adelaide. I was in a big hall eating breakfast while all the foster-parents came to pick up their evacuees. All the time I was eating, this lady kept smiling at me. Later that day, I was put to bed for a rest with my 'foster-sister'. She shut me in a wardrobe and I had to pretend I was a radio! . . . I was easily bullied.'

Of course, it was not only evacuees who suffered when relationships were difficult in these early weeks and months. A thirteen year old ex-Australian evacuee writes that she was 'quite happy' with her uncle and aunt, but 'seemed to quarrel with my cousins.' After three months, she was moved to another uncle and aunt 'owing to the illness of the first aunt.' Was the perpetual quarrelling at the root of the aunt's illness? Many evacuee record cards note that moves were made because of 'hostess's illness,' and, in some of these cases, at least, the difficulties of looking after a CORB child must have contributed to the illness.[7]

Another aspect of the upheaval in family dynamics caused by the arrival of an evacuee, is highlighted by Mrs F Scott-Miller, who hosted fourteen year old Edinburgh evacuee Angus Macleod. She points out that her two daughters were not accustomed to having a brother and thus 'they were apt to spoil him.' Mrs Scott-Miller realized she had to try to treat Angus 'exactly like my daughters', but her relatives, friends and neighbours tended to feel so sorry for the boy 'so far away from home', that they 'felt it their duty to entertain him, give him presents of sweets, and invite him to their parties.' The girls, meanwhile, were left out of the fun, even though they had readily agreed to give up things like going to the cinema, 'to help the family budget, and had given over personal things for Angus's use.'

As a member of the Wellington Contact Committee, Mrs Scott-Miller was in an ideal position to speak about this 'thoughtless generosity' as she terms it. The result was that the British High Commissioner in New Zealand, Sir Henry Battersbee, held a party to which he invited all the evacuees who could get there, with all the young members of their host families. It was a most successful affair and, says Mrs Scott-Miller, 'led the way to getting the balance right in New Zealand.'

What could have been a highly significant contribution to good relationships between evacuees and their host families was an article that appeared in the American social services journal *Survey Mid-Monthly*. Directed towards American hosts to privately evacuated British children, the article, entitled 'On Becoming a Foster-Parent', was written by New York social worker Marion Gutman.[8]

This article was distributed by Mr Blois, Nova Scotia's Director of Child Welfare, to all homes hosting CORB children in his Province. He also sent a copy to Mr Keith Jopson, then CORB's liaison officer in Ottawa, who promptly sent copies to all the other Provincial Child Welfare Departments, hoping that they would follow Mr Blois' example. But, it is doubtful whether this ever happened.

Marion Gutman stressed that making evacuees happy would require more than determination on the part of the foster-parents. Foster-parents would need patience to understand an evacuee. Having understood, and only then, they could start to help with any emotional problems underlying a child's apparent stoicism. She warned that foster-parents must expect different temperaments. Some children would settle more easily; be more ready to adapt, and even to share affection with the host family. Others would be more reserved, often withdrawn, because of their loneliness. These would need sympathetic and gentle treatment, rather than pressuring or shaming them into being less detached.

As it was, prospective hosts received virtually no advice before receiving their charges and the advice they had thereafter varied tremendously even from area to area within the same Dominion. Widely applied, Ms Gutman's psychology and Mr Garnett's placement guidelines could have prevented many misplacements and moves. As one boy evacuated to Tasmania says: 'I went to grandmother and an unmarried uncle. It lasted a short week! Then I was moved to another aunt and uncle!'

Another source of difficulty was that the Dominion authorities seemed to ignore the likelihood of people offering foster-homes simply to acquire status in the local community. But some of these offers came from people already highly respected in political and commercial circles. As one former Canadian host writes: 'All four children were originally taken by a wealthy lumber merchant and his wife. After seven months, however, his wife's health problems increased and the glamour had worn off; so the family dispersed — and we took the oldest.'

In another similar case, two Canadian evacuees were taken from their temporary Distribution Centre by a Minister of the Provincial Government. They stayed with this family very happily for a few months until, without any choice, they were moved to separate homes. The children received no explanation for this move.

The Education Authorities in the Dominions experienced quite considerable problems in placing many of the evacuees in the correct grade or year group at school. To complicate matters, many of the older evacuees were ahead of youngsters of their own age in subjects like English and French, but behind in Maths and, sometimes, Science. For some evacuees, unhappiness at the local school added to their difficulties in settling down in their new land. A former Canadian evacuee says, simply, 'We didn't like being different and standing out . . . It took us quite a few months to get over that.' The Harris twins, also in Canada, comment: 'We found it most difficult to adapt to school in a class in which all the others were two years older.'

Ten year old Brenda Mallett, evacuated to a bush region of Victoria, Australia, — 'a vast contrast to London, SW20' — describes her situation very succinctly: 'I was odd man out in a number of ways. I went to a one teacher school, cycling several miles to and from the school on bush roads

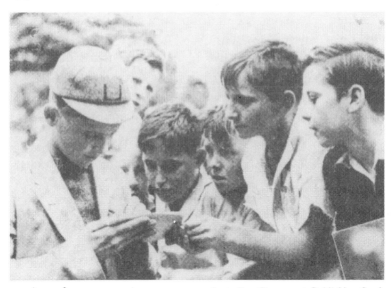

Australian Government Publishing Service

Fig 26: *A CORB boy is pressed for his autograph by new schoolmates at his Australian school.*

each day.' York City ten year old Muriel Evans found herself slightly better off in the West Australian bush: 'I attended a little weather-board, tin-roofed school with its two tanks for drinking water, two rooms and two teachers, with under fifty children.'

Those arranging CORB placements, both in foster-homes and at school, were severely handicapped by the lack of information available about many of the children. Miss Maxse, CORB's Director, later described the records sent to the Dominions as 'scanty and inadequate', explaining that this was because of the 'overwhelming speed and pressure of work under which the CORB team operated.'[9]

In the majority of cases the Headteacher's report required about each child did not reach CORB Headquarters soon enough to be sent to the Dominion Authorities ahead of the child's arrival. This was nobody's fault. Most requests for these reports had to be made during the British schools' summer holidays in July and August, 1940. To make things more difficult, some requests went to schools in evacuation reception areas because the children concerned were still evacuated when the parents applied to CORB. But, by the time the request arrived, the child was back in the home area where, holidays or not, most inner city schools were closed anyway as an air-raid precaution.

Whilst this lack of information explains some of the problem of placing the CORB children correctly at school, it also helps to explain why some moved quickly from their first placement in foster-homes overseas, particularly those whose record cards say that they moved because they 'did not fit in', 'had difficulty adjusting to life in higher social environment', or because 'child wanted a simpler home'.

But, for all the suffering some social mismatching caused, there was an inevitable lighter side to it. For example, Peter Beams, aged ten, and his two older brothers, sons of a Glasgow draughtsman, were taken home by the Manager of the General Motors Car Assembly Plant in New Zealand. They drove with their newly acquired foster-father to his huge mock-Tudor house set in five acres of gardens. There, the large staff of servants paraded on the steps, in stately home fashion, to greet the evacuees' arrival. John Fethney, then aged thirteen, son of a Bradford municipal clerk, was occasionally given a lift to school by his first Australian host, Senator H S Foll, Minister for the Interior, travelling in the Senator's chauffeur driven, Government-registered Buick. One day, John arrived at North Sydney High School late for class. In response to a master's tetchy objection, he said — with suitably deadpan face — 'Sorry, Sir! The chauffeur was late today!'

More seriously, however, the ruling that hosts must be financially responsible for the CORB evacuees caused anguish for hosts and evacuees alike. In Australia alone, there were nineteen cases of early moves where the records state the reason as 'financial problems of hosts.'[10] The ruling also added to the tendency to place children with families of a higher social class than the homes they had left in Britain: inevitably, placement officials were more likely to find 'well-off' Dominions families better able to cope with the expense of hosting evacuees. True, each Dominion gave a tax concession to evacuee hosts, but, deliberately, the concession was not large enough to encourage people of limited means to host evacuees in order to gain financially.

Fig 27: *The author and his brother, John, play Chinese Chequers with three of Senator Foll's daughters, watched by Senator and Mrs Foll. The Senator, Federal Minister for Information and the Interior, was the boys' first host.*

For a variety of reasons already outlined, in the months October, 1940 to July, 1941, eighty five children moved from their first placements in Australia, (out of 577); eighteen out of two hundred and two in New Zealand; and thirty six out of two hundred and ninety five surveyed in South Africa. But these are only minimum figures, as not all moves recorded are given a date, nor were all the moves actually recorded.

On the other hand, the majority of CORB evacuees stayed permanently in their first placements for the rest of the time they were overseas — although they stayed in varying degrees of happiness.[11] In some cases, a very unpromising start developed into a very successful and happy long-term stay.

One outstanding example of massive, early difficulties resolved happily must be instanced. The story is told by a Canadian lady, whose parents hosted two CORB children in Vancouver. She writes: 'My brother and I went to the Jericho Deaf and Blind School in West 4th Avenue to pick them up. We saw two very scared, forlorn-looking children with only the clothes they had on, as all else had been lost on the trip. All I wanted to do was let them know we would be good to them.

'The boy was fine; but the little girl was terrified of all that happened. They were the youngest children in the group and very upset. In addition to losing all their belongings, they had had 'shots' (ie., injections) and were very unhappy.

'The girl just didn't speak to us for a month. One bath-night, I asked her why she wouldn't. She just said she didn't because she didn't know us and was scared. But her brother said we were "all right", so, finally she did speak . . .

'Our little girl only weighed thirty pounds on arrival, and was very undernourished for her age. We had quite a time with head lice and had to get her head shaved. She also wet the bed. Between the social worker and ourselves, we came up with the idea of a teaspoon of boiled parsley water at bed-times, and told her she wouldn't wet the bed. It took about six months, then she didn't wet the bed any more. She had a poor time for the first year, then everything went fine . . .'

Others can testify, both ex-evacuees and ex-hosts, that some placements went well right from the outset. For example, New Zealand hostess Mrs J R Osbaldiston, who originates from Aberdeen, writes about her delight when she learned she was to foster two CORB boys aged twelve and thirteen and discovered they were 'two Scotties who had been to the same school as myself!' She and her husband collected the boys from the Presbyterian Orphanage in Wellington, 'and of course,' she writes, 'When they found out I was from "the Silver City by the Sea" they seemed pleased. Robbie's first words when we got home were: "Are we gan tae bide here a' the time?" Knowing the language was a great help to the boys, and must have made the settling-in so much easier for them.'

Again, Rita Patterson, who arrived in Australia aged eight, recalls: 'I was met by my great aunt and great uncle, and also by neighbours of theirs, at a school in Sydney. We travelled to Wollongong by train that night, and I found they had toys, dolls, prams, etc., and had gone to a lot of trouble. They had obviously looked forward greatly to my arrival.

'My foster-parents were middle-aged and childless. As an active eight year old I probably caused them more trouble than I was caused emotional upset! There was a special social evening at our local church to introduce me, and a great deal of sympathy came my way, both at school and at church, which I think I enjoyed very much, and which eased my homesickness ... I enjoyed a normal, full and happy life in Australia.'

Mrs M Rhind, a New Zealander with two boys of her own, became hostess to six year old Heather Johnston. She writes: 'We had to go to the Anglican Children's Home in Christchurch to get Heather and found her a delightful, shy little girl. I picked her up and cuddled her, and we have been great friends ever since!'

Some foster-parents, aware that they should not supplant the parents' affections, and conscious that they should not appear to reject their own children, tended to avoid overt expressions of affection. But, following Mrs Rhind's spontaneous action in 'cuddling' Heather, it is no surprise to learn, both from Heather and Mrs Rhind, that the relationship blossomed.

Writing in 1942, Geoffrey Shakespeare referred to the permanently good impressions the CORB children were making in the Dominions 'by their courage, self-possession, poise and conduct,' and admitted he was pleased that his own farewell words to CORB batches seemed to have borne fruit.[12]

Similarly, in her account of CORB's work written in 1944, Miss Maxse said: 'The reserve, bearing and intelligence of these children, some drawn from the poorer quarters of the cities, impressed their new circles deeply and added a measure of admiration and understanding of the British to their foster-parents.'[13]

Fine. But, jutting chins and stiff upper lips do not encourage motherliness in foster-mothers. Instead, they suggest aloofness and independence, creating barriers and, as Marion Gutman warned, making overt affection seem out of place. Thus, whilst it was good for the CORB children to be encouraged to stand on their own two feet, it did little to help caring foster-parents who had expected to welcome an uprooted child who would feel dependent upon them.

Finally, we have seen that most hosts and their families had inadequate preparation for coping with their evacuee guests. But, it is too easy to forget that the children had had even less adequate preparation for accepting the status of foster-children. The position for both hosts and evacuees was, therefore, fraught with numerous complications. Even so, despite unhappy first placements and too much movement during the early months, strong and happy bonds were forged. And some host families did, indeed, come to regard their CORB evacuees as 'the Crown Jewels' after all.

15

STINGS IN THE TAIL

On the 3 November, 1940, whilst the CORB evacuees were still finding their feet in their new homes, a party of twenty two former CORB escorts left Sydney aboard the Polish ship *Batory* on the first stage of their voyage home. For those who had sailed with batch C1 aboard the ship earlier, the voyage to Wellington proved bitter-sweet. They enjoyed the now spacious accommodation with only forty passengers on board. But, they felt lost and lonely without the children.

After two weeks of royal entertainment in Wellington, the escorts went to Auckland and lived for five days aboard the *Rangitane*, which previously appeared in the CORB story when she landed batch Z3 in Liverpool in September. At last, on Sunday, 24th November, the CORB escorts were joined by about a hundred other passengers, many of them New Zealander volunteers for the Fleet Air Arm; the ship's Master, Captain H L Upton, DSC, RNR, conducted a short service in the lounge and, soon afterwards, the ship set sail.

At 2.50 am on the 27 November, the ship's Second Officer called Captain Upton to the bridge. He arrived, overcoat on top of his pyjamas, and soon picked out the shapes of two ominous looking vessels, one on each side of the *Rangitane*. At once, he ordered a warning message to be radioed: 'Sighted suspicious vessels.'[1]

The two raiders, for it was the German ships *Komet* and *Orion* alongside him, responded to his signal immediately with warning shots. Minutes later, when Captain Eyssen, commander of the *Orion*, realized that the *Rangitane* was refusing to heave-to, he ordered the two German ships to

M Slabosz

Fig 28: *The Polish ship "Batory" after safely bringing 477 CORB children to Australia, briefly entered the CORB story again when she took some former CORB escorts on the first stage of their return voyage.*

aim to hit and stop her.

For a few seconds there was the screech of shells. Then, aboard the *Rangitane*, there came the crash of smashing glass; the crunch of cabin walls caving in; screams for help. Briefly, bewilderment and chaos prevailed.

Sisters Edge and Sandbach, ex-members of *Batory's* medical staff, had started dressing on hearing the first warning shots. Now thrown to their cabin floor by a shell exploding nearby, they were both badly concussed. They came to, in total darkness, to hear a man shouting, 'Help me! My arm's blown off!'[2]

In a neighbouring cabin, Mrs Sutcliffe-Hay, formerly CORB dentist aboard the *Batory*, was blown clean out of her cabin by the explosion, and found herself in the dining room eight feet below.

In another nearby cabin, ex-*Batory* escorts Mrs Elsie Davies and Miss Eleanor Pearson grabbed their slacks in the darkness and made for the cabin door. 'Wait,' shouted Miss Pearson. 'I'll get our pullovers.' But, Mrs Davies did not wait. She stepped into the corridor just as the next shell exploded and was blown to pieces.[3]

Pinned to the cabin floor by wreckage, Miss Pearson tried unsuccessfully to move. Through a terrifying sheet of flames, she could see Miss Elspeth Herbert-Jones, the youngest ex-*Batory* escort, lying badly injured. Miss Pearson remembered screaming. Then, she heard a man's voice encouraging her to crawl. Putting her life-jacket around her head as protection from the fire and smoke, she found strength to 'wriggle like a reptile' to the corridor. Some timbers crashed onto her leg, breaking a bone in her foot, she discovered later. But, 'half crying, bruised and bleeding,' she made it to the open deck.

There, Miss Pearson found Fr Denis Kelly, the *Batory's* former RC chaplain-escort. He laughed when he first saw her blackened face. But when she gasped out the news about Miss Herbert-Jones's plight, he sprang into action and immediately organized a group of men to the rescue with hoses and flash-lights.

Meanwhile, Sisters Edge and Sandbach, still concussed, and blinded by smoke, found their first route blocked by an impassable fire. At the heart of the inferno stood the cabins of other CORB escorts. No-one there could have survived. Retracing their steps, they found a small group of survivors in the purser's square. Several were badly cut. By the light of a single torch, a crew member took them in tow to the boat deck.

Some sailors carried Elspeth Herbert-Jones on deck in a blanket. She was calling for water, and Eleanor Pearson was able to give her a few drops of brandy.

'Can you make it?' asked Miss Pearson.

'Of course I can,' she replied, smiling. 'I'll have to!'

Miss Herbert-Jones had a splinter of glass through a lung, though no-one knew at this point how grievously hurt she was. 'Aged twenty one,' recorded Eleanor Pearson, later, 'she was the bravest girl I have ever known. Despite her injuries, she insisted on walking to a life-boat, "provided", she said, "someone will give me a little bit of help!" '

Ablaze fore and aft, the *Rangitane* was already sinking on an even keel. In the faint light of dawn, therefore, Captain Upton gave the order to take to the boats. By this time, boarding parties from both the *Orion* and the *Komet* were on board the *Rangitane*, hastily removing as much as they could of the ship's cargo.[4]

As the life-boats pulled away from the sinking ship, the survivors now discerned the shapes of three enemy ships. One, the *Orion*, dirty and black, was flying the swastika. The other two, the *Komet* and the supply ship *Kulmerland*, were flying Japanese flags — though Japan was still, supposedly, a neutral country at the time. On reaching the German ships, the survivors were courteously helped aboard, those injured being treated with especial care. By now, the only intimation that the *Rangitane* had sunk through an act of war was the presence on deck of armed naval personnel.

Miss Elspeth Herbert-Jones died of her wounds on board the *Orion*. Fr Ernest Ball, ex-Anglican chaplain to CORB batch C2 aboard the *Nestor*, received orders to conduct the burial service. He had to write out the service from memory as best he could and, on the Captain's instruction, submitted it for censorship.

Captain Weyher of the *Orion* made a long oration at the committal, moving from praise to propaganda in almost imperceptible steps. 'I believe, my German comrades,' he said, 'that not one of us would wish our women and children to be exposed to the dangers of war at sea, no matter for what reason. If another country, however, sees fit to do so, it is not our task to pass judgment . . . We regard Miss Herbert-Jones as having fallen in the service of her country . . .'[5]

Then, to the tune of *Ich hat ein Kamarad* — *I had a friend* — played by the *Orion's* band, the service came to an end. One of the ship's officers turned to Miss Pearson. 'Don't British women cry?' he asked. 'We can't,' she replied, 'as we have no handkerchiefs!'[6]

Soon, the Germans redistributed the prisoners among the

ships, all belonging to Allied Armed Forces, together with
Fr Ball, being collected aboard the *Orion*. Now, the CORB
personnel were able to work out for the first time who had
survived the sinking of the *Rangitane*, realizing with sadness
that six colleagues had met their death.[7] In addition, Miss
Phyllis Matthews and Miss Florence Mundy — both ex-
Batory nurses — were both grievously wounded. Miss
Matthews was hit by large shell fragments, and lost so much
blood in her life-boat that her friends did not expect her to
survive. But, she did — thanks to the German doctor
aboard the *Komet*, who amputated her right arm, set her
badly injured left arm, and treated the burns on her face.

Miss Mundy had had the clothes burnt from her back,
suffered facial burns, and had severe damage to her lower
jaw. For several days, she did not know the extent of her
injuries. But later, 'When she knew,' said Fr Denis Kelly,
'she accepted the news bravely, asserting that she could still
be a useful member of the community.'[8]

Meantime, the only news about the *Rangitane* was that she
had disappeared without trace after her brief radio message
before being attacked. There followed rumours and bitter
accusations in Australia and New Zealand that the ship had
sunk as the result of spy activity, and some unpleasant mud
was thrown in the direction of *Batory* crew members,
alleging poor security on their part. But, official inquiries
completely exonerated them, dismissed the spy theories as
highly unlikely, and demonstrated that enemy raiders' crews
only had to tune in to Australian and New Zealand news
bulletins to piece together sufficient intelligence about ship
movements for their purposes.[9]

At last, on Christmas Day, 1940, news came. In a coded
cable timed 2100 hours, the UK High Commissioner in
Wellington contacted the Dominions Office to report there
was news of survivors. Two days later, London had full
details of survivors, injured and dead. Thus after weeks of
anxiety, during which some escorts' relatives had accused
Miss Maxse of withholding information, CORB was able to
telegram the next of kin: 'I share your joy and relief at
survival of . . .' Or, in the six less fortunate cases: 'I deeply
regret to inform you that . . . is not amongst those reported
rescued . . .'

Very soon afterwards, the strange story of the survivors emerged, first of all in the Australian and New Zealand press: the hours spent as prisoners below decks; the correctness of the Germans; the discomfort — 'four weeks seemed like six months!' and 'bed for four weeks was the iron deck of the hold', although 'the women prisoners were all in bunks in cabins.' There were stories about the constant anxiety, which reached crisis point whenever the prisoners heard the gun covers being removed, and the ammunition lifts working, denoting that the raiders were sailing into action again.

But the story that caught the world's imagination was that of Emirau Island. On the 8 December, 1940, Captain Robert Eyssen, Commander of the German Far East Raider Squadron, ordered his three ships to converge on Emirau Island in the Bismarck Archipelago in order to release the accumulated prisoners. By now, there were 153 in *Komet*, 257 in *Kulmerland* and 265 in *Orion*, virtually doubling the number of mouths the Germans had to feed.

Disembarkation of prisoners eventually began on the 21 December, the prisoners landing in ships' life-boats. But, the *Orion* landed only three of her 265 prisoners, the three being unwell, which explains why Fr Ball, the only CORB escort aboard the ship, had the misfortune to remain a prisoner. In fact, he and the other *Orion* civilian prisoners were the victims of a disagreement amongst the Germans. Captain Weyher of the *Orion* felt that his superior, Captain Eyssen aboard the *Komet*, was breaking security by landing the prisoners and releasing them. He complained to his masters in Berlin, who promptly radioed all raiders ordering them to 'avoid mass releases in future.' But Eyssen's action must rank as an outstanding instance of humane treatment of the enemy by Germans in the whole of World War II.[10]

An advanced party of eleven heavily armed Germans had landed on Emirau the previous day, met the four Europeans who lived there, and asked about food supplies. Mr and Mrs Cooke, who managed the island's plantations, said they had enough to feed two or three people for three months. When questioned about their launch, Mr Cooke said, truthfully, that two Seventh Day Adventist missionaries, who sometimes lived on the island, had gone on three months leave to Rabaul in New Britain. What he did not reveal was that Mr Collett, who with his wife was looking after the missionary station in the Atkins' absence, had sent some natives in another launch to nearby Mussau Island to pick up supplies. So, sea transport was quite near at hand.

As the prisoners landed, the officer in charge of the German sailors ordered one group to search for a radio transmitter and another group to catch and kill five working bullocks. Three of these they left for Mrs Cooke and Mrs Collett to prepare for a stew in forty gallon oil drums. On smelling their evening meal in preparation, the crowd of prisoners began to feel that they had landed on the most idyllic tropical isle on earth. When night fell, with myriads of attacking mosquitoes, many felt a bit less enthusiastic; but it was still wonderful to be on shore and free.[11]

As the Germans left the island, they warned the Cookes to make no attempt to get help for forty eight hours. Otherwise, they threatened, they would return and 'blast Emirau to kingdom come.' But, Mr Collett had already sent a native canoe across to Mussau to get the launch back. Exactly forty eight hours after the Germans rejoined their ships, this launch started the eighty mile crossing from Emirau beach to Keviang and the nearest radio transmitter.

The tense wait that ensued was relieved for all by the hospitality of the Cookes and Colletts and the native inhabitants of Emirau; and by the hectic and happy preparations to celebrate Christmas. Given some calico by Mrs Cooke, a group of ex-*Batory* stewardesses made an alb, stole and chasuble in which Fr Kelly would celebrate Midnight Mass. A massive choir of men and women rehearsed carols, and teams of helpers assisted Mrs Cooke and Mrs Collett prepare the food.

Before the Mass began, the choir processed through the palm trees collecting the congregation as they sang, leading them to the Cooke's jetty, where some sailors had helped Fr Kelly rig up an altar, with one of the Cook's hurricane lamps at each end, and Fr Kelly's small crucifix mounted on a cross of white wood, driven into a bag of damp sand behind.

There were four hundred people at the Mass. The

wounded and ill had asked to be present, and were assisted there by friends. One ex-prisoner wrote: 'The light of the lanterns lit up the solemn faces of the men and women brought together by a common impulse, to give thanks for deliverance and to pray for their less fortunate companions.'

Appropriately, the Christmas Mass was just beginning when a light shone from far out at sea. Suddenly, signals flashed: the island's launch was escorting the Government ship *Leander* to Emirau. She had two doctors, medical supplies and food on board.

So, at 2 pm on Christmas Day the *Leander* left for Keviang with the women and children on board, and all the men gathered at the jetty to cheer them on their voyage. At 1.30 on Boxing Day morning, the *Leander* transferred its passengers to the luxury of the *SS Nellore*, a liner anchored in Keviang Harbour, with all its lights ablaze as though it were peacetime, 'waiting for us with cabins for all — and a meal. What a lovely night,' wrote Sister Edge later.[12]

Later that day, the *Nellore* sailed to Emirau to rescue the men. Then, after many expressions of thanks to the people on the island, the survivors sailed on to Townsville in Queensland and a tumultuous welcome. In fact, the welcome continued at every stop they made on the train journey southwards, reaching a climax with an official reception on 4 January, 1941, at Government House, Sydney. The whole of Australia hailed the survivors as war heroes, and mourned their dead companions.

In St Andrew's Cathedral, Sydney, on the 6 January, there took place a service 'in memory of those who lost their lives in the Pacific Ocean in 1940 through the action of enemy raiders.' Dr Mowll, the Archbishop of Sydney, gave an appropriate address. But no words spoken there in praise of the six brave CORB escorts who had lost their lives could surpass those in which Fr Kelly praised all of his fellow escorts, living and dead, singling out the women for special recognition. 'The women's morale was excellent,' he wrote. 'These were the sort of women to lead children overseas. How heroically they would have behaved if disaster had overtaken us when the children were still with us . . . Even without any disaster overtaking us, I am of the opinion that their services to the children were truly heroic.'[13]

Heroines or not, CORB in London warned that any escorts staying longer than the first available ship home would not be paid the CORB subsistence allowance, amounting to six shillings and three pence per day; and those staying beyond three months would have to pay their own fares home.

This does not quite end the story of the disasters and triumphs surrounding the CORB scheme in its early days. There was another sting in the tail.

Only three days after the sinking of the *Rangitane*, the German raider *Pinguin*, last mentioned in connection with convoy WS2 and the *Batory*[14] and still commanded by Captain Ernst-Felix Krüder, overhauled the British merchant ship *Port Wellington* in the Indian Ocean nearly 1,000 miles west of Fremantle. When a mile distant, the *Pinguin* opened fire, immediately destroying the British ship's radio room and killing the ship's Master.[15]

Eight ex-CORB escorts were on board the *Port Wellington*, and the first intimation that there were any survivors, did not reach Britain until the 15 April, 1941.[16] Those interminable five months proved a weary and desperately anxious time for relatives and friends, who concluded that no news was a bad sign, pointing to the sinking of the ship without trace and with no survivors.

But, the eight ex-escorts aboard the ship were fortunate. All escaped serious injury and were safely picked up from their life-boats by the *Pinguin*. Within a few days, Captain Krüder radioed Berlin, reporting that he was sending his prisoners to Europe aboard the supply ship *Storstad*. In fact, Captain Krüder was desperate as a result of his own success. Already, he had sunk over 100,000 tons of Allied and neutral shipping, leaving him with four hundred and fifty prisoners aboard his ship.

The *Storstad*, to which most of the prisoners were transferred, proved a grim prison ship. She had poor cooking facilities; the sanitary conditions were appalling; prisoners were only allowed half an hour on deck on alternate days; and the rest of the time they 'stared up at the hatch for either food or water to be lowered to them.'

After notification from the International Red Cross that

the escorts were safe in Germany, eventually, in May, 1941, came brief messages written by each of the people concerned, announcing they were safe and well, and giving the address of their respective prison camps. Then, very sadly, news reached CORB from the Foreign Office in the Autumn of 1941 that Miss Joan Fieldgate, ex-*Nestor* escort, had died in Ravensburg Hospital on the 9 October. She was twenty seven years old.[17]

A little later, Miss Maxse received a letter from Miss Mabel Wood, a *Port Wellington* survivor, and another former escort aboard the *Nestor*. Miss Wood had been interned in the same prisoner-of-war camp as Miss Fieldgate, and she explained that her colleague had suffered from dysentery for several weeks, leading to her admission to hospital in mid-September. There, she was 'most kindly treated by German nuns.' Mrs Best and Miss Wood were both allowed to attend the funeral, at which the Anglican Burial Service was read, and 'there were flowers, including some from the nuns.' Miss Wood added: 'Joan Fieldgate showed a fine, high courage and fortitude, a shining example to all ... She was simply slendid.'[18]

In November, 1942, news came from South Africa, by way of a cable from the CORB liaison officer, Miss Thompson, that a possible repatriation of CORB prisoners was afoot. She reported: 'Best, Fox, MacKenzie, Maclean, Sharp now in Cairo proceeding home via South Africa.' They had apparently arrived in Egypt through Ankara and Palestine; but, indicative of the complications surrounding the repatriation of prisoners, over a month later Mr A G Ponsonby of the Foreign Office POW Section told Miss Eleanor Nicholas at CORB Headquarters that he knew of no party of civilians expected to leave Germany via Turkey.

At last, on the 30 January, 1943, over two years after they had first been made prisoners, Miss Thompson was able to cable from South Africa: 'Party of repatriates have arrived Durban.' A few days later, Mrs Best, Miss MacKenzie, Mrs Maclean and Miss Sharp sailed for Britain from Cape Town aboard the *Nestor*. Mrs Fox was not well enough to travel until the end of April, her active yet gentle personality had taken so great a punishment during her imprisonment. Meanwhile, Miss Wood, who had declined the original offer of repatriation, came out of Germany via Lisbon, whence Thomas Cook's arranged a flight for her to London on the 11 February by courtesy of BOAC.[19]

Fr Ernest Ball, it will be remembered, was the one escort sunk in the *Rangitane* who did not land on Emirau Island, being imprisoned instead aboard the *Orion*. In January, 1941, he and his fellow prisoners were transferred to a raider supply ship, the *Irmland*. Aboard this ship, the prisoners plied their way across the Pacific, rounded Cape Horn, meeting up with another raider ship and the pocket battleship *von Scheer*. Thus escorted, they sailed without incident to Bordeaux, arriving there in April, 1941.

Fr Ball and the other prisoners went to POW camp at Sandbostel, and, later, at Milag Nord between Bremen and Hamburg. There, Fr Ball had a pleasant surprise when he met Brigadier Best of the Salvation Army, who had been his chief escort aboard the *Nestor* with batch C2.

After two and a half years, during which time he acted as prisoners' Chaplain, Fr Ball was recommended for repatriation. He wished to stay to minister to his flock of prisoners; but, he had developed a tubercular lump that was badly affecting his voice. Furthermore, the German authorities insisted that an Anglican Naval Padre in a neighbouring camp, whose members were shrinking, should take over Fr Ball's duties. Consequently, he travelled by train and ferry with other sick and wounded prisoners to Malmo in Sweden, and thence in a hospital ship to Scotland, where the party had a 'tumultuous welcome' in Edinburgh.

A few days later, Fr Ball visited his mother in London. Learning what she and other Londoners had endured during the war so far, he wrote: 'The true heroes were those who so generously gave a heroes' welcome to many of us who had done so little to earn it!' But, the calibre and resilience of that brave band of men and women, the CORB escorts, is epitomized in some words Miss Mabel Wood wrote from prison camp to Miss Maxse: 'Faced with the question to go or not to go, I should still choose to go. For it has been a great experience which has taught me much I needed to know.'[20]

16

LIFE OVERSEAS — THE BRIGHTER SIDE

'I adored my years in Australia. I shall never forget the kindness and hospitality of the people. It was incredible!' So wrote former CORB evacuee Freda Stout, over forty years after her return to peace-time England. And Freda is by no means alone in her enthusiasm.

Former New Zealand evacuee Peter Beams also retains very favourable memories and, although he returned to England after the war, he has been resident in New Zealand for many years now. 'As far as I can recall,' writes Peter, who was hosted together with his two brothers by the same family, 'we had no problems whatsoever. We were not separated. Our foster-home was superb. We fitted into school life very easily. I feel certain we had no emotional or physical difficulties, or anything else that bothered us or our foster-parents.'

John Doughty, fifteen years old when he arrived in Tasmania, comments: 'I had no worries: a fifteen year old is a heartless creature!' He admits he is 'still rapt' with Australia, and that he 'never contemplated repatriation to England.' Instead, when the war was over, he persuaded his family to emigrate and join him overseas.

Another former New Zealand evacuee, who, like Peter Beams returned to the country to settle permanently, is Heather Johnston. She went back to her former foster-parents in 1949, and lived with them until her marriage in 1956. Heather cherishes very happy memories of her earlier years in New Zealand as a CORB girl, being 'fostered by a family who treated me,' she writes, 'like the daughter they did not have.' The only war-time worry she can recall was temporary: during the last year of the war, her mother went to live with a friend from work. Heather was anxious that her mother aimed to re-marry, 'as she did not tell me at first that her friend's name was "Lily"!'

Apart from this, Heather asserts, 'I spent five extremely happy years with my host family, as part of the family. I suppose my foster-father took the place of my own father whom I had never known.'

Heather's mother, widowed before the war, but entitled to no pension and therefore forced to work full-time, opted to send her only child overseas 'as I was afraid for Heather's life.' Without a trace of bitterness she writes of those evacuation years: 'There were many advantages: Heather had a good home, was well looked after, better fed, and safe. Her foster-parents were wonderful people.' Mrs Johnston herself emigrated to New Zealand in 1959, after the death of her mother.

Mrs Rhind, Heather Johnston's foster-mother, not only during the war years, of course, but also after 1949 when Heather returned to school in New Zealand, completes this particularly happy CORB story, stressing the 'great pleasure' she and her family experienced in looking after their evacuee. She points out that the social worker from the Welfare Department visited occasionally at first, 'then decided it was a waste of time, saying that Heather could not have been in better hands or happier.'

Other former CORB children can recall very happy years of evacuation, with former hosts and their own parents sharing the happiness of the venture. Barbara Spence, who went from York to Canada aged ten, recalls only the briefest problem after arriving to live with her uncle and aunt in Sault Ste Marie: she was put in Grade 4 at school the first day, Grade 5 the second day, and Grade 6 a few days later. But she felt 'instantly accepted by the other children, and they looked after me. People were very kind.'

Barbara's mother says she would send Barbara to Canada again, given similar war-time conditions. Her daughter grew up 'free from the threat of air-raids. She was very happy in Canada, and was welcomed into people's homes.'

Mrs Constance Fairbairn, Canadian widow of the Rev R K Fairbairn, gives a valuable insight into some of the difficulties they had to overcome in order to give their nine and eleven year old niece and nephew a war-time home. But, she obviously looks back with pleasure on the experience, too.

Mrs Fairbairn writes: 'Our three children accepted the evacuees quite willingly. I think it helped that their ages were such that they could have been my own children. Our home was a six room apartment, so it meant that my oldest girl had to have a couch in the dining-room: Betty and Rosemary (her niece) together, Benson and John (her nephew) sharing a room. We were on minimum salary so that I could not afford help; but the fact that the children had come from a similar environment — (John and Rosemary were the children of a Methodist Minister) — made a big difference to their accepting what we had.'

When the time eventually came for the two evacuees to leave, Mrs Fairbairn recalls, 'it was quite an event, as many friends joined with us in wishing them Godspeed. The folks at the Church had been exceedingly kind to them and they had made many friends. Johnnie vowed he would return to Canada some day . . .'. He did so, in 1959, and has lived there permanently since.

John writes about his experience 'as an integrated member of my adoptive family' and retains the happiest of memories: the holidays the family spent with young people from Mr Fairbairn's Church at the summer camp at Hudson Beach, Quebec; skating and skiing at Mount Royal; and 'my first bike ride through melting ice in the early spring; converting an old flat-bottomed boat for sailing; the first kiss . . .'. He also records the pleasure he felt, one day, when his beloved uncle said, 'Why, Johnnie, you're quite a philosopher!'

John's sister Rosemary adds to the picture, mentioning the widespread kindness and friendliness they both received. And she also acknowledges the strain their stay imposed upon their host family. 'Our poor older cousin had a bed put in the dining-room. I didn't appreciate it at the time, but ever since I've realized what a burden the addition to their family had been. Money was short, too. I can never repay their kindness and generosity.'

Clearly, many host families must have made generous

sacrifices in much the same ways as the Fairbairns in Montreal. Strictly speaking, of course, had CORB's guide-lines on placements been followed scrupulously, John and Rosemary would not have been able to stay with their uncle and aunt, as CORB stipulated that evacuees should not have to share bedrooms with members of host families. Yet, despite accommodation and financial difficulties, the place-ment worked happily for all concerned.

Parents left at home in Britain add testimony to the success of placements overseas. Mrs Edith Penwarden, whose son Douglas went to close family friends in Canada at the age of eight enthuses: 'Douglas received the great advantage of being able to get away from the war terrors of Britain, and being treated royally by every person whom he came into contact with in Canada. I understand that the other children did too!'

This sort of contentment is echoed by Mrs Mary Webster, whose son Derric aged nine, and daughter Catherine aged seven went from Bradford to Melbourne. 'The Australian hospitality was amazing,' she says, 'and the children made many friends. They enjoyed school. They became confident and self-reliant.'

Mrs Mary Hume, mother of Tom, twelve, and Roy, six, who went from Edinburgh to New Zealand, states: 'Our sons had the advantages of security, freedom from fear, plenty of good food for growing bodies, and the opportunity to learn, by personal experience, about another country and a different people. We corresponded regularly and, in the exchange of letters, soon came to know a great deal about each other and our respective families. A relationship was established which has lasted throughout the years .... Their lives and ours were enriched by the relationship with these wonderful people.'

Crucial to the success of any placement was the development of good relationships between an evacuee and the fostering family. Many genuinely caring foster-parents, helped often by their own children and other relatives, worked very hard to achieve this. It required great effort, especially as the war began to drag on so much longer than most people had ever envisaged.

A delightfully happy story, illustrative of the profound

love and patience given to evacuees in some foster-homes, concerns the continuing care for the two sad children collected by a Canadian lady and her brother from the Vancouver Deaf and Blind School in 1940. The girl, aged five at the time, had serious problems initially,[1] even finding it impossible to talk to her hosts. But, the hosts' daughter writes: 'Our whole family valued the pleasure gained by helping two very young people from a different environment. The nine year old boy was fine and well adjusted. His sister had a poor time the first year, even had to stop out of school because her health needed a lot of attention, and emotionally she was not ready for school. But, happy to say, everything went fine then. They went everywhere with us, enjoyed the lacrosse games we went to at that time, entered school activities, and in general mixed well. When they left, they were two lovely children, and well adjusted. It was wonderful to have them, and our parents would have adopted them if it had been possible. Our only unhappy day with them was the day they left for England: it was a sad time to see them go . . .'

Particular mention is due to those people who willingly accepted evacuees into their homes, knowing that there had probably been problems over relationships, as they had already been billeted elsewhere. Such children could prove 'difficult'. A former Canadian host writes about giving a CORB girl her second placement: 'I think she was happy to live in a modest home where there were no great demands on her behaviour. In her previous foster-home, there were "appearances", and too many bosses . . . Now, our own daughter had a companion. They enjoyed each other's company skating, swimming, hiking . . .'

The daughter of a Winnipeg couple who welcomed another unsettled evacuee, writes about the experience after her parents were contacted by the Children's Aid Society who were trying to place the girl, a fifteen year old, who had not adjusted to her first two foster-homes. The Society warned that things might not be at all easy, but the foster-parents were not to hesitate to contact the CAS and seek help with any problems. 'But, mother never did that,' writes the hosts' daughter. 'All she did was contact the families who had Peggy's sisters, and talk things over with them. My mother had actually wanted a girl about eight years of age. She had never thought about a fifteen year old!'[2]

'When the girl arrived in this, her third home, she cried and insisted, "No-one wants me!" But, my mother was very kind-hearted, and this cry went right to her heart. She took her in.' It was never easy, but for the next three years Peggy's foster-family worked hard to help her adjust to Canadian life, never allowing themselves to feel they had made a mistake in giving her a home. When her mother became seriously ill, in 1943, CORB arranged for Peggy's repatriation to Britain.

In a somewhat ironic, yet meaningful way, a death in the host family could demonstrate the deeply mutual confidence that had developed between an evacuee and the host family. When Gwen Laycock's aunt died of cancer in New Zealand, she competently ran the home for her uncle and young cousin for many months until her uncle was able to arrange for his own daughter to attend boarding school. Similarly, when the hostess of three CORB sisters died in South Africa, they remained with their host and his married daughter, helping to look after the home. Then, when their host remarried, in 1944, he took the youngest evacuee to his new home in Natal, arranging for the oldest, now eighteen, to work in his office, and for the middle sister to be with friends in Bloemfontein, because she had started a college course there.

On a more evenly happy note, some evacuees, mostly girls, became engaged whilst evacuated. The official number of those who married was recorded as ten in February, 1946.[3] But, the numbers could well have been higher, partly because CORB records, with too small a Headquarters staff, were not always kept up to date, and partly because some got married after they had withdrawn from CORB's jurisdiction, though they were still living abroad. One such instance involved Keith Langdale, Mrs Fox's capable King's Scout aboard the *Batory*, who joined the British Army in India when he was eighteen, and rose to the rank of Major. Keith married an Army Nursing Sister at the end of the war.

In Canada, eighty per cent of eligible CORB boys joined

Fig 29: *The author (left) and Michael, youngest son of Dr Palmer, second host to the author and his brother, about to scooter off to their smallest private school in Bulli, NSW.*

the Forces, roughly equal numbers joining British and Canadian Services. In South Africa, seventy two per cent joined one of the Services, and in Australia, seventy eight per cent. The South African proportion was a little lower because the opportunities presented for Higher Education were rather better than in Canada or Australia. In New Zealand, the call-up age was twenty one; thus, fewer CORB boys became eligible for service there than in the other Dominions, but several under twenty ones arranged passages home from New Zealand in order to join the British Forces. Australian evacuees were given an option of direct entry to the British Army in India, usually with the guarantee of an Officers' Selection Board six weeks after arriving in India. Several boys availed themselves of this scheme, and received commissions in British Regiments. A good sprinkling of CORB girls joined the Women's Auxiliary Services, too.[4]

Of course, the majority of CORB children did not reach military service age before the end of the war. The commonest experience for almost all of them was some form of education, however briefly it lasted for some of the oldest. When the CORB scheme first started, it was announced in Britain that children evacuated overseas 'would be given the same educational opportunities as those available to Dominion children in the district where an evacuee went to live.' As Miss Maxse said in her 1944 summary of CORB's work, 'that promise was very fully implemented.' In some cases, the provision was even better than that available for local Dominion children, as when generous foster-parents or a local reception committee paid the fees for evacuees to attend independent schools, including boarding schools.[5]

In Canada, many CORB children who might have expected to leave school at the age of fourteen in Britain, stayed on to reach junior matriculation level because of the prevalence of staying on in that Dominion. Indeed, some CORB children who had already left their elementary schools in Britain restarted school on arrival in Canada — occasionally under protest — and acquitted themselves well.

The highest proportions of older children staying at school were to be found in New Zealand and South Africa where, consequently, a higher proportion took university degree courses. Up to 1944, when Miss Maxse made her analysis, some forty CORB children (about eight per cent), across the four Dominions had taken — or embarked upon — University, Teacher Training and Technical College Higher Certificate Courses.

The Welfare Departments in the various Dominions tried to ensure that evacuees seeking employment went to jobs with an opportunity for some training. But, it was not always easy for them to help, because some evacuees made their own, local arrangements, leaving school on hearing of a nearby vacancy that seemed suitable.

In all Dominions, but especially Australia and New Zealand, many boys took up farming. In New Zealand, this included some boys who joined the Youth Farm Settlement Scheme, which gave five years training, money saving inducements, and prospects of assistance in owning their own property eventually.

Perhaps the most important educational advantage that came to CORB children is the one emphasized by Miss Maxse. As she said, in terms of 'social education' CORB youngsters benefited by 'taking their place alongside their fellow students and living as young members of a Dominion society'. Furthermore, many evacuees had memorable and educative holidays in some of the most famous and attractive places in the world: the Rockies in Canada, game reserves in South Africa, the Rotorua Mountains in New

L. Fethney

Fig 30: *The author (left) and brother (right) holidaying in Bondi with the relatives they had expected to live with in Australia. (The boys spent much more time in swimming trunks than suits as the famous Bondi surfing beach was nearby).*

Zealand, the Blue Mountains and some of the world's best surfing beaches in Australia. Some of these holidays were arranged by charitable organizations, such as Rotary, in order to give foster-parents a rest from looking after their evacuees, as well as to give the evacuees a good holiday.

During the long years of separation from home, a great aid to both parents and evacuees keeping in touch was the monthly free cable, generously introduced in September, 1940, by Sir Edward Wilshaw, Chairman of Cable and Wireless Ltd.[6] Each parent and each evacuee received a card containing a selection of forty messages. These covered most eventualities from the mundane 'Love to all at home: All well here', to the more unusual 'So glad you like your new school. Writing. Love.' All the sender had to do was to write the code letter of the required message on a cable form at the Post Office each month. The full text was then delivered at the receiving end.

Occasionally, as some evacuees remember, the messages caused bewilderment. One recalls, for instance, that the message 'New sister just arrived. All well,' was dismissed as

STANDARD TEXTS

From PARENTS.

A. *Letter and contents received. Thanks. Writing.*

B. *Letter received. Glad know you are well. Love.*

C. *Parcel received. All well at home. Writing.*

D. *Have received your telegram. Glad know you are safe. Write soon.*

E. *Hope you received letters. Please write. Love.*

F. *No news from you for some time. Love. Writing.*

G. *Thanks for telegram. Convey best wishes to your host. Love.*

H. *Happy Birthday Greetings. All well here.*

I. *Best Birthday wishes. Parcel sent. Love.*

J. *Am sending Birthday present. Hope you will like it. Love.*

From PARENTS—continued.

K. *Love and Greetings from all at home. All well here.*

L. *Loving wishes for Christmas and New Year to you and your hosts.*

M. *Congratulations. We are proud of you. Love.*

N. *Sending photos. All well here. Love.*

O. *How are you getting on? All well at home.*

P. *Glad know you are now happy. All well here.*

Q. *Is there anything you specially want?*

R. *Glad you like your new surroundings. Write again soon.*

S. *So glad you like your new school. Writing. Love.*

T. *Always with you in thought. Love. Write often.*

U. *Sorry to learn news. Love. Writing.*

Crown Copyright

Fig 31: *Standard texts from which parents could select a monthly cable to CORB children and send at no cost. The children had identical provision overseas.*

a misuse of code letters. But, some months later, a letter arrived by surface mail giving details about his mother's new baby.

A former New Zealand evacuee writes: 'Sometimes, it was difficult to find a message that would exactly suit. On receipt of one simply saying, "Congratulations. We are proud of you" from my father, and being perplexed, my foster-mother suggested it must be because she had informed my parents that I had attained womanhood at around thirteen years. I was mortified beyond belief that she should have done this, and the fact that my father knew deeply embarrassed me . . .'

The 'airgraph' letters, introduced in 1943, were another boon to the matter of maintaining contact between families. These involved writing a letter onto a specially prepared form which was then photographed and reduced in size, then sent by airmail. This not only speeded up communications, but guaranteed more certainty of letters reaching their destination.

But former CORB evacuees, their parents and their hosts

remember the Cable and Wireless monthly service as paramount in keeping in touch. However unsystematic families might have become about letter-writing, they usually made sure to send a cable once a month. In this way, gulfs were bridged, anxieties reduced, and — for a brief time — life was seen to be continuing with some normality.

Meanwhile, however, anxiety was never far beneath the surface of many a young CORB child's mind, anxiety increased by the nagging realization that they could no longer call to mind an image of their parents, nor any other people who had been close to them at home. This added to the uneasiness of guilt they felt, at times, if they were enjoying the life overseas.

17

LIFE OVERSEAS — THE DARKER SIDE

'I ran away from my uncle's place: I didn't seem to get on with my aunt. In fact, I didn't seem to fit in with any relations, and I wasn't very happy until 1946 when I went to live with some strangers who at least acted like I was a human being, and not something that had to earn its keep all the way.'

The writer, a CORB evacuee from Wales, arrived overseas aged ten. He discloses more detail of the agony he endured during the war years. 'One foster-parent,' he writes, 'used to hit me with a poker because I wouldn't go to the toilet at a specified time. This one wanted me to love her like my mother who was still very much alive — so I couldn't. Another family made me the butt of their jokes for two years. It's a wonder I'm sane at all; but, being stubborn by nature makes one very self-reliant!'

The cruelty this CORB boy alleges was extreme, but his experience is a reminder that happy memories are not universal. The amount of movement that occurred from first homes overseas,[1] pointed strongly to the probability of continuing unhappiness, both on the part of evacuees and their host families.

In her 1944 summary of CORB's work, Miss Maxse acknowledged that changes of foster-home were 'inevitable', through what she called 'temperamental difficulties' of either children or foster-parents, or through 'bad or restrictive placements' and, sometimes, 'through bad behaviour or moral failing of the children themselves.' She went on to claim that in most cases 'a second home was able to settle those difficulties and no further moves were necessary.'

On the other hand, she admitted, where evacuees failed to adjust suitably to the second home, 'it would have been wiser to bring the children back.' According to Miss Maxse, between 1940 and 1944, seventy per cent of the children overall stayed in their first home and, of those taken into a second home, half stayed there.[2]

But, unfortunately, Miss Maxse's summary does not reveal the excessive movement, and the degree of suffering, experienced by a significant minority of evacuees. In Australia, for instance, 106 (eighteen per cent) of the CORB evacuees lived in three or more different homes. But, of those 106, twenty three lived in four homes, and ten in five homes. 'Top scorers' were four youngsters who had eight different homes, and one who had nine.

In New Zealand, with its centralized Child Welfare provision, the situation was rather better. Although eighty two children (forty per cent) moved home at least once, only twenty three lived in three or more homes; and two 'top scorers' lived in five and seven homes apiece.

But, of course, movement statistics alone cannot give the full picture either of happy or unhappy placements. There were instances where the situation for evacuee or hosts — or both — was tolerable, but only just. Nevertheless, because no move took place, such placements would appear statistically as 'happy'.

For example, an eleven year old London boy, picked up from the distribution centre for un-nominated evacuees at North Head Quarantine Station in Sydney a few days after arriving in Australia, admits that 'although happy at work and technical college — once started — I was not happy at home with my host family, and tried many times to live with another family who had befriended me. But my hosts would not release me, and that was that.' He is part of the apparently happy seventy per cent who stayed in one foster-home.

Similarly, a former South African evacuee, a Londoner aged fourteen when evacuated with her sister, twelve, and brother, six, describes the mixed feelings she experienced with her hosts. Her foster-father was sixty four and his wife in her fifties. 'She was a demanding, strong personality. He was quiet, retiring, and very kind, but not interested in rearing another family. I don't think any of us children can say we were very happy. We each had educational problems, too, and battled until we finished school.' Her brother had bed-wetting problems for some time after arriving in South Africa. Although he was only six, he had to wash his own sheets, his sisters being forbidden to help him: 'that was his punishment!' Yet astonishingly, perhaps, this ex-evacuee insists: 'We were wonderfully cared for, and had everything we could ask for. The South African authorities just could not do enough for us.'

In the natural course of events, all children, whether evacuees or not, might expect to meet some unsettling experiences just by virtue of growing up. But, a difficult problem for welfare workers and CORB liaison workers to contend with was the existence of a continuing undercurrent of unhappiness amongst evacuees. This undercurrent could often only be sensed by those directly involved, and was not plain for all to see, even if they were actually looking for it. Evacuees living in these circumstances could also find it difficult to verbalize their unease and, even if they tried to, sometimes had difficulty convincing a welfare worker that anything was wrong.

A former CORB girl's parents readily expressed their gratitude to the family who cared for her during the war. Yet, there existed that undercurrent of unhappiness and, over forty years later, the former evacuee writes: 'Physically, we were well looked after, well fed, worked hard on the farm, and we enjoyed it. But there was very little love to spare for us — although this made me self-reliant. We were always in the wrong. We had no privacy. All our letters to home were read first by our foster-mother, and any mail for us from home was read first, too. I developed a nervous cough. But I bounced back; and I developed an attachment to the youngest daughter of the family: we were like sisters.'

Another apparently happy story was a case where a girl went to the family nominated by her parents, and her brother did not. Nearly two years after the two children had arrived overseas, their parents declared how fortunate they both were in their foster homes. However, the daughter in particular experienced a perpetual undercurrent of unhappiness, some of which she identifies. She found her nominated foster-parents 'very formal people.' A teenager, this CORB girl had to share a room with her hosts' small son: 'no privacy.' She continues: 'I was well cared for, but not loved. I felt I was someone for them to "show off", their "war effort". I was always introduced as "our war evacuee", and they were furious because I once told a neighbour I had been in tears, homesick after three years.' Even so, despite her unhappiness, this former evacuee insists that all was not bad. She and her family returned to that Dominion after the war as permanent residents. She still sees her former foster-parents regularly and says, 'We are much closer now. I love them very much.'

How very complex some of these host family and evacuee relationships were. The two girls and brother whose reluctant arrival in Tasmania has already been described,[3] eventually found their experiences disconcerting enough for the older sister to contact the welfare authorities, although she now writes about her former hostess with praise. 'She was a fine character of the old school, honest, God-fearing, strict and extremely patriotic. I doubt if she had ever had to deal with children before. She was very good to us indeed, and must have been sorely tried.'

But, the former evacuee then describes some aspects of their strange life in that foster-home, and her mixed feelings about it. 'We led a very healthy life,' she writes. 'Our ponies were our first loves. Our hostess was a no-nonsense countrywoman. One instance I clearly remember was when she started shouting at my brother saying he was the untidiest boy she knew and to go out to the stable and hang the bridle he had left on the ground on its hook. He knew he'd hung it up; but, in the end, to keep the peace, he marched out looking furious and came racing back: there was a new pony on the ground, not a bridle!' This was a strange way of introducing someone to a generous present.

The older girl had a pet kid whose mother had died giving birth. She reared the kid herself and says: 'I adored this animal, but he grew into a great Billy goat and a proper menace to everyone. Our hostess was always threatening to have him put down. Later, when I was sent away to school and came back for the holidays, I looked everywhere for Jacob, calling and calling.' But the writer says, the goat was dead although the girl was left to discover this for herself when she found his hide hanging up to dry.

After living on this farm for eighteen months, the girl wrote to the authorities 'saying that we were most unhappy and that we should like to be placed in a home where we could attend better schools.' The result was 'an immediate grand visit from the Nabobs, about six of them, all middle-aged and admonishing us about our ingratitude, how we had a wonderful home, and our hostess was a pillar of the State, well respected by everyone.'

Nevertheless, a few months later, the two girls did go to boarding school and their brother to a farm boarding school. They enjoyed their schools, and 'worked hard to justify the hullabaloo we had stirred up.' The three continued to return regularly to their hostess's farm every month and for school holidays. And, apparently, there was a happy outcome apart from their improved schooling. The hostess 'realized long before we came home to England that it hadn't all been in vain, that we had gradually acquired for her a deep affection, and were grateful. Certainly, the three who sailed home were nicer people, I think, than the three "horrors" who arrived!'

Welfare workers have to be wary of children who fantasize or complain unnecessarily. But, social workers responsible for CORB children seemed too ready, sometimes, to assume that evacuees were simply being ungrateful when they complained. A CORB boy called Ted[4] illustrates this point. His first placement was with an uncle in a seedy city area which the Child Welfare Department deemed unsuitable. Thus, after a few months, they transferred him to a family in a desirable suburb. There he had to live in a gardener's hut and, he states, single-handedly look after some two acres of garden, although he was only eleven years old when he arrived.

The following year, Ted's host left his wife, taking his teenaged daughter to live near his place of work. On occasions, Ted's hostess took to whipping him when she was dissatisfied with his work or attitude. Not surprisingly, he ran away. But, some weeks later, having worked on two farms he was arrested by the police, and subsequently taken back to his foster-home.

In due course, a welfare worker lectured the boy about his ungrateful behaviour, and he found he could convince no-one that he had any cause for unhappiness, let alone that he was being cruelly treated. In later life, his own wife admitted that she was not totally convinced about his long ordeal, finding it hard to accept that such treatment could continue without detection. But, in the 1970s she accompanied him on an overseas holiday during which she met the hostess's son, who had served with the Forces throughout the war.[5] He confirmed his mother's harsh streak. 'Why do you think I never visited her when I was on leave?' he asked Ted's wife.

Ronald, evacuated overseas aged twelve, recalls much happiness in his evacuation years, but can also pinpoint specific sources of unhappiness. First, his younger brother was placed with the son and daughter-in-law of his hosts, 'so I lived with people much older than my own mother and father, whilst he was lavished with a bike and a pony and holidays at the summer cottage; and I was expected to work at my foster-parent's grocery store after school and at weekends in the summer. So, I had some feelings of unfairness.'

Secondly, he states, 'I yearned for room for self-discovery, room to make some mistakes without feeling I had committed the unforgivable sin. Maybe I became a bit neurotic about the whole thing. I remember going to my hosts' church (Baptist: I had been nominally C of E) and the Minister preaching about the Prodigal Son, except in this sermon the Prodigal was an Englishman. I took great exception, feeling that maybe my foster-parents and he were in "cahoots".'

Shortly after this incident, Ronald was moved to another foster-home thirty miles away from his brother. His new hosts were 'nice people' but, again, 'quite a bit older than my mother and father.' Soon, the generation gap led to another phase of unhappiness. He writes: 'One young lady in particular became a beautiful part of my life . . . It was a pure, simple relationship. We enjoyed skating together, going to the pictures, and all the innocent fun things. But, my foster-parents grew concerned and, though I was top of my class, they set restrictions and left little Salvation Army tracts around on what happens to girls and boys when they get too familiar. I was upset by this lack of trust.'

Yet, for all that there were difficulties, Ronald holds 'happy memories of a lot of wonderful people' and, in retrospect, 'the genuine concern' of the people who took care of him is clear. His love for the country is shown by his being a resident there for many years now.

Perhaps the welfare authorities in the four Dominions could have done more to seek out and deal tactfully with the continuing undercurrent of unhappiness that obviously existed in an appreciable number of foster-homes.

Geoffrey, evacuated from northern England aged ten, with a young sister, went to nominated relatives. He was totally happy at school, and enjoyed the opportunity to go Scouting at weekends. But, 'there was great tension at home' where his uncle and aunt 'ran affairs with a very strict Edwardian outlook: "*Fly, jump, run* when I speak to you BOY!" '[6]

This evacuee experienced a long phase of enuresis, was permanently afraid in his host's house, and felt extremely lonely. He had 'lots of chores to do always', and found the family dog his 'closest friend'. He and his sister often felt like running away. 'Once,' he writes, 'when I'd saved some birthday money, we were going to leave. When this was realized, the attitude in the house suddenly changed for a while.'

Geoffrey marks a deficiency in the care system, at least in some areas. 'We often wished,' he says, 'that the "CORB inspector" would see us at school rather than at home, so we could discuss things, instead of having to put on a good front at home.'

Running away did arise, sometimes with a very serious cause as instanced by Ted, the boy who lived in a gardener's hut and was beaten by his foster-mother. But sometimes the motivation was more a matter of 'high spirits' or 'a sense of adventure' — the sort of characteristics that explained why some of these CORB youngsters had been excited at the prospect of going overseas in the first place.

Examples of high spirited adventurers who absconded are to be found in all the Dominions. There was a fourteen year old Yorkshire boy evacuated to Australia. The State Welfare Department decided to move him from his first un-nominated home in February, 1941 noting simply that 'he did not settle down.' A year later, they moved him again 'to be in a home with another boy', and, soon afterwards, he went to a training farm for boys, from which he duly absconded. He then received permission to work on two farms, having 'expressed an interest in farming.' Still clearly unsettled and restless, the boy joined the Australian Militia (Home Defence) Forces, soon transferring to the AIF, the volunteer Australian Army, which undertook to serve in any theatre of war where required.

However, in July, 1944, the boy was discharged from the AIF 'because he was under eighteen,' although he had already managed to serve for ten months. Still, on reaching his eighteenth birthday a month later, he immediately volunteered for service with the British Army, and CORB arranged his passage back to England where he joined up in October, 1944.[7]

Two adventurous Canadian evacuees ran away from their foster-parents and even managed to get back to Britain without help from the authorities. The first of these, Ian Hamilton, left his foster-home 'where he was quite happy', state CORB records, in the summer of 1941, when he was fifteen and a half. He hitch-hiked from Ontario to Halifax, Nova Scotia, signed on aboard a merchant ship, and arrived safely in Newcastle-on-Tyne.

The other boy, Dennis Furnish, a permanent resident in Canada for the past twenty years — and prior to that in South Africa — writes about his experiences: 'All in all, I was very lucky to be with such a nice family who provided for me and were able to introduce some culture into my life. They were interesting and intelligent people. I think the war situation must have deteriorated, or I was influenced by war movies, or something. I don't think I was *so* unhappy — though it's a long time ago. I think there may have been a touch of adventure, perhaps. But, I wanted to join up. I had *always* wanted to go to sea. I had tried to join the Royal Canadian Navy as a midshipman to no avail. Hence, I gave up my job and hitch-hiked to Halifax to see if I could go to sea and, maybe, to the UK. Obviously,

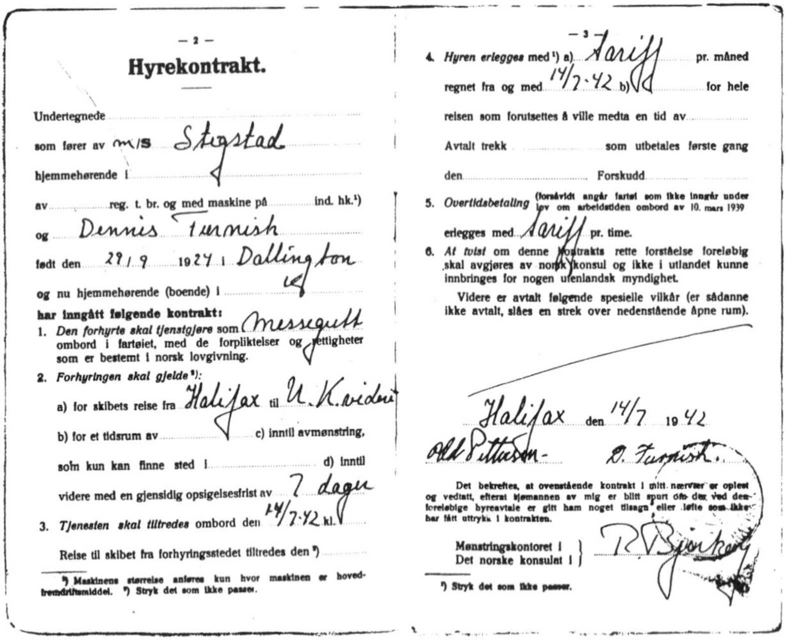

— 2 —

Hyrekontrakt.

Undertegnede

som fører av m/s Stigstad

hjemmehørende i

av reg. t. br. og med maskine på ind. hk.¹)

og Dennis Furnish

født den 29/9 1927 i Dallington

og nu hjemmehørende (boende) i

har inngått følgende kontrakt:

1. *Den forhyrte skal tjenstgjøre* som Messegutt ombord i fartøiet, med de forpliktelser og rettigheter som er bestemt i norsk lovgivning.
2. *Forhyringen skal gjelde*²):
   a) for skibets reise fra Halifax til U. K. wide
   b) for et tidsrum av c) inntil avmønstring,
   som kun kan finne sted i d) inntil
   videre med en gjensidig opsigelsesfrist av 7 dager
3. *Tjenesten skal tiltredes* ombord den 14/7·42 kl.
   Reise til skibet fra forhyringsstedet tiltredes den ²)

¹) Maskinens størrelse anføres kun hvor maskinen er hovedfremdriftsmiddel. ²) Stryk det som ikke passer.

— 3 —

4. *Hyren erlegges* med ¹) a) Tariff pr. måned regnet fra og med 14/7·42 b) " for hele reisen som forutsettes å ville medta en tid av
   Avtalt trekk som utbetales første gang den Forskudd
5. *Overtidsbetaling* (forsåvidt angår fartøi som ikke inngår under lov om arbeidstiden ombord av 10. mars 1939 erlegges med Tariff pr. time.
6. *At tvist* om denne kontrakts rette forståelse foreløbig skal avgjøres av norsk konsul og ikke i utlandet kunne innbringes for nogen utenlandsk myndighet.
   Videre er avtalt følgende spesielle vilkår (er sådanne ikke avtalt, slåes en strek over nedenstående åpne rum).

Halifax den 14/7 1942

Olaf Pettersen — D. Furnish.

Det bekreftes, at ovenstående kontrakt i mitt nærvær er oplest og vedtatt, efterat sjømannen av mig er blitt spurt om der ved den foreløbige hyreavtale er gitt ham noget tilsagn eller løfte som ikke har fått uttrykk i kontrakten.

Mønstringskontoret i } R. Bjørkeng
Det norske konsulat i }

¹) Stryk det som ikke passer.

Fig 32: *The "signing-on" papers of CORB boy Dennis Furnish who made his own way back from Canada to England aboard the Norwegian ship "Stigstad" in order to join the Commandos.*

Dennis Furnish

today, I regret any inconvenience I must have caused my hosts. They had a big responsibility in looking after me, and I failed them.'

Having reached Halifax, Dennis managed to sign on as a messboy aboard the Norwegian ship *Stigstad*, sailing in convoy across the Atlantic. He arrived home in Darlington just as his parents received a letter from CORB informing them that he was missing from his foster-home, but reassuring them that owing to various restrictions, it would not be feasible for him to leave Canada under existing war-time conditions, and they should not worry unduly. Soon after returning, Dennis joined the Commandos.

Another absconder presents a sadder story. Evacuated to New South Wales from an English public school at the age of twelve, the Welfare Department moved him from elderly foster-parents in his first, un-nominated home. Mr Bavin had already been involved on hearing that they seemed 'too old to cope' — which raises the question, again, as to why an evacuee was originally sent there. In quick succession, the boy moved to two more homes — 'now becoming undisciplined' — and then went for 'compulsory training' at a Farm Home. But, after a few months there, he absconded and lived rough for some time.

The root of the boy's rebellion, now, was his strong desire to go to the Royal Australian Naval College and take the midshipman's course. His father refused to permit this. Instead, he offered to pay the fees for his son to attend an independent boarding school. But, the boy attended for only a short time. Then, in some desperation, Mr Bavin permitted him to start work, but he drifted through various jobs, doubtless with several chips on his shoulder by this stage. Just as the war ended, he was arrested 'for housebreaking and stealing'. He sailed for England as speedily as CORB could arrange a passage, and duly arrived in September, 1945.[8]

Former Canadian evacuee Keith Austin gives a humorous slant to the matter of running away. He claims that he 'settled easily and well' when, aged six, he arrived in small town Bruno, from Kent although he admits he had 'a bed-wetting problem in the early days' and some initial antagonism from local people of German descent. In addition, he found his bank manager uncle 'a martinet'. Thus, says Keith, 'I ran away twice — but returned when hungry!'

Keith's uncle later put affairs into humorous perspective, too. When the day came for Keith to leave the locality and return to England, he gave him a silver dollar and, says Keith, 'a scrapbook of my major japes. Broken windows, a broken clock, etc., were all documented — with the cost!'

Many of the CORB children, with their restlessness and difficult behaviour, illustrate, in rather extreme forms, the emotional disturbance created by being uprooted from home, travelling across the high seas in war-time; and also the difficulties of adapting to a totally new environment. Some of the older boys tried very hard to join the Forces under age, or showed a particularly strong urge to go back to sea. Perhaps the care authorities took too little account of the fact that many evacuees were bound to be disturbed, rebellious and high-spirited young people.

Some of the cryptic reasons given in CORB records for moving evacuees to new foster-homes have quite a tragi-comic ring about them suggesting, occasionally, that hosts would do almost anything to be rid of their troublesome charges. 'Because host joined army' is quite common, as is 'hostess had a baby'. One South African evacuee had had three moves in the first eighteen months after arrival there. Records show that the Johannesburg rector who prepared him for confirmation eventually gave the boy a home with him. But, before the end of that year, his record states: 'Rector joined the Army'.[9]

An intriguing note explaining one evacuee move is 'parent-hostess called to Pretoria on Government business'. One might wonder whether looking after an evacuee could rate as 'Government business', but, to be fair to this particular hostess, she arranged for the girl concerned to attend a boarding school.

Unfortunately, owing to the insuperable problems CORB Headquarters had in trying to keep complete records, it is not possible to obtain an accurate picture of the proportion of CORB evacuees who suffered really serious problems whilst overseas. Many of the comments on record cards tell virtually nothing about the circumstances. A look at just a few cases where truly harrowing experiences occurred, compared with the bland remarks on record cards, suggests that there was probably an appreciable amount of unde-tected harshness, as well as the undercurrent of unhappiness mentioned already.

For example, the record card of the boy whose horrific experiences opened this chapter, contains only one untoward note: 'Ill adjusted'. Similarly, a South African boy's card has only one entry of any kind: 'Hospital treatment for poisoned thorn in foot'. But, forty years afterwards this boy wrote: 'The five years of my evacuation left scars on my soul. I was billeted at first with a middle-aged, eccentric English couple who hated everything South African. As a ten year old, I was terrified of them and hated them as only a child can, especially as I took to the South African way of life like a duck to water ... My official guardian was a kind Scots lady. She did all in her power to have me shifted; but this was overruled politically. However, she had me sent to a farm for the holidays.'

The farmer and his wife became 'Grandfer' and 'Grandma' to the boy every holiday. Then, after he had started secondary school, having by now spent three years living with the anti-South African couple in term-time, the school matron discovered he was suffering from 'Natal sores', a malnutritive disease unheard of in a European child. 'There was a storm of protest,' explains this ex-CORB boy. 'I became a "train boy", and commuted from Grandfer's to school each day. Life became wonderful. The joys of a farm: riding, shooting, working with the ox-teams; and love! But,' he adds, 'how I longed for someone to kiss me at Christmas-time for myself, and not say "for your mother!" '

A girl amongst the 'top scorers' in number of foster-homes — seven placements — arrived in Australia aged eleven. By May, 1941, she had already moved twice 'at request of host'. Soon afterwards, she was referred to a psychiatrist at a children's hospital, whose recommendation, after administering tests, was that 'every endeavour be made to find a suitable home with a motherly woman. She has suffered badly from homesickness.' Despite the slightly fuller records in this girl's case, the notes say nothing, of course, about the depth of anguish she must have been enduring, and nothing at all about the host families who tried to help. They probably felt very sad and inadequate when they were unable to make the girl feel more settled.[10]

Again, what misery lay behind the case of the boy in New Zealand whose relatives in his first, nominated home, accused him of being untruthful and dishonest? Investigation showed that 'all charges were unfounded, and his new hosts have found him of good character'. When old enough, the boy took up farming, and apparently did well.[11] But what scars did those accusations leave? Similarly, what unhappiness motivated the evacuee living in the far north of Queensland to earn the comment: 'Pilfering: stole small sums of money from his foster-parents, January, 1945'. By then, this boy was in his third foster-home; but he had only just reached his thirteenth birthday after four and a half years away from home.[12]

The record card gives little detail, beyond her changes of

address, about the girl who felt, after three months abroad, that she must join the family nominated by her parents, to whom she had not been sent originally owing to some oversight.[13] Life for her continued to be bewildering and harrowing when, after a year, she found herself in her third foster-home. She was now billeted with a couple who had one son at home and another son posted 'Missing' overseas. The girl was given this son's room — 'But I was not allowed to touch anything of his, or use the drawers to put my clothes in.' After only a few days in this home, she started a letter to her previous foster-mother, pouring out her heart to her. A couple of days later, a Child Welfare representative was waiting for her as she arrived home from school. 'She told me I was very ungrateful for having written such a letter, and I was shocked that the half written letter had been read. However, I guess it was ungrateful of me, and I wished I hadn't upset that kind woman so.'

The girl was quickly sent to a Children's Home where she spent the next few months in a depressing atmosphere with girls whose parents could not control them. Then, one day, she was introduced to a couple who had lived in the same village as her grandparents and knew them well. They asked her to live with them, and she gladly accepted.

But, by this time, depression had taken a hold on her. 'It was so wonderful to hear a familiar accent again,' she writes, 'that I cried all over the place. I think I spent quite a lot of time crying, and became "nervy".' Perhaps this contributed to her foster-mother's illness. Whether or not, when this evacuee was sixteen and a half her foster-mother was taken ill. Child Welfare became involved again, and she went to a Girls' Hostel where the other girls were all in care for being 'unmanageable' or 'in trouble with authority'. 'The stories they told about running away from home, living with men, stealing, etc., really shocked me, and I hated the place,' she adds.

Becoming 'obsessed with thoughts of suicide', she eventually decided to write to her parents about all her problems. But, having written her letter 'with many sobs', she realized it would only distress them, so she tore it up into small pieces which she 'threw into the wood bin outside the back door.' She was still contemplating suicide when the Matron invited her to sit down and chatted to her 'like an old friend.' The girl was now worried by the change in the woman's manner. 'Then,' she continues, 'she produced my letter, all pieced together and glued on to a piece of cardboard. I was terrified as I knew I had criticized her in my letter. I thought I was going to be sent to Borstal, which was the threat hanging over all the girls at the hostel.' However, Matron grew kinder, producing cakes and tea and, in the ensuing weeks, developed a more solicitous attitude toward the girl. On reaching the age of seventeen, the CORB girl arranged to live at a pleasant YWCA hostel, and stayed there until she was joined by some of her family after the war.

This case is a very rare one. It is made the more unusual because the girl's area rightly earned an excellent evacuee care record. Only four CORB children went into any kind of institution, other than hospitals, in the whole of her Dominion. So it is strange that she could be treated as thoroughly wayward when she seems to have been largely the victim of circumstances.

The unpleasantest experience of any CORB evacuee must surely be that of the girl who arrived overseas aged eight. She and her brother were amongst an unfortunate minority whose foster-parents forbade them ever to open their mail unsupervised. But, far worse than that, the girl states that she was sexually assaulted by her host during the whole time she was evacuated. Like many sexually abused children, she kept the matter to herself until later in life. At the time it was happening, her suffering was intensified by the rural isolation in which the family lived. She had no friends of her own age for over two years. Her foster-father — a man of good standing in the locality — was, this ex-CORB girl reports, gaoled for sexual offences after the war. The girl's own parents, not surprisingly, felt that the CORB story would be better left untold.[14]

In a somewhat contrary direction, a few CORB girls caused anxiety to their host families and welfare authorities owing to their sexual attachments. This seems to have been a particular problem in South Africa where Miss Thompson, the CORB liaison officer, reported that several had 'boyfriend trouble'. Towards the end of the war, she negotiated for one 'precocious girl' to return to Britain where she joined the WRNS. An instance of an unmarried CORB girl giving birth to a baby is recorded on one Australian evacuee's record card. This girl had an unsettled time: five different foster-homes and, although she had wanted to be a journalist, she worked at a nearby factory.[15] A Canadian evacuee also had a baby during her time overseas.[16]

Very sadly, eight CORB youngsters lost their lives whilst abroad. Four of these, two from Australia, two from Canada, were young men killed in action whilst serving with the Air Force of their Dominion as aircrew. Of the other four deaths, one boy in Canada died as a result of an accident when out shooting; another boy in Canada died of TB after a long illness. A young man in New Zealand, studying science at University, lost his life in a climbing accident during a vacation; and a girl, also in New Zealand, died after undergoing three operations for the removal of a cancerous tumour of the face. Her two sisters were looked after by the same foster-parents.[17]

Some fifty evacuees received news whilst overseas that one or other parent had died. In a few cases, this had been the only surviving parent when they left the UK. A very few parents appear to have died as a result of the war: a handful on active service, another handful during air-raids. Some fifty evacuees received news that their parents had separated or divorced during the war — though, in one or two cases, they were not made aware of this change in family circumstances until their return to the UK after the war.[18]

In spite of the educational advantages gained by many CORB children in their Dominion,[19] a significant minority, especially amongst those in Australia, felt they made limited progress compared with what they had expected to achieve. For the most part, Australian evacuees lived in an environment where the majority of children were expected to leave school and start work as soon as they were old enough.

An extreme example of the difficulty was that of a CORB girl from Wales. The aunt with whom she lived held strong

Tel: MAYFAIR 8400.
Ref: No. *120*
Please quote.

CHILDREN'S OVERSEAS RECEPTION BOARD,
45, Berkeley Street,
W.1.

March 1941

Dear Sir or Madam,

     I have no doubt that you have very much in mind the future education, training and career of *John*.

     The Dominion Authorities are anxious to give the children from this country the best chance they can, taking into consideration the opportunities available in the district in which they are living, their own wishes and special abilities and the wishes of parents in this country.

     It will be very helpful to us as well as to your child's hosts and to the Dominion Authorities, if you will write to us giving information on the following points and any other information that you think will be useful:-

1. <u>EDUCATION:</u> How long would your child have remained at school in this country?
   What examination did you expect him/her to take?

2. <u>TRAINING:</u> Had you intended that your child should take any special course of training at school, or after leaving school, e.g. commercial training, or technical training in any particular trade?

3. <u>CAREER:</u> What are your views on the kind of work for which your child is most suited?

     You will realise that in some ways it may be necessary or desirable to modify plans that you have made in view of special opportunities or difficulties that may obtain in the districts in which your child is now living.

     Would you at the same time please let us know if you have expressed any wish on these matters to your children's hosts.

Yours faithfully,

Elspeth Davies

A.C.26.

Fig 33: *CORB's circular to parents concerning an evacuee's future.*

views against higher education for women. The girl wished to study medicine. Her school reports indicated that she had exceptionally high academic ability. But, her aunt was so adamant that, despite parental pressure, CORB pressure, and the involvement of Mr Bavin and the NSW Child Welfare Department, the evacuee had to leave her girls' high school at the age of fifteen to become an office clerk.[20]

Several other evacuees write that they would have liked to take their schooling further than they did, but felt it was right, in view of the generosity of foster-parents, that they should find a job and contribute to the host family budget. In South Africa, the local child-guest committees usually advised evacuees about employment. Miss Maxse claimed that, although well-intentioned, the women who made up these committees for the most part had limited expertise to offer. In educational terms, this had a beneficial side-effect: they tended to recommend youngsters to stay on longer at school 'for the sake of keeping them occupied', though several boys did start suitable apprenticeships. Throughout the Dominions, it was the CORB girls who suffered most educational deprivation, the majority of them starting work on reaching school leaving age in offices and banks as shorthand-typists, clerks, book-keepers, and telephonists, though the vocational tests they underwent quite often indicated that their capability made them suitable for training in more challenging careers.[21]

As could be expected, most CORB children experienced some anxiety about their families during the war years. Realizing this, parents were usually cautious about the news they included in letters, but, at the same time, tried to maintain a regular flow. As former Australian evacuee Joan Dixon says: 'My family in the UK wrote to me every week and told me all the news. So, I always felt part of the family although I was so far away.' But, she explains, being told 'all the news' does not necessarily mean straight away. 'My mother was seriously ill with pneumonia at one time — but I was not told about it until she had recovered. My two brothers, one in the RAF and the other in the Royal Navy, came through safely, though my RAF brother was shot down twice — but I was not told about it until afterwards.'

444

Bradford
"Telegraph & Argus"

Fig 34: *(above) Mr and Mrs Fethney and their daughter, Barbara, in Bradford listening to the author and his brother sending messages recorded by the Australian Broadcasting Commission and broadcast by the BBC.*

Fig 35: *(below) CORB's circular inviting parents to use the opportunity given by the BBC to send messages to their children overseas.*

Crown Copyright

CHILDREN'S OVERSEAS RECEPTION BOARD.

45, Berkeley Street,
W.1.

28.8.41.

BROADCAST MESSAGES.

If you have not already recorded a message to be broadcast to your child/children and would like to do so, you should write to Miss Maxwell, Broadcasting House, W.1, mentioning your name and address, your child/children's names and addresses overseas and the dates of birthdays.

If you have already applied to the B.B.C. and have heard nothing for some months, you should write again mentioning your previous application.

Former Canadian evacuee Marion Freedman points out that it was impossible, for parents to include much 'significant' news, both to avoid upsetting their children and also to avoid the censors' scissors. 'It was after the war,' she writes, 'when we saw them again, that we learned of their experiences: bombed out of three homes; father blown up — had a heart condition and lost all his body hair as a result.'

Former evacuees admit that, even more difficult than 'scratching about' to find things to say in their own letters, was finding suitable things to say in the 'two-way broadcasts' arranged by the BBC and the Dominion radio authorities. The hope that these links would increase morale by bringing evacuees and parents into direct contact, if only for half a minute, was well meant. But, too many found the arrangement 'an embarrassment: what was there to say?', as one now puts it.

Unfortunately, the effect was often the opposite of that intended. One ex-Australian evacuee is not alone in saying: 'When we had the chance to talk to our parents in a radio telephone broadcast, I broke down when I heard their voices and had to be cut off. It upset me for weeks.' After Miss Maxse and Mrs Davies expressed CORB's concern about the harmful effects of these broadcasts, the healthier practice grew of arranging recorded messages between children and parents. This relieved the strain, including the fear of breaking down in mid-broadcast.

Many of these youngsters had much to worry about, and many worried stoically, silently, anxieties often unshared, with the customary stiff upper lip. Former CORB girl Theresa Dawson, still only thirteen years old when the war ended, writes with feeling about this: 'I loved the fruit trees with the fruit still warm from the sun; the holidays by the sea in a shack on stilts; the kindness of the people, especially at Christmas and Easter; and the nuns at school. But, the main hurt was homesickness in bed at night, under the covers. The worrying over the family left behind developed as one got older and became more aware of exactly what was happening, especially through newsreels — and tied to the memories of the family nights spent in the air-raid shelter, and the ARP Warden calling to see if all was well . . .'

18

CORB INSPECTS — AND PROBLEMS ABOUND

On the 17 February, 1942, Geoffrey Shakespeare gave a speech to a Kinsmen's Lunch in Grosvenor House, London, held to set up a Trust for needy children in North America. He felt that this Trust would give a chance for British people to repay some of the kindness given by foster-parents to British evacuees.[1]

In his speech, he took the opportunity of reporting in detail on the trip he had recently made to Canada, making the eight hour journey from Scotland in an RAF *Liberator* during the 1941 parliamentary Christmas recess. He had attended a reception in each Provincial capital, where he met evacuees, foster-parents, members of the Provincial Governments, and child welfare officials.

Mr Shakespeare was quite euphoric. He spoke of the 'lavish care bestowed on the evacuees.' He also answered critics in Britain who argued that those evacuated overseas would miss a great deal that 'other British children will acquire here through their war experiences.' He said he doubted whether air-raids, bombing, interrupted sleep and rationing were anything like as valuable an education 'as travel and the opportunity of studying new conditions and different customs and scenery.' He claimed that, when CORB children returned, they would have acquired 'a breadth and independence of outlook and a wider vision that may well put them ahead of those children to whom these opportunities were denied.'

Mr Shakespeare's customary enthusiasm was evident in this assessment. But perhaps he was a little too ready to assume that the officially organized receptions in the

Fig 36: *Geoffrey Shakespeare (left) with CORB boy Douglas Penwarden and his hosts during Mr Shakespeare's Canadian tour in 1941.*

Canadian Provincial capital cities were a reliable yardstick for measuring the continuing success of the CORB scheme overseas. He claimed, for example, that in ninety per cent of cases, the children had made 'good adjustment' in Canada; that only a small percentage 'have failed to adjust'.

He quoted in his speech one of his favourite examples of a CORB boy who overcame initial setbacks. He met 'George', who was now in his third placement, and talked to his farmer host on his Canadian farm. He learnt that the first foster-parents had said, 'We'll make any contribution to the war — except George!' But the third foster-parent told Mr Shakespeare: 'He is a grand boy. If he goes on like this, I shall leave him my farm, as I have no children myself.'[2]

Just over two years later, Miss Marjorie Maxse also visited Canada during the months April to June in order to make an appraisal of evacuee care. Even allowing for a natural wastage in euphoria about the CORB scheme during the intervening years, it is possible to see a more realistic picture in the report Miss Maxse produced than in Mr Shakespeare's Kinsmen's speech at the end of 1941.

Whilst Miss Maxse conceded that the children with whom she made contact seemed 'mostly well-placed', she suspected that she was shown 'a well-trodden path of acceptable homes and standards.' In general, Miss Maxse felt that for each Province to have 'very autonomous control of CORB matters' created 'inadequacies' in evacuee provision. Provincial autonomy was fine for the CORB children in British Columbia where, she reported, the standard of child welfare was 'undoubtedly the highest in the country and recognized as such.'[3]

Quebec, also, Miss Maxse considered 'outstanding' in its welfare organization and provision for CORB children, and she was glad that CORB was not affected 'by the tension' there. In Manitoba, she found trained social workers, as in British Columbia, were 'the norm'. The other Provinces received a mixture of praise and constructive criticism — except one. This Province received almost total castigation and, despite the passing of over forty years, it seems fairer not to name it. However, Miss Maxse's comments are worth summarizing because they provide, not only an insight to her analytical powers, wit, and frankness, but also underline the sort of chaos that might well have existed elsewhere with so much of the welfare of CORB children left to local discretion.

Miss Maxse considered child care in the Province 'practically non-existent' and, worse still, 'so dangerous where it does exist, that it was not fit to assume charge of British children.' She explained that 'an amateur friend of the Minister was appointed. Her zeal outran her knowledge, and a breakdown eliminated her from the CORB picture.' This unfortunate person apparently handed over to someone who, in Miss Maxse's opinion, 'suffered an overwhelming emotional instability . . . With these handicaps she has tried her best . . . and expended herself without stint.'

But, incredibly, this was not all that Miss Maxse found distressing. There was 'little method; an absence of planning, standards or reliable supervision. Only by supreme luck has nothing serious occurred.' Some of the placements she had seen 'were intolerable'. Is it surprising to learn that, in this same Province, Miss Maxse found 'the whole atmosphere was squalid' and she left it 'equally angry and anxious about the supervision of CORB children'?

Before leaving Canada, Miss Maxse reported her findings to the National Advisory Committee for Children from Overseas. The Committee's welfare adviser, an experienced British Columbia man, promised to take such steps as he could, but warned of 'political scandals in the offing.' These, he added, might well 'side-track even genuinely concerned people from the real issues that cried out for improvement.'[4]

It is a great pity, though doubtless it was a relief to some at the time, that CORB was unable to send Miss Maxse to report on evacuee provision in the other Dominions. Her views, one feels, would have been both fair and illuminating.

Geoffrey Shakespeare did visit South Africa in September, 1944, though not as an official representative of CORB. Now Sir Geoffrey, and no longer a Government Minister, he had handed over the chairmanship of the Overseas Reception Board into the capable hands of Mr Paul Emrys-Evans, MP. It was Mr Emrys-Evans who suggested that Sir Geoffrey might incorporate a tour for CORB into a South

African visit he was organizing for British MPs, all of whom belonged to the Empire Parliamentary Association, of which Sir Geoffrey was chairman.

The prickliness in certain South African quarters to the Empire Parliamentary group's visit gives a pointer to the way things operated in the Union. Whilst Captain Maurice Green of the EPA in Cape Town was quite amenable to British MPs coming on behalf of the Association, he gave 'less than lukewarm support' for the idea that Sir Geoffrey should incorporate CORB engagements in his itinerary.[5]

To be fair to Captain Green, his guarded response was the natural reaction of someone who knew how keenly the various departments of national and provincial governments preserved their spheres of influence. Equally, the local Guest Committees for the care of overseas children were 'very local' indeed, and prepared to resist any possible interference from anywhere.

In the end, Miss Thompson, the CORB liaison officer, threw all protocol to the wind. She contacted directly those Guest Committee secretaries she could trust to make fully private plans for Sir Geoffrey Shakespeare to meet parent-hosts, child-guests, and Guest Committee members. Meantime, Miss Thompson warned CORB in London that, if anyone let the cat out of the bag, there would be dire trouble because she was 'never supposed to tell the Committees anything except through the Department of Social Welfare.'

However, a little later Miss Thompson reported to London that successful parties had taken place for evacuees, hosts and Committee members in all the major cities of the Union. And, she added, the Pietermaritsburg Guest Committee Secretary, writing about their 'informal gathering for "Uncle Geoff" said the event would not have been possible if I'd depended on Pretoria!'[6]

Both Miss Maxse's visit to Canada and Sir Geoffrey's visit to South Africa highlight some of the relative problems facing the CORB liaison officers in each Dominion. By comparison with the other three Dominions, New Zealand was fortunate in having no States nor Provinces nor powerful local committees to complicate its evacuee welfare arrangements. What is more, Miss Kyrsty Page, the liaison officer, found it possible to maintain close and regular links with the national welfare body on the one hand, and just about all the foster-parents and the 202 CORB children on the other.

The situation in the other Dominions was nowhere so tidy. Miss Thompson had to deal with national government, four provincial governments, numerous local Guest Child Committees, and about the same number of local magistrates and 'proxy' children's guardians, as well as her own High Commissioner, the foster-parents and 355 evacuees.

Likewise, Mr Jopson — and later Mrs Snow who replaced him as CORB's liaison officer in Canada — had to contend with a Federal Government Minister, a National Advisory Committee for Overseas Children, nine Provincial Government Child Welfare Departments, voluntary agencies such as the Children's Aid Society, and local ad hoc reception committees. Furthermore, he had 1,535 CORB children under his wing; and Ontario alone cared for almost twice the number of evacuees in the whole of South Africa, and three times the number of those in New Zealand.

Mr Bavin's task in Australia was similarly spread over large territory and, like his Canadian counterpart, he had the disadvantage of being based near the eastern edge of that territory — in Sydney. He had to deal with a Federal Minister, as well as six State Governments and, in Western Australia and Tasmania, with local reception committees like those in South Africa. His 577 CORB children were also quite widely spread.

In her 1944 summary of CORB's work, Miss Maxse extolled the good relationships that had been established between many CORB parents and their children's foster-parents overseas. Very few instances arose where the parents disagreed with the actions or attitudes of foster-parents. One of these — rather a sad case — involved a girl in South Africa whose parents expressed alarm on hearing that she was showing interest in the Roman Catholic Faith. Yet, they had themselves nominated a Roman Catholic family for her to live with. What made the dispute sadder is that the host family, realizing the girl was a very slow learner, kindly arranged for her to work in a Children's Home attached to a Convent when she reached school leaving age.

It was hardly surprising that the kindness her hosts and the nuns showed the girl inclined her towards their beliefs.[7]

Another dispute involved a boy living with relatives in Australia. His mother had a disagreement with the boy's aunt and insisted he be moved to another home. The boy protested that he was very happy to stay where he was, and that his mother should not have interfered. His mother then claimed that this was evidence that the relatives were coming between the boy and his own mother. Rightly or wrongly, the boy was moved elsewhere.[8]

There are also a few recorded cases where parents received letters indicating that their children were unhappy in their homes overseas, and asked for them to be moved. In these cases, however, further enquiries usually led to a decision to keep the children where they were.

In such cases as these, and in many, many more — some of them involving a greater degree of seriousness — Mrs Elspeth Davies, CORB's Welfare Director at London Headquarters, played an active and often vital part. During the course of the war, she met hundreds of parents, sometimes privately by appointment, at other times in groups, after notifying those living in certain areas that she would be 'holding court' in the offices of the nearby Local Education Authority. In these sessions, she would give what advice she could about approaches to be made to foster-parents or various bodies in the Dominion concerned, or discuss educational, employment, health or other worries.

A small number of particularly anxious or demanding parents could sometimes make Mrs Davies' life very trying. But, calm, charming and diplomatic person that she still is, Mrs Davies won the admiration and affection of the vast majority of CORB parents. Sometimes, as Welfare Director, she had unenviable tasks to perform: maybe to inform parents about an unexpected change of home for a child, perhaps caused by the death of a foster-parent; or notifying parents of a child's serious illness or, even, the death of a child. Amongst the most serious ilnesses and misfortunes she had to communicate was the case of a boy in Canada who required the services of an eminent surgeon to remove a brain tumour. The operation was a success, though the boy lost his sight and had to attend the Blind Institute in

January, 1941.

2 2 JUL 1942

Dear Sir/Madam,

Next of Kin

A number of parents have written to tell us that, in the event of their death, they wish their children to remain overseas under the guardianship of the foster-parents. Any such arrangement should of course first be agreed by the foster-parents.

You will no doubt also realise that to have legal validity, the appointment of a guardian must be made in proper legal form. If you wish to be sure of the wording you should consult a solicitor and refer him to the Guardianship of Infants Act, 1925, Sections 5(1) and (2).

It follows, of course, that the fact that you have furnished the Board with the name and address of your next-of-kin does not mean that the person named would necessarily be recognised legally as your children's guardian.

Yours faithfully,

Maynie Maxse

D 32472-1 1,500 D/d 101 1/42

Fig 37: *Miss Maxse, CORB's Director, raises the sombre matter of next-of-kin in the event of CORB parents' death.*

Winnipeg until his return in 1944 to the UK.

There was a boy who kept having fits after a head injury; a boy hit by a truck; a boy who lost an eye in an accident, although he later served in the Australian Air Force as a clerk; and a typhoid and a malaria case, both in South Africa. In each eventuality, Mrs Davies had to break the news with care and sympathy.[9]

After the war, Geoffrey Shakespeare wrote warmly about the three women who shouldered the major CORB responsibilities — Miss Maxse, Miss Nicholas, and Mrs Davies: 'These three rendered splendid service and set an example to all Government Departments of efficient and humane administration.'[10] Typically modest, Mrs Elspeth Davies questions his judgement. But, hundreds of satisfied CORB parents would doubtless echo his praise.

19

GOODBYE AGAIN

'I had wanted to go home so much. But, when the time came, I didn't really want to go. I'm afraid I cried a great deal — but, as so much was happening, I didn't have time to be sad!' So writes Jean Cheyne who, now aged fourteen, was a member of the first peace-time Canadian CORB batch to sail home, in April, 1945, aboard the *SS Cavina*.

In the ten months between the end of war with Germany in May, 1945, and CORB's closing down in February, 1946, 1,405 CORB evacuees returned home, representing just over half the total who arrived overseas in 1940. As might be expected, many who returned had mixed feelings — often shared by their Dominion host-families.[1]

Mr Robert Dickinson, Canadian host to Jean Cheyne and her brother George, states: 'When we had to say goodbye it was heartbreaking for the children, my wife, and myself.' These feelings are echoed by other hosts and their evacuee guests.

Mrs M Rhind, who had hoped that she and her husband could have adopted Heather Johnston, whom they hosted in Christchurch, New Zealand, agrees with the Dickinsons. 'It was a heartbreaking business,' she writes, 'when the time came for her to leave; but we tried to comfort her, in that she might be able to come back.' Mrs Rose Gofsky, hostess to Bernie Conn in Edmonton, Alberta, says: 'The least happy occasion of those years was to say "goodbye". There were lots of tears.' And Australian hostess Mrs E Gill, who looked after Joan Dixon at Nambucca Heads, NSW, recalls: 'The unhappiest day was when my family said "goodbye".'

Former evacuees recall the torn emotions they experienced

230

when their return to Britain became imminent. They wanted to see their families back home, but would have liked to stay in their adopted land which they had come to love. Peter Wilde, leaving Canada, and still only twelve years old, must speak for many: 'I had very mixed feelings,' he remembers, 'which are difficult now to describe; but I loved my foster-mother very much.' Similarly, another twelve year old, Keith Parker: 'I felt pain at leaving what had become my "family"; but also anticipation of the journey to England, and meeting my real family again.'

Norman Standage writes: 'At the end of the war, it was a case of return to England for those who wanted to go. In our case — (his older sister was with him) — we liked Australia. However, it was right that we should return to our parents in England.' But, in 1957, Norman went back to Australia, and has resided there permanently ever since.

A few admit to having no regrets. One of the youngest Canadian evacuees, Kenneth Austin, still only eleven on returning, states: 'It was no hardship. I remember finding a small patch of melting snow for a final ski!' And fourteen year old Denis, about to leave New South Wales, states succinctly: 'I had no regrets.' In view of the anxiety-ridden life he and his young sister had endured, it is not surprising. And another ex-Australian evacuee who had not enjoyed the happiest relationship with her aunt recalls: 'My brother and I only had a week's warning of our sailing for home. The day my aunt told me, she was very upset. I think this was the first time my guardians displayed any emotion since I had been with them!'

But, for the most part, it was a wrench both for evacuees and their host families; and former New Zealand evacuee, Edna Chase, who left the country aged fifteen, reminds us that the hardship could be greater for the hosts. 'I remember vividly,' she writes, 'as we left Port Lyttelton with half a dozen of the Christchurch evacuees my foster-mother and her daughter Shirley were still with us. As the ferry pulled away from the wharf I felt very sad. Up until then I think I had almost hurt my foster-mother with my excitement and desire to be off. I can remember as we left home to go to the station her saying to me: "If there are reporters there, you will let them know you have been happy in New Zealand, won't you?" ' Edna's former hostess, Mrs Eileen Ede confirms: 'I think this was one of the saddest days in Shirley's life. The parting was hard.'

For a variety of reasons, other evacuees felt more than sad to leave. Catherine Webster, thirteen years old when the time came to leave her uncle and aunt in Melbourne, remembers: 'It was as traumatic as the parting from my parents had been carefree! I was five years older, had more idea of what the parting meant, and had transferred all my love and affection to my aunt and uncle whom I thought of as my parents. My uncle and aunt, too, were terribly upset to part with us. It was awful.' Her aunt agrees, writing: 'It was a very sad day indeed. When we arrived home from seeing them off and saw the empty bedrooms, we both had a few tears.'

Peter Beams, about to sail home from New Zealand aged fifteen, was even more desolate: 'Because I had wanted to stay and be adopted by my foster-parents, I was very sad, and to this day I am very sorry that, for some reason or other, this could not be done. Perhaps our parents had a say — I don't know.'[2] To add to Peter's grief, he knew, even before being evacuated in 1940, that relations between his mother and father were not good, and they were likely to separate.

A few evacuees mention the pain of leaving a special friend. Geraldine Robb, sixteen when scheduled to leave Auckland, says: 'The worst part was leaving my boyfriend from school. It was a very strong friendship, very much frowned upon by my foster-family, who feared the worst possible outcome — understandably, in retrospect. But, in fact, it was a totally innocent relationship . . . He followed me to England within eighteen months to join the Navy; but a lot of the magic had gone for us both.'

Similarly, an Australian evacuee, devastated five years earlier when she had to part from her soldier boyfriend aboard the *Batory* at Singapore, was saddened to face another such parting before sailing for England aboard the *Aquitania* in November, 1945. 'I'd at last got a boyfriend and didn't want to go home any more. I couldn't have cared less, but had to return because our parents wanted us to go back.'

Australian Government Publishing Service

Fig 38: *The first peace-time batch of CORB evacuees to leave Australia saying farewell to Mr Cyril Bavin, CORB liaison officer in the Commonwealth, before setting sail aboard the "Andes".*

For some the actual day of departure seems to have been just about as distressing as the parting from parents in 1940. Rita Patterson, aged thirteen, was with the CORB party that sailed from Sydney aboard the *Andes* in August, 1945. 'It is one of my saddest memories,' she records. 'My relatives took me to the ship and insisted on going past the guard at the gangway to see my cabin. I was inspecting everything excitedly, and when I turned round they had gone. I ran after them but wasn't allowed ashore. I know great-uncle had taken my aunt away because she was so distressed, and I think that's the only way he could do it.'

Foster-parents Mr and Mrs George Goddard, who gave a home to Bob Bullard in Western Australia, remember clearly the events surrounding his departure. 'He wanted to take everything, including a push bike which required, together with everything else, a box six feet by five feet by one and a half feet. When he left he said, "I'll just have a look at everything in England and come straight back;" but it took thirty years before we had that pleasure.

'Bob went aboard the *Stratheden* the afternoon before

departure,' continues Mrs Goddard, 'and we were down at the wharf by 6 am next morning to say our farewell. I watched that ship and Bob until he was only a speck. I remember being numb with sadness. We were trying to adopt a baby, and the Welfare Department gave us a two year old to mind two weeks before Bob sailed. So, after returning from the boat, I tried to concentrate on making her a frock. But even though we got the new baby, it took me months to get over Bob going away.'

Reflecting on his reluctant departure from New Zealand, sixteen year old Colin Crafer recalls happy memories of his three different foster-homes: his 'continuing desire to own a pianola like the one in my Mount Pleasant home; the school at Little River and my friendly contact with Maori children; learning the "facts of life" — that a dozen chickens can pick a cooked sheep's head clean in under fifteen minutes'; and finally, as a worker in Christchurch, 'fitting and turning; collecting wages; my first bicycle . . . and leaving it all to come "Home". I often wonder why!'

20

HOME — SWEET HOME?

By the end of the war with Germany on the 8 May, 1945, well over a quarter of the CORB evacuees had already returned to Britain, 680 from Canada alone, and 72 from South Africa. Over 200 were still serving in the Dominions or British Forces.

Ten months later, when CORB closed down its Headquarters, and Miss Maxse presented her final report to the last meeting of CORB's Advisory Council on the 22 February, 1946, she disclosed the following figures:

Returned to UK (or about to return):[1]

Canada	1,326 out of 1,535
Australia	446 out of 577
South Africa	284 out of 355
New Zealand	153 out of 204[2]

A mid-war drift home had started in 1942 owing to several parents of Canadian evacuees requesting CORB to repatriate their children. These requests stemmed from the growing realization that the invasion was not now going to happen, whilst the blitz had eased considerably, thus making the continued separation pointless for their children. Furthermore, some evacuees were clearly unsettled, not least some of those approaching the age for military service, and therefore old enough to resent the accusation that they had 'run away from the war.'

At this same period, CORB was also receiving calls to help repatriate children privately evacuated to Canada and the USA. These evacuees, including some accompanied by mothers, had often been badly hit by the ban on sending sterling to the dollar area. As a result, CORB arranged for some of these stranded, privately evacuated youngsters to return under the 'White Ensign Scheme', which entitled Commanding Officers of Royal Navy ships to take on board 'suitable' civilian passengers, usually interpreted as young men old enough for military service, and return them to Britain. Gradually, CORB arranged for a small trickle of older Canadian CORB evacuees to use the White Ensign Scheme, too, if they wanted to join the British Armed Forces.

Then, in 1943, CORB encouraged further movement home from Canada by informing parents that they would consider arranging the return of any boys aged sixteen and girls aged seventeen. This provision was agreed for CORB children in the other Dominions, but was never publicized because of the additional problems of getting them home from farther away.[3]

With the end of the war against Germany, CORB was anxious to fulfil its promise to ship the evacuees back home, and began to book passages for them as quickly as berths came available. The high speed with which most CORB batches sailed to Britain, compared with their war-time voyages, and the relatively small number in each batch, characterize the pattern of most of the CORB return voyages. These peace-time travellers also comment about the comparative luxury of the conditions, and the welcome degree of freedom they were allowed, both on board their ships and in ports of call.

Two CORB batches celebrated victory whilst at sea. Those aboard the *Cavina* had actually left Halifax, Nova Scotia, on the 26 April, 1945, in convoy. Thus, they were in mid-Atlantic when news broke about the Nazi surrender, and joined in the celebrations with the rest of the passengers. A couple of days later, there was great excitement again when five German U-boats surfaced alongside the convoy and surrendered to the Commodore. The submarines sailed with the convoy into British waters, where Royal Naval escort vessels met them.

Similarly, the *Ruahine* left Auckland with returning New Zealand evacuees in August, 1945, just before VJ Day.

Thus, a few days out of Auckland news broke of the Japanese surrender, the CORB youngsters joined in the celebrations, and also enjoyed the sudden transformation to peace-time conditions, with the blackout abolished and the ship sailing with lights ablaze and portholes unsealed.

The quickest homeward voyage was accomplished by the CORB batch aboard the *Ile de France*. Among the group was eleven year old Kenneth Austin — 'again I was in trouble for not washing my neck!' — and twelve year old Keith Parker. Keith describes life aboard a troopship 'with all the happiness of the war being over, and all going home. No convoy. No blackout. No danger. Amateur shows. Welcome by Fleet Air Arm planes in the Clyde.' The *Ile de France* docked in Greenock only five days after leaving Halifax.

Without doubt, the longest homeward voyage was endured by the thirty five CORB youngsters aboard the *TSS Nestor*. Setting sail from Sydney on the 21 November, 1945, they eventually arrived in Liverpool ten and a half weeks later on the 4 February, 1946, having broken by one day the previous record of longest CORB voyage held by the *Batory*. To be fair to the *Nestor*, she was hit by a dockers' strike for a week in Fremantle. Then, three days out into the Indian Ocean, feed pipes to her main boilers burst, reducing the ship's speed to between three and five knots for the rest of the voyage. Their 'record low' for a day's journey was nineteen nautical miles in the Irish Sea.

A handful of evacuees returning from Australia had lucky meetings with their fathers who were serving with the Armed Forces in the Middle East. One of these, Norman Standage, aboard the *Stratheden* with his sister Brenda, says his father did not know exactly which CORB ship they were aboard, but knew they were on their way home and likely to pass through Suez. So, he enquired of every passenger ship that went through the Canal. Eventually, his persistence paid off. They had an emotional reunion, and spent a few hours together, not meeting again until 1947.

The last escorted groups of CORB evacuees to return were the fifteen youngsters who left Wellington aboard the *Rangitata* in late January, 1946, and a party of nine who sailed from Sydney early in March aboard the *Rangitiki*.

CORB escorts with each returning peace-time batch had

"New Zealand Herald"

Fig 39: *CORB batch about to leave New Zealand attend a reception with Sir Patrick Duffy, British High Commissioner. Kyrsty Page (centre), CORB's liaison officer in New Zealand, was to be their escort aboard the "Ruahine".*

instructions to give guidance about life on reaching home. For instance, they were to warn them about serious shortages, especially of food; that they might meet people who resented their 'running away from the war', leaving others to face the blitz and possible invasion. Sir Patrick Duffy, the UK High Commissioner in New Zealand at the end of the war, always gave similar warnings about the hazards to each CORB batch whom he entertained just before departure. He would end his homily by saying: 'Those who have not seen death, or streets shaken under bombs, or houses cascading down in a roar of falling stones, tiles and glass, or who have not felt hunger in the pit of the stomach, or sleeplessness in their whole body, just have no idea . . .'[4]

One group of CORB girls returning from abroad took the

warnings about food shortages so much to heart, that they tried to cut down drastically on the food they ate on board ship in order to acclimatize themselves to food rationing. But their escort wisely suggested they should avail themselves of the good food on the ship whilst they still could.

A very varied picture emerges of the experiences of ex-CORB evacuees who arrived home after the war, even the first moments of reunion with their families eliciting contrasting responses.

Writing enthusiastically about first seeing her family again, Nora Lupton says: 'My parents, two sisters, niece and a friend met the train at Darlington Station. It was a very joyous occasion. Inevitably, my family all appeared smaller to my fourteen year old eyes — as did "Home". But this feeling soon passed, along with my broad Aussie accent!'

Others echo this enthusiasm. Madge Harris, twenty years old now, who had left her twin brother behind in the Canadian Air Force, speaks of 'the tremendous joy and excitement all round.' John Hillier, arriving in London from Australia with his young brother Frank, says: 'We met our parents at Waterloo, and I think we recognized each other straight away. It was a tearful reunion, but they were tears of joy. Of course, we wanted to know so many things about what had happened, and we spent a long time talking.'

Rita Patterson, returning to north east England from Australia, shares her emotion: 'In the dusk, we rolled across the Tyne Bridge. Through the window of the train, I saw Mum and Aunts start running alongside the train as they caught sight of me. As we stood there, embracing and crying, I looked over their heads and saw my father at the gate. And, as I write this, I'm crying again — I will never forget that meeting as long as I live!'

Sometimes, it is the ordinariness, the trivial incident, even the sense of anticlimax, or things not being as expected, that linger in the memory. 'We reunited at Waterloo Station,' says ex-Australian evacuee Bob Bullard. 'My younger brother seemed a real Cockney to me, and the family were very amused with my school winter uniform: a trilby hat!'

A former Canadian evacuee recalls: 'I was surprised at my mother's white hair. She had brown hair when I left in 1940.' Joyce Hazeldon, arriving at Waterloo from Australia, says: 'I knew my father straight away, he had not changed; and also my brother. But my mother was strange! It seems that she had had new teeth whilst I was away.'

For some, recognition was difficult. 'My parents hardly knew me,' writes Jean Cheyne, 'and I only recognized them because my brother George (who had returned from Canada earlier) was there with them.' A thirteen year old, arriving back from Australia, with younger brother and sister says: 'We were twenty four hours late owing to storms in the Bay of Biscay. Boat train to London. Everyone gone. We three standing by our luggage; a man hurrying along the platform. It must be our father, he's the only one about. It's cold, it's misty, it's December, it's dark. We board a packed train and head for the north . . .'

There were families for whom conversation was hard. Heather Johnston, who had wanted to remain in New Zealand, recalls the meeting with her mother and an uncle in London: 'We were stilted in our conversation when crossing London, and the taxi driver helped us greatly.' Sixteen year old Betty Deeley, arriving back from Australia on a foggy day at Birmingham's New Street Station, reports: 'It was very depressing. And our parents were like strangers. They looked different. My father was ill. And we hardly spoke for the first day.'

Such difficulties apart, some of the ex-evacuees recall that they warmed quickly to the welcome awaiting them as they reached their homes. The greeting frequently belied the warnings given on the voyage about possible hostility towards them from those who had stayed behind. On arriving home in Hornchurch, John and Joan Hare found 'there were flags and bunting decorating our street, and a "Welcome Home" party for us!' Similarly, Nora Lupton, back in Darlington, received a box of chocolates from a friend who worked in a confectioner's shop, 'which I didn't fully appreciate until the full impact of sweet rationing hit me. Then, an almost unheard of tin of salmon was produced for that first meal — again, not fully appreciated at the time.'

Former New Zealand evacuee Elizabeth Taylor, on arrival in Cheam with her parents, was greeted by the next-door neighbour ringing her ARP bell from an upstairs

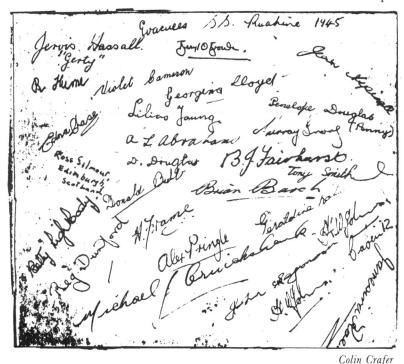

Colin Crafer

Fig 40: *Memories. Some of Colin Crafer's autographs of the other CORB evacuees returning with him from New Zealand aboard the "Ruahine".*

window. And also back from New Zealand, Geraldine Robb received a truly northern welcome back in Manchester, where the family home was bursting at the seams for a party attended by all her relatives and 'many childhood friends.' She admits that the warmth of this reception quickly dispelled fears she had had about the possible reaction she would meet on reaching her home city.

Derric Webster, back in Bradford from Melbourne with his sister Catherine recalls: 'Arriving home was a joyous occasion. Sister Elizabeth, whom we had not previously seen, was peering out of the front room window — a little, fair, four year old with long plaits. Mother rushed out and hugged us both.'

Alas, for some there was neither warmth nor joy in getting home. Peter Beams, one who had not wanted to leave New Zealand, remembers it all as 'fairly unemotional.

Nearly five years out of a fifteen year old life makes early memories fairly dim. Certainly, we knew our parents on sight, but they meant very little to me. They had already broken up by this stage, so we boarded with a relative . . .'

Colin Crafer, also back from New Zealand, motherless since he was a baby and brought up by an aunt until his evacuation, says that 'because of the age difference my family had either left home and married or, where not yet married, were still in HM Forces . . . Try as I might, I cannot recall the first instance of meeting; but, on arriving "home" I felt like the proverbial fish out of water!'

Fifteen when she arrived back from Australia, Brenda Mallett recalls: 'I felt strange and strained. It was early winter. Everything was cold, dark and drab. Our house seemed much, much smaller than I remembered it. I was pretty uncomfortable with my mother for some reason, though not with my father.' And a thirteen year old girl back from Canada writes poignantly: 'I did not recognize my parents. I felt very uneasy; and hurt and shocked by their shabbiness. When my father came into our bedroom on the first evening and told us that he had become rather deaf, I felt a violent "Fallen Idol" shock.'

One of the most desolate homecomings of all must be that of the two sisters and a brother who arrived back from Australia, where they had lived with the eccentric spinster whose exploits are described earlier. [5] They expected to be met at Southampton when the *Stirling Castle* docked. But, there was no-one there; simply instructions from an official to proceed on the boat train to London.

'Another blow fell then,' writes the older sister, now aged eighteen. 'We were informed that we were not going to Kent but to my mother in North Wales. Our parents' marriage had broken down. I knew she was living and working in North Wales, but naïvely assumed this was because of doing war work. Apparently our hostess in Australia knew; but, for some unknown reason, kept it to herself. It was a dreadful shock. My father met us in London. He seemed very old, sad and frail. We stayed overnight in London and went by rail to Liverpool next day, where my mother was waiting to meet us. We were very idealistic and naturally expected her to return to Kent.

But, this was not to be . . .'

Whilst some evacuees can recall with pleasure the early days after getting home and report no particular crises, probably at least as many did begin to feel some strain and experience problems. Amongst those who settled most easily were those who had served in the Armed Forces. At least their parents seemed able to recognize more readily that they had grown up and severed the parental apron strings. In the case of younger children, parents had much more difficulty in adjusting to their age and level of development. Some evacuees resented the way mothers in particular treated them as though they were the same age as they were when evacuated in 1940.

Another widely experienced family problem was the resentful attitude of brothers and sisters, usually younger ones, who felt their noses pushed out of joint on the return of CORB members of the family. Yet another quite widespread difficulty was adjustment to British schools. In this, Canadian evacuees in particular tended to find large gaps in their academic education compared with British pupils. As a result, some ex-Canadian evacuees who had been one or two years younger than the other children in their Canadian classes, suddenly found themselves odd-man-out in the opposite direction, and resented the situation. The youngsters returned from Canada also seemed to provoke the most amused or mocking reaction to their informal attitude and strange-sounding accents, with those returned from Australia close behind.

In fact, former Australian evacuee Muriel Evans says that her first impression on returning home to York was that people were more interested in her Australian accent than they were in her. She is echoed by Dorothy Graham, who returned to Tyneside from Australia and remembers 'being a curiosity for a while because of my Aussie accent.'

A serious factor impeding the rehabilitation of former evacuees, and their parents' efforts to help them settle down, was that bomb-scarred Britain, with its shortages of food, fuel and clothing, its dowdiness and sheer exhaustion, compared very unfavourably with the colour, the plenty and the warmth of life in the Dominions. Furthermore, by voicing their opinions, some ex-evacuees bred resentment

Fig 41: *Hazel and Howard John shortly after their arrival in New Zealand from Bristol in October, 1940. (Compare with Fig 42).*

"New Zealand Herald"

Fig 42: *Hazel and Howard John shortly before leaving New Zealand in August, 1945. These pictures illustrate how long five war-time years were in terms of a CORB evacuee's development; and both were taken at a time of uncertainty about the future.*

"New Zealand Herald"

both in parents and in other members of the family.

Edna Chase describes a common experience: 'My mother seemed resentful of my feelings for New Zealand and the extravagant "habits" I'd acquired. My whole desire became to return to New Zealand.' She did so, in 1948. In lighter vein, but on the same matter, the father of an ex-Australian evacuee (who claims he had 'no problems' in settling down to life in England) wrote to the boy's former foster-mother, asking: 'Haven't you really any faults? And does the sun shine ALL the time in Australia?'

Back in Bradford from Australia, Catherine Webster recalls: 'I took a long time to settle and was very resentful at having to return to the UK. I was moody, awkward, and extremely difficult for about two years. Fortunately, my parents were extremely patient.' Her mother writes, phlegmatically: 'Derric settled more quickly than his sister Catherine who was in her early teens. The standard at the Girls' Grammar School was higher than in Melbourne, and she took longer to make friends. But, it all straightened out in due course.'

In the final analysis, the patience with which parents were able to deal with their children on return must have been a major factor in determining whether they settled to life in Britain or eventually decided to return overseas. Some parents were able to be remarkably patient, some were not. But, who can blame the parents who were not?

When Miss Maxse made her final CORB report in February, 1946,[6] she stated that nine per cent of the overall total of CORB children were remaining overseas intending to make their homes there. Her figure did not include those still in Dominion Forces, some of whom would also stay abroad when demobilized. Of the nine per cent staying, sixty two children were staying 'irrespective of parents' plans' and one hundred and fifty nine were going to stay permanently 'if joined by their parents.' These figures mask some considerable problems and anguish.

The case of Mrs E M Purdy, a widow from Tyneside, is hard, though not as heartbreaking as some. Her daughter and two sons were evacuated to Vancouver. Mrs Purdy could not afford to emigrate at the end of the war. She writes: 'Enid being just fourteen had to return. But the boys were working and wanted to stay in Canada. Ellen Wilkinson, the MP for Jarrow at that time, helped them to stay.' Mrs Purdy thus bowed to the inevitable in agreeing to split up her family and, perhaps, her avoidance of conflict paid off. In 1956, the younger son came home, married and settled in England. 'But,' ends Mrs Purdy, 'the older brother, Peter, has made a happy life in Canada.' She seems very philosophical about it all.

An example of a much more complex case, but typical of a small minority's difficulties, is that involving two sisters aged twelve and thirteen as the war ended. They had settled very happily in their second foster-home in Vancouver and the arrangement agreed was that the two sisters should stay in their foster-home until their mother and father were able to leave England to visit them and discuss the family's future. The older girl writes: 'My parents first joined us in Vancouver in 1946, and stayed a few months. My mother was unhappy and resented the degree to which we had become part of our foster-family — a large family with many relatives.'

Her sister adds: 'When my mother and father were in the same room as Auntie and Uncle, my sister and I didn't know who to ask if we wanted to go out, or to church, or whatever. If we asked Auntie, Mum would be mad. If we asked Mum, our Auntie would be hurt. It was very awkward and also very emotional.'

Eventually, the parents decided to return to England, and did so in 1947, having stipulated that their daughters must follow them as soon as arrangements could be made. Says the older girl: 'My sister and I did not wish to return and appealed against the decision . . . However, we did return under CORB, (although the scheme had expired), after a judge decided we were to return to our parents.'

Predictably, the heartbreak did not end there. The sisters' return to London was disastrous. 'We resented having to come back to England and didn't like our parents, especially our mother,' says the older girl. 'Meanwhile', her sister continues, 'my mother and father forbade us to receive any letters or to write any, or to have anything at all to do with Canada.' A further, distressing complication was that the parents had sold their house — (and having been

bombed out of their home several times during the war, to
sell their house took great self-sacrifice) — in order to pay
for their Vancouver visit. As they had to queue for council
accommodation, they arranged for the girls to live with
other relations for a year after their return.

Utterly disillusioned with London, the two girls decided
they would return to Canada as soon as they came of age,
and regarded the years in between as simply a painful
waiting stage. The older concludes: 'The evacuation scheme
separated us emotionally from my mother for the rest of her
life. We could not discuss the subject with her. I believe it
was her greatest sorrow that she did separate from us for
this long period of time.'

Affairs were not guaranteed to work out smoothly even
when parents consented to former evacuees staying abroad,
and agreed to join them. Rose Burder, aged thirteen as the
war ended, together with her three sisters aged ten, sixteen
and nineteen, did not return to Scotland. Their father, who
suffered lung trouble, had died in 1941, and their mother
decided to bring their seven year old brother to New
Zealand with her. Rose writes: 'My mother and brother
came to New Zealand in 1946. I remember this time as a
very strained period, as there was such a gap between us.
My mother resented the affection we had for our foster-
mother. It was really a very difficult time, and I remember
wishing that we did not have to go and live with our
mother as she seemed such a stranger to us.'

A relatively happier story is that of 'Billy' Diane Clarke,
who was evacuated from Liverpool to Australia with her
older sister. Both stayed put after the war, almost
irrespective of their parents' wishes, because their mother
and father had separated and divorced whilst the children
were evacuated. When the war ended, Billy was training to
be a nurse; her sister was already married. 'So,' writes Billy,
'we had no home to go back to. Father was a Squadron-
leader in India by this time, and mother, having joined the
WAAF, was a Section Officer in Algeria.' Billy's mother
arrived in Australia on a visit in 1947, and Billy was able to
meet her for a time in Sydney. 'Then in 1972,' she writes, 'I
managed to get to England and met my father. It was
thirty two years, three weeks and five days since I'd seen

him. He hadn't changed a bit!'

One of the most confused, as well as a protracted and painful case, involved four sisters evacuated to Canada from East Anglia. They were the girls whose mother warned them that their father would not bother to see them off when they left home in 1940, although, in fact, he did. It is evident that tensions continued to exist within the parents' marriage for, at the end of the war, the sisters received instructions to remain in Canada, because their mother intended to emigrate to Canada when she could, and bring three younger daughters with her. But, eight more years elapsed before she was able to sail to Canada — and, even then, it could only be for a visit, during the course of which she arranged for the youngest of her ex-evacuee children to be formally adopted by her host family. This girl was, by now, aged eighteen and the oldest of the ex-evacuees was married. This oldest 'girl' writes, over forty years after the event: 'I felt a sense of rejection at this time. We never returned to England because my mother did not want us back. I was upset at this time in my life, but I was also pleased that I could remain in Canada and continue my education.'

The father of this family died in the mid-1950s never having seen his four evacuee daughters again, and his widow went to live permanently in Canada in 1956, taking the youngest children with her. The four ex-evacuee daughters have done well in Canada. They have each experienced particularly happy marriages and enjoyed raising large families. But, as one so cogently writes: 'The experience led to the total fracture of our family. I have three sisters whom I do not know. My father died alone in England without ever seeing the four daughters evacuated to Canada. And I have never returned to the city of my birth. But, some day I will! You ask how long was I homesick? The answer is: I still am!'

For some of those who sailed home reluctantly at the end of the war difficulties continued as might be expected. The experiences of one start with a happy foster-home in Australia. Her former host writes: 'After the war ended, Joan became very unsettled and unhappy about the prospect of returning to her parents, and her Headmistress said she was equally unsettled at school. She had forgotten her parents — (Joan was seven years old when she left England in 1940) — and was very upset when she left us. She was still only twelve years old, and we feel it was a very traumatic experience for her. During her time with us, we had a son and a daughter, and she regarded us all as her own family. My last view of her as the *Stratheden* sailed was of her face purple with crying and waving in the wrong direction, as she couldn't see us for tears!'

Joan's mother takes up the story. 'My husband and I considered emigration. We would have liked to, but couldn't afford it, as there was no emigration scheme just after the war.' So, the parents asked for Joan, who was their only child, to return home. But, she did not settle at all well. 'Life was so different for her,' continues her mother, 'that she couldn't adjust and we had a difficult time with her for three or four years. In fact, it continued until she was married — just before she was seventeen.' Twenty three years later, still cherishing her happy memories of the evacuation days in Australia, Joan at last returned to settle there with her husband and children.

The mother of Heather Johnston, another who would have preferred to remain abroad, outlines the kind of problems facing several evacuee parents at the end of the war. She writes: 'Heather was only eleven years old when she returned and didn't know me. She cried every time she had a letter from New Zealand, and, as I still had to go out to work, there was no warm welcome for her when she came home from school. Also, food and fuel were hard to come by, which was not in my favour. She longed to return to New Zealand.

'When she was fifteen, a new scheme came from the UK Government for any of the evacuees to return. So I reluctantly let her go. She returned to her foster-parents and was very happy — and so were they . . . I came out to New Zealand after my mother died in 1959. I have since returned for visits to the UK. My heart is there; but my home is in New Zealand now.'

Some of those who stayed abroad at the end of the war can write of a happy outcome. John Doughty, in the top age group of CORB evacuees, and therefore fifteen on arrival in Australia, became enamoured of Tasmania virtually from the start. As soon as he was eighteen he enlisted in the AIF, turning down an offer to transfer to the British Army in India. 'When on final leave before going overseas,' he writes, 'I think, in retrospect, that even at that stage I felt naturalized. Then, when I was demobilized, the process crystallized. I married a Tasmanian girl, and I don't think I ever contemplated repatriation to England; rather the effort was directed towards getting my parents and sister to emigrate — which they eventually did.' The whole family settled well, becoming part of Australian society.

Others who elected to stay can tell similarly happy stories, although some of them will always feel torn between home in the land where they live, a land which they love, and 'Home' in the Old Country, which they left in 1940, a land which they also love.

Thus, writes Brenda, thirteen when the war ended and the youngest of the four children in her family evacuated by CORB: 'We simply stayed in New Zealand till our parents arrived after the war. My happiest memory is of seeing Mum and Dad on the deck as the ferry arrived at Lyttelton! But,' she confesses, 'I love the UK. To me it is still "Home" after all these years!'

21

MORE THAN FORTY YEARS ON

'There has not been sufficient time or research to judge the effects of the CORB scheme upon the children and parents, and upon their relationship to each other,' wrote Miss Marjorie Maxse in her summary of CORB's work compiled in 1944.[1] 'Time might show,' she continued, 'that the disruptive effect upon the children, and the absence of parental control during the formative years, was a drawback which might leave a mark.'

Miss Maxse then went on to outline the other side of the coin: 'Transfer of children of this age from the horrors of war, the restrictions on food, clothing and fuel, and the effects of the blackout, to the freedom of open-air life, and to their new and warm experiences of affection and friendship, may prove to be of incalculable benefit. These, and many other features of the scheme can only be assessed later.'

Once again, Marjorie Maxse demonstrated her powers of perception and analysis. And, more than forty years on, the comments and recollections of former CORB evacuees show that both aspects of Miss Maxse's antithesis can be argued — though with what degree of equality it is impossible to say.

First, a look at some of the benefits ex-evacuees claim to have derived from taking part in the scheme all those years ago.

A few speak about social benefits. In doing so, they bear out a prediction of possible gains, made earlier than Miss Maxse's, by the writer Alfred Body in his book *Children in Flight*, published in February, 1940. Writing about the

internal British evacuation of 1939, Mr Body forecast that
when the serious analysis was made at a future date of the
effects of evacuation on children, one of the most interesting
and most important aspects would be the increased social
awareness that would accrue from life in advantaged homes.

Mr Body would have been interested in the comments of
a former Australian CORB evacuee who wrote: 'My
guardians were financially very comfortable — no expense
spared. My great uncle's only interest was in me and my
school work. He spent every week night helping and
encouraging me. At home, I would have been one of five, in
a family just finding its feet financially. But,' she adds, 'set
against this, I was very much spoiled and took a lot of
convincing, when I got home, that I wasn't all that
wonderful — and I didn't like it!'

A former New Zealand evacuee also writes about social
benefits: 'I enjoyed many advantages. I was taught music,
elocution and had a better education than I would have
had in Scotland. I lived with people much better off
financially than my parents. Up to my evacuation, we lived
in two rooms, and I shared a bed with two sisters in a
tenement.' And, similarly, a former South African evacuee
says: 'Certainly we had better opportunities in coming to
South Africa. All of us (she refers to a brother and sister as
well as herself) have done well. What we have today could
never have been achieved had we remained in England.'

Much more common than observations about financial
and social benefits are those about the broadening experience gained. As a former Australian evacuee says: 'It
enabled me to see different countries and appreciate people
of all races. Travelling so far as we did broadened our
outlook.' This view is shared by many: 'I gained knowledge
of other countries and their ways of life,' says one. And
another, 'It helped the broadening of my outlook and
understanding of other countries.'

A former Canadian evacuee puts it like this: 'Vancouver
was a good place to spend five years. Whilst there, I
experienced a different way of life, another continent, and
received a different way of looking at England. I feel free of
the dread "stratification" of English society.'

Predictably, some former evacuees attribute their continuing love of travel to their evacuation days. One, evacuated to Australia, writes: 'With my husband and family I enjoyed travelling to many countries. I like to think the evacuation gave me a good general education and a love of travelling. Two of my grown-up children work overseas — encouraged by their mother's attitude to travel!'

A former Canadian CORB boy, who is a serving officer with the Royal New Zealand Air Force, having previously served with the Royal Air Force and the Sultan of Oman's Air Force, states: 'The long-term advantages gained from my evacuation are that my general education was enhanced, and that I have no qualms about travel or moving and, perhaps as a result of the evacuation, I have the "Wanderlust".'

A former New Zealand evacuee reiterates the point about concepts being enlarged, although he reserves judgment on whether evacuation alone was responsible for this. 'It made me aware that the world and its problems are bigger than my own backyard,' he writes. 'I suspect, though, that my time in the Royal Navy' (he was a full, time-serving regular) 'is the reason for most of this realization.'

An ex-South African evacuee is very specific about the broadening effects of his evacuation: 'I became very "colonial" in outlook, eg., "Jack's as good as his master" — though life has not always proven that theory! I have a home and standard of life which could not have been mine if I'd stayed in the UK.' (He is now a permanent resident in New Zealand.) 'I also feel that life in South Africa helped me to understand the events now bedevilling that beautiful and misunderstood country. I, for one, have a deep knowledge of the fears, reasoning, hopes and frustrations which go to cause Apartheid — today's political nightmare.'

Many of the CORB evacuees, in addition to a healthy broadening of outlook and useful general education, see beneficial effects to their personalities resulting from the evacuation years. Their comments about this tend to repeat a common set of advantages, with interesting and occasionally original variations.

Says one: 'I developed the ability to stand on my own feet in adversity; to mix with all types; an open and enquiring mind with few prejudices; and tolerance, especially with young people.' But, quite rightly, another writing on similar lines gives a reminder that it is always difficult to analyse the crucial determinants in one's own personality. 'I think those of us already into our teens, who came from a secure home background, probably developed the ability to mix — though this may derive as much from our original home background. I can imagine the total experience was probably very different for the younger evacuees, especially for those belonging to larger families that had to be split and go to different foster-homes.'

A selection of different angles on the theme of effects on personality, include these comments: 'I appreciated being one of a family instead of being an only child.' Another: 'New Zealand made me more independent, which I don't think I would ever have been if I'd stayed in England — because the death of my foster-mother thrust independence upon me.' Again: 'Being brought up in a large, happy foster-family in Canada had lasting effects. It made me a stronger person and determined to support myself and succeed. I have an excellent relationship with my own daughter, and have a greater insight into people's problems.'

It is very clear that, more than forty years after Miss Maxse wrote about the possibility of the CORB scheme presenting 'incalculable benefits', there are former CORB evacuees who would agree strongly. These are the ones who write about the advantages in finding a philosophy of life, a broader understanding of the world, of different peoples and their cultures; the riches gained in independence, self-reliance, the ability to mix with others, to adapt, to win through.

On the other hand, Miss Maxse also warned that the 'disruptive effect' of the scheme could prove 'a drawback which might leave a mark.' And, once again, the evidence is forthcoming from the testimony of former CORB evacuees. For all the benefits claimed by some, there are others who give harrowing reports of the permanent marks left upon them, and of psychological scars that still produce ill effects.

These 'disruptive effects' are apparent in the following comments: 'I still have a feeling I took part in something special. I would not have travelled at all if I had not been evacuated. But I believe it had a great effect on me. I find that all travelling is a very great strain. I get claustrophobia in cars and coaches, and lose my self-confidence very easily.' And another: 'My evacuation demanded too many emotional adjustments from me, exacerbating my shyness, slowing down my emotional maturity and resulting in uncomfortable school years in particular.'

And, inevitably surely, the 'identity problem': 'I had to be how people wanted me to be, so I think I lost my own personality somewhere during this time. I became very self-conscious and had no confidence in myself, as a lot more was expected of me than I was capable of giving. I wanted praise when I did something well; but I only seemed to get a reprimand when I did something wrong. It was a sad time for me, and I really wonder what sort of person I would have been if I had not been evacuated.'

Or, the 'hardening' effect: 'I became very self-sufficient and found family life, when married, (ie., in-laws, etc.,) a little hard to put up with. Even today, I have no real feelings towards anyone except my own direct family — ie., my children. I have surviving parents, but where I do not know.'

A former South African evacuee says: 'We had to pay the price in the loss of love and affection from our parents during the most formative years. I would never have done the same for my children had the circumstances been the same.' This writer goes on to explain that she was, indeed, in a very similar situation when, with her husband and children, she lived in Zimbabwe from 1964 to 1978. There they were caught up in the war for independence, yet, she says, 'we all remained together, and are a very close family.'

Many former CORB children return to the decision their parents made to send them overseas. One evacuated to Canada writes: 'As my own children reached the age of ten I wondered to myself how I would have handled the situation mother had to decide: to send her two youngest boys about 4,000 miles to a different country, not knowing when next she would see them.' Another says: 'It must have been a very difficult decision for my parents to make. Would I have been brave enough to send three of my children into the unknown like that? God knows — I don't, and thankfully never will!'

Some express, not only amazement at their parents' decision, but a hint of disapproval as well. For instance, a former Canadian evacuee writes: 'Since reaching maturity and having my own children, I can't conceive of sending my children away.' And others link their feelings of rejection with their disapproval: 'I feel a slightly "displaced person",' states a former Canadian evacuee. 'I feel there was an element of rejection in being sent off, and also in never being part of Canadian society either.' And an ex-Australian evacuee puts the rejection case even more strongly: 'The bad things were the desperate homesickness and uncertainty and, in my case, the estrangement from my mother. I was convinced that she had found an easy way of getting rid of me.'

The feeling of rejection was probably more widespread than the conscious memories of former evacuees would suggest. In addition, there certainly were a few parents using the CORB scheme simply in order to be rid of their children. When looking briefly at CORB in her book *Children of the Empire*, Lady Wagner mentions that some of the evacuees who developed behavioural problems overseas came from homes where 'the parents had ridded themselves of their children.'[2] Mrs Elspeth Davies, one of Lady Wagner's sources, holds this view and, in her position as CORB's Director of Welfare she is in the best position of anyone to know that some parents did behave in this way — and that some of the children who were deliberately rejected became 'problem children' whilst abroad.

But, as we have just seen, the small number whose parents did get rid of them were by no means the only ones to feel a sense of rejection. And this problem was another that was forecast in 1940, just before the CORB plan came into existence. Dr John Bowley, a psychiatrist attached at that time to the Child Guidance Training Centre in Cambridge, writing on 'Psychological Aspects' in the Survey of the 1939 British Evacuation (compiled by Drs Padley and Cole for the Fabian Society)[3] warned that a small child could find it very difficult to accept that he had been evacuated purely for safety's sake. 'Not all children can believe the truth,' he wrote, 'and it is difficult for a child not to interpret his being sent away as a desire on the parents' part to be rid of him.' And this fear that his parents wanted rid of him Dr Bowley described as being 'as real as the fear of bogey-men.'

Commenting on this recently (in 1983), Mrs Elspeth Davies said:[4] 'Everyone at CORB realized that separation from parents was serious. It was commonsense. And they realized this whether or not they had read any of the Evacuation Surveys appearing at the time. We knew there were bound to be emotional risks. But, we have to remember: the whole scheme was born out of a desperate situation.' Very true. And, in looking at CORB, we do have to remember — and try to understand — the desperation of British parents in June, 1940, facing the prospect of a Nazi invasion with what seemed total certainty. Better to lose your child to a life of freedom overseas, than to the effects of Nazi oppression at home. It was this argument that led over 211,000 parents to apply to CORB in the two weeks that applications were being accepted. And it was this argument, this 'desperate situation', that produced the CORB scheme.

Moreover, Geoffrey Shakespeare himself felt so strongly about the potential emotional dangers of an overseas evacuation scheme that he initially opposed the very idea, saying that the British Government had 'gone to the limits of prudence in disrupting family life by providing the well-planned evacuation within the United Kingdom itself.'[5] So, as Elspeth Davies points out, CORB organizers did not dismiss lightly, nor in ignorance, the obvious hazards to the children's emotional development and the family's relationships.

Paramount amongst these hazards was not only the possibility of children believing that their parents had taken the opportunity to get rid of them, but also the likely harm to accrue merely from severance from parents. Both the Fabian Evacuation Survey of Padley and Cole, and the slightly earlier Survey compiled by Dr Susan Isaacs[6], whilst analysing the harmful effects of the 1939 Evacuation, stressed the need to encourage regular parental visits to evacuees in any future evacuation scheme. This idea went contrary to popular belief, many people believing that visits by parents had a harmful, unsettling effect on evacuated

children. But the Cambridge Survey in particular demonstrated that regular visits from parents, far from being a
disturbing influence upon the relationships between children
and their foster-parents, for instance, actually contributed
enormously to the happy adjustment of the majority of
evacuee children.[7]

This view was supported by Dr Bowley in the Fabian
Survey.[8] He gave evidence that adolescent evacuees were
capable of 'a surprising stability' provided they were visited
regularly by their parents. The reassurance that their homes
were safe and their parents well, could help them to cope
with the stresses of being away from their families, he said.

But, obviously, in planning an overseas evacuation
scheme, CORB had to rule out the possibility of regular
parent visits — or, indeed, the hope of parental visits at all.
Straightaway, therefore, a crucial stabilizing factor, mentioned by two of the weightiest guides available to
evacuation organizers in 1940, had to be completely
discounted. The fact that they were discounted is testimony,
again, to the sickening fear felt by British parents for their
children, when Britain looked certain to be occupied by the
Nazis. But, the emotional risks remained enormous.

Predictably, therefore, many ex-CORB evacuees echo the
words of the girl evacuated to Australia aged eight: 'From a
child's point of view, knowing what I went through
mentally, I would never do it with my children — no, not
even send them to boarding school. Our family life never
was — never could be — the same again.' And a boy, also
evacuated to Australia, in his case aged ten: 'If another war
did come, I believe I would rather face it with all my
family than have them go through what I did.'

In addition, many who speak of the effects on the family,
are conscious of the sadness it brought their parents,
especially mothers. A ten year old evacuated to Canada
says: 'It certainly destroyed a true relationship with my
mother, and God knows what it did for her, poor woman.'
Another ten year old, evacuated to Australia, writes: 'My
parents suffered stress through our parting, and the lack of
sympathy from relatives and local people, who said they
could not understand how a loving parent could send a
child abroad.'

Yet another states, very sadly: 'The shock of us both leaving reflected very much on our mother. Shortly after we left, she experienced a nervous breakdown and was very ill for a long time — besides having to cope with the blitz on London.'

In some form or other, the recognition that it produced permanently harmful effects for the family to be missing regular, physical contact, is mentioned over and over again. 'I did not get on with my mother on my return,' writes a former CORB evacuee in typical terms, 'since I had grown up and away from her. I was definitely closer to my foster-mother. I tended to say, "In Canada we always did . . ." and, of course, this upset her. But it took me years to discover this.' Psychiatrist Dr Bowley had forecast this, too. 'Mothers of younger evacuees,' he wrote with staggering accuracy, 'will, at the end of hostilities, find themselves greeting home children who do not know them, and who regret leaving their foster-parents.'[9]

So, Dr Bowley would not have been surprised by comments such as these, all made by former CORB evacuees: 'The unfortunate thing was parting from parents. Then, when one returned to them, not knowing each other.' Or: 'I would have known my parents, especially Father, a lot better if I'd not been evacuated — and it would have saved them from a very traumatic experience.' And another: 'I would not have missed Canada and my foster-home for the world. But, I do wonder how relations with my family might have differed.' Yet another: 'One impression stays with me: a child can put up with practically anything if he has his parents near . . . I have many happy memories of Canada, but being uprooted twice whilst still a child was upsetting.' And, finally: 'The really traumatic part was having to return at the age of thirteen. It was an awful tearing up of roots, and one which took me many years to recover from. In hindsight, I wonder if I would be a different person now if I'd not gone — and how I would be different.'

Hindsight also shows that the majority of foster-parents were in an impossible situation both in regard to their own emotions and those of the children they cared for. If foster-parents loved the child as their own, and tried to give him total security, they ran the risk of usurping the place of the natural parents in the child's emotions. However, if the foster-parents tried to be 'correct' and avoid taking over from the parents, they ran the equally dangerous risk of leaving the child feeling unwanted and unloved. As a former Australian evacuee says, 'Although my Aunt did her best, a little motherly love would have helped over the difficult years.' And, similarly, a New Zealand evacuee whose foster-parents were not relatives, points out: 'I had a good foster-home; but I remember how I wished I was some kind of blood relative of theirs, as I felt at times not one of them.'

Another former New Zealand evacuee says: 'In retrospect, with children of my own, I do see that it is immensely difficult to take the place of natural parents, temporarily, over an unknown length of time, and make a success of it.'

Another perceptive comment about the possible effects of evacuation upon children, appeared in 1940.[10] Dealing with problems encountered in the 1939 internal evacuation, the author, Mrs St Leo Strachey, quoted from an unpublished paper by a psychiatrist who insisted that any re-billeting of an evacuee 'should be regarded as a far more important step than a simple physical transfer. The child has to face afresh all the difficulties of settling into a strange house and, with each change, will feel less confident and take longer to settle.'

Comments from three ex-CORB evacuees illustrate that the business of moving homes, or even the fear of having to do so, did present problems, though none of the three was regarded as a 'problem child'. The first, evacuated to Canada aged twelve, writes: 'I have so many favourable memories of my evacuation that I came back to live in this land with my wife and son in the 1950s. My one unfavourable memory is having to move from one foster-home to another, and having to re-establish friendships.'

The second, evacuated to New Zealand aged eight, stayed in a foster-home which she describes as 'a good home'. But, she states, 'I lost my security in being sent away. I had a great fear that, if I did not behave as they wanted me to, my foster-parents would send me off to someone else. After all, I was not their kin, so had, I felt, no right to be there at all.' The third comment, from a former Canadian evacuee, implies this same, latent fear of being moved. 'I lacked confidence — and still do — from years of trying to be no bother to my foster-parents and to cost them as little as possible. Why I should feel like this I don't know' — (she was happy in her foster-home, and still calls it 'my second home') — 'but I always chose the most practical pair of shoes, for example, rather than the ones I really wanted.'

Other effects of the CORB scheme are even more difficult to assess than effects on individuals and families. For instance, did any of those children evacuated by CORB have a 'safer' war? The official Home Office casualty figures state that 15,358 children were seriously injured or killed in air-raids on Britain, representing about ten per cent of the total casualties. But, even the total casualties in air-raids represent only about 0.02 per cent of the British population. CORB's evacuee casualties in the *City of Benares* débâcle represented some 2.8 per cent of the total sent overseas.[11]

Since the majority of CORB evacuees came from specially designated 'vulnerable areas', there is some justification in the feeling expressed by a few ex-CORB children, over forty years after the war, that their evacuation was beneficial from the point of view of avoiding the blitz. Writes a former CORB girl: 'I think the Evacuation was a good thing. It saved us from the dreadful effects of the bombing and air-raids, and allowed us to grow up away from the war. My mother said that, whenever there was an air-raid, she would thank God I was in Australia.' To be sure, ex-CORB evacuees report that their home areas suffered during the blitz: 'A house was bombed at the end of our road. The family was killed,' writes one. 'My parents were bombed out twice,' writes another. 'The second time, they had to leave their badly damaged house for about a year.' One states: 'Raids were constant during the Battle of Britain. My family had three bombs and a land-mine on Christmas Eve, 1940, on a corner of the house and garden.' Yet another: 'Our parents were bombed out of three homes.'

However, the CORB scheme was designed as much to save children from a German invasion as from the blitz. In fact, the scheme only made sense if it was a response to the threat of invasion, for evacuation within Britain was coping quite well with providing refuge from bombing, and the majority of the population would always have to hope that this provision would continue to be adequate. So, the 'war benefits' of the CORB scheme were pretty minimal.

In a totally different direction, what about the 'migration' aspect of the CORB scheme? During his tour of South Africa in 1944, Geoffrey Shakespeare noted, rather typically, in his Diary: 'South African parents have treated these children as their own. No more can be said. A large number of our children will return one day, I hope, and settle there.'[12] This is one of several instances of his lingering interest in migration to the Empire — an understandable 'lapse' considering that he was touring South Africa as Chairman of the Empire Parliamentary Association.

However, despite Geoffrey Shakespeare's personal interest in 'migration and the redistribution of population within the Empire' — to use his own words[13] — and despite some hope, undoubtedly, on the part of Dominion Governments, that their invitation to Britain to send evacuees might result in some permanent settlers after the war, the CORB scheme was not planned with the intention of adding permanent settlers to the Dominions. As Mrs Elspeth Davies said recently (1983): 'There was no whiff of a long-term migration scheme. The atmosphere of the time was "blitz and invasion". No-one had *time* to think migration — though the Dominions might have had an eye on this.'[14] Miss Maxse was clearly of exactly the same mind. At the end of her 1944 summary of CORB's work she wrote: 'The CORB scheme was launched under the threat of imminent invasion and air bombardment. The determining motive of the parents was the safety of the children . . .'[15]

Nevertheless, scattered throughout the Dominions, is a sprinkling of former CORB evacuees, some of whom never returned to Britain to live, even for the briefest time, and others who decided to return at some stage to make their homes there. The enormous happiness some of these former evacuees have enjoyed in their adopted countries would doubtless have gladdened Geoffrey Shakespeare's heart, as well as the hearts of the Dominion politicians who first invited the British Government to send evacuees to them.

'If it were not for the Evacuation,' writes one, 'I would probably never have lived in Australia, which I love dearly.' Similarly, another states: 'But for the Evacuation, I would probably never have come to Canada — a country I love.' And yet another, a former Australian evacuee: 'The evacuation scheme changed my whole life — and that of my family. After my brother, parents and married sister joined me here, it was very much to our benefit. I know I wouldn't have wanted things to be otherwise.'

A different style of comment comes from a former Canadian evacuee: 'I think, personally, that the evacuation was a crazy scheme, although I consider myself one of the lucky ones. I have had thirty three years of happy marriage in Canada, and love British Columbia as much as when I first arrived. In my own case, I feel more Canadian than British.'

Unfortunately, as we have seen,[16] some of the ex-evacuees' families did not settle well after emigrating. Problems sometimes arose from a feeling of divided loyalty between members of the family left in the UK, and those now living in the particular Dominion. An ex-CORB girl writes describing how her parents sold their house in England in order to join her in 1951 in New Zealand. 'Father settled well; mother not at all.' After a couple of visits back to Britain, her mother persuaded her husband to return with her to live there in 1967. But, by that time, the former evacuee's two brothers and one of her sisters were permanently resident in New Zealand, leaving only one sister in England near her parents. The ex-evacuee comments: 'So, I feel my evacuation is still affecting our lives, because I know that, if my mother comes to New Zealand again, she will still yearn for England and her younger daughter!'

Probably a majority of former CORB evacuees, whether settled overseas or living in Britain, suffer some degree of divided loyalty themselves. In this respect, they would share the sentiments of writer Anthony Bailey, who was evacuated privately to the USA in 1940. In a fascinating section of one of his books[17] he describes how he returned to England after the war, did his National Service, went up to Oxford, and then returned to America, 'looking for the continuation of the life that my American childhood might have prepared for me, and where I lived for the next fifteen years . . .' His four daughters were born during those years; more recently, they have all lived in England. So, he believes, 'I have lost America again. And, as before, I feel a need — which, perhaps, I will always have to try to satisfy — to regain and rediscover it.'[18]

Geraldine Robb, evacuated from Manchester aged eleven, who has re-visited New Zealand, but who has lived permanently back in England since the war, expresses this same, divided feeling, too: 'I feel always that my childhood roots are in New Zealand, and always have a great longing to be there.' And another, who never returned to Britain from Canada, can speak of it: 'Eventually, I married the one, shy, quiet boy who did not laugh at my English accent when first I entered Canadian school.' She enthuses about 'this great country Canada — my home!' But then, she reveals her yearning, her unrealized dream: 'Some day, I will walk up the steps of City Hall and show my husband all the places I remember, like the castle, the cathedral and old St Mark's Church . . .'

Maybe, amongst the CORB 'children' scattered across the world, the happiest of all will be those who are able to relate to one or other of the two statements that follow. Each has had an element of travel in his life since CORB days; one finally opted for a home in the Dominions, the other in Britain. Both show a grasp of perspective in regard to their CORB experiences, though in different ways, and a talent for balance. John, evacuated aged eleven, writes: 'My early stay in Canada has never struck me as a special event but as an integrated part of the way in which my life has unfolded, and continues to unfold. Of course, being evacuated to Canada has entirely changed my life, for I have made "my Dominion" my home. This was almost by chance. Once I had readapted to England, I loved it there. Dissatisfaction with my first job after University led me to a couple of years in Ethiopia. After my tour of duty there, I just decided, as I was "on the move", to revisit Canada, since I had fond memories of the place from my evacuation days. Although I have been in North America ever since and am now a Canadian citizen, I never immigrated in the usual sense of rejecting the "old country" to find "new life" in the land of promise. Rather, it seems, I was looking for my roots, left here, when I was torn away to return to England . . .'

The other, Derric, evacuated aged nine, returned to England, left school at sixteen to join the Merchant Navy as a deck apprentice and, during twenty two years in the service, became a Ship's Master. During the five years of evacuation, he had been very happy with an aunt and uncle, and was able to pay them a brief visit in Melbourne during his seafaring days. His links with the sea in recent years have been at a shipping company desk in Southampton. Derric writes: 'I do not relate very much to my five years' evacuation. For instance, I look upon myself as a Bradford Grammar School Old Boy, not as a Northcote High School Old Boy — even though I was at BGS for only a year after returning to England. I sometimes feel that nothing would have been lost had it not happened — if you understand me.'

However, there will be many who cannot identify with the philosophy of either of these ex-CORB boys. For some, the evacuation remains the highlight period of their lives. For some, the evacuation was the starting point for a totally new life that would have been impossible for them otherwise. For some of these, the years since have been mostly happy, whilst for others, there has been continuing grief and suffering.

Wherever they stand on this spectrum, there will be many associated with CORB, in whatever capacity, who agree with ex-CORB girl Catherine Webster's succinct verdict: 'Looking back, the whole thing appears to me as a well-intentioned but ill-conceived scheme, put into operation in a great hurry and with scant organization.'

Supporting her viewpoint are people who were heavily involved and committed, such as Miss Kyrsty Page, former *Rangitata* escort on both outward and return CORB voyages and who, in the meantime, served as CORB's highly effective liaison officer in Wellington. She said recently (1982): 'With hindsight, the scheme should not have taken place.'[19] This is despite her belief that, in her own Dominion, the New Zealand Welfare Authorities took better care of the CORB evacuees than it actually did of its own children in need of care.

Mrs Elspeth Davies, CORB's Welfare Director throughout the hectic war years, agrees with Miss Page: 'The scheme was a mistake from the start,' she said (in 1983). 'There was a desperate atmosphere at the time. This, alone, can explain what now appears so absurd.'[20] She also regrets, looking back, that the Ministry of Health and the Board of Education turned down CORB's suggestion, at the end of 1945, that there should be a probe into the effects of the scheme upon CORB evacuees and their families.[21] Mrs Davies explains that CORB did not press the idea because the tiny, over-worked Headquarters staff were so relieved when the war ended and, once the majority of evacuees had returned to their homes, felt justified in 'closing the shop', and picking up the threads of a normal life themselves.

So, in desperation, amidst an atmosphere of gloom and panic as France capitulated in 1940, the CORB scheme was planned and executed. Treated by Cabinet Ministers with suspicion, and by the Prime Minister with detestation and alarm, the scheme was suspended before it even started. Yet, start it did, despite grave warnings from the Admiralty that adequate naval protection for CORB ships was impossible.

There followed tragic loss of life, unnecessary loss, as events proved. The scheme had many sad consequences besides bereavement and injury: broken relationships, bitterness, divided families, occasional cruelty, and permanent psychological damage. Yet, it also gave expression to much generosity and kindness in the Dominions, especially amongst the host families, some of which drew from deep reserves of love to care for the children. And it brought forth much bravery amongst parents, escorts, foster-parents and the CORB children alike. On occasions, this brave element rose to the supreme heights of heroism and, for all its many faults and absurdities, the CORB scheme deserved better recognition from the British Government than the one British Empire Medal awarded to escort Mary Cornish, thoroughly deserving as she was.

However, whether enthusiastically for the CORB scheme or emphatically against it, there can be few who would disagree with Marjorie Maxse's comment made, with an eye to any future crisis, in Autumn, 1944: 'It would certainly appear that, with the end of CORB, the word "finis" could also be written on any large-scale evacuation of children from private homes in the UK to foster-homes in the Dominions.'[22]

Nevertheless, the harrowing dilemma will continue to face parents in each generation, desperate for the safety of their children, amidst the indiscriminate killing of modern war, whether civil or international. Should they keep their children with them, to face all dangers together as a family; or send them to a dubious safety with total strangers, in places far away? This dilemma must remain one of the strongest arguments for striving to maintain peace in the world.

22

THOUGHTS ON THE SIXTIETH
ANNIVERSARY

Ken Humphrey writes:

In 1990, Michael Fethney organised a reunion of overseas evacuees. I was privileged to be at that reunion.

As a child of thirteen, I had sailed during wartime to South Africa, totally oblivious to the dangers that lurked beneath the water. As children, we were confident that the invincibility of the Royal Navy would protect us and that we would arrive safely at our destination. My parents, who were living in the South East of England, would be safe — because they had an air raid shelter. Such innocence. Apart from the occasional bout of homesickness, my life in South Africa was bliss. Freedom, sunshine, fruit, sea, surf, sand, sport, the list is never ending.

Return home in 1945 was to be heaven — the stories I could tell them all! My surreal attitude of mind was soon tempered whilst en route home, by one lovely sixteen to seventeen year old girl who buttonholed me one day and in floods of tears, admitted she could not go home — she had forgotten her parents and had grown to love her host parents. She was almost suicidal and begged to be allowed to go back on the next ship.

Reaction in general to my own homecoming was strangely casual but I soon realised I had lived five wonderful years, whilst those who had stayed at home had lived through hell. I clammed up on my experiences and hardly ever spoke of them again until shortly before the 1990 reunion. Fifty years was too long to hold all these wonderful experiences inside — they were bursting to break out. The reunion gave me an opportunity to release my pent-up feelings and to re-live some of my experiences.

For this opportunity, I shall be ever grateful to Mike Fethney — life has never been, nor will ever be, quite the same. For so much of this book, it is like looking into a mirror of my own life. Thank you, Mike.

However, the more I consider and thank God for my own good fortune, the more I am haunted by the tragedy of all those children and parents, whose lives were shattered in September 1940.

Ken Humphrey

Margaret Wood writes:

During the last three years I have received a number of letters from fellow evacuees and talked to many more. Bearing in mind our own personalities and backgrounds, the crucial factors affecting the outcome of evacuation seem to have been the quality of the family life we joined, the values nurtured by the host parents and the reasons why homes were offered.

Host parents, as they were called in South Africa, either looked upon us as children in need, as hands to do work or as part of their 'war effort'. Warm, caring people welcomed evacuees with open and loving hearts, drawing them into their family life. Valmai Allies, in her second placement, commented "Uncle George had felt that his own four children had so many benefits that it would be good for them to share with an evacuee ... I was treated the same as the other children."

Some people had hoped for extra workers, such as a farmer in the vast and arid Karoo, who asked for six healthy strong young men to help him on his farm[1]. The CORB authorities did not comply with this sort of request although, despite their efforts, a number of children did become 'an extra pair of hands'.

Other evacuees were labelled 'My war effort' by the host parent, which did nothing for the child's self esteem. For those who experienced the negative effects of evacuation throughout the sensitive years of adolescence, the legacy has been a lifelong effort to cope with the feelings of isolation, loss of love and affection, a numbness, a deep searching for home and belonging.

Returning home to the UK at the end of the war created its own set of challenges. For many, their familiar homes were gone, maybe relatives too. Returning to London, I remember having to get used to my family again. They were still recovering from the ravages of war but I seemed to be floating, not quite sure what to do. After five and a half years in South Africa there were no familiar school friends and no one with whom I could share all the vivid experiences. There were no 'pieces to pick up' because I had changed and any pieces that remained were no longer of use. I had to forge a new life again just as I had needed to do in South Africa. In a way that had been easier, it had all been new. Back home again there were memories, but they seemed meaningless, everything was different.

I know that many people felt, and still feel, the same way from what they have told me. Even after sixty years some people are still reluctant to talk about their evacuation.

Although I am writing from a South African point of view, these remarks are common to many evacuees regardless of where we were sent. Some evacuees found their only real home had become their new country of adoption so returned as soon as they could and made a new and happy life there.

Dr Martin Parsons[2] of Reading University and colleagues from other universities, are making studies of the long-term effects of the evacuation.

At this point, I would like to pay tribute to our twenty-three Escorts. We travelled to our new homes through dangerous waters as our Escorts knew only too well. It was 1940 and they knew the *City of Benares* had just been sunk. They were indeed 'the Brave' and many, in other parts of the world, lost their lives. Some older children were conscious of the danger but the younger ones had no idea what was happening to them. War had no meaning for them so they looked upon it all as a marvellous adventure. Some were very homesick.

The crew and Escorts worked so hard to make the voyage as much fun as possible. They entertained us with games, 'Crossing the Line' ceremonies, fun menus for meals, regular lessons about the new country and, of course, daily lifeboat drill. Some evacuees were treated to the particular thrill of the ship's machinery or the bridge.

I have been able to contact Madge Wear (née Paine) and Freda Levson (née Troup), two of the Escorts who cared for us on the *Llanstephan Castle*. Ken Humphrey has also been in contact with Barbara Ethel Tuck (née MacPhee) in Vancouver. They have shared their memories and experiences and have provided documents and photos relating to their work on board. How they avoided losing any of their exuberant charges overboard is still a miracle!

Evacuation to South Africa offered an added angle to our education. Afrikaans was a required subject in every school, in fact, it was the only language used in some areas up-country. In Cape Town, I was allowed to substitute French but was still encouraged to learn Afrikaans. To this day, I say "wag-'n'-bietjie" (wait a minute) when under stress! I shall never forget the wonderful scenery, the outdoor life and those people who were so kind to me — people of all colours.

I have been told that many records relating to those who were evacuated were lost so I, and many others, never heard about the valuable reunion at York in 1990 organised by Michael Fethney. Down the years, reunions have played an important part in giving evacuees the opportunity to talk, share and reminisce; in fact, for some they have been of great therapeutic value, perhaps being the first occasion after more than 50 years, when old emotional traumas have been released.

On 3rd September 1999, UK evacuees gathered for the 60th Anniversary of the mass evacuation of three and a half million children from towns and cities to safer areas of the UK. A service of commemoration in Westminster Abbey and the Reunion afterwards was organised by the Evacuees Reunion Association.[3]

Representatives from Australia, Canada, New Zealand and South Africa joined with the thousands of UK evacuees.

This Millennium year coincides with the 60th Anniversary of the work of CORB. The South African group of CORB (SACORB[4]) is celebrating with a reunion in Liverpool on the 23rd August 2000, the 60th anniversary of our embarkation on the *Llanstephan Castle*.[5] In mid-September, the Canadians are planning a reunion at 'Pier 21', their arrival point in Halifax, Nova Scotia.[6]

On the 17th September 2000, at the National Memorial Arboretum, near Lichfield, a plaque will be dedicated and placed beside the tree planted to commemorate the day in 1940 when the *City of Benares* was sunk. This tragedy, when more than 250 lives were lost including 77 evacuees and five escorts, is described on pages 135–145. Details of this Service of Dedication and the ongoing Arboretum Appeal, can be found by contacting David Childs.[7] A grove of trees, which will grow to be a tribute to all Evacuees, has also been planted in the Arboretum.

Looking back, this mass evacuation to distant parts of the UK and abroad does seem 'absurd' and we pray it will never be repeated, but Britain believed her population was in imminent danger of indiscriminate bombing and invasion. Evacuation, despite all it would entail, seemed a desperate but necessary measure. Millions of parents were convinced it was the only way to ensure their children's safety.

Publication of this updated edition of *The Absurd and the Brave* has been arranged to coincide with the 60th anniversary of the CORB evacuations in August and September 1940. In his new foreword, Lord Asa Briggs describes it as a 'rounded social history' so we trust the references and contacts listed below will make it of lasting value.

Our thanks go to Michael Fethney and all those who have contributed to this book.

Margaret Wood (née Banyard)

References

1 *Cape Times*, 26 September 1995
2 Dr Martin Parsons, School of Education, University of Reading, Bulmershe Court, Reading, RG6 1HY.
   Tel: 0118 931 8870   Fax: 0118 931 6804
   e-mail: m.l.parsons@reading.ac.uk
3 Evacuees Reunion Association, (ERA), Secretary, James Roffey, Goodbody's Mill, Retford, Notts., DN22 6JD.
   Tel:/Fax 0177 771 9800
   e-mail: era@evacuees.org.uk
4 'SACORB', Secretary, Ken Humphrey, 11 Crouch Close, Willingdon Village, Eastbourne, E. Sussex, BN20 9EL.
   Tel/Fax: 0132 350 3697
   e-mail: kenhumphrey@compuserve.com
5 After 38 years of continuous service, the *Llanstephan Castle* was sold in 1952 for scrapping.
6 'Pier 21', P.O. Box 611, Halifax, Nova Scotia, B3J 2R7. Canada.
   Tel: 001902 423 7770   Fax: 00190 2423 4045
   e-mail: info@pier21.ns.ca
7 David Childs, Director, National Memorial Arboretum, PO Box 10, Tisbury, Salisbury, SB3 6TH.
   Tel: 01722 716310   Fax: 01722 716839
   e-mail: aboretumnma@waitrose.com

Useful contact addresses

Australia: Paul Farquharson, 17 Allspice Street, Bellbowrie, Queensland, 4070, Australia.
Tel: 00617 3202 6843

Canada: Margaret G. Smolensky (née Beal), 35 Whitehall Road, Toronto, Ontario, M4W 2C5, Canada.
Tel: 00141 6924 6084   e-mail: smolensky@sympatico.ca

New Zealand: Mim Mackisack (née Whitehorn) 27 Westpark Glen, Warkworth, New Zealand.
Tel: 0064 9425 7499   e-mail: mackisacklm@xtra.co.nz

South Africa: See SACORB, ref. 4 above.

UK: See E.R.A. ref. 3 on page 274.

Extensive Documentary and Sound Archives concerning evacuation both within Britain and overseas, are held in the:
Imperial War Museum, Lambeth Road, London, SE1 6HZ. Open - Mon. to Fri. 10.00 am to 5 pm. Admission free.

For access to these records, which is free of charge, contact:-

Keeper of the Department of Documents (at the above address) Tel: 020 7416 5220   Fax: 020 7416 5374 e-mail: docs@iwm.org.uk

Keeper of the Sound Archive (at the above address) Tel: 020 7416 5360   Fax: 020 7416 5379 e-mail: sound@iwm.org.uk

The Museum is always glad to discuss or receive records which may have historical value.

AUTHOR'S NOTES

When acknowledging a quotation from a book for the first time, the author's name is given followed by the title of the book and page number. In subsequent quotations from any book, only the author's name is given followed by the page number. All the books from which quotations are taken appear in the Bibliography on page 288

Explanation of the code letters for documentary sources appears on page 289

Chapter 1

1 R M Titmuss, *Problems of Social Policy* in *History of the Second World War* ed. Hancock, pp 3ff
2 *Hansard* Vol. 293 28/11/34
3 Titmuss pp 29ff
4 DO35/529/B277/4
5 DO35/529/B305/4
6 DO35/529/B305/8
7 DO35/529/B305/8
8 DO35/713/M562/130
9 DO35/529/B305/13
10 DO35/529/B305/13
11 Titmuss p 246

Chapter 2

1 DO131/4 (16/7/40)
2 *The Times* 1/6/40 (In the event he did, to the author and his brother, to whom he was foster-father from Oct 1940 to Feb 1941)
3 *The Times* 1/6/40
4 G Shakespeare, *Let Candles be brought in* p 18
5 G Shakespeare, p 243
6 G Shakespeare, p 244
7 DO131/43 (Appendix I)
8 DO35/688/M213/147 — Memo (10/7/40) from civil servant R F Wiseman. See also CAB67/6(40)152 and DO3/162/M562/14

9 See Appendix I on p 284, and DO131/43, Appendix I
10 DO131/43 Appendix I
11 Shakespeare p 245
12 See Appendix II on pp 285ff
13 CAB65/7/170(40)11
14 CAB65/7/170(40)11
15 Shakespeare p 245
16 Shakespeare p 245
17 CAB65/7/170(40) — (17/6/40)
18 Shakespeare pp 245-6
19 Shakespeare pp 245-6 gives an account of this decision and of Maurice Hankey's gifts in dealing with 'inconclusive discussion' in his time as Cabinet Secretary.
20 See, eg., *The Times* reports for June, 1940
21 DO35/529/B277/4

Chapter 3

1 Shakespeare p 249
2 DO35/713/M562/65 (17/6/40)
3 Shakespeare p 247
4 See Appendix IIIa on p 287
5 See Appendix IIIb on pp 288ff
6 DO131/43
7 DO131/43
8 Shakespeare p 249
9 DO131/43

Chapter 4

1 CAB65/174(40)9 (21/6/40)
2 Shakespeare p 265
3 *The Times* 22/6/40
4 CAB65/174/(40)9 (21/6/40)
5 DO131/2 and DO131/43 both give text of this speech
6 CAB65/189/(40)7 (1/7/40)
7 *The Times* 29/6/40
8 CAB65/189/(40)7 (1/7/40)
9 CAB65/189/(40)7 (1/7/40)
10 CAB65/189/(40)7 (1/7/40)
11 CAB65/189/(40)7 (1/7/40)
12 Shakespeare pp 245-6. The child concerned stayed in Britain.
13 *The Times* 3/7/40

Chapter 5

1 CAB66/8/242 (19/6/40)
2 *The Times* 25/5/40
3 R Collier *1940: The World in Flames* p 128
4 R Collier p 129

5 DO131/4 The civil servant's estimate was that there would be 440,000 children aged between 5 and 14 in 1940. The work was based on the Census of 1931.

6 CAB67/179/(40)7 (6/7/40) Note: In her summary of CORB's work (DO131/43) Marjorie Maxse states that 'mention of the use of fast, unescorted liners was raised several times, the argument being that they would be safer (ie., than ships in convoy), but this view was always rejected "in view of the public criticism that might arise".'

7 CAB67/179/(40)7 (9/7/40)

8 *The Times* 17/7/40

9 The *Arandora Star* was not carrying CORB children as implied in Professor Carlton Jackson's book *Who will take our children?* pp 100-103 because, of course, the CORB scheme was by no means operative yet.

10 *The Times* 17/7/40

11 *The Times* 18/7/40 See, eg., the comment of Mr Lindsay, MP for Kilmarnock, that the scheme was 'not properly thought out'.

12 *The Times* 19/7/40

13 *The Times* 19/7/40

14 W S Churchill *Their Finest Hour* p 570 (footnote)

15 See below Chapter 13, p 153

16 DO131/4 At the meeting of the CORB Advisory Council on 16/7/40, Geoffrey Shakespeare reported the suspension of the scheme because of difficulties over 'proper protection', but said there were 'definite instructions to proceed with all arrangements so that parties might be sent to the Dominions whenever possible.' This was the tenor of the Cabinet decision to suspend on 9/7/40, announced to the House of Commons on 16/7/40. But, whether 'to proceed' meant going so far as to embark and send children overseas before Admiralty clearance about safety was given, is very dubious.

17 DO3/M562/116 (11/7/40) eg., the message from the South African High Commissioner that offers of homes were dropping because of uncertainty about the future of the scheme.

18 DO131/4 (23/7/40)

19 MT9/2234/7 See pp 91-3 below for details of this attack.

20 ADM199/2108

21 ADM199/2165 Naval Intelligence analysis of the Battle of the Atlantic, contained in this document, states that 'July, 1940, marks the beginning of serious attacks on convoys even while anti-submarine vessels were actually present. These ships were still scarce, however, and a large convoy might only have two of them in company.'

Chapter 6

1 See Appendix IV pp 290-1

2 DO131/43 Appendix 6

Chapter 7

1 Meta Maclean *The Singing Ship* pp 5-7

2 See p 7 above

Chapter 8

1 DO131/43 (General Survey part 2)
2 DO131/74
3 Shakespeare p 256
4 DO131/43 (General Survey part 2) See also DO35/713/M562/65
5 DO131/43
6 DO131/3, 4 and 43 (General Survey part 2i, *Policy*)
7 Letter from Miss Finlayson to the author
8 DO131/5 (19/10/40) mentions the case of a Scottish boy rejected by Canadian representatives 'on civil grounds' on 26/8/40. The Scottish CORB Advisory Council complained to the Canadian authorities about this rejection.
9 DO131/43 (General Survey part 7)

Chapter 9

1 Information from Mr Marian Slabosz in conversation with the author, 1981
2 Ditto
3 ADM199/1136
4 Jean Lorimer *Pilgrim Children* p 16
5 Shakespeare p 257
6 Source is a newspaper clipping, unfortunately unnamed and undated and, so far, untraced.
7 Shakespeare p 260

Chapter 10

1 The figure includes two Canadian batches torpedoed (See Chapter 12 below) and one New Zealand batch returned to a British port (See Appendix VIII p 297).
2 See Appendix VIII below
3 MT9/3290
4 DO131/75
5 ADM199/217
6 ADM199/2133
7 ADM199/217
8 ADM199/1941
9 ADM199/1941
10 The *Batory* was carrying batch C1 to Australia. The group was fed on a fable that they were in the largest convoy — 60 ships — yet to leave Britain. On leaving Liverpool, they overtook convoy OB194 destined for Canada with CORB batch D2 in its midst aboard the *Hilary*. The presence of this convoy hid the fact that there were only sixteen ships in the *Batory's* convoy.
11 DO131/75
12 These included Spencer Tracy in *Boy's Town* and Laurel and Hardy in *Swiss Miss*.
13 *The Times* 5/8/40

14 OB = Outward bound from Liverpool or Greenock across the Atlantic and 'fast', ie., up to a speed of about nine knots; OA = Outward bound, but 'slow', ie., up to a speed of about six knots.
15 ADM199/23 (convoy reports, Aug-Oct, 1940)
16 ADM199/23
17 ADM199/23
18 WS = Sailing to West Africa with naval escort
19 ADM199/1136 (6/8/40)
20 ADM199/1136 (6/8/40)
21 ADM199/1136 (15/8/40)
22 ADM199/1136 (7/8/40)
23 ADM199/1136 (2-9/9/40)
24 Appropriately, HMS *Cornwall*, which had orders to hunt the *Pinguin* on leaving the *Batory's* convoy, eventually sank the raider in August, 1941. This was off the coast of Madagascar to which the *Pinguin* had returned after sinking many ships off the Australian coast. Muggenthaler pp 71ff
25 See Chapter 12 below, p 127
26 DO131/15
27 MT9/2234
28 Shakespeare p 259
29 See Meta Maclean, *The Singing Ship* for the full text of the song. (Miss Maclean requested the author not to quote directly from her written work).
30 John is the author's brother. The South African press reported with delight that the C1 CORB children when entertained at a sports stadium by the Mayor of Cape Town and local charities consumed 8,000 oranges, 1,000 apples, 5,000 ice creams and 300 lbs of sweets 'with no serious after effects!'
31 DO131/5
32 Father E Ball *One Man's War*, an unpublished manuscript
33 ADM199/23
34 DO131/15
35 See Chapter 12 below, pp 126ff
36 M Maclean p 107
37 Written by Mr Oats to the author

Chapter 11

1 MT9/3324
2 DO131/3 and 4 deal with the Advisory Council's work in detail.
3 Shakespeare p 254
4 Article by Polly Toynbee, *The Guardian* 10/11/86
5 DO131/43
6 Incident mentioned in Shakespeare p 259. He repeated the incident in Lorimer to which he wrote an introduction. The sentiment is implied in Phyllis Bottome's novel *London Pride* p 26.
7 See Appendix Va and b on p 292
8 DO131/5
9 See Appendix Vc on p 292

10 DO131/4 and 43
11 In conversation with author, 1983
12 DO131/43
13 DO131/3, 4, 23, 29 and 43 give details of CORB's administration
14 DO131/43 (General Survey part 2ii)
15 DO131/51
16 See Chapter 13 below, p 156
17 DO131/72
18 DO131/29
19 See Appendix VI on p 293

Chapter 12

1 ADM199/372 (30/8/40)
2 ADM199/2037
3 ADM199/2134
4 *Yorkshire Evening Post* 5/9/40
5 DO131/5
6 ADM199/2134
7 *Yorkshire Evening Post* 5/9/40
8 ADM199/372
9 The clothing shopping list for the 321 children, most of whom had lost all their day clothes, cost CORB a total of £205/7/2½. DO131/20
10 Shakespeare p 270
11 *Yorkshire Evening Post* 5/9/40
12 DO131/42
13 *The Times* 2/9/40
14 Shakespeare p 269
15 MT9/3461 refers to the matter of rescue ships during the inquiry into loss of life in the sinking of the *City of Benares*. One result of the inquiry was the decision to 'supply special rescue ships' to convoys. See also ADM199/2165 for a discussion of the slow development of naval escort and convoy rescue procedures, July 1940 to January 1941.
16 ADM199/372
17 Part of the introduction to *Atlantic Ordeal* by Elspeth Huxley, one of the original team of selectors at CORB Headquarters.
18 DO131/20
19 DO131/20
20 ADM199/2165
21 See HMSO *Merchant Shipping UK lost by enemy action* for the positions of ships sunk in Aug–Sept, 1940. At least six merchant ships were sunk by U-boats in August, 1940, beyond 21°W, and four of these were beyond 25°W.
22 ADM199/142 and MT9/3461
23 ADM199/2165 records a U-boat attack on a convoy in mid-August, 1940, 'as far out as 27°W.'
24 ADM199/1707
25 ADM199/1707
26 Collier p 242

27 ADM199/1707
28 ADM199/1707
29 E Huxley, passim
30 DO131/79
31 ADM199/142
32 DO131/79
33 See p 145 below
34 ADM199/142 and 2037
35 Letter to author, 1982
36 Quoted in full in *Exodus of Children* p 120, by D E Johnson
37 Recounted by Huxley
38 See Appendix IX p 298
39 DO131/88 The total cost to CORB of providing clothing for evacuees rescued was £19/5/3½. This included toothbrushes and paste.
40 DO131/80
41 DO131/80
42 DO131/80
43 It is a sad reflection of the Government's view of CORB's endeavours (however much Cabinet members might have deprecated the panicky circumstances in which the scheme was born) that Mary Cornish was the only CORB escort to receive any 'official' recognition of her work. The rest of the escorts, including those held as POWs, were even refused the widely, and almost indiscriminately issued, Defence Medal on the grounds that it 'required six months' continuous service to the nation.' See DO131/42

Chapter 13

1 DO131/20 G Shakespeare's notes written after his letter to R H Cross 7/12/40
2 DO131/20 Press notes
3 Widely reported in newspapers 23/9/40
4 DO131/20 Press cuttings, particularly from US and Canadian newspapers
5 DO131/20 Information sent to Miss Maxse at CORB Headquarters by Miss D Neville-Rolfe of the Ministry of Information
6 DO131/20; MT9/3461; ADM199/142 The comments made by Davies, Dean and Nagorski were treated with utmost seriousness by the Admiralty and the Ministry of Shipping.
7 The findings summarized here and on pp 149-151 are in ADM199/142, MT9/3461, DO131/20
8 MT9/3461
9 CAB65/10/254(4)3 When the news first reached the Cabinet on 19/9/40, there was discussion about the advisability of continuing the scheme, but general agreement not to announce the suspension of it when the Ministry of Information released news of the disaster to the public.
10 *Yorkshire Evening Post*, Leader 23/9/40
·11 *Yorkshire Evening Post*, Leader 23/9/40
12 DO131/79

13 Conversation with author, 1983
14 Shakespeare p 274
15 CAB65/10/257(40)6
16 CAB65/10/257(40)6
17 CAB67/8 Letter from G Shakespeare to Home Secretary 25/9/40. Mention of 'Slow convoy' hints at lack of Admiralty/CORB cohesion. No CORB ships sailed in officially designated slow convoys, only in fast convoys. Perhaps the knowledge that the *City of Benares* was sailing well below her top speed led Mr Shakespeare to believe that she sailed in a slow convoy.
18 CAB65/10/261(40)6 (30/9/40)
19a CAB65/10/261(40)6 (30/9/40)
19b The trickle of private evacuation continued; eg., 343 under 18's, and 286, to Canada in 1941 and 1942 respectively. DO131/27.
20 G Shakespeare to Home Secretary 25/9/40 (CAB67/8)
21 Ditto
22 Ditto
23 CAB67/8 Memo from John Anderson, Home Secretary, to Cabinet on ·26/9/40 relating to G Shakespeare's letter of previous day.
24 DO131/5 and ADM199/23
25 DO131/5 and DO131/43 and 75
26 DO131/30
27 See Chapter 15 below, pp 181-5ff
28 ADM199/1941 (No. 380, 21-22/9/40)
29 CAB65/10/261
30 CAB66/12/393

Chapter 14

1   Note: South African reception authorities used the term 'parent-host'; Australian reception authorities used 'custodian', whilst New Zealand and Canadian used CORB's term 'foster-parent', although this had legal and psychological flaws. 'Custodian' was probably the most accurate description of the role, but in this book the more familiar terms 'foster-parent' and 'host/hostess' are most commonly used.
2   Information on pp 160-3; 165-7; and 169-171 comes from DO131/3, 4, 23, 43, 53 and 106-112, as well as from ex-CORB evacuee and host accounts given to the author.
3   See Appendix VII below, pp 295-6
4   'Nominated' and 'un-nominated': all parents of CORB children had the option to nominate a relative or friend whom they would like to host their children.
5   DO131/106-112
6   DO131/106-112
7   DO131/106-112
8   DO131/45 Ms Gutman's article is typed out in this file, but is undated.
9   DO131/43
10 DO131/106 Dr Charlotte Whitton, Director of the Canadian Welfare Council stated that it would cost a foster-parent at least two hundred

dollars a year for food, clothes, medical/dental care, and 'hidden costs' (extra room, bedding, fuel, light, etc) — DO131/45
11 See Chapters 16 and 17 below
12 DO131/32
13 DO131/33

Chapter 15

1   A K Muggenthaler *German Raiders of World War II* p 64
2   Sandbach and Edge *Prison Life on a Pacific Raider* p 98
3   Miss E Pearson's private papers
4   The cargo included 24,881 cases of butter, 32,255 cases of meat, and 23,646 cases of cheese. Captain Eyssen estimated that the butter would provide fifteen and a half million Germans with their weekly ration. — Muggenthaler p 65
5   DO131/16-19
6   Pearson papers
7   See Appendix X below, p 299
8   DO131/16
9   Spy stories appeared, eg., in *Sydney Morning Herald* 4/1/41 and *New Zealand Herald* 6/1/41. Muggenthaler p 73 mentions that German raiders found news bulletins useful for naval and shipping movements.
10 Muggenthaler p 65
11 Pearson papers
12 Sandbach and Edge p 186
13 DO131/16
14 See Chapter 10 above, pp 96-7
15 Muggenthaler p 71
16 See Appendix X below, pp 299
17 DO131/73
18 DO131/76
19 DO131/17-19
20 E Ball, unpublished manuscript

Chapter 16

1   See Chapter 14 above, pp 177-8
2   'Peggy' is not the girl's real name
3   DO131/43
4   DO131/43
5   But see Chapter 17 below: some CORB children suffered educationally
6   Sir Edward sent a letter to all CORB parents explaining the scheme

Chapter 17

1   See Chapter 14 above, pp 168-171
2   DO131/35 and 43
3   See Chapter 14 above, pp 167-8
·4 'Ted' is not the boy's real name
5   Conversation with the author in 1981

6   'Geoffrey' is not the boy's real name
7   DO131/29
8   DO131/106
9   DO131/112
10   DO131/106
11   DO131/111
12   DO131/106
13   See Chapter 14 above, p 170
14   Letter to the author from the ex-CORB girl concerned
15   DO131/3 and 68
16   DO131/107-110
17   DO131/43
18   DO131/106-112
19   Mentioned in Chapter 16 above, p 199
20   DO131/94
21   DO131/43

Chapter 18

1   DO131/28
2   DO131/28
3   DO131/33 — a long and detailed report
4   DO131/33
5   DO131/34
6   DO131/34
7   DO131/112
8   DO131/106
9   Conversation with author in 1983
10   Shakespeare p 274

Chapter 19

1   DO131/27 and 43
2   Peter is right: CORB could not consider adoption without written
     agreement of the next-of-kin.

Chapter 20

1   DO131/27
2   DO131/27 See Appendix XII below, p 301, for the summary of statistics
     Miss Maxse presented to the Council.
3   DO131/27
4   Conversations between Kyrsty Page and author in 1982
5   See Chapter 17 above, pp 206-7
6   See Appendix XII summary below, p 301, and DO131/27

Chapter 21

1   On Professor Hancock's invitation, Miss Maxse wrote a summary of fifty
     foolscap pages for his official history of non-military aspects of World

War II. He compressed this into three pages of his book. See DO131/43 for her work.

2 G Wagner *Children of the Empire* p 251
3 Padley and Cole *Evacuation Survey*, Chapter 16
4 Conversation with author, 1983
5 Shakespeare p 243 (and see Chapter 2 above, p 33)
6 S Isaacs *Cambridge Evacuation Survey*, Appendix 2
7 Isaacs — Memorandum on practical recommendations
8 Padley and Cole Chapter 16
9 Ditto
10 S L Strachey *Borrowed Children* p 96
11 T O'Brien *Civil Defence* Appendix 2 in Hancock's *History of the Second World War*
12 Shakespeare p 331
13 Shakespeare p 244
14 Conversation with author
15 DO131/43
16 See Chapter 20 above, p 249
17 Anthony Bailey *America: Lost and Found*
18 Bailey — p 150-1
19 Conversations with author
20 Ditto
21 DO131/70 — After seeking civil servants' advice, Miss Ellen Wilkinson gave this as the final verdict of the Ministry of Education: 'Any enquiry such as is suggested would involve a great deal of labour which would not be commensurate with the results that would accrue.'
22 DO131/43

Appendices

1 DO131/43
2 DO131/43
3 Shakespeare p 248
4 DO131/3
5 DO131/43 Appendix 7
6 DO131/106, 111 and 112
7 DO131/29
8 DO131/10-14
9 DO131/5, 42, 43, 75 and ADM199 series (individual ships catalogue)
10 DO131/20 and 113
11 DO131/16, 17 and 18
12 Several copies kindly sent to author by former evacuee host families
13 DO131/43 — (facsimile)
14 DO131/113
15 DO131/106 (Australia); DO131/107-110 (Canada); DO131/111 (New Zealand); DO131/112 (South Africa).

BIBLIOGRAPHY

Bailey A *America: Lost and Found.* Faber & Faber, 1981.
Bennett J W *John Anderson, Viscount Waverley.* Macmillan, 1962.
Body A H *Children in Flight.* ULP, 1940.
Bottome P *London Pride.* Faber & Faber, 1941.
Calder A *The People's War.* Jonathan Cape, 1969.
Churchill W S *The Second World War, Vol II, Their Finest Hour.* Cassell, 1949.
Collier R *1940: The World in Flames.* Penguin, 1980.
Graves C *Women in Green.* Heinemann, 1948.
HMSO *Merchant Shipping, UK, Lost by Enemy Action.* 1947.
Huxley E *Atlantic Ordeal.* Chatto & Windus, 1941.
Isaacs S (Ed.) *The Cambridge Evacuation Survey.* Methuen, 1941.
Jackson C *Who will take our Children?.* Methuen, 1985.
Johnson B S *The Evacuees.* V Gollancz, 1968.
Johnson D *Exodus of Children.* Pennyfarthing Publications, 1985.
Lorimer J *Pilgrim Children.* F Muller, 1942.
Maclean M *The Singing Ship.* Angus & Robertson, 1941.
Madge C *War Begins at Home.* (Mass Observation). Chatto & Windus, 1940.
Muggenthaler A K *German Raiders of World War II.* Robert Hale, 1978.
O'Brien T *Civil Defence.* (In *History of Second World War* Ed. Hancock). HMSO & Longmans, 1950.
Padley & Cole *Evacuation Survey.* Routledge, 1940.
Perry C *Boy in the Blitz.* Leo Cooper, 1972.
Sandbach & Edge *Prison Life on a Pacific Raider.* Hodder, 1941.
Shakespeare G *Let Candles be Brought In.* Macdonald, 1949.
St Leo Strachey *Borrowed Children.* Murray, 1940.
Taylor A J P *English History, 1914-1945.* OUP, 1965.
Titmuss R M *Problems of Social Policy.* (In *History of Second World War* Ed. Hancock) HMSO & Longmans, 1950.
Wagner G *Children of the Empire.* Weidenfeld & Nicolson, 1982.
Wicks B *No Time to Wave Goodbye.* Bloomsbury, 1988.
Wicks B *The Day They Took the Children.* Bloomsbury, 1989.

DOCUMENTARY SOURCES

AVAILABLE IN THE PUBLIC RECORD OFFICE, KEW, SURREY,
UNLESS OTHERWISE STATED.

ADM (Admiralty) 199 series, files 17; 23; 142; 372; 1136; 1941; 2037; 2108; 2133; 2134; 2165.
CAB (Cabinet) 65, 66 and 67 series for May-October, 1940.
DO (Dominions Office) 3 series, (Messages/Communications, May-October, 1940).
DO 35 series, ('M' = Migration, and 'B' = Defence files for 1940).
DO 131 series, (the CORB files, indexed and titled, Nos. 1 to 113).
MT (Ministry of Transport) 9 series, files 3290; 3324; 3355; 3461.
Hansard 'Parliamentary Debates', 1934, 1938, 1939, 1940.
Minutes of Leeds City Education Committee, 1940, in Leeds City Reference Room.
The Times; *Yorkshire Evening Post* in Leeds City Reference Room.
Private Papers kindly made available to the author:
The Diaries of Dorothy Loft and Gwen Staynes; Eleanor Pearson's Collection, (by kind permission of her sister, Mrs M I Cross); *One Man's War*, an unpublished MS by Fr E Ball, SSM, (by kind permission of the writer and his Father Superior, Fr Edmund Wheat, SSM).
I owe my thanks to the Staff of the Public Record Office at Kew and of the Leeds City Reference Library for their help and advice about documents, and to the Staff of the Harrogate Reference Library for tracing many books long out of print.

Other Sources

My thanks to all the following for sharing their experiences and thoughts:
Former Evacuees: Mrs W M Alder (née Harris); Mrs M Auburn (née Freedman); K P Austin; Mrs B N Atkins (née Hooper); G Budgern; R C Bullard; P D Beams; Mrs B Browne (née Turner); Mrs C D Caine (née Fletcher); Mrs J F Carr (née Dixon); C G Crafer; E V Crozier; Mrs G Campbell (née Robb); Mrs F M J Clarkson (née Godfrey); J A Cruddas; Mrs E Davidson (née Chase); Mrs J Dorman (née Clout); G K J Doughty; G A Eccles; Miss M Evans; Mrs N Fernie (née Lupton); Rev J G Fethney; Mrs J Flewers (née Hare); Mrs M D Forster (née England); Miss T Freedman; D H Furnish; Mrs D M P Fisher (née Magrath, evacuated by CORB to India); Mrs J Frost (née Godfrey); J F Hare; R Harris; Mrs J Hay

(née Board); Mrs J M Hazeldon (née Briant); J Hillier; R C Harris; A F Hedgecock; Mrs F Isherwood (née Stout); Mrs R Jackson (née Patterson); Mrs B Jeffrey (née Deeley); Mrs E Jenkins (née Wheatley); G Jepson; Mrs D Laing (née Loft); Mrs A Lowes (née Bradley); Mrs B Murray (née Mallett); Mrs J Morton (née Cheyne); Rev A H Macleod; W Nicholson; Mrs B D Nizette (née Clarke); Mrs B Neal (née Hamilton); Mrs E O'Connor (née Kershaw); Mrs R Oxberry (née Udy); K A Parker; M A Pike; Mrs R Rawson (née Jones); Mrs J Singleton (née Cole); N Standage; Mrs M W Smith (née McKeon); Rev R Smith; Mrs G Staynes (née Laycock); Rev G D Staff; Mrs C G Turner (née Webster); J Udy; Mrs R Waters (née Burder); Mrs H Walls (née Johnston); D G Webster; P J Wilde; J Wood; and the following who were evacuated privately overseas: R D Gilbert; Mrs S Ivinson (née Kniveton); R S M Ling; Mrs E D Watson (née Alway).

Some twenty other ex-CORB evacuees also kindly supplied information, some of it very detailed, but I have not named them in deference to their wishes. The request for anonymity was almost always made in order to avoid hurting relatives or foster-parents. If anyone is surprised not to have been mentioned by name, either in the above list or in the text of the book, it will be because I have tried to err on the side of preserving anonymity where a person's instructions on the matter were at all in doubt. If, on the other hand, anyone is surprised to have been named who did not wish to be, I apologize: it will be because of an unintended lapse.

Parents of former CORB evacuees: Mrs E Churchman; Mrs V M Dixon; Mrs M L Fethney; Mrs G Hedgecock; Mrs M Hume; Mrs M Latham; Mrs E Penwarden; Mrs E M Purdy; Mrs F Sharp; Mrs F G Spence; Mrs M Webster.

Former Hosts Overseas: Mr & Mrs E Browne, Mr C D Denney; Mr & Mrs K W Cooper; Mrs D M Dryden; Mr & Mrs R Dickinson; Mrs G Eastwood; Mrs E D Ede; Mrs F Elkins; Mrs R K Fairbairn; Mrs R Gofsky; Mrs J (Pippy) Graham, daughter of former hosts Mr & Mrs Pippy; Mr & Mrs R Goddard; Mrs R M Goyen; Mrs E Gill; Mr & Mrs R Lucas; Mrs G Millin; Mrs E Scott Miller; Mrs J R Osbaldiston; Mrs E Pease; Mrs M Rhind; Mrs M Steeds; Mrs D Taylor; Miss R G Turner daughter of former hosts; Mrs C Thornton; Miss S Trites; Mrs F Webster; Mr D Willock, son of former hosts.

Former CORB Escorts (unless otherwise indicated): Mrs D Berringer (Home escort); Mrs E Clothier; Brig. V Chalmers (Salvation Army); Mrs G M Conquest (née Macpherson); Mrs B Daley; Mrs Elspeth Davies (Welfare Director, CORB Headquarters Staff, London); Miss G B Finlayson (assistant at Glasgow CORB hostel); Miss E R Golding (CORB ship's nurse); Miss E Gray; Mr & Mrs S Kociucki (Catering staff, *MS Batory*); Mrs N K Lewis (née Belgrove); Mrs D McClelland (née Close); Miss R Morton; Mr W N Oats; Miss K Page (ship's escort & CORB liaison officer, New Zealand, 1941-46); Lt Col D N Rendell (Salvation Army); Mrs E M Slassor; Mr M Slabosz (Assistant Purser *MS Batory*).

APPENDIX I[1]

MEMBERS OF THE INTER-DEPARTMENTAL COMMITTEE
CONVENED ON 7 JUNE, 1940, TO PLAN A GOVERNMENT
OVERSEAS EVACUATION SCHEME:

Mr Geoffrey Shakespeare, MP, Under-Secretary for Dominion Affairs, Chairman.

Miss Florence Horsbrugh, MP, Parliamentary Secretary to Ministry of Health.

Mr J Chuter Ede, MP, Parliamentary Secretary to the Board of Education.

Civil servants representing various Government Departments were:

Mr R A Wiseman and Mr C W Dixon both of the Dominions Office.

Mr L G Duke and Mr H A Montmorency both of the Ministry of Health.

Mr E A Hogan of the Scottish Department of Health.

Mr A P Sharam of the Board of Education.

Mr J W Parker of the Scottish Board of Education.

Mr B W Gilbert of the Treasury.

Mr F J Ralfe of the Home Office.

Mr T M Snow and Prof. T N Whitehead both of the Foreign Office.

Mr P H Brind of the Ministry of Labour & National Service.

Miss M S Cox of the Ministry of Pensions.

The Hon. J G Simon and Mr F H Norman both of the Ministry of Shipping.

Mr J P Dodds and Mr G Kimber both of the Dominions Office, Secretaries.

APPENDIX II[2]

SUMMARY OF THE REPORT (Cmd 6213) OF GEOFFREY
SHAKESPEARE'S INTER-DEPARTMENTAL COMMITTEE —
DISCUSSED BY WAR CABINET, 17 JUNE, 1940:

Committee's brief was to consider the offers made from overseas 'to care for
children from the European war zone residing in Great Britain.' At this
Committee stage, the scheme was intended to cover Allied refugee children
then in Britain, as well as British children. The Report recommended:

1. Children would not finally be approved for evacuation by CORB until
   they had passed the medical tests required and approved by 'the receiving
   Governments'. (This provision was written into the scheme to ensure that
   no child would be returned on medical grounds after arrival in a
   Dominion).

2. Shipping facilities would be investigated by the Ministry of Shipping. The
   Committee expressed the view that 'it should be possible to arrange
   passages for a considerable number of children without any alteration in
   the present schedules of shipping.' (Events proved this a wildly over-
   optimistic forecast. The phrase 'considerable number of children' shows
   that the early intention of the Committee was to evacuate large numbers
   of children — a ridiculous concept).

3. 'Certain risks must attend travel by sea,' said the Report, especially as the
   Committee was agreed that the Nazis would 'continue the war in an
   unprincipled manner.' But, such risks, they decided, must simply be
   weighed 'against the risks of attacks upon this country.' (Once CORB was
   set up, this emphasis on the risks remained part of official policy, with
   reminders to parents that they alone could decide the issue).

4. Financing the scheme: the Report was adamant that there should be
   'no direct financial transactions' between the evacuees' parents and the
   receiving families, though parents were to help defray costs of the scheme,
   paying nine shillings (forty five pence) per week if children were in state
   schools — towards 'the billeting costs'. (This was reduced to six shillings
   per week when the scheme started). Parents of other children were to pay
   'a somewhat larger contribution' at CORB's discretion. The cost of
   shipping was to be met by the British Government. (In the event, the
   financial aspect of the Report led to much controversy and confusion
   early in 1941 when parents of CORB children discovered that, their
   payments having been refused by three of the four Dominions involved,
   instead of helping with 'billeting costs', were being diverted by the British
   Government to help pay general costs of the scheme. This upset illustrated
   that the planners had not thought through the financial ramifications as
   thoroughly as they might have done).

5. Children accepted by CORB would be aged between five and fifteen

inclusive. The age of five was considered the lowest at which children could reasonably be separated from parents. No parents were to be allowed to accompany their children 'for the time being', although it was hoped that war widows might later receive special consideration. (The scheme was permanently suspended before any war widows had been selected for CORB evacuation).

6. The upper age limit of fifteen was easily determined: emigration laws operating in 1940 forbade anyone aged sixteen to sixty to leave Britain, unless making a journey 'of national importance'. The only permitted exception was that of mothers accompanying young children abroad.

7. Children from any part of the British Isles were to be eligible for inclusion in the scheme, though it was agreed that if large numbers of applications were received preference would be given to children from 'vulnerable areas.'

8. The Report recommended the adoption of a 'nomination' scheme. (On first arriving overseas, sixty three per cent of the CORB evacuees went to 'nominated' homes. But, it was soon being admitted privately, both by CORB Headquarters and welfare workers overseas, that the nomination aspect of the scheme had done nothing beyond reassuring the parents left behind. Some of the happiest placements involved children sent to complete strangers; and some of the unhappiest of all were in nominated homes).

9. It was to prove a serious oversight that the planners made no mention at all in this Report of legal guardianship matters.

APPENDIX IIIa[3]

APPENDIX IIIb[4]

REPRESENTATIVES ATTENDING THE INAUGURAL MEETING OF
CORB'S ADVISORY COUNCIL ON THE 18/6/40:

Lord Snell, CBE, Ll.D., who took over the Chair from G Shakespeare.
Miss Florence Horsbrugh, MP, Parliamentary Secretary, Ministry of Health.
Mr J Chuter Ede, MP, Parliamentary Secretary, Board of Education.
Mr J Westwood, MP, Parliamentary Under-Secretary for Scotland.
Miss Ellen Wilkinson, MP, Parliamentary Secretary, Ministry of Pensions.
E R Appleton, Founder of the Silent Fellowship.
Cyril Bavin, OBE, Secretary, Community Services, YMCA, (later CORB's
   liaison officer in New Zealand then, from March, 1941, in Australia).
Rev John Bennett, Catholic Council for British Settlement Overseas.
Countess of Bessborough, Chairman of Council of Society for the Overseas
   Settlement of British Women.
Miss Grace Browning, Commissioner for Kindred Associations, The Girl
   Guides Association.
Laurence Cadbury, OBE, Chairman of Cadbury's, (with a known interest in
   school and welfare affairs).
Lt Col Culshaw, Salvation Army Headquarters Staff, London.
Miss E Doggett, OBE, League of Empire.
Miss E Evans, Principal, Glamorgan Training College.
Capt. G F Gracey, General Secretary, Save the Children Fund.
Gordon Green, Secretary, Fairbridge Farm Schools.
W A F Hepburn, OBE, MC, Ll.D., Director of Education, Argyle.
Rev. S W Hughes, General Secretary, National Free Church Council.
Canon H E Hyde, C of E Advisory Council for Empire Settlement.
Miss M F Jobson, JP, Fife County Council Education Committee.
Miss E A Jones, MA, Headmistresses' Association.
P J Kirkpatrick, General Superintendent, Barnardo's Homes.
Harold Legat, Boy Scouts' Association.
Rt Hon. Sir Ronald Lindsay, GCB, GCMG, CVO, British Ambassador to
   Washington, 1930-39.
W A Markham, MA, Member of Executive, National Children's Homes.
Mrs Montagu Norman, Vice-chairman, WVS.
Mrs E V Parker, Ex-President, National Union of Teachers.
Donald Paterson, MD, FRCP, Physician, Children's Hospital, Great Ormond
   Street. *Miss Gladys Pott*, CBE, Ex-Chairman, Council of Society for
   Overseas Settlement of British Women.

Brendan Quin, Assistant Secretary, 1820 Memorial Settlers' Association.
Sir W Reardon Smith, Bt, Director of Shipping Companies.
Miss Edith Thompson, MBE, Chairman of Executive, Society for Overseas
    Settlement of British Women, (later CORB's liaison officer in South
    Africa).

APPENDIX IV[5]

CORB'S 'SUGGESTED OUTFIT FOR EACH CHILD UNDERTAKING THE JOURNEY':

BOYS
Gas Mask
1 overcoat & mackintosh if possible
1 suit
1 pullover
1 hat or school cap
2 shirts (coloured)
2 pairs stockings
2 undervests
2 pairs pants
2 pairs pyjamas
1 pair boots or shoes
1 pair plimsolls

6 handkerchiefs
1 comb
1 toothbrush and paste
1 face flannel or sponge
1 towel
1 suitcase — about 26" x 18"
Stationery and pencil
Ration card
Identity card
Birth Certificate (if possible)
Bible or New Testament

GIRLS
Gas Mask
1 warm coat & mackintosh if possible
1 cardigan or woollen jumper
1 hat or beret
1 pair warm gloves
1 warm dress or skirt & jumper
2 pairs stockings
1 change of underclothes, including vests, knickers, etc.
1 pair strong boots or shoes
1 pair plimsolls
2 cotton dresses or overalls with knickers
2 pairs pyjamas
1 towel
6 handkerchiefs
1 hairbrush and comb
1 toothbrush and paste
1 face flannel or sponge
Sanitary towels
1 linen bag
1 suitcase — about 26" x 18"
1 attaché case or haversack
Sewing outfit
Stationery and pencil
Ration card
Identity card
Birth Certificate (if possible)
Bible or New Testament

NO trunk will be permitted. All clothing should be clearly marked in indelible ink . . .

Note: The above list was issued to parents of children departing for Canada. The list for those bound for Australia, New Zealand and South Africa varied slightly, requiring the addition of 1 pair of khaki knickers (sic) for boys, 1 panama hat for boys, 2 towels (both boys and girls, instead of 1), 1 shady hat for girls, 1 swimming suit (boys), 1 bathing costume and cap (girls), — and omitted mention of any 'pants' (ie., underpants) for the boys.

APPENDIX V[6]

THE HOME BACKGROUND OF CORB EVACUEES:

(a) The attempts of CORB's selectors to give preference to 'average, normal families' were successful, as evidenced in 1,074 CORB children's record cards closely examined — (those of the 577 evacuated to Australia, the 202 evacuated to New Zealand, and 295 of those evacuated to South Africa). Over 460 of these 1,074 children had fathers engaged in manual occupations. These 460 include 40 whose fathers are described simply as 'labourer', 8 as 'docker' and 13 as 'miner'. The figure also includes 17 bus drivers, 5 trolley bus drivers, and 121 children whose fathers are described as engineers, tool-makers, fitters and 'electrical workers'. The fathers of another 59 children are listed as 'clerks', and a further 38 as 'civil servant', most of whom were probably clerks as well.

(b) In the relatively higher salaried occupations, as might be expected, the figures are considerably lower. Of the 1,074 children, 4 had fathers who were doctors, 4 dentists, 3 ministers of religion (middle class, rather than higher income), 2 architects, and 9 accountants. These 22 'professional' fathers between them sent only 36 of the 1,074 children whose record cards were examined. Similarly, the total of 26 schoolmaster parents sent only 35 children.

(*Note*: Some of the occupations mentioned point to changes in recent social patterns. In addition to the 5 trolley bus drivers, there was a 'mantle manufacturers' manager', a 'sailmaker', a 'Gas Co Hand', and two described as 'railway fire-dropper'.)

(c) The extent of Miss Power's success in selecting from 'vulnerable areas' is illustrated in these figures compiled for the Public Accounts Committee in March, 1941. Of the 3,075 children who set sail for overseas with CORB, 278 came from Middlesex; 258 from Glasgow; 209 from Essex; 148 from Middlesborough; 143 from Kent; 125 from London; 94 from Durham; 78 from Grimsby; 75 from Lancashire; and 62 from Darlington.

The proportion of children evacuated from the south-east of England is fairly reasonable. But the numbers from Grimsby and Darlington are surprisingly high, especially considering that nearby Hull and Newcastle-on-Tyne sent such small numbers as not to be mentioned in the report at all. Similarly, the Lancashire number is very small, considering that Manchester and Liverpool were beginning to receive heavy bombing whilst the CORB scheme was in operation.

APPENDIX VI[7]

FACTS PRESENTED TO THE PUBLIC ACCOUNTS COMMITTEE
OF THE BRITISH TREASURY IN MARCH, 1941:

The following information is from a long report presented by CORB's
Director-General, Mr Arthur Mullins. The presentation of the report was
somewhat delayed, as the Committee agreed to wait until Mr Mullins had
recovered from the injuries and shock he sustained in a London air-raid the
previous summer.

Salaries and travel expenses had totalled £38,176/8/8. To this, he pointed
out, should be added a further £22,372 in salaries to civil servants loaned to
CORB, but paid by the Department which loaned them. He suggested that
the total cost of salaries looked disproportionately high for the relatively
small number of children safely evacuated by CORB: 1,532 had arrived
safely in Canada; 577 in Australia; 353 in South Africa; and 202 in New
Zealand. (A further 838 had gone to the USA under the auspices of the US
Committee for the Evacuation of European Children — 'with the
collaboration of CORB', but not, of course, in any way under CORB's
jurisdiction or responsibility.)

Mr Mullins stressed that the high salaries bill sprang from the need to
employ 620 staff, 'the size of machine necessary to cope with the public's
unforeseen' response to the CORB scheme.

Apart from salaries, other CORB costs were remarkably low: Local
Authority expenses: £1,132/16/5; hostel expenses in Glasgow and Liverpool:
£2,835/3/7; payment of allowances to CORB ship escorts: £8,067/17/3. Even
the amount paid to the Ministry of Shipping for the children's voyages to the
Dominions and, in most escorts' cases, for the two-way journey, was not
exorbitant: £52,756 for the children; £15,007 for the escorts.

Furthermore, receipts were accruing all the time, reported Mr Mullins:
£14,917/1/11 from parents; and many goodwill gifts, notably £7,500 from
the Nawab of Bahawalpur and £25,000 from the Fiji Government.

Of the 211,448 applications received by CORB during the two weeks that applications were accepted, 199,746 were on behalf of children in state schools.

APPENDIX VII[8]

GUARDIANSHIP LEGISLATION PERTAINING TO CORB EVACUEES:

(i) In Britain, The Temporary Migration of Children (Guardianship) Act of June, 1941 — made the Secretary of State for the Dominions responsible for agreeing the guardians for children overseas. 'Children' meant 'under sixteen years of age'. The Act was to apply to children who had left the UK before the passing of the Act, provided they were not accompanied by parents.

(ii) In Australia, The National Security (Overseas Children) Regulations, 1939 and 1940 — appointed the Minister for the Interior the guardian of all overseas children, a position he automatically delegated to the Child Welfare authorities in all states except Western Australia and Tasmania, where the delegation was to Overseas Children's Reception Committees.

(iii) In New Zealand, the British Children's Emergency Regulations, 1940 — placed all evacuees under the care of the Superintendent of Child Welfare, an officer of the National Department of Education.

(iv) In South Africa, The Control and Care of Overseas Children Regulations, 1940 - appointed the Minister of Social Welfare the children's guardian, with the specified assistance of the National Advisory Committee of the Overseas Children's Administration, and with the regulation that local magistrates should exercise jurisdiction over the local reception committees.

(v) The Canadian position remained uncertain until August, 1941. By that time, several Canadian surgeons had performed appendectomies on their own initiative. One of these cases involved a girl with peritonitis who was very seriously ill. Fortunately for the surgeons as well as the patients, all operations had a happy outcome. In August, 1941, Mr Clement Attlee, now British Secretary of State for the Dominions, used the powers he had under the Temporary Migration of Children Act to nominate the UK High Commissioner in Ottawa (Mr Malcolm MacDonald, co-founder of the Inter-Departmental Committee that planned CORB) as legal guardian of CORB children in Canada.

(vi) By the summer of 1941, CORB was embarrassed by enthusiastic discussions overseas about the permanent adoption of overseas children, particularly in the event of their being orphaned as a result of enemy action. However, Mrs Jennie Adamson, Parliamentary Secretary to the British Ministry of Pensions, came to CORB's rescue. She announced to the press on the 27 June, 1941: 'We shall not consider any adoption until after the war,' and proceeded to make clear that, until then, the British Government would say 'No' to any requests for permanent adoption, whether at home or overseas.

(vii) A serious loophole observed in the area of guardianship, and never legally resolved, was this. The various Acts at home and abroad defined 'children' as being 'under sixteen', simply because that covered all CORB children at the time they left Britain. But, who was legally their guardian after that age? Fortunately, the question was not often asked. When it was, the various delegated authorities in the Dominions were brave enough to assume that they were, and acted accordingly. A CORB decision made in 1943 supported this action: 'If pressed, CORB would argue that the delegated authority was responsible up to the age of twenty one.'

APPENDIX VIII[9]

THE CORB SHIPS OF 1940:

(*Note*: There is no complete list of ships and CORB batches in the CORB files. This information has had to be compiled from various sources, mostly Admiralty files which, again, are not complete.)

Ship	Sailed	Convoy	Arrived	Evacs. Abroad		Escorts Aboard	Code
Anselm	21/7/40	OB189	3/8/40	39B	43G	1Dr, 2N, 7Esc	D1
Hilary	6/8/40	OB194	?	70B	84G	1Dr, 2N, 12Esc	D2
Batory	5/8/40	WS2(f/s)	16/10/40	477 total		2Dr, 1de, 10N, 38E	C1
Oronsay	10/8/40	ZA	21/8/40	187B	166G	2Dr, 4N, 29Esc	D8
Antonia	10/8/40	ZA	21/8/40	145B	139G	1Dr, 3N, 21Esc	D5
Duchess of York	10/8/40	ZA	21/8/40	256B	238G	2Dr, 5N, 36Esc	D7
Bayano	16/8/40	OB199	28/8/40	45B	44G	1Dr, 2N, 7Esc	D3
Ruahine	16/8/40	OB199	27/9/40	58B	31G	— 2N, 7Esc	Z1
Llanstephan Castle	24/8/40	OB203	20/9/40	308 total		2Dr, 6N, 23Esc	U1
Nestor	24/8/40	OB203	20/10/40	82 total		— 2N, 8Esc	C2
Volendam	28/8/40	OB205	Torpedoed	320 total		2Dr, 3N, 26Esc	D10
Rangitata	28/8/40	OB205	3/10/40	113 total		1Dr, 2N, 12Esc	Z2
Nerissa	8/9/40	OB210	?	16B	18G	— 1N, 3Esc	D12
Newfoundland	8/9/40	OB210	?	4B	7G	— 1N, —	D?
?	8/9/40	OB210	6/10/40	26B	19G	1N, 3Esc?	D?
City of Paris	10/9/40	?	13/10/40	45 total		1Dr, 1N, 5Esc?	U2
City of Benares	13/9/40	OB213	Torpedoed	47B	43G	1Dr, 1N, 6Esc	D11
Diomed	17/9/40	OB215	?	18 total		?	C3
Nova Scotia	21/9/40	OB217	3/10/40	29 total		1N, 1Esc	D?

Note: The CORB ships' code = D for (Dominion of) Canada; C for (Commonwealth of) Australia; U for (Union of) South Africa; and Z for New Zealand.

In addition to the ships listed above, D4 and D9 did not sail; similarly, C4 boarded the *Largs Bay* and U3 the *Llandaff Castle*, only to disembark after the sinking of the *City of Benares*, and Z3 sailed aboard the *Rangitane*, returning some hours later to disembark. Thirty-seven children were also disembarked from the *City of Simla* which was sunk early on 21 September.

APPENDIX IX[10]

CORB SURVIVORS FROM THE *CITY OF BENARES* DISASTER:

Escorts: Miss Marjorie Day (chief escort); Miss Mary Cornish, BEM; Fr D O'Sullivan; Mrs Lillian Towns.

Children: Rescued by *HMS Hurricane* — John Baker, 7; Elizabeth Cummings, 14; Jack Keeley, 8; Rex Thorne, 13; Bessie Walder, 15, and Louis Walder, 10; Eleanor Wright, 13. Rescued by *HMS Anthony* — Derek Capel, 12; Howard Clayton, 11; Paul Shearing, 12; Kenneth Sparks, 13; Harry Steel, 11; Billy Short, 9.

THOSE LOST IN THE DISASTER:

Escorts: Miss Sybil Gilliat-Smith; Nurse Dorothy Smith; Mr Michael Rennie; Dr Margaret Zeal; Rev. William H King.

Children: Elizabeth Allan; Robert Baker; Kathleen Barrett; Vera, Phyllis, and Edna Beesley; Michael Brooker; Enid Butlin; Alan Capel; James and Lewis Came; Beryl and Derek Carr; Sheila and Michael Chase; Geoffrey Crawford; Pauline and Sheila Crawley; Cynthia Dadds; Maureen Dixon; Derek and Christopher Goodfellow; Augusta, Violet, Constance, Edward and Leonard Grimond; Patricia and James Harrington; Bruce and Jeffrey Hillyard; Terence Holmes; Joan and Florence Irving; Peter Langdon-Lloyd; Derek Leigh; Audrey Mansfield; Robin Miller; Phillip Mollard; William Moon; Aileen, Marion and Rita Moss; Ailsa Murphy; Audrey Muncey; Beryl Myatt; Dorothy and Patricia Nolan; John Pemberton; Roger Poole; John, Charles and Donald Pugh; Anita and William Rees; Colenso Rodda; Leighton Ryman; Edith and Irene Smith; Henry Smoolovitch; Joan and James Spencer; Rosemary and John Spencer-Davies; June and Anthony Taylor; Marion Thorne; Betty Unwin; Gordon Walsh; Thomas and Ann Watson.

APPENDIX X[11]

CORB ESCORTS SUNK DURING RETURN VOYAGES ABOARD
SS RANGITANE AND *SS PORT WELLINGTON*:

Rangitane — Killed during the raider attack, or died owing to injuries: Miss Beeston; Mrs Davies; Mr Dixon; Miss Herbert-Jones; Miss Scott; Mr Tocher. Survivors: Miss Alston (went to India); Mrs Clothier (returned to England); Miss da Costa (stayed in Australia); Fr Kelly (stayed in Australia); Miss Osborne (stayed in Australia); Miss Pearson (stayed in Australia); Misses Matthews and Mundie (both seriously injured in the attack), and Nurses Child, Dunsmuir, Edge, Golding, Sandbach, and Willis (all returned to UK); Fr Ball (held as POW).

Port Wellington — Brigadier and Mrs Best, Majors Sharp and MacKenzie (all Salvation Army Officers), Miss Fieldgate (subsequently died during imprisonment); Mrs Fox; Mrs Maclean; Miss Wood: (all were held POW).

APPENDIX XI[12]

QUEEN'S LETTER OF THANKS SENT TO ALL HOST-FAMILIES
WHO ENTERTAINED CORB EVACUEES IN THE DOMINIONS:

*'I wish to mark, by this personal message, my gratitude for the help
and kindness which you have shown to the children who crossed the
sea from the United Kingdom many months ago. Since the early days
of the War, you have opened your doors to strangers and offered to
share your home with them. In the kindness of your heart, you have
accepted them as members of your own family, and I know that to
this unselfish task you and all your household have made many great
sacrifices. By your generous sympathy you have earned the true and
lasting gratitude of those to whom you have given this hospitality,
and by your understanding you have shown how strong is the bond
uniting all those who cherish the same ideals.*

Elizabeth'

APPENDIX XII √3 COPY OF INFORMATION SUMMARY PRESENTED BY MISS MARJORIE MAXSE TO EACH MEMBER AT THE LAST MEETING OF CORB'S ADVISORY COUNCIL, FEBRUARY, 1946:-

CHILDREN'S OVERSEAS RECEPTION SCHEME

POSITION at 14th FEBRUARY, 1946

POSITION	EVACUATED from U.K. (including additions overseas)	WITHDRAWN from SCHEME				RETURNED to U.K. (or about to return)	REMAINING OVERSEAS			
		DIED	MARRIED	JOINED by PARENTS	PARENTS making own ARRANGE-MENTS		TEMPORARILY to complete course or training or until fit to travel	SETTLING irrespective of parents' plans	SETTLING if joined by parents	SERVING in DOMINION FORCES
CANADA	1,535 (1)	4 (6)	5	14	24	1,326	18 (7)	34	54	56 (9)
AUSTRALIA	578 (2)	2 (6)	3	3	11	446	15 (8)	14	62	20 (9)
SOUTH AFRICA	353 (3)	–	1	9	3	284	16	4	14	24 (9)
NEW ZEALAND	204 (4)	1	1	2	3	153	3	10	29	2 (9)
TOTAL	2,670 (5)	7	10	28	41	2,209	52	62	159	102 (9)

(1) 1532 + 3 added after arrival in Canada

(2) 577 - 1 transferred to New Zealand

(3) 353 + 2 added after arrival in S. Africa

(4) 202 + 1 transferred from Australia + 1 added after arrival in New Zealand

(5) 2,664 + 6 added overseas.

(6) 1 killed in action - 1 missing believed killed.

(7) 2 for health reasons

(8) 1 " " "

(9) Some already demobilised. At some time in 1945, the numbers were as high as:-

Canada 69 - Australia 35 - South Africa 39
New Zealand 3 - Total 146

APPENDIX XIII[14]

ADULT ESCORTS ON CORB SHIPS, 1940:

Note: On receiving an application to serve, CORB Headquarters staff opened a file and allocated a number to the applicant. The following list is given in CORB's file number order. With the exception of the seventeen names at the end of the list, all CORB escort files were destroyed under statute in April, 1959.

31 Linck, Eleanor; 41 De Boissiers, Constance; 51 Thomson, Miss G E; 63 Searight, Miss M; 102 Troy, Mary; 123 North, Helen; 140 Aherne, Dorothy; 155 Needham, Violet; 206 Moon, Emilie de Ronsenay; 210 Hamilton-Pearson, Mrs Isabelle; 212 Fellows, Mrs Mabel; 247 Bell, Iris; 256 Winter, Reginald; 257 Speirs, Beryl; 259 Herring, José; 261 Allright, May; 282 Walwyn, Frances; 331 Ede, Marion; 355 Henne, Barbara; 365 Clarke, Kathleen; 368 Day, Grace; 379 Hatfield, Ann; 417 Brown, Isabelle; 441 Scott, Alice; 451 Maclean, Meta; 453 Baxter, Sheila; 492 MacGillivray, Mrs Beatrice; 506 Sotham, Eileen; 543 McDonald, Annie; 561 Scott, Mrs Ada; 568 Anderson, Robert; 578 Thomas, Barbara; 586 Cuthbertson, Frances; 608 Dunham, Dorothy; 640 Da Costa, Eileen; 651 Leitch, Isabel; 654 Marshal, Phyllis; 667 Anderson, Mrs A; 683 Cooper, Marjorie; 707 Searle, Irene; 719 Davy, Phyllis; 729 Casty, Viola; 736 Engel, Hilda; 756 Rushforth, Doris; 761 Craig, Marjorie; 794 Hornsby, Anna; 850 Alston, Christianna; 858 Ritchie, Elizabeth; 948 Towns, Mrs Lillian; 958 Skelton, Esther; 975 Gresham, Rosalie; 1025 Illington, Marjorie; 1034 Kilby, Charles; 1207 Chesney, Horace; 1254 Douglas, Mrs Florence; 1360 Smith, Dorothy; 1396 Vidal, Edward (Entertainer); 1416 Evans, Margaret; 1563 Tribe, Enid; 1588 Page, Margaret (Kyrsty); 1621 Bolton, William; 1658 Robinson, Ruby; 1702 Peters, Wilhelmina; 1713 Lawton, Graham; 1731 Rees, Gwyneth; 1791 Sharp, Mabel; 1796 Scott, Muriel; 1800 Trenholme, Mary; 1837 Herbert-Jones, Elinor; 1850 Biggs, Ethel; 1940 Nott, Lilian; 1940A Bentley, Walter; 1942 Close, Diana; 1960 Burton, Mrs Margaret; 1981 Thistle, Ethel; 2028 McSweeney, Mrs Norah; 2041 Morgan, Nesta; 2138 Oats, William; 2218 Tarrant, Minnie; 2230 Nash, Pauline; 2248 McIntyre, Jean; 2386 Godfrey, William; 2527 Bryant, Muriel; 2553 Forward, Ivy; 2563 Elgie, Dorothy; 2783 Bryant, Henry; 2786 Hale, Mrs Fordes-Robertson; 2807 Allen, Pauline; 2839 Baker, Josephine; 2860 Brooke, Mrs Norah; 2888 Elliott, James; 2895 Osborne, Margaret; 2920 Budge, David; 2954 Jolly, Mary; 3020 Dixon,

James Yeomans; 3173 Phillips, Florence; 3205 Lennon, Patricia; 3322 Borrow, Carlton; 3537 Bancroft, Mrs Beryl; 3543 Wade, Mary; 3559 Clothier, Mrs Annabella; 3576 Gill, Doris; 3693 Kendall, Doreen; 3736 Harrington, Mrs Kathleen; 3824 Paine, Madge; 3827 Sandilands, Mrs Marion; 3864 Prior, Sybil; 3882 Kirkwood, Helen; 3901 Stump, Walter; 4079 Selson, Viola; 4110 Gillison, Effie; 4384 Williams, Nina; 4385 Beeston, Doris; 4412 Horton, Mrs Isabel; 4436 Bennett, Rev. John; 4458 Cross, Walter; 4442 Ross, Mrs Vera; 4559 Martin, Rev. Geoffrey; 4656 Stead, Mrs Ellen; 4658 Gerson, Phyllis; 4659 Brown, Mrs Mabel; 4660 Belgrove, Nora; 4662 Lenerson, Jane; 4739 Loe, Florence; 4740 Noise, Amelia; 4741 Reardon, Eleanor; 4755 Tippen, Kermande; 4828 Clough, Mrs Ada; 4893 Dromgool, Winifred; 4895 Dewhurst, Alice; 5098 Jones, Rev. Peter; 5127 Fraser, Mary; 5210 Redmayne, Pamela; 5227 Lester, Roland; 5230 Hockley, Mary; 5282 Prest, Maisie; 5309 Paterson, Ian; 5603 Shaw, Minnie; 5656 Illiff, Charles; 5755 Hungerford, Helen; 5779 Crocker, Vera; 5822 Gaffikin, Phillipa; 5829 Ball, Rev. Ernest; 5837 Goode, Muriel; 5844 Cumber, Ellen; 5877 Baldwin, Doris; 6055 Patrick, Frances; 6081 Mills, Alan; 6245 Fazan, Iris; 6256 Durrant, Mrs Ada; 6259 Burbeck, Edith; 6274 Simons, Walter; 6353 MacPhee, Ethel; 6369 Guest, Steven A R; 6382 Haggard, Charles, W; 6458 Craven, Major E; 6468 Fluellen, William H; 6468A Evans, John; 6498 Jennings, Mary; 6499 Low, John; 6518 Hatfield, Mr & Mrs George; 6531 Hillman, Mrs M G; 6538 Marshall, Laura; 6621 Bullard, Audrey; 6625 Cole, Josephine; 6925 Moran, Dr Frederick; 6927 Kelly, Fr Denis; 7845 O'Connor, Agnes; 8120 Sharpe, Marjorie; 8411 Brain, Elizabeth; 8839 Evans, Mrs F; 9745 Norton, Rev. John; 9746 McKenzie, Major Florence; 10162 Johnson, Victor; 10679 Dunlop, Enid; 12115 Allen, Joan; 12617 King, Rev. John; 12912 Sutcliffe-Hey, Mrs; 12997 Frith, Roger; 13219 Rolfe, Colonel Mrs Brunhilde; 13220 Woods, Major Ethel; 13221 Chalmers, Adjutant Violet; 13222 Stewart, Major Mary; 13224 Fouracre, Major Eva; 13225 Knights, Adjutant Agnes; 13226 Cullum, Adjutant Hannah; 13227 Ticklepenny, Col. Symonia; 13228 Trendell, Adjutant Evangeline; 13229 Ware, Brigadier Mabel; 13655 Hindley, Charles; 13719 Rider, Robert; 14484 Evans, Adjutant Mrs F; 14552 Best, Brigadier Mrs A; 14554 Best, Brigadier, Mr Arthur; 14582 Troup, Winifred; 14555 Evans, Adjutant Frances; 14673 King, Rev. William; 14704 Shaw, Capt. K; 14975 Muir, Rev. Anthony; 15468 Foy, Sister M; 15475 Shackleton, Miss E H.

Nurses:

32 Newill, Barbara; 302 Bingham, Kathleen; 303 Boath, Beatrice; 354 Heathcot, Beatrice; 359 Holliger, Blanche Bella; 362 Howsen, Stella; 369 Katkooff, Maria; 383 Maunsell, Eva; 386 Miller, Mabel; 391 Moore, Katherine; 443 Webb, Ethel; Westerman, Ida; 450 William, Joan; 518 Truckett, Pat; 519 Mills, Mary; 520 Rimmer, Margaret; 521 Ogilvie, Helen; 522 Vincent, Irene; 523 Golding, Rosalie; 525 Child, Florence; 526 Dunsmuir, Mary; 528 Foulkes, Francesca; 529 McKeigh, Linda; 534 Bryan, Emily; 535 Dean, Elizabeth; 536 James, Alice; 537 Jarvis, Eileen; 538 Pummel, Evangeline; 539 Williamson, Ellen; 544 Richardson, Honor.

Selected by the Scottish Branch of CORB:
Spiritual — 14181 Murray, Rev. Thomas; 14366 Rogers, Rev. Gerard; 14400

Kelly, Rev. D L; 14649 Noon, Rev. John.

Medical — 17001 Warden, Dr Agnes; 17002 Cossar, Dr George; 17003 Ross, Dr Lily.

Nurses — 402 Fairweather, Mary; 403 Foy, Mary; 430 Struthers, Celia; 431 Frame, Elizabeth; 432 McAdam, Agnes; 448 Stewart, Agnes; 454 Ferguson, Annette; 455 Fielding, Beatrice; 2648 Williamson, Ruby; 2652 Robinson, Stella; 2653 Eadie, Alice; 2670 Young, Jean; 2619 Lefevre, Violet.

Escorts — 41 Douglas, Alison; 209 Bell, William; 219 McChesney, Mary; 235 Moncrieff, Elsie; 242 Guthrie, Agnes; 256 Johnson, Jean; 2229 Scott, Helen; 2293 Fraser, Margaret; 2298 Green, Nellie; 2308 Gray, Marjorie; 2316 Ray, Rev. Stanley; 2344 Ahrens, Elsie; 2360 Cassie, Sheila; 2412 Fleming, Mary; 2444 Stewart, Mrs W; 2445 Maclean, Rachel; 2446 Robertson, Mary; 2519 Campbell, Charles; 2573 Durning, Margaret; 2919 Hossack, James; 2947 Forest, Irene; 2964 Maitland, Joan; 2965 Shanks, Jean; 2966 Murray, Margot; 2969 Budge, Rena; 2992 Buchan, Alexander; 2994 Moffat, James; 4064 Stewart, John; 4154 Lang, Archibald; 4167 Crowe, Edith.

The following also served as escorts aboard CORB ships. Their files were preserved as 'samples', and are classified at the PRO as DO131/71 to 87: 71 Calvert-Langton, Ruth; 72 Sherring Dr Jean M; 73 Fieldgate, Jean; 74 Cartwright, Roland; 75 Gowans, Edith; 76 Wood, Mabel; 77 Fox, Mrs Constance; 78 Davies, Mrs E M; 79 Day, Marjorie; 80 Rennie, Michael; 81 Feust, Francis; 82 O'Sullivan, Fr R; 83 Edge, Nurse G; 84 Maclean, Mrs E B; 85 Maud, P M; 86 Mundie, F E H; 87 Sandbach, B.

APPENDIX XIV[15]

THE CORB CHILDREN WHO ARRIVED SAFELY
IN THE DOMINIONS:

Note: Whilst all applications made by parents and guardians to CORB received an index-coding, it was not until a child had been firmly allocated to a batch due to sail overseas that CORB Headquarters issued his/her CORB Official Number. The child received this Number, enclosed in a small, transparent, perspex disc attached to a string, on reaching the pre-embarkation hostel. From that moment onwards, the disc had to be worn at all times. It was this disc, in most cases, that made it possible to identify those evacuees who did not survive the ordeal in life-boats after the sinking of the *City of Benares*. As they were wearing night clothes only, the disc was the only means of identification — and this proved the wisdom of placing such importance on the number, and wearing it always.

The names that follow are listed exactly as CORB recorded them; ie., they are in 'ship-batch order', with the number as allocated just before embarkation took place in Liverpool or Greenock. A '+' = same family follows. Place from which evacuated is given, and the age on leaving home, if recorded.

The CORB Children — Australia

87 HARRIS, Eleanor, 15, Barry +
88 HARRIS, Melvin, 13, Barry +
89 HARRIS, Reginald, 10, Barry +
90 HARRIS, Ruby, 7, Barry
91 MATTHEWS, Margaret 15, Barry
92 DAVIDSON, Frederick, ?, Bridlington
93 SCHULTZ, Phillip, 6, Hull +
94 SCHULTZ, Hester, 5, Hull
95 BROWN, Joan, 11, Birmingham
97 DEELEY, Betty, 12, Birmingham +
98 DEELEY, Philip, 14, Birmingham
99 JONES, Sheila, 7, Swinton
100 HAWLEY, Anthony, 10, Barnoldswick
101 SALT, Albert, 12, Birmingham
102 SPINKS, Iris, 9, Birmingham +
103 SPINKS, George, 7 Birmingham +

104 SPINKS, Joan, 5, Birmingham
106 BRENNAND, Anthony, 13, Blyth
107 BROWN, Evelyn, 11, Blyth
110 PATTERSON, Elsie, 9, Blyth +
111 PATTERSON, Jean, 13, Blyth
112 PATTERSON, Rita, 8, Blyth
113 WOODS, Francis, 12, Blyth
114 WOODS, Isabella, 11, Blyth
115 BULLEN, Donald, 9, Liverpool
118 DUFFY, Francis, 13, Bradford
119 FAREY, Doreen, 12, Bradford
120 FETHNEY, John, 13, Bradford +
121 FETHNEY, Michael, 9, Bradford
122 FIELD, May, 14, Bradford
123 HARDISTY, Helen, 13, Bradford +
124 HARDISTY, Ian, 10, Bradford

125 LANGDALE, Keith, 15, Bradford
126 LEE, Allan, 12, Bradford
127 METCALFE, Kenneth, 15, Bradford
128 RUSSELL, Jack, 13, Bradford
129 STANWAY, Robert, 14, Bradford
130 WEBSTER, Derric, 9, Bradford +
131 WEBSTER, Catherine, 7, Bradford
134 LITTLE, Phyllis, 14, Cardiff +
135 LITTLE, Isobel, 11, Cardiff
136 JONES, Lewis, 12, Cardiff +
137 JONES, Lillian, 7, Cardiff
138 RICHARDS, Ruth, 12, Cardiff +
139 RICHARDS, Barbara, 11, Cardiff
140 THOMAS, Denis, 12, Cardiff
141 WILLIAMS, Dorothy, 11, Cardiff
142 COLE, Jean, 15, Grays
143 CORNISH, Patricia, 10, Loughton
144 COX, Gerald, 9, Chelmsford +
145 COX, David, 8, Chelmsford
146 DIXON, Joan, 11, Chelmsford
147 LAMBLEY, Winifred, 10, South
    Benfleet +
148 LAMBLEY, James, 5, South Benfleet
149 SOLE, Kathleen, 12, South Benfleet
150 BOWCOCK, Arnold, 13, Colchester
151 BURRELL, Dennis, 14, Colchester +
152 BURRELL, Trevor, 10, Colchester
153 CAPPS, Victor, 13, Colchester
154 GRAY, Michael, 9, Colchester
155 HADDOCK, Vernon, 7, Colchester
156 WARD, Michael, 15, Colchester
157 WIGHT, Richard, 12, Colchester +
158 WIGHT, Rex, 10, Colchester
159 WHITTEN, David, 13, Southall
160 WILKINSON (Twins), Sidney, 12,
    Colchester +
161 WILKINSON, Philip, 12, Colchester
166 BAKER, Dulcie, 14, Darlington +
167 BAKER, Arthur, 10, Darlington
168 BELL, Margaret, 8, Darlington
169 COOPER, Launa, 9, Darlington
173 WILLIAMS, Doreen, 10, Manchester
174 KERSHAW (Cousins), Evelyn, 11,
    Darlington +
175 LUPTON, Nora, 9, Darlington
176 McLEISH, Margaret, 14, Darlington
177 SIMPSON, Jean, 12, Darlington
178 SNAITH, Sheila, 13, Darlington +
179 SNAITH, Noreen, 12, Darlington

180 THOMPSON, Sylvia, 8, Darlington
181 ANSELL, John, 11, Doncaster +
182 ANSELL, Julie, 9, Doncaster
183 HIGGINBOTTOM, Geoffrey, 8, Doncaster
184 HOGARTH, Stanley, 10, Doncaster +
185 HOGARTH, Betty, 9, Doncaster
186 HOWARTH, Brenda, 13, Doncaster
187 LOXTON, Joan, 7, Doncaster
188 SMITH, Geoffrey, 9, Doncaster
189 WARD, Eric, 11, Liverpool +
193 WARD, Phyllis, 13, Liverpool
190 FLOWERS, Edward, 13, Chester-le-Street
191 HOLMES, Violet, 12, Newcastle-on-Tyne
192 ROBINSON, Rosemary, 13,
    Middlesborough +
194 ROBINSON, Lilian, 8, Middlesborough
195 TEMPLETON, John, 11, Hartlepool
196 WILLIAMS, Marie, 13,
    Newcastle-on-Tyne
197 ASCOTT, Kenneth, 12, Greenford
198 BERNARD, Robert, 10, Hanwell, W7
199 BYFORD, Iris, 12, Hanwell +
200 BYFORD (Twins), Lawrence, 7,
    Hanwell, +
201 BYFORD, Maureen, 7, Hanwell
202 COLES, Richard, 13, Greenford
203 GIBSON (Twins), Janet, 9,
    Wycombe Marsh +
204 GIBSON, Robert, 9, Wycombe Marsh
205 GRANT, Olive, 13, Northolt +
206 GRANT, Roy, 10, Northolt
207 GREENING, Patricia, 13, Northolt +
208 GREENING, Terence, 14, Northolt +
209 GREENING, Shaun, 9, Northolt +
210 GREENING, Maureen, 7, Northolt +
211 GREENING, Dominic, 6, Northolt
213 HILL, Patricia, 8, W. Ealing
214 HILLIER, Frank, 13, Hanwell +
215 HILLIER, John, 12, Hanwell
216 JOHNSON, Robert, 12, Greenford
219 OWEN, Roderick, 8, Greenford
220 ROSS, Gordon, 13, Hanwell
221 SAUNDERS, Stella, 8, Ealing
222 WOOLLEY, John, 11, Hanwell
225 BARKER, Derek, 9, Enfield
226 HARKNESS, Deirdre, 12, Enfield
227 HENRY, John, 7, Enfield +
228 HENRY, Pamela, 6, Enfield
235 BERTRAM, Doreen, 13, Durham +

236 BERTRAM, Robert, 10, Durham
237 CLOUGH, Greta, 10, Gateshead
239 LAIDLER, Margaret, 13, Felling
240 SIMPSON, Derek, 13, Gateshead
241 STONE, Lillian, 13, Felling
242 TIMMINS, Alan, 11, Gateshead
243 WAUGH, Wilfred, 13, Gateshead
244 WEATHERBURN, Peter, 7, Gateshead
247 BRYDGES, Mary, 12, Grimsby
248 BUDDERY, Leonard, 10, Grimsby
249 CORMACK, Kenneth, 11, Grimsby
250 CUCKSON, Peggy, 13, Grimsby
252 SMITH, Iris, 13, Grimsby
253 SMITH (Twins), Nan, 14, Grimsby +
254 SMITH, Sheila, 14, Grimsby
261 BARRETT, Edward, 13, Hull
262 BORRILL, Herbert, 10, Hull
263 CRAWFORD, Brenda, 10, Doncaster
264 FARROW, John, 12, Hull
265 GOODFELLOW, Rita, 12, Hull +
266 GOODFELLOW, Barbara, 10, Hull
267 SCARBOROUGH, Jean, 9, Hull
268 TAYLOR, Maurice, 13, Hull
271 WHYTE, Cynthia, 10, Ilford
272 BARTON, Patricia, 11, Carisbrooke, IOW
273 EEDLE, Donald, 12, Sandown, IOW
274 KENCHINGTON, Agnes, 12,
    Newport, IOW
275 PENNY, Michael, 14, Undercliffe,
    IOW +
276 PENNY, David, 12, Undercliffe,
    IOW +
277 PENNY, Margaret, 9, Undercliffe, IOW
278 PIGGOTT, Bernard, 8, Freshwater, IOW
279 TOWNSEND, Norman, 13, Newport, IOW
280 WHILLIER, Jean, 14, Gatcombe,
    IOW +
281 WHILLIER, Joan, 12, Gatcombe, IOW
282 ALEXANDER, Joseph, 11, Canterbury
283 ANDREWS, Elizabeth, 12, Leeds +
284 ANDREWS, Audrey, 13, Leeds
285 BELMAR, Leon, 15, Eltham, SE9
286 BOWMAN, Terence, 8, Welling
287 BRIANT, Joyce, 14, Ashford
288 CLOUT, Jacqueline, 12, Ashford +
289 CLOUT, Yvonne, 10, Ashford +
290 CLOUT, Alan, 9, Ashford
291 COLEMAN, John, 12, Bexley +
292 COLEMAN, Frederice, 10, Bexley +

293 COLEMAN, Anthony, 8, Bexley
294 PERREN (Step-sisters), Doreen, 12,
    SE9 +
295 DEACON, Joan, 7, SE9
296 EDNEY, Frank, 14, Tonbridge
297 GALE (Twins), Audrey, 9, Edenbridge +
298 GALE, Shirley, 9, Edenbridge
299 GOLLOP, Joyce, 11, Bexley
300 HADAWAY, Bernard, 13, Sittingbourne
301 HANSON, Frederick, 12, SE9 +
302 HANSON, Richard, 10, SE9 (+ 304)
303 WALSHAM, Doris, 11, Liverpool
304 HANSON, Derek, 5, SE9
305 HARRIS, Geoffrey, 5, Bexley Heath +
306 HARRIS, David, 11, Bexley Heath
307 LLOYD, Verna, 13, Bromley +
308 LLOYD, Clarice, 11, Bromley
309 LOFT, Dorothy, 15, Bromley +
310 LOFT, Reginald, 13, Bromley
311 PACKMAN, Betty, 13, Ashford
312 PARRETT, Joan, 15, Sevenoaks
313 PEMBERTON, Leo, 11, Bromley
314 PUXTED, Robert, 14, Tenterden
315 ROACH, Yvonne, 9, Welling
316 ROSE, Arthur, 12, Dartford +
317 ROSE, Jean, 6, Dartford
318 SMITH, Anthony, 13, Glasgow
319 WASTELL, George, 14, Mottingham +
320 WASTELL, Alan, 13, Mottingham +
321 WASTELL, Edna, 11, Mottingham +
322 WASTELL, Colin, 7, Mottingham
323 SHARP, Joan, 6, Pendlebury
324 WHITTAKER, Patricia, 13, Orpington
335 COATES, Alan, 11, Leeds +
336 COATES, Dorothy, 13, Leeds
337 JONES, Margaret, 13, Manchester
338 CLARKE, Patricia, 14, Liverpool +
339 CLARKE, Billie Diana, 11, Liverpool
340 HARDCASTLE, Shirley, 7, Leeds
341 HARDCASTLE, Harry, 11, Leeds
342 HELLIWELL, Barbara, 9, Leeds
343 MACDONALD, Jessie, 15, Leeds
344 MORRIS, Irene, 8, Leeds
345 RATCLIFFE, Annie, 9, Leeds +
346 RATCLIFFE, Phyllis, 14, Leeds
347 CARTHEW, Roland, 13, Peckham
348 COHEN, Sidney, 14, Hackney +
349 COHEN, Ralph, 12, Hackney
350 DICKENSON, Audrey, 12, Charlton

351 GLASS, Sarah, 13, E1 +
352 GLASS, Braham, 7, E1
353 GOLDRING, Pamela, 6, E5
354 HOUGHTON, May, 13, E3
355 McGINTY, Patricia, 8,
    Liverpool
356 JEFFREY, Alan, 10, SE9 +
357 JEFFREY, Brenda, 9, SE9
358 KEEN, William, 5, N16
359 LEWIS, John, 6, W. Kensington
363 MILLS, Teresa, 13, Blackwall
364 NOAH, Rachel, 12, W. Kensington
365 PALLIS, Elsie, 11, Dalston, E8 +
366 PALLIS, Patricia, 9, Dalston, E8
367 POTTER, Theresa, 14, SE18
368 RANDALL, June, 13, N16 +
369 RANDALL, Howard, 10, N16
371 SCHULTZ, Jean, 10, E1
372 STEVENSON, Cyril, 14, W6
373 STROUD, Joan, 10, SW7
374 WATERS, Kenneth, 8, SW1
377 AUSTIN, Laura, 13, Newcastle-on-Tyne
378 GRAHAM, Dorothy, 13,
    Newcastle-on-Tyne
379 HUDSON, Valerie, 5, Newcastle-on-Tyne
380 QUINN, Robert, 13, Newcastle-on-Tyne
381 SMITH, Joan, 6, Newcastle-on-Tyne
382 STEPHENSON, Robert, 9, Belford,
    Northumberland
383 TRIGG, Charles, 13,
    Newcastle-on-Tyne +
384 TRIGG, William, 12, Newcastle-on-Tyne
385 BARRETT, George, 13, Dereham +
386 BARRETT, John, 12, Dereham
394 BROWNE, Ann, 8, Norwich
395 KNIGHTS, Ronald, 12, Norwich
396 POWELL, Elizabeth, 11, Merthyr Tydfil
397 BARRETT, Norman, 13, Plymouth
401 HOOK, Laura, 13, Port Talbot +
402 HOOK, Trevor, 11, Port Talbot
403 DWYER, Patrick, 11, Romford
404 KERSHAW, Rosemary, 7, Romford +
405 KERSHAW, Judith, 6, Romford +
406 KERSHAW, Anna, 5, Romford
407 PROCTOR, Elizabeth, 13, Gidea Park,
    Essex +
408 PROCTOR, Andrew, 5, Gidea Park, Essex
413 DINGWALL, George, 14, Sheffield +
414 DINGWALL, Audrey, 12, Sheffield +

415 DINGWALL, Kenneth, 8, Sheffield +
416 DINGWALL, Yvonne, 6, Sheffield
417 LOWE, Kathleen, 11, Sheffield
418 SLINGSBY, Joseph, 9, Sheffield +
419 SLINGSBY, Sheila, 6, Sheffield
420 STACEY, Jack, 14, Sheffield
421 STEVENS, Geoffrey, 11, Sheffield
423 FUDGE, Judith, 6, Southampton
424 HOLWAY, Eileen, 10, Portsmouth
427 WILLIAMS, John, 9, Southampton +
428 WILLIAMS, Jean, 7, Southampton
430 DUFF, Irene, 14, South Shields +
431 DUFF, Laura, 12, South Shields
432 STAFF, Denis, 11, South Shields +
433 STAFF, Heather, 9, South Shields
434 THOMPSON, Gordon, 14, South Shields
435 CLAMPS, Stanley, 11, Stockton
436 COLLINS, George, 15, Stockton
437 DAWSON, Theresa, 8, Stockton +
438 DAWSON, Marie, 7, Stockton +
439 DAWSON, Peter, 6, Stockton
441 WALTERS, Vera, 10, Liverpool
442 HANDYSIDE, Sylvia, 10, Stockton
443 HARVEY, Ronald, 15, Stockton
444 MACAULAY, John, 12, Stockton
445 RILEY, William, 8, Stockton
446 SHUTE, Charles, 9, Sheffield
451 BOARD, Joyce, 13, Swansea
452 BUDGEN, Gerald, 12, London
456 PERKINS, Rosina, 12, Tottenham +
457 PERKINS, Albert, 10 Tottenham
458 WHEATLEY, Eileen, 8, Tottenham
459 GREGORY, Kenneth, 10, Willesden
460 TWEED, Leonard, 11, NW10
461 ASH, Douglas, 14, Wimbledon
462 HEATH, Patricia, 13, Wimbledon +
463 HEATH, Derek, 12, Wimbledon
464 JUDD, Arthur, 8, Wimbledon, +
465 JUDD, Douglas, 10, Wimbledon
466 McCAPPIN, Joan, 14, Wimbledon
467 SHARPE, David, 12, Wimbledon
470 LOCKWOOD, Roger, 12, York
471 RICHARDSON, Terence, 11, York
472 VARLEY, Robert, 10, York
473 EVANS, Muriel, 10, York
474 SPELLER, John, 8, York
475 STOUT, Freda, 13, York
476 YOUNG, Raymond, 14, Hessle +
477 YOUNG, Julia, 12, Hessle +

478 YOUNG, Albert, 7, Hessle
480 PAGE, Jean, 14, Middlesborough
481 RUSSON, Christine, 11, Redcar +
482 RUSSON, Doreen, 7, Redcar
483 SKINNER, James, 13, Thornaby +
484 SKINNER, Rhoda, 11, Thornaby +
485 SKINNER, William, 9, Thornaby
486 WILSON, Ruth, 13, Sunderland
487 FOGGAN, Blanche, 12, Blyth +
488 FOGGAN, Joseph, 10, Blyth +
489 FOGGAN, June, 8, Blyth
490 LAST, Hetty, 12, Brightlingsea
491 DOMMERSON, Kenneth, 13, Rayleigh
492 CHAMBERS, Kathleen, 12, Liverpool
493 STONE, Geoffrey, 14, Manningtree +
494 STONE, Michael, 12, Manningtree +
495 STONE, Philip, 9, Manningtree
496 BISHOP, Ronald, 10, Hornchurch
497 DRAKE, Pauline, 15, Tollesbury
498 HUMBER, Leslie, 13, Romford +
499 HUMBER, Geoffrey, 10, Romford
500 HARE, Peggy, 13, Hornchurch +
501 HARE, Betty, 12, Hornchurch +
502 HARE, Joan, 10, Hornchurch +
503 HARE, John, 7, Hornchurch
504 BUNDOCK, Trevor, 8, Thundersley
505 BLAKEMAN, Charles, 13, Birmingham
506 ROBINSON, Philip, 14, Birmingham
509 DONALD, George, 13,
        Bishop Auckland +
510 DONALD, Barbara, 11,
        Bishop Auckland +
511 DONALD, Harry, 10,
        Bishop Auckland (See No. 514)
512 HARDING, Elsie, 12, Billingham +
513 HARDING, George, 10, Billingham
514 DONALD, Martha, 13, Bishop Auckland
515 WEEKS, Leslie, 14, Durham
516 RUDGE, Raymond, 13, Gateshead +
517 RUDGE, Alan, 8, Gateshead
518 MUNRO, Joseph, 14, Tyneside +
519 MUNRO, Charles, 9, Tyneside
520 WINDER, Terence, 10, Bristol
522 WALKER, David, 13, N21
524 HIBBERT, Edwin, 9, Teddington
525 LANG, Benedict, 12, Ashington
526 DIXON, Charles, 12, Whitton, Middlesex
527 LE GROS, Daphne, 14, Teddington
528 EDWARDS, Eileen, 12, Hampton

529 VINCENT, Ann, 11, Hampton
531 RUMENS (Twins), Terence, 10,
        Wembley +
532 RUMENS, Geoffrey, 10, Wembley
533 EDKINS, Peter, 11, Hayes, Middlesex
534 DOUGHTY, John, 15, Holloway
535 URSELL, Marjory, 11, Hampton
536 PALMER, Pamela, 14, Harrow
537 BURROW, Enid, 7, Salford (See No. 552)
538 TONGE, James, 13, Wembley +
539 TONGE, Anthony, 10, Wembley +
540 TONGE, Michael, 6, Wembley
541 PLENTY, Anthony, 7, Wembley
542 BULLARD, Robert, 8, Wembley
544 WIX, Dennis, 13, Teddington
545 STOREY, Roy, 15, Teddington +
547 STOREY, Michael, 8, Teddington
548 TOFT, Philip, 6, Ruislip
549 FARQUHARSON, Paul, 12, Ashford +
550 FARQUHARSON, Reginald, 10, Ashford
552 BURROW, Marion, 11, Salford
554 PIPER, Kenneth, 9, Edgeware
555 ROGERS, Anthony, 9, Twickenham +
556 ROGERS, David, 6, Twickenham
563 DAVIES, Cyril, 12, Walsall +
564 DAVIES, Philip, 10, Walsall
565 COOPER, Douglas, 11, Walsall
566 MITCHELL, Albert, 13, Walsall
567 COCKER, Donald, 9, Oldham
733 MALLETT, Brenda, 9, Raynes Park
1982 VOS, Kenneth, 12, Harrow +
1983 VOS, Theodora, 14, Harrow
1984 FREEBORN, Mary, 13, Wimbledon +
1985 FREEBORN, John, 9, Wimbledon
1986 GUTHRIE, Donald, 13, Liverpool
1987 MACLAGAN, Robert, 9, Chertsey +
1988 MACLAGAN, Ian, 10, Chertsey +
1989 MACLAGAN, Catherine, 12,
        Chertsey +
1990 MACLAGAN, Sheila, 14, Chertsey
1991 BIRTWISTLE, Shirley, 5, Stockport
1992 HIGGINS, John, 8, Stockport
1993 FAGEN, William, 8, Cheadle Hulme +
1994 FAGEN, Arthur, 5, Cheadle Hulme
1995 HUME, Peter, 11, Manchester
1996 CHADWICK, David, 10, Stockport
1997 WILLIS, John, 13, Stockport
1998 GARNER, Jack, 12, Manchester +
1999 GARNER, Ann, 6, Manchester

2000 KENYON, Charles, 10, Stockport
2001 SCOTT, Florence, 13, Stockport
2002 ELLIS, Leonard, 13, Manchester +
2003 ELLIS, Alan, 9, Manchester
2004 ORWIN, Joan, 11, Cheadle
2005 JAMES, Geoffrey, 9, Stockport
2006 ECCLES, George, 12, Stockport
2007 JONES, Janet, 6, Stockport
2008 EMBLING, Barbara, 15, Stockton
2010 MANNING, Dulcie, 9, London
2011 VICKERY, John, 5, Tiverton
2012 BESWICK, Audrey, 14, Oldham
2013 BARNARD, Ernest, 13, Ealing +
2014 BARNARD, Margaret, 9, Ealing
2016 JENKINS, Gwyneth, 12,
    Bury St Edmunds
2017 BOOCOCK, Joan, 10, Bradford +
2018 BOOCOCK, Clarice, 13, Bradford
2021 WATKINSON, Roger, 10,
    Thornton Heath
2022 REED, Martin, 11, Banstead +
2023 REED, Derek, 9, Banstead
2024 O'DOWD, Pamela, 15, Surbiton
2025 CLEWES, Mary, 13, Orpington
2027 HAMMOND, Sheila, 11, Tolworth
2028 TILLMAN, Robert, 13, Mortlake
2029 STANDAGE, Brenda, 12, N. Cheam +
2030 STANDAGE, Norman, 9, N. Cheam
2031 MINTER, Beryl, 10, Purley
2032 EDWARDS, Derek, 11, Worcester Park
2033 LOWE, Ernest, 13, Coulsdon
2035 PAWSEY, Derek, 8, N. Cheam +
2036 PAWSEY, Sylvia, 12, N. Cheam +
2037 PAWSEY, Peter, 6, N. Cheam
2039 WATTS, Hilary, 13, Epsom
2040 MORAN, John, 10, Mitcham
2041 HEDGECOE, Kathleen, 12, Cheam
2044 DUBERY, Mervyn, 13, Epsom
2045 BOLING, Michael, 11, Surbiton +
2046 BOLING, John, 6, Surbiton +
2047 BOLING, Geraldine, 13, Surbiton
2048 LONGWORTH, Joan, 14, Sutton +
2049 LONGWORTH, Iris, 6, Sutton
2050 ROGERS, Janet, 10, Bristol
2051 JARRITT, Frieda, 14, Bristol
2052 CASTLE, Pauline, 14, Bristol
2550 MORGAN, Maurice, 7, Liverpool +
2551 MORGAN, Freda, 12, Liverpool +
2552 MORGAN, Percy, 14, Liverpool

2553 FLETCHER, John, 7, Liverpool +
2554 FLETCHER, Geraldine, 8, Liverpool
2555 CLARKE, Thomas, 12, Liverpool +
2556 CLARKE, Gladys, 10, Liverpool +
2557 CLARKE, John, 5, Liverpool
2564 HACKETT, John, 12, Liverpool +
2565 HACKETT, Sheilagh, 9, Liverpool
2566 DUFF, Gordon, 13, Bolton
2567 GARDNER, Beryl, 9, Manchester +
2568 GARDNER, William, 6, Manchester
2569 PRINCE, Marjorie, 5, Manchester
2570 HODGSON, Margaret, 13, Prestwich +
2571 HODGSON, Joan, 8, Prestwich
2572 CLIPSTONE, Patricia, 11, Nottingham
2573 CRAWSHAW, Nellie, 12, Bolton
3129 MILLINGTON, Kenneth, 12, Warrington
3130 HOUGHTON, Ernest, 14, Warrington +
3131 HOUGHTON, David, 11, Warrington
3132 NAYLOR, Stuart, 11, Warrington
3134 RIMMER, Henry, 13, Southport
3137 WILSON, Harry, 13, Rochdale
3138 GARFAT, Frank, 12, Rochdale
3140 RILEY, Leslie, 11, Manchester
3141 THOMPSON, Gordon, 13, Manchester
3142 MASSEY, David, 11, Liverpool
3143 CARDY, John, 12, Lancaster
3144 BEECH, Arthur, 13, Oldham
3145 HUMPHREYS, Clifford, 12, Oldham
3146 TOMLINSON, Jess, 12, Blackburn
3148 EASTHAM, Alan, 13, Foulridge
3149 MITCHELL, James, 13, Colne
3150 PHILLIPS, Anthony, 13, Colne
3501 FERN, Lloyd, 12, Dundee
3502 HERD, Ian, 11, Methil +
3503 HERD, Andrew, 9, Methil
3504 KILPATRICK, George, 10, Burnbank +
3505 KILPATRICK, Emerson, 8, Burnbank
3506 LAUGHLAN, Samuel, 11, Bellshill +
3507 LAUGHLAN, Duncan, 8, Bellshill
3510 RUNDLE, Douglas, 8, Motherwell +
3511 RUNDLE, Gregor, 12, Motherwell
3512 SCOTT, John, 14, Ayr
3513 BARCLAY, Robert, 13, Edinburgh
3514 BRALSFORD, David, 7, Edinburgh
3515 CRUDDAS, John, 13, Enfield
3516 GLASIER, William, 8, Edinburgh
3517 MACKIE, David, 8, Edinburgh +
3518 MACKIE, Walter, 9, Edinburgh
3519 McINTYRE, Peter, 13, Edinburgh

3520 NICHOLSON, William, 13, Edinburgh
3521 ROBERTSON, George, 12, Edinburgh +
3522 ROBERTSON, William, 10, Edinburgh
3523 ROBERTSON, William, 10, Leith
3524 SMITH, David, 12, Edinburgh
3525 VALVONA, Ralph, 9, Edinburgh
3526 AITCHISON, Thomas, 14, Dumbarton
3530 HILL, Ian, 9, Glasgow
3531 HOOPER, Brian, 9, Johnstone
3532 LAIRD, John, 8, Glasgow
3533 MILLAN, William, 11, Glasgow
3534 McDONALD, Ramsay, 10, Glasgow
     (See Nos. 3578 & 3579)
3535 McNEIL, Thomas, 11, Glasgow
3536 PATERSON, Samuel, 12, Baillieston
3537 TIERNEY, Albert, 11, Glasgow
3538 TURNBULL, Robert, 12, Glasgow
3539 WIGG, Arthur, 9, Glasgow
     (See No. 3599)
3540 YOUNG, Andrew, 10, Glasgow
3541 BLANCHE, Adina, 11, Edinburgh +
3542 BLANCHE, William, 7, Edinburgh
3543 CAMERON, Sheila, 14, Edinburgh
3545 GLASIER, Dorothy, 11, Edinburgh
     (Sister of No. 3516)
3546 LAW, Annie, 14, West Calder
3547 PATERSON, John, 5, Glasgow +
3548 PATERSON, Margaret, 9, Glasgow
3549 RENNY, Mabel, 7, Arbroath +
3550 RENNY, Maureen, 8, Arbroath
3551 RICHARDSON, Elizabeth, Edinburgh
3552 ROBERTSON, Constance, 12,
     Edinburgh +
3553 ROBERTSON, George D, 5, Leith
     (Brother of No. 3523)
3554 SINCLAIR, Margaret, 7, Edinburgh
3555 TROTTER, Margaret, 11, Edinburgh
3556 CUTHBERT, Helen, 9, Glasgow +
3557 CUTHBERT, Katherine, 7, Glasgow
3558 FARMAN, Harriet, 12, Bridge of Don
3559 GOUGH, Christopher, 6, Edinburgh
3560 HOOPER, Kathleen, 11, Johnstone
     (See No. 3531) +
3561 HOOPER, Winifred, 5, Johnstone
3562 HOWE, Ethel, 12, Glasgow
3563 KILPATRICK, Margaret, 7, Burnbank
     (See Nos. 3504 & 3505)
3564 LOW, Helen, 5, Dundee
3566 MILLAN, Terence, 7, Glasgow

     (See No. 3533)
3568 SOMERVILLE, Isabella, 12, Ruthenglen
3569 TIERNEY, Joseph, 6, Glasgow
     (See No. 3537)
3570 WYLLIE, Jessie, 10, Mauchline
3578 McDONALD, Mary, 14, Glasgow
     (See No. 3534) +
3579 McDONALD, Margaret, 12, Glasgow
3580 McINTYRE, Mary, 11, Edinburgh
     (See No. 3519)
3581 SWAN, Ruby, 9, Leith
3583 VALVONA, Caroline, 6, Edinburgh
     (See No. 3525) +
2584 VALVONA, Doreen, 13, Edinburgh
3585 WALKER, Janet, 8, Edinburgh
3586 BARTON, Roberta, ?, Glasgow
3587 CUNNINGHAM, Annie, 10, Glasgow +
3588 CUNNINGHAM, Esther, 7, Glasgow +
3589 CUNNINGHAM, Isabella, 12, Glasgow
3590 LAUGHLAN, Jeanie, 10, Bellshill
     (See Nos. 3506 & 3507) +
3591 LAUGHLAN, Jessie, 14, Bellshill
3592 MACKIE, Lois, 10, Glasgow
3593 MILLER, Mary, 13, Glasgow
3595 McINTYRE, Rachel, 10, Glasgow
3596 McNEIL, Jessie, 12, Glasgow
     (See No. 3535)
3597 ROSS, Irene, 12, Cambuslang
3598 TIERNEY, Agnes, 12, Glasgow
     (See Nos. 3537 & 3569)
3599 WIGG, Elizabeth, 7, Glasgow
3600 WILLIAMSON, Nessie, 11, Glasgow
3601 WHITE, Margaret, 10, Bonnybridge
3602 FULLERTON, Jack, 9, Glasgow +
3603 FULLERTON, Marion, 14, Glasgow
3605 DAVIDSON, Annie, 13, Glasgow +
3606 DAVIDSON, Margaret, ?, Glasgow
3607 GAIRDNER, William, 12, Glasgow
3610 OSWALD, John, 6, Edinburgh
3611 YOUNG, Grace, 11, Edinburgh
3612 CREEVY, Charles, 8, Glasgow +
3613 CREEVY, Mary, 11, Glasgow
3614 GRAVIL, Sydney, 14, Glasgow
3720 BOYD, Ross, 12, High Burnside

The CORB Children — Canada

2 PARRY, Martin, 12, Bristol +
3 PARRY, Eva, 8, Bristol +
4 PARRY, John, 6, Bristol
5 MALLABY, George, 5, Middlesborough
6 McIVOR, Robert, 8, Middlesborough
7 LANGFORD, Joyce, 10, Middlesborough
8 BURTON, Thelma, ?, Middlesborough
9 SAYERS, Denis, 6, Middlesborough +
10 SAYERS, Gerard, 8, Middlesborough
11 MASTERMAN, Elizabeth, 11,
   Middlesborough +
12 MASTERMAN, Harold, 6,
   Middlesborough +
13 MASTERMAN, John, 12,
   Middlesborough +
14 MASTERMAN, Marion, 9,
   Middlesborough
15 GRANT, Joan, 8, Middlesborough +
16 GRANT, Maureen, 10, Middlesborough
18 LAVILLE, Georgina, 10, Middlesborough
19 DICKENSON, Aileen, 11, Middlesborough
20 MIZON, Bessie, 8, Middlesborough +
21 MIZON, Ronald, 10, Middlesborough
22 POLLARD, Celia, 13, Middlesborough
23 DICKINSON, Marjorie, 9,
   Middlesborough +
24 DICKINSON, Kenneth, 10,
   Middlesborough
25 WHITTLE, Audrey, 10, Middlesborough
26 ROE, Sheila, 10, Middlesborough +
27 ROE, Monica, 13, Middlesborough
28 THORNE, Adrianne, 8,
   Middlesborough +
29 THORNE, Corinne, 13, Middlesborough
30 REID, Frank, 14, Middlesborough +
31 REID, Donald, 10, Middlesborough
32 WHITEHEAD, Dennis, 14,
   Middlesborough
33 BARKHOUSE, Joyce, 11,
   Middlesborough +
34 BARKHOUSE, Margaret, 13,
   Middlesborough
35 COVERDALE, Olive, 15,
   Middlesborough
36 HUTCHINSON, Kathleen, 14,
   Middlesborough +
37 HUTCHINSON, Marian, 9,
   Middlesborough

38 SMITH, Ronald, 13,
   Middlesborough +
39 SMITH, Gordon, 8, Middlesborough
40 WILSON, John, 10,
   Middlesborough +
41 WILSON, Barbara, 8, Middlesborough
44 CALVERT, Kenneth, 13, Tynemouth +
45 CALVERT, James, 15, Tynemouth
46 YOLE, Richard, 10, Middlesborough +
47 YOLE, Raymond, 13, Middlesborough
48 HARLOW, Anita, 9, Middlesborough +
49 HARLOW, Joan, 13, Middlesborough
50 PARR, George, 13, Middlesborough +
51 PARR, Doris, 9, Middlesborough +
52 PARR, Betty, 11, Middlesborough
53 HINTON, Rita, 9, Middlesborough +
54 HINTON, Kelvin, 13, Middlesborough
55 ROWLANDS, Alan, 11,
   Middlesborough +
56 ROWLANDS, Philip, 5,
   Middlesborough +
57 ROWLANDS, Peter, 8, Middlesborough
58 WHYMAN, Margaret, 14, Middlesborough
59 WHENRAY, John, 10, Middlesborough
60 GOAT, Ronald, 8, Middlesborough +
61 GOAT, Robert, 13, Middlesborough +
62 GOAT, Maisie, 11, Middlesborough
64 WILLIS, Margaret, 13, Leeds
65 STOKER, Frederick, 13, Blackpool
66 WHEATMAN, Alfred, 13, Middlesborough
67 JARVIS, William, 8, Middlesborough +
68 JARVIS, Brenda, 6, Middlesborough +
69 JARVIS, Sara, 13, Middlesborough +
70 JARVIS, Denis, 10, Middlesborough
71 GLASPER, George, 11, Middlesborough
72 SMITH, Rhoda, 9, Middlesborough +
73 SMITH, Raymond, 13,
   Middlesborough +
74 SMITH, Arthur, 8, Middlesborough
75 HADFIELD, Jean, 10, Middlesborough
76 BURKE, Winifred, 11,
   Willington Quay +
77 BURKE, Maureen, 7,
   Willington Quay +
78 BURKE, Elizabeth, 13, Willington Quay
79 CHARLTON, Robert, 9,
   Willington Quay +
80 CHARLTON, June, 11, Willington Quay

81 DODDS, Dorothy, 8, Worksop +
82 DODDS, David, 10, Worksop
83 GILRAY, Vilma, 10,
   Wallsend-on-Tyne +
84 GILRAY, Ronald, 13,
   Wallsend-on-Tyne +
85 GILRAY, Kenneth, 8, Wallsend-on-Tyne
86 BRUCE, Beverly, 9, West Wickham
568 LEIGHTLEY, Thomas, 13, Wimbledon +
569 LEIGHTLEY, Margaret, 12, Wimbledon
572 NORRIS, Ronald, 8, Liverpool
573 DOBSON, Brenda, 13, Liverpool
574 ORR, Elaine, 8, Manor Park, E12
575 ROISSETTER, Pamela, 8, Ilford +
576 ROISSETTER, Sheila, 12, Ilford
577 LARDENER, Peter, 12, Ripon
578 FRENCH, Joan, 13, Manor Park
579 BROWN, Evelyn, 12, Forest Gate
580 CARTER, Joyce, 13, Greenfield
581 RAYMENT, Kenneth, 11, Enfield +
582 RAYMENT, Margaret, 12, Enfield
583 AMBRIDGE, Joan, 10, Enfield
584 ASHFORD, Hazel, 10, Enfield
585 CONMETT, Audrey, ?, Enfield
586 PASCAL, Anne, 15, Enfield
587 DAVIS, Roy, 11, Enfield +
588 DAVIS, Rita, 10, Enfield
589 FINDLAY, Peter, 11, Enfield
590 YOUNG, Ian, 10, Enfield
591 SIMMONS, Eileen, 5, Enfield
592 BLACKMAN, Percy, 7, Enfield +
593 BLACKMAN, Grace, 8, Enfield
594 PARKER, Keith, 6, Hull
595 BURGE, Iris, 10, Hull +
596 BURGE, Terence, 8, Hull +
597 BURGE, Kenneth, 12, Hull
598 EDWARDS, Roland, 11, Hull
599 McALLISTER, Evelyn, 11, Hull
600 ROYDHOUSE, Clifford, 13, Hull
601 SEAMAN, Mary, 10, Hull
602 BAILLIE, Richard, 7, Fulwell
603 ENTWISTLE, Grace, 8, Sunderland
604 DAVIES, Esther, 5, Liverpool
607 LAMB, Hilda, 11, Sunderland
608 TAIT, Gladys, 13, Sunderland +
609 TAIT, Sylvia, 7, Sunderland
610 TAYLOR, Dorothy, 6, Sunderland +
611 TAYLOR, John, 10, Sunderland
612 WAUGH, Eileen, 5, Fulwell +

613 WAUGH, Thomas, 11, Fulwell
614 FRANCIS, George, 7, Tottenham +
615 FRANCIS, Henry, 12, Tottenham
616 WALFORD, Raymond, 9, Tottenham
617 BILDING, Constance, 10,
   Wood Green +
618 BILDING, Patricia, 11, Wood Green
619 ARCHER, Jean, 8, Tottenham +
620 ARCHER, John, 6, Tottenham
621 HARDING, Gloria, 6, Tottenham
622 JOLLY, Jean, 6, Tottenham
624 SIMPKINS, Robert, 14, Tottenham
625 JONES, Robert, 9, Liverpool
626 COOK, Thomasina, 14,
   North Shields +
627 COOK, George, 10,
   North Shields +
628 COOK, Donald, 7, North Shields
629 GIBBONS, Joan, 12, North Shields +
630 GIBBONS, Alan, 7, North Shields
631 HALL, Donald, 10, Bridlington +
632 HALL, Mildred, 15, Bridlington
633 POLTZ, Margaret, 12, North Shields
634 WALKER, Marguerite, 15, Cullercoats
635 SHIPPEN, Enid, 8, Durham +
636 SHIPPEN, Kenneth, 11, Durham +
637 SHIPPEN, Peter, 12, Durham
638 BATESON, Mary, 10, Gateshead
639 BRECKON, Pamela, 8, Gateshead
640 BROWN, William, 7, Gateshead
641 COWAN, John, 12, Gateshead +
642 COWAN, Thomas, 14, Gateshead
643 CURTIS, Robert, 11, Gateshead
645 O'KEEFFE, Peter, 9, Liverpool 10 +
646 O'KEEFFE, Bernard, 10, Liverpool
647 MAYNE, Raymond, 5, Gateshead
649 SANDERSON (Twins), Lilian, 9,
   Gateshead +
650 SANDERSON, Robert, 9, Gateshead
651 JONES, William, 13, Liverpool
653 TYSON, Florence, 11, Gateshead
654 JONES, Alan, 13, London
655 PHILLIPS (Twins), Richard, 8,
   Overton +
656 PHILLIPS, Robert, 8, Overton
657 FENESON, Stanley, 13, London
658 HAINSWORTH, Veronica, 5, Harrow
659 TULLY, Margaret, 6, Blackpool
660 BATTENBURG, Eunice, 15, London

661 COHEN, Jeffrey, 13, London
662 SIMMONS, Rose, 12, Liverpool
663 NARDELL, Daphne, 15, Aldgate +
664 NARDELL, Laila, 9, Aldgate
665 O'KEEFFE, Kathleen, 7, Liverpool 14
666 NORRIS, William, 12, Liverpool
667 SIMMONDS, Pauline, 14, London
668 DICKINSON, Peter, 14, London
669 KELLEHER, Jean, 14, London
670 RAE, Anthony, 6, Fulham +
671 RAE, Janette, 5, Fulham
672 EADES, Eileen, 9, Brixton
673 DURNFORD, Olivia, 12, W. Norwood
674 TURVEY, Patricia, 14, London +
675 TURVEY, Heather, 15, London
676 ARNOLD, Lavinia, 8, London
677 WOOD, John, 13, London
678 BOLTON, Helen, 11, London
679 CURLEY, Mavis, 14, Grimsby +
680 CURLEY, Patricia, 14, Grimsby
681 FAIERS, John, 12, Grimsby
682 DOBSON, Henry, 6, Liverpool
683 MANN, Iris, 14, Lincs +
684 MANN, Roy, 12, Lincs
686 HUNTER, Terence, 9, Grimsby +
687 HUNTER, Audrey, 15, Grimsby
688 BELLAMY, Beryl, 14, Grimsby +
689 BELLAMY, Donald, 13, Grimsby +
690 BELLAMY, Byron, 10, Grimsby
691 YOUNG, Kenneth, 13, Grimsby +
692 YOUNG, George, 14, Grimsby
693 PRESCOTT, Joyce, 9, Grimsby +
694 PRESCOTT, Anthony, 8, Grimsby
695 MURPHY, Eileen, 13, Grimsby +
696 MURPHY, Peter, 11, Grimsby
697 COY, Gwendoline, 7, Grimsby
698 GILBERT, John, 13, Grimsby +
699 GILBERT, Donald, 10, Grimsby
700 CRAN, Diana, 13, Grimsby
701 EVERARD, Ronald, 15, Grimsby +
702 EVERARD, Marjorie, 13, Grimsby
703 BEASLEY, Douglas, 11, Fleetwood
704 MARGARSON, Geoffrey, 12, Grimsby +
705 MARGARSON, Maud, 15, Grimsby +
706 MARGARSON, Olive, 14, Grimsby
710 JUPE, Brian, 9, Bodmin +
711 JUPE, Daphne, 11, Bodmin
712 PEPPERDINE, Ronald, 10, Grimsby
713 CALLAGHAN, Walter, 8, Grimsby

714 HOLLINGTON, Myra, 10, Grimsby
715 GRESSWELL (Twins), Maria, 10, Grimsby +
716 GRESSWELL, Mavis, 10, Grimsby
717 CRAWFORD, Jean, 11, Grimsby +
718 CRAWFORD, Dorothy, 13, Grimsby
719 BALLS, Betty, 6, Grimsby +
720 BALLS, Lilian, 11, Grimsby +
721 BALLS, Marjorie, 9, Grimsby
722 HEWITT, Barbara, 12, Grimsby
723 HEALY, Ruth, 13, Alford
725 MARTIN, Raymond, 13, Grimsby +
726 MARTIN, Gladys, 10, Grimsby
727 MACKRILL, Bernard, 13, Grimsby
728 MARTIN, Ralph, 9, Grimsby
729 SHARP, Mavis, 11, Grimsby
731 KALSON, Ivan, 13, Grimsby +
732 KALSON, Yvonne, 6, Grimsby
735 FRENCH, Peter, 12, Chelmsford
736 ROBINSON, Sylvia, 9, Chelmsford
737 CARR, Lilian, 13, Chelmsford +
738 CARR, Joseph, 11, Chelmsford
740 HUME, Mary, 12, Chelmsford
743 BRADLEY, Joan, 14, Chelmsford +
744 BRADLEY, Richard, 8, Chelmsford
745 BEDFORD, Norma, 11, Chelmsford +
746 BEDFORD, Robert, 10, Chelmsford
747 BROWN, Dennis, 13, Chelmsford
748 SIMMONDS, Eileen, 8, Chelmsford +
749 SIMMONDS, Albert, 7, Chelmsford
750 HUME, Brian, 13, Chelmsford +
751 HUME, Marjorie, 7, Chelmsford +
752 HUME, Ronald, 5, Chelmsford
753 HARMSWORTH, Victor, 8, Chelmsford +
754 HARMSWORTH, Charles, 9, Chelmsford
755 NUTTER, Peter, 12, Colchester
756 MOLES, Doreen, 10, Colchester +
757 MOLES, Beryl, 9, Colchester +
758 MOLES, Basil, 8, Colchester
759 HYNES (Twins), Sheelagh, 10, Colchester +
760 HYNES, June, 10, Colchester
763 JOHNSON, John, 12, Darlington
764 KIRTON, Neville, 11, Darlington
765 NICHOLSON, William, 13, Linthorpe +
766 NICHOLSON, Eleanor, 11, Linthorpe
767 SCARRE, Dorothy, 5, Darlington

768 TALLENTYRE, Sylvia, 11, Darlington

769 METCALFE, Brian, 14, Darlington

770 JACKSON, Walter, 11, Darlington

773 TIDYMAN, Thelma, 13, Darlington +

774 TIDYMAN, John, 9, Darlington +

775 TIDYMAN, Peter, 6, Darlington

777 BELL, Norman, 12, Darlington

778 HAYWOOD, John, 8, Darlington

779 PENWARDEN, Douglas, 8, Darlington

780 BYGATE, Harold, 11, Darlington +

781 BYGATE, Josephine, 10, Darlington

782 FOX (Twins), William, 9, Darlington +

783 FOX, Horace, 9, Darlington +

784 FOX, Derek, 8, Darlington

786 HENDERSON, William, 12, Darlington +

787 HENDERSON, Robert, 11, Darlington

788 JACKSON, John, 9, Darlington

789 FURNISH, Dennis, 15, Wooler

790 HAMMOND, Geoffrey, 13, London

791 GLOVER, Joyce, 13, London

792 WATTS, Pauline, 13, Southgate

793 LATHAM, Joan, 13, London

794 BROWN, Lucy, 15, Cambridge

795 GUTTERIDGE, Betty, 14, Cambridge

796 CATTELL, Vera, 12, Sutton

797 BORHAM, Roger, 13, Colchester +

798 BORHAM, Gillian, 12, Colchester

799 STAMP, Alfred, 13, Hornchurch

800 COOK, David, 15, Chelmsford

801 STITT, Agnes, 10, Dagenham

802 JACOBS, Charles, 9, Dagenham

803 PRINCE, Albert, 12, Dagenham

804 OAKLEY, Philip, 7, Billericay +

805 OAKLEY, Kathleen, 15, Billericay

806 DADD (Twins), Valerie, 9, Epping +

807 DADD, Carol, 9, Epping

808 BAKER, Stuart, 15, Faversham

809 MARSH, John, 11, Faversham +

810 MARSH, Ralph, 13, Faversham

811 DEWIS, Joan, 13, Faversham +

812 DEWIS, Geoffrey, 11, Faversham

813 SPINKS, Sylvia, 8, Faversham +

814 SPINKS, Gladys, 12, Faversham

815 PARSONSON, Patricia, 9, Faversham

816 BRANNAN, Margaret, 11, Hebburn-on-Tyne

817 WEBSTER, Frederick, 11, Hebburn-on-Tyne +

818 WEBSTER, Elizabeth, 12, Hebburn-on-Tyne

821 ROBSON, Kenneth, 12, Hebburn-on-Tyne

822 BAMBRIDGE, Isabel, 13, Hebburn-on-Tyne

823 WISHART, Gwendoline, 10, Heston +

824 WISHART, June, 13, Heston

825 MILNER, William, 11, Hounslow

826 BRICE, Margery, 8, Ilford +

827 BRICE, Joan, 12, Ilford +

828 BRICE, Leonard, 10, Ilford

829 HARRISON, Anthony, 8, Dagenham

830 HOWE, James, 8, Ilford +

831 HOWE, Isabel, 11, Ilford

832 YARE, Eric, 14, Bexley Heath

833 DUNNAGE, Cynthia, 9, Bexley Heath

834 HARRIS (Twins), Richard, 15, Gravesend +

835 HARRIS, Madge, 15, Gravesend

836 WILLIAMS, Bernard, 11, Faversham

837 BENTLEY, John, 14, Maidstone

838 TIDBALL, Joan, 11, Maidstone

839 GUY, David, 10, Maidstone +

840 GUY, Ruth, 14, Maidstone

841 HAYES, Marion, 8, Bearsted

842 WISEMAN, Shirley, 11, Maidstone

843 PAGE, Peter, 15, Maidstone +

844 PAGE, Dorothy, 11, Maidstone

845 WARD, Yvonne, 12, Bexley Heath

853 GARGRAVE, Anthony, 14, London

854 WALKER, Mary, 13, Brixton

856 BLACK, Robina, 9, London +

857 BLACK, Margaret, 7, London

861 JESSOP, Charles, 7, London

862 GRIMWOOD, Clifford, 13, London

866 SLADE, Gerald, 15, London

867 RICHARDSON, Thomas, 13, West Norwood

868 APPLEYARD, Denis, 7, West Norwood +

869 APPLEYARD, Edward, 11, West Norwood

872 THORN, John, 11, London

888 BOWERS, Brian, 11, London

894 BARBER, Allan, 13, Clapham Common

895 BROWN, Brenda, 10, Streatham

896 EASTWOOD, James, Maidstone

897 HAMMOND, James, 12, Maidstone

898 ROGERS, Kenneth, 10, Maidstone +

899 ROGERS, Ronald, 13, Maidstone

900 AUSTIN, Kenneth, 6, Bridgwood
901 CROUCHER, Michael, 10, Cranbrook +
902 CROUCHER, David, 8, Cranbrook
903 WOOD, John, 11, Maidstone +
904 WOOD, David, 13, Maidstone
905 BAKER, Joyce, 14, Maidstone +
906 BAKER, Keith, 12, Maidstone +
907 BAKER, Shirley, 7, Maidstone
908 SAWARD, Gillian, 9, Maidstone +
909 SAWARD, Rhoda, 6, Maidstone
910 SMITH, Donald, 8, Middlesborough
911 TANN, Raymond, 13, Middlesborough +
912 TANN, James, 11, Middlesborough +
913 TANN, Sylvia, 15, Middlesborough
914 BURT, Peter, 5, Middlesborough +
915 BURT, Kendal, 8, Middlesborough +
916 BURT, Doris, 10, Middlesborough +
917 BURT, Margaret, 13, Middlesborough
918 SWASH, Vera, 14, Middlesborough +
919 SWASH, Rosena, 12, Middlesborough
920 GRIGGS, Marjory, 14,
    Middlesborough +
921 GRIGGS, Marion, 15,
    Middlesborough +
922 GRIGGS, Dorothy, 9, Middlesborough
925 WATSON (Twins), Jean, 9,
    Middlesborough +
926 WATSON, Joan, 9, Middlesborough +
927 WATSON, Ralph, 12,
    Middlesborough +
928 WATSON, Irene, 14, Middlesborough
929 HART, John, 10 Bradford +
930 HART, Ronald, 11, Bradford
932 LANE, Joan, 14, Middlesborough +
933 LANE, Edith, 12, Middlesborough
934 KYTE-POWELL, Maude, 12,
    Middlesborough +
935 KYTE-POWELL, Noel, 11,
    Middlesborough
936 RIDLEY, John, 7, Middlesborough +
937 RIDLEY, June, 8, Middlesborough +
938 RIDLEY, Hazel, 10, Middlesborough
939 COBBOLD, Kenneth, 12,
    Middlesborough +
940 COBBOLD, Marion, 9, Middlesborough
941 JONES, Betty, 13, Middlesborough +
942 JONES, Henry, 7, Middlesborough
943 DICKENSON, Leslie, 13, Middlesborough
944 ANDERSON, Enid, 5, Ormesby

945 DERMONT, Richard, 5, Middlesborough
946 DUNNING, Jean, 9, Middlesborough
947 LAWSON, Margaret, 15, Middlesborough
948 GIBSON, Rosemary, 12,
    Middlesborough +
949 GIBSON, Evelyn, 13, Middlesborough +
950 GIBSON, Maureen, 9, Middlesborough
951 WILLIAMSON, Francis, 15,
    Middlesborough
952 ALMOND (Twins), John, 13,
    Middlesborough +
953 ALMOND, Peter, 13, Middlesborough
954 FORGAN, Mary, 13, Middlesborough +
955 FORGAN, Thomas, 11,
    Middlesborough +
956 FORGAN, Sheila, 5, Middlesborough
958 SHIPPEY, Brenda, 10,
    Middlesborough +
959 SHIPPEY, Mason, 15, Middlesborough
960 WOODRUFF, Hilda, 12,
    Middlesborough +
961 WOODRUFF, Enid, 9, Middlesborough
962 OLDFIELD, Joan, 7, Middlesborough
963 IRVING, Jean, 9, Acklam
964 WYNN, Marie, 13, Acklam +
965 WYNN, Donald, 10, Acklam
966 HARE, John, 7, Middlesborough
967 PROFITT, Margaret, 15,
    Middlesborough +
968 PROFITT, May, 11, Middlesborough +
969 PROFITT, Joan, 13, Middlesborough
970 BISHOP, William, 9, Nottingham
971 BROUGHTON, Eric, 13, Middlesborough
972 PITCHER, Brenda, 12,
    Middlesborough +
973 PITCHER, Edna, 9, Middlesborough
974 HOLIDAY, Betty, 11, Middlesborough
975 EMPSON, Charles, 14,
    Middlesborough +
976 EMPSON, Leslie, 12, Middlesborough
992 CREE, Mary, 10, Newark +
993 CREE, Lewis, 13, Newark
994 ROGERS, Ralph, 12, Newark +
995 ROGERS, Josephine, 8, Newark
996 LALE, Roma, 14, Newark
997 LEE-SILVEY, Margaret, 6, Newark
998 HAMILTON, William, 14,
    Newcastle-on-Tyne
999 HOLMES, Walter, 13, Newcastle-on-Tyne

1000 UDY, John, 11, Newcastle-on-Tyne +
1001 UDY, Rosemary, 10, Newcastle-on-Tyne
1002 YELF, Gordon, 15, Newcastle-on-Tyne +
1003 YELF, Sheila, 12, Newcastle-on-Tyne
1004 HAYES, Maurice, 15, Scarborough +
1005 HAYES, Albert, 14, Scarborough
1006 PARSONS, Deirdre, 10, Scarborough +
1007 PARSONS, Peter, 12, Scarborough
1008 BEAL, Margaret, 14, Scarborough
1009 SINNOTT, Thomas, 12, Doncaster
1010 BURROWS, Olga, 14, Scarborough
1011 GAUNT, Jeanne, 15, Scarborough
1012 MORLEY, Michael, 10, Scarborough +
1013 MORLEY, Shirley, 7, Scarborough
1014 CHARLTON, John, 6, Scarborough +
1015 CHARLTON, Patricia, 12, Scarborough
1016 ARNOLD, William, 11, Scunthorpe
1017 GOODGER, Jean, 10, Walsall
1018 MORGAN, William, 8, Leiston +
1019 MORGAN, Barbara, 10, Leiston
1020 TINKLER, Paul, 11, Scarborough
1021 SOWERBY, George, 12, Scarborough
1022 WELLOCK, Maureen, 12,
        Scarborough +
1023 WELLOCK, Margaret, 5,
        Scarborough +
1024 WELLOCK, Allen, 7, Scarborough
1025 MIDDLETON, Mercia, 9, Scarborough
1026 BANNING, John, 9, Norton-on-Tees
1027 MARSH, Jean, 13, Stockton-on-Tees
1028 DAVIES, Shirley, 5, Norton +
1029 DAVIES, William, 7, Norton
1030 HOBSON, Mary, 14, Stockton
1031 CADWALLADER, George, 10,
        Stockton +
1032 CADWALLADER, Joan, 12, Stockton
1033 CHAMBERS, Thomas, 9, Stockton
1034 LONG, Joan, 9, Tottenham
1035 LAWRENCE, Royston, 12, Tottenham
1036 CONN, Ivan, 13, Tottenham +
1037 CONN, Bernhard, 8, Tottenham
1038 OLDHAM, Margaret, 9, Haringey +
1039 OLDHAM, Ada, 14, Haringey +
1040 OLDHAM, Horace, 11, Haringey +
1041 OLDHAM, Violet, 8, Haringey
1042 WOOD, William, 14, Tottenham
1043 FITCH, Ronald, 15, Tottenham
1044 BAUMER, Josephine, 10, Finsbury
1045 CAVE, Peter, 15, Southgate

1046 COWANS, Margaret, 6,
        Wallsend-on-Tyne
1047 SOONES, David, 6, Wallsend-on-Tyne +
1048 SOONES, Peter, 10, Wallsend-on-Tyne
1049 WAFER, James, 7, Wallsend-on-Tyne +
1050 WAFER, Thomas, 9, Wallsend-on-Tyne +
1051 WAFER, Patricia, 11,
        Wallsend-on-Tyne +
1052 WAFER, Mary, 13, Wallsend-on-Tyne
1053 MILL, Elizabeth, 8, Wallsend-on-Tyne +
1054 MILL, William, 15, Wallsend-on-Tyne
1055 OSSELTON, Thelma, 8,
        Wallsend-on-Tyne +
1056 OSSELTON, Catherine, 15,
        Wallsend-on-Tyne +
1057 OSSELTON, Francis, 12,
        Wallsend-on-Tyne
1058 DEARY, James, 14, Forest Gate
1059 RIDGWELL, Anita, 12, Forest Gate
1060 THIRKETTLE, Mavis, 9, Windsor
1061 HENSON, Doris, 13, Windsor
1062 PHILLIPS, Kathleen, 14, Datchet
1063 ELLIOT, Elise, 14, Bletchley +
1064 ELLIOT, Peter, 12, Bletchley
1065 GRUBB, Sheila, 6, Windsor
1066 MERRETT, Joan, 14, Windsor
1068 BRISTOW, Doris, 14, Windsor +
1069 BRISTOW, Henry, 13, Windsor +
1070 BRISTOW, James, 11, Windsor
1071 HARRISON, Martin, 10, York
1072 SPENCE, Barbara, 10, York
1073 BENTON, Neil, 9, York
1074 FORD, Leslie, 14, York
1075 SKRINE, Brian, 14, York
1076 PROCTOR, Jean, 11, York +
1077 PROCTOR, Brian, 8, York
1078 LEATHER, Elizabeth, 5, York
1079 ADAMSON, Malcolm, 6, York +
1080 ADAMSON, Richard, 10, York
1081 COLMAN, Margaret, 9, York +
1082 COLMAN, Henry, 15, York
1083 RUDDOCK, Betty, 8, York +
1084 RUDDOCK, Marjorie, 11, York
1085 SHIPPEN, John, 13, Scarborough
1086 GIBSON, George, 15, Pickering +
1087 GIBSON, Michael, 12, Pickering +
1088 GIBSON, John, 7, Pickering
1089 LLOYD, William, 6, Catterick
1090 TOWNSHEND, Roderick, 9, York

1091 PARKER, Sheila, 8, York
1092 FENWICK, Arthur, 12, Whitby +
1093 FENWICK, Bruce, 6,
1094 NORMAN, George, 13, South Bank, Yorks +
1095 NORMAN, Audrey, 11, South Bank, Yorks +
1096 NORMAN, Stanley, 10, South Bank. Yorks
1097 HUGHES, Anthony, 14, Catterick +
1098 HUGHES, Maureen, 12, Catterick
1099 HAMILTON, Rosemary, 13, Middlesborough
1100 MUIR, Pamela, 8, Manchester
1101 McVEY, Jean, 7, Manchester
1102 HOBSON, Vincent, 11, Blackley, Lancs
1103 McALLISTER, Dorothy, 13, Manchester
1104 McCANN, Dorothea, 11, Manchester +
1105 McCANN, Dennis, 7, Manchester
1106 OWENS, Oliver, 11, Manchester
1107 FRANKLAND, John, 12, Manchester
1108 WILSON, Margaret, 7, Manchester +
1109 WILSON, Thomas, 5, Manchester
1110 ROBINSON, Joan, 9, Manchester
1128 BILLS, Edna, 14, Barking
1129 HAMMOND, Doreen, 8, Barking +
1130 HAMMOND, Richard, 11, Barking
1131 FLAUM, Reginald, 12, Dagenham
1132 WOOLGAR, Roy, 12, Beckenham +
1133 WOOLGAR, Derek, 9, Beckenham
1134 COLLIE, Doreen, 9, Selby
1136 TAYLOR (Twins), May, 13, W. Wickham +
1137 TAYLOR, Christine, 13, W. Wickham
1139 HAYMAN, Peter, 10, W. Wickham
1140 WOOD, Bernard, 13, Sydenham +
1141 WOOD, John, 9, Sydenham
1142 BARDELL, Audrey, 14, Beckenham
1143 HINES, Peter, 13, Beckenham
1144 KIRBY, Dorothy, 15, Bristol +
1145 KIRBY, Geoffrey, 9, Bristol
1146 JEFFRIES, Frank, 15, Bristol +
1147 JEFFRIES, Marguerite, 9, Bristol
1149 SILVER, Patricia, 5, Bristol
1152 LOVELL, Hugh, 9, Weston-super-Mare +
1153 LOVELL, John, 8, Weston-super-Mare
1154 DENFORD, Gordon, 13, Bristol
1155 WHITEHEAD, Roy, 9, Bromley

1156 JOSLIN, Clifford, 14, Chelmsford +
1157 JOSLIN, Elizabeth, 12, Chelmsford +
1158 JOSLIN, Cedric, 8, Chelmsford
1159 SPOONER, John, 10, Chelmsford
1160 COVE, Ronald, 13, Chelmsford
1161 LANGDON, Mavis, 14, Chelmsford +
1162 LANGDON, Christopher, 6, Chelmsford
1163 ROSSINGTON, Ronald, 12, Chelmsford
1164 GIRTON, Victor, 12, Chelmsford
1165 BAGGS, Roland, 8, Chelmsford +
1166 BAGGS, Barbara, 6, Chelmsford
1167 HOWELL, John, 6, Chelmsford
1168 CURTIS, Hazel, 13, Chelmsford +
1169 CURTIS, Muriel, 11, Chelmsford +
1170 CURTIS, Frederick, 9, Chelmsford +
1171 CURTIS (Twins), Anthony, 7, Chelmsford +
1172 CURTIS, Jeffrey, 7, Chelmsford
1173 HUNTER, Agnes, 9, Chelmsford +
1174 HUNTER, Mildred, 6, Chelmsford
1175 ALLEN, Denise, 11, Chelmsford +
1176 ALLEN, Granville, 10, Chelmsford +
1177 ALLEN, Terry, 8, Chelmsford +
1178 ALLEN, Gerry, 5, Chelmsford
1185 HUTTON, John, 7, Colchester
1186 WILSON, Hazel, 15, Colchester +
1187 WILSON, Harry, 13, Colchester
1188 LEE, David, 8, Colchester +
1189 LEE, Barbara, 6, Colchester
1193 LAW, Janet, 5, Colchester +
1194 LAW, Ann, 6, Colchester
1195 McVEIGH, Donald, 6, Blackpool +
1196 McVEIGH, Colinette, 10, Blackpool +
1197 McVEIGH, Audrey, 12, Blackpool
1198 STRUTT, Diane, 9, Colchester +
1199 STRUTT, Rayleign, 7, Colchester +
1200 STRUTT, Paul, 6, Colchester
1207 GREEN, Anthony, 12, South Croydon
1209 SMITH, Doris, 15, Greenford
1210 BOOTH, Brian, 14, Hanwell
1211 PURKISS, Frank, 9, Greenford
1213 CROWTHER, Donald, 11, Leicester
1217 CHAPMAN, Eunice, 7, Enfield
1218 SARGENT, Lilian, 11, Enfield +
1219 SARGENT, Irene, 9, Enfield
1221 DERV, Adrienne, 9, Enfield +
1222 DERV (Twins), June, 11, Enfield +
1223 DERV. Yvonne, 11, Enfield +
1224 DERV, Ada, 13, Enfield

1227 NEWTON, John, 11,
    Winchmore Hill +
1228 NEWTON, Marjorie, 13,
    Winchmore Hill
1236 BAKER, Thelma, 11, Romford
1237 FORD, Irene, 13, Romford +
1238 FORD, Phyllis, 11, Romford
1239 JARVIS, Margaret, 13, Romford
1240 KEEBLE, William, 15, Maldon
1241 GLOVER, Barbara, 15,
    Saffron Walden +
1242 GLOVER, Hugh, 13, Saffron Walden
1245 PARKER, Bruce, 9, Gillingham
1246 SAUNDERS, James, 11, Hornchurch +
1247 SAUNDERS, Gwendoline, 13,
    Hornchurch
1249 ROYSTON, Denis, 14, Romford
    (Step-brother of:) +
1250 SEAGRIEF, Margaret, 7, Romford
1251 BROWN, Doreen, 11, Epping
1254 RICHARDSON, Frederick, 14, Witham
1255 WHITE, Betty, 11, Upminster
1256 MINNIS, Alma, 14, Upminster
1257 PYE, Pamela, 10, Upminster +
1258 PYE, Dorothy, 12, Upminster
1259 ROBSON, Josephine, 11, Romford +
1260 ROBSON, Dorothy, 9, Romford
1261 ROBERTS, David, 8, Romford
1264 DAVIE, Dennis, 8, Hornchurch
1265 WEST, Pamela, 13, Upminster +
1266 WEST, Peter, 12, Upminster +
1267 WEST, Margaret, 11, Upminster
1268 HAWKES, Elsie, 12, Loughton
1269 HALTON, John, 10, Romford
1271 TAGG, Ronald, 12, Dagenham
1272 LOVEGROVE, Brian, 11, Romford +
1273 LOVEGROVE, Kathleen, 12, Romford
1274 OATS, Peter, 9, Dagenham
1276 WYER, David, 6, Finchley
1277 BLAND, John, 10, Finchley +
1278 BLAND, Pamela, 8, Finchley
1279 KORN, Denis, 12, London
1280 ENRIGHT, Peter, 15, Finchley +
1281 ENRIGHT, Joseph, 11, Finchley
1282 SAUNDERS, Robert, 13, Finchley +
1283 SAUNDERS, Eric, 11, Finchley
1284 ELRICK, Ina, 8, Whetstone
1285 McCRINDELL, Edward, 10, London +
1286 McCRINDELL, Robert, 8, London

1287 BARNARD, Stanley, 13, Finchley +
1288 BARNARD, Desmond, 12, Finchley +
1289 BARNARD, Anthony, 10, Finchley +
1290 BARNARD, Doreen, 7, Finchley
1291 CLARK, Grace, 12, Finchley
1292 TREWINNARD, Edwin, 13, Finchley
1293 DOOLEY, Vernon, 13, Finchley
1295 HOROBIN, Reginald, 13, Finchley
1296 PERRY, Horace, 10, London +
1297 PERRY, Gwendoline, 13, London
1298 MELTON, Jean, 8, Finchley
1299 CLAYTON, George, 14, Lyminge, Kent
1300 THOMSON, Anne, 14, Gillingham
1301 GREY, Janet, 8, Heston
1302 COOK, Douglas, 11, Hounslow
1303 HUTSON, Vera, 8, Hounslow
1304 COE, Valerie, 10, Hounslow +
1305 COE, Josephine, 12, Hounslow
1306 GRANT, Ivy, 12, Hounslow +
1307 GRANT, David, 11, Hounslow
1308 HARRIOTT, Derek, 10, Hounslow +
1309 HARRIOTT, Cyril, 12, Hounslow +
1310 HARRIOTT, Alfred, 14, Hounslow
1311 CRAWSHAW, John, 11, Isleworth
1312 IRWIN, Joan, 7, Heston +
1313 IRWIN, Iris, 13, Heston +
1314 IRWIN, Constance, 9, Heston
1315 HOARE, Ivy, 12, Isleworth +
1316 HOARE, Dorothy, 10, Isleworth +
1317 HOARE, Margaret, 9, Isleworth
1319 HOGWOOD, Geoffrey, 15, Hounslow
1320 JORDAN, Margaret, 9, Lowestoft +
1321 JORDAN, Peter, 10, Lowestoft +
1322 JORDAN, Sidney, 12, Lowestoft
1323 MOONEY, Bernard, 10, Hounslow +
1324 MOONEY, Gerald, 8, Hounslow
1325 GIBBONS, Olive, 14, C. Tyrone, NI
1326 JOHNSON, Edwyn, 15, Liverpool
1329 DENHAM, Winifred, 11, Hounslow +
1330 DENHAM, Mavis, 9, Hounslow
1331 BEENHAM, Leslie, 9, Hounslow +
1332 BEENHAM, Sydney, 10, Hounslow
1333 GARDINER, Rita, 12, Hounslow
1334 GOMM, John, 7, Hounslow
1335 FOSBROOKE, John, 10, Isleworth
1336 WICKS, Brenda, 8, Ilford +
1337 WICKS, Eileen, 11, Ilford +
1338 WICKS, Jean, 14, Ilford
1339 BUCKMAN, Sheila, 13, Islington

1340 BEDFORD, Eileen, 6, Ilford +
1341 BEDFORD, Norman, 12, Ilford
1342 WALKER, Robert, 12, Romford +
1343 WALKER, William, 13, Romford
1344 PERT, Constance, 10, Ilford +
1345 PERT, June, 15, Ilford
1346 SENIOR, Edward, 10,
    Chadwell Heath +
1347 SENIOR (Twins), Joan, 13,
    Chadwell Heath +
1348 SENIOR, Jean, 13, Chadwell Heath
1350 CHANDLER, David, 11, Dagenham +
1351 CHANDLER, Dorothy, 9, Dagenham
1352 LEEKE, Frederick, 13, Barkingside
1354 PENGLASE, Ian, 10, Cliffe-at-Hoo +
1355 PENGLASE, Ann, 6, Cliffe-at-Hoo
1356 ROKER, Brian, 8, Erith
1357 ECKFORD, Joan, 9, Dartford
1358 NUNN, Barbara, 15, Welling +
1359 NUNN, Sylvia, 11, Welling
1360 MILLS, Pauline, 14, Sidcup +
1361 MILLS, Joyce, 12, Sidcup
1362 SWADLING, Beatrice, 13, Worthing +
1363 SWADLING, Richard, 12, Worthing
1364 STYLES, John, 13, Tunbridge Wells
1365 NEWTON, George, 13, Aylesford +
1366 NEWTON, Albert, 12, Aylesford
1370 LYNN, Peter, 8, Petts Wood +
1371 LYNN, Shirley, 5, Petts Wood
1372 FRANKLIN, Joyce, 11, Luton +
1373 FRANKLIN, Brenda, 8, Luton
1376 STEVENS, Bryan, 14, Luton
1377 ROBSON, Nora, 14, Luton +
1378 ROBSON, Harold, 11, Luton
1379 LUFF, Harold, 8, Luton +
1380 LUFF, Jessie, 12, Luton
1381 WAGHORN, Mary, 7, Maidstone
1384 ROBERTS, May, 8, Maidstone +
1385 ROBERTS, Francis, 6, Maidstone
1388 KENT, Peter, 10, South Harrow
1389 WEST, Terence, 13, North Harrow
1390 GURNEY, Peter, 15, South Harrow +
1391 GURNEY, Muriel, 12, South Harrow
1392 NEVILLE, David, 10, Kenton
1393 GOFF, Phyllis, 12, Southall
1394 HOWARTH, Geoffrey, 9, Southall
1395 LOVELL, Peter, 10, Southall
1396 MERRIFIELD, A M, 12, Feltham
1397 GARE, Beryl, 11, Wembley +

1399 GARE, Teddy, 7, Wembley
1400 SWEETMAN, Jean, 6, Southall
1402 MACDONALD, Gaynor, 10,
    Whetstone +
1403 MACDONALD, Gordon, 6, Whetstone
1406 GOODCHILD, William, 7,
    Palmers Green +
1407 GOODCHILD, Jean, 9,
    Palmers Green +
1408 GOODCHILD, Dorothy, 5, Palmers Green
1409 RAGBOURN, Victor, 12, New Southgate
1410 TANNER, Peggy, 15, Stanmore
1411 RICHARDS, Olive, 13, Twickenham
1412 GOODHAM, Terence, 8, Southall
1413 SMITH, Eric, 11, Southall
1414 BLACKSHAW, Harold, 13, Palmers Green
1415 GEBHARD, David, 6, Southall +
1416 GEBHARD, Joan, 9, Southall
1417 PICK, May, 12, Hanworth
1418 PHELPS, Brenda, 15, Harrow +
1419 PHELPS, Patricia, 9, Harrow
1420 PITT, Audrey, 12, S. Harrow +
1421 PITT, Olive, 9, S. Harrow
1424 WEBBER, Gordon, 8, Southall +
1425 WEBBER, Eileen, 9, Southall +
1426 WEBBER, Cyril, 11, Southall
1427 RAVEN, Peter, 13, Yeovil
1428 PICKERING, Stella, 6, Kingsbury +
1429 PICKERING, Barbara, 8, Kingsbury
1430 MARTIN, Margaret, 12, Edgware
1431 JOYCE, Malcolm, 7, Wembley
1432 FRENCH, Doris, 11, Wembley +
1433 FRENCH, Patricia, 10, Wembley
1434 DALE, Michael, 11, Harlesden
1435 FRANK, Joan, 14, London
1436 CALLEAR, Olga, 15, Oxford +
1437 CALLEAR, Ilona, 14, Oxford
1438 PERKINS, Sheila, 13, Oxford
1439 LANE, Thomas, 9, Oxford +
1440 LANE, Christine, 6, Oxford
1441 TAYLOR, Gordon, 14, Southsea
1444 HILTON, Peggy, 11, Basingstoke
1445 JESSOP, Mervyn, 6, Liverpool
1446 ELEY, Miriam, 15, Basingstoke +
1447 ELEY, Joan, 14, Basingstoke +
1448 ELEY, Florence, 6, Basingstoke
1450 HARE, Doris, 11, Fareham
1451 FOSTER, Neill, 9, W. Clandon +
1452 FOSTER, Pamela, 5, W. Clandon, Surrey

— 1 PARRY, Ann, 14, Bristol (CORB No. of this child suggests delayed sailing)
1453 GRIFFIN, Edwina, 13, West Molesey
1454 AUSTIN, Henry, 12, Tolworth
1455 HINSHELWOOD, Cyril, 13, Surbiton
1456 KISSENGER, Anthony, 14, Kenley
1457 CORNISH, Donald, 13, Coulsdon
1460 SHINE, Anthony, 15, Sompting
1461 GOACHER, John, 12, Reigate +
1462 GOACHER, Geoffrey, 10, Reigate
1463 HOLMES, Enid, 8, Telscombe Cliffs +
1464 HOLMES, Freda, 10, Telscombe Cliffs
1465 MURPHY, Doreen, 10, High Wycombe
1466 COOK, Joyce, 13, Tottenham
1470 LEFEVRE, Doris, 13, Harlesden +
1471 LEFEVRE, Sheila, 10, Harlesden
1472 KING, Nordra, 9, London +
1473 KING, Billy, 7, London
1475 HARRISON, William, 8, London +
1476 HARRISON, Gladys, 6, London
1477 TEMPLE, Robert, 12, Southgate +
1478 TEMPLE, Walter, 7, Southgate
1479 BENNETT, Norman, 14, Palmers Green
1482 SHIERS, Roy, 14, London
1483 PROWSE, Joyce, 13, Wood Green +
1484 PROWSE, Dorothy, 12, Wood Green
1485 PYER, Audrey, 8, Wood Green
1486 HALVERSON, Eric, 12, London
1487 HEALES, William, 13, Wood Green
1488 SMITH, Ivor, 13, Palmers Green
1489 MAYNARD, Alan, 14, Wood Green
1491 GAIR, Robert, 13, Bowes Park +
1492 GAIR, Walter, 14, Bowes Park
1493 COOMBER, Ronald, 13, Bowes Park
1494 JOHNSON, Patrick, 14, Windsor
1496 WARREN, Peter, 11, Yeovil +
1497 WARREN, Clifford, 13, Yeovil +
1498 WARREN, Joan, 10, Yeovil
1499 RATTLE, Glen, 13, Yeovil +
1500 RATTLE, May, 10, Yeovil
1501 LARAMY, Theodore, 11, Yeovil
1504 CREEK, Douglas, 13, Yeovil +
1505 CREEK, Robert, 11, Yeovil +
1506 CREEK, Ronald, 8, Yeovil +
1507 CREEK, Edward, 7, Yeovil
1508 LEADER, Robert, 13, Islington +
1509 LEADER, Grace, 11, Islington
1512 PERRY, Marjery, 14, E. Finchley
1513 ADSHEAD-POPE, Dennis, 14, London

1515 GIBBS, Rosemary, 9, Holloway +
1516 GIBBS, Jean, 8, Holloway
1517 PARKER, Stanley, 8, Camberwell
1518 RAWLINGS (Twins), Donald, 14, London +
1519 RAWLINGS, Stanley, 14, London
1520 ROPER, June, 7, London
1521 COSTELOE, Robert, 14, Stockport
1522 EVES, Frederick, 13, Stockport
1523 CROMPTON, Henry, 12, Stockport
1524 HIGGINSON, Arthur, 12, Stockport
1525 HOLROYD, Peter, 10, Hazel Grove
1526 STORER, Doris, 13, Stockport
1527 COLLISTER, Joan, 14, Wilmslow
1528 COLLINS, Harry, 12, Stockport +
1529 COLLINS, William, 9, Stockport
1530 HUMPLEBY, Sylvia, 13, Stockton-on-Tees
1531 McKEAN, Marjory, 12, Stockton-on-Tees +
1532 McKEAN, Betsy, 9, Stockton-on-Tees
1533 PASSMORE, Elizabeth, 13, Stockton-on-Tees
1534 BATES, Clifford, 11, Stockton-on-Tees
1535 DINSLEY, Jean, 8, Stockton-on-Tees +
1536 DINSLEY, Clarice, 11, Stockton-on-Tees
1537 BLACKBURN, Gladys, 13, Stockton-on-Tees
1538 EMMERSON, Margaret, 15, Stockton-on-Tees
1539 PHILLIPSON, Annie, 13, Gateshead +
1540 PHILLIPSON, Doreen, 9, Gateshead
1541 HAGAN, Doreen, 12, Gateshead
1542 MURRAY, Alan, 10, Hull +
1543 MURRAY, John, 12, Hull
1544 ASHTON, Ada, 10, Hebburn-on-Tyne +
1545 ASHTON, Sylvia, 9, Hebburn-on-Tyne
1546 BELL, Fenwick, 15, Hebburn-on-Tyne +
1547 BELL, William, 10, Hebburn-on-Tyne
1550 ROBERTS, Minnie, 6, Hebburn-on-Tyne
1551 STEPHENSON, Sylvia, 10, Hebburn-on-Tyne +
1552 STEPHENSON, Leonard, 7, Hebburn-on-Tyne
1553 HORNBY, Malcolm, 5, Hebburn-on-Tyne
1554 AMER, Raymond, 14, Hebburn-on-Tyne +
1555 AMER, Clifford, 7, Hebburn-on-Tyne
1556 BLAKEY, Donald, 13, Hebburn-on-Tyne

1557 IRWIN, Muriel, 9, Hebburn-on-Tyne +
1558 IRWIN, Olive, 8, Hebburn-on-Tyne
1559 ROY, William, 13, Hebburn-on-Tyne
1560 SCOTT, Alan, 11, Hebburn-on-Tyne
1561 TAYLOR, John, 13, Hebburn-on-Tyne +
1562 TAYLOR, James, 11, Hebburn-on-Tyne +
1563 TAYLOR, Humphrey, 10,
    Hebburn-on-Tyne
1564 WILSON, Alan, 11, Hebburn-on-Tyne
1567 HENDERSON, Robert, 13,
    Hebburn-on-Tyne
1568 BARKER, Charles, 10, Darlington
1569 TURNBULL, Nance, 13, Darlington +
1570 TURNBULL, Ronald, 8, Darlington
1571 OWEN, Hunter, 12, Darlington +
1572 OWEN, James, 10, Darlington
1573 BRASS, Margaret, 8, Darlington
1574 BRETT, James, 14, Darlington +
1575 BRETT, Albert, 11, Darlington +
1576 BRETT, Doris, 9, Darlington
1578 LAMB, Margaret, 11, Darlington
1583 SMITH, Peter, 10, Darlington
1584 RACE, Dorothy, 14, Darlington +
1585 RACE, David, 11, Darlington
1586 BRENTLEY, Thomas, 11, Darlington
1587 WINDALE, Dorcea, 13, Darlington +
1588 WINDALE, Eric, 6, Darlington
1589 ANDREW, William, 9, Darlington
1590 CRAGGS, John, 13, Darlington +
1591 CRAGGS, Colin, 12, Darlington +
1592 CRAGGS, Kathleen, 9, Darlington
1593 THOMAS, Margaret, 12, Darlington +
1594 THOMAS, Hilda, 10, Darlington +
1595 THOMAS, Edward, 8, Darlington
1596 CLIFF, Ronald, 10, Darlington
1597 TIPLADY, Norman, 14, Darlington
1600 SMITH, Raymond, 13, Darlington +
1601 SMITH, Freda, 11, Darlington
1602 BURRELL, John, 11, Darlington +
1603 BURRELL, Margaret, 12, Darlington
1604 VOKES, William, 13, Darlington +
1605 VOKES, Colin, 9, Darlington
1607 MARTIN, Frank, 12, Darlington
1610 ECKFORD, Sheila, 15, Darlington
1611 COSTLEY, William, 12, Gateshead +
1612 COSTLEY, Betty, 8, Gateshead
1613 TATE, Edna, 10, Gateshead
1614 CLEVERLEY, Gordon, 13, Gateshead +
1615 CLEVERLEY, Joan, 12, Gateshead

1616 NEIL, Myra, 13, Gateshead
1617 BLAKE, Joseph, 11, Gateshead
1618 BARKES, Ernest, 15, South Shields +
1619 BARKES, Margaret, 13, South Shields
1640 HOLLINRAKE, Doris, 11, Burnley
1641 HINDLE, Yvonne, 14, Whalley
1646 ABEL, Marjorie, 13, Stretford
1647 GIBSON, Margaret, 12, Stretford
1648 STANFORD, Ronald, 11, Manchester +
1649 STANFORD, Betty, 12, Manchester +
1650 STANFORD, Constance, 8, Manchester
1651 BROCKBANK, Joan, 8, Manchester +
1652 BROCKBANK, Edwin, 10, Manchester
1653 SHEEHAN, John, 13, Manchester +
1654 SHEEHAN, Winifred, 10, Manchester
1655 WYATT, Margaret, 10, Manchester +
1656 WYATT, Stephen, 8, Manchester
1657 LONGMAN, Jean, 12, Manchester +
1658 LONGMAN, Ronald, 11, Manchester +
1659 LONGMAN, John, 9, Manchester
1660 WARDLE, Sheila, 8, Manchester
1661 STEVENSON, Eva, 9, Manchester
1662 CONDY, Trevor, 13, Manchester +
1663 CONDY, Norman, 14, Manchester
1664 DALEY, Peter, 6, Manchester
1665 MAXWELL, Sheena, 13, Manchester +
1666 MAXWELL, Andrew, 9, Manchester
1669 JOLLEY, Irene, 14, Manchester
1670 McWALTER, Kenneth, 9, Manchester +
1671 McWALTER, John, 13, Manchester
1672 HILL, David, 13, Manchester
1673 PINDER, Brian, 7, Manchester
1674 GOODFELLOW, Audrey, 9, Manchester
1675 KIERNAN, Phoebe, 12, Rochdale
1676 NEELY, Helen, 13, St Helens +
1677 NEELY, Betty, 12, St Helens
1678 INGRAM, Rose, 13, St Helens
1679 ORRELL, Jennie, 15, St Helens
1680 ORMEROD, John, 14, St Helens +
1681 ORMEROD, Barbara, 11, St Helens +
1682 ORMEROD, Augustine, 9, St Helens
1683 HUNTER, Robert, 14, St Helens
1684 FRODSHAW, William, 11, St Helens
1685 BURGESS, Reginald, 8, St Helens +
1686 BURGESS, Sylvia, 7, St Helens
1687 BOARDMAN, Norah, 10, St Helens
1688 NUNN, Olive, 11, Salford
1689 CHARLESWORTH, Irene, 13, Salford
1690 DIBBLE, Marjorie, 11, Salford

1691 OWEN, Kenneth, 11, Southport
1692 SCOTT, Winifred, 15, Southport
1693 WILSON (Twins) Anthony, 13,
    Southport +
1694 WILSON, William, 13, Southport
1695 JARVIS, Michael, 10, Southport +
1696 JARVIS, John, 5, Southport
1697 ANDREWS, Joyce, 15, Southport
1698 KIDD, Hugh, 11, Grimsby
1699 LANCASTER, Barbara, 15, Grimsby
1700 CLARKE, Esme, 12, Grimsby +
1701 CLARKE, George, 5, Grimsby +
1702 CLARKE, Peter, 8, Grimsby
1703 MUDD, Anthony, 6, Grimsby +
1704 MUDD, George, 9, Grimsby
1705 WHITLEY, Tom, 13, Grimsby +
1706 WHITLEY, Raymond, 12, Grimsby +
1707 WHITLEY, Sheila, 9, Grimsby +
1708 WHITLEY, Ida, 5, Grimsby
1709 TUMBER, John, 13, Grimsby +
1710 TUMBER, Frederick, 10, Grimsby
1711 BALLARD, Roy, 6, Grimsby +
1712 BALLARD, John, 5, Grimsby
1713 YORSTON, May, 5, Grimsby
1714 WHYTE, Pearl, 11, Grimsby
1715 HALLIWELL, Colin, 14, Grimsby
1716 SPACKMAN, Marie, 9, Grimsby +
1717 SPACKMAN, David, 13, Grimsby
1718 BURCHELL, John, 14, Grimsby +
1719 BURCHELL, Mae, 10, Grimsby
1720 READ, John, 7, Grimsby
1723 GAGE, Eileen, 13, Grimsby
    (Step-sister of:) +
1724 WHITTINGTON, John, 14, Grimsby
1726 GRANT, Bruce, 7, Grimsby
1727 GIFFORD, Sybil, 13, Grimsby
1729 LAND, Colin, 11, Caister-on-Sea +
1730 LAND, Nigel, 8, Caister-on-Sea
1731 KEMP, Eric, 12, Norwich +
1732 KEMP, David, 6, Norwich
1733 WOODS, Barbara, 12, Norwich +
1734 WOODS, Geoffrey, 7, Norwich
1735 ALDHAM, Ivy, 13, Norwich +
1736 ALDHAM, Joan, 11, Norwich +
1737 ALDHAM, Brenda, 8, Norwich +
1738 ALDHAM, Margaret, 6, Norwich
1739 CARLTON, Beryl, 9, Norwich +
1740 CARLTON, Joan, 15, Norwich
1741 LONG, Dennis, 13, Norwich +

1742 LONG, Bernard, 11, Norwich
1743 ALLEN, Diana, 15, Norwich +
1744 ALLEN, Rosalind, 13, Norwich +
1745 ALLEN, Elaine, 10, Norwich
1746 SMITH, Victor, 12, Norwich +
1747 SMITH, Kenneth, 11, Norwich +
1748 SMITH, Geoffrey, 8, Norwich
1749 CAREY, Ronald, 12, Norwich +
1750 CAREY, Alan, 8, Norwich
1751 HALL, Baden, 15, Norwich
1752 SILLETT, Leslie, 12, Norwich +
1753 SILLETT, Ronald, 11, Norwich
1754 TASKER, Kathleen, 9, Norwich +
1755 TASKER, Frederick, 14, Norwich
1756 GOWING, Brenda, 7, Norwich +
1757 GOWING, Beryl, 6, Norwich
1758 GEORGE, Michael, 5, Norwich
1759 STEWARD, Philip, 8, Norwich +
1760 STEWARD, Arthur, 11, Norwich +
1761 STEWARD, Cecilia, 13, Norwich
1762 HARRIS, Olive, 10, Norwich
1763 EDWARDS, Frederick, 11, Norwich +
1764 EDWARDS, Frank, 10, Norwich
1765 DYSON, Nancy, 12, Norwich +
1766 DYSON, David, 8, Norwich
1767 DENNIS, Cedric, 12, Norwich +
1768 DENNIS, Kenneth, 9, Norwich
1769 HAWES, Margaret, 6, Norwich
1770 DAWSON, Gerald, 6, Norwich +
1771 DAWSON, Neville, 12, Norwich +
1772 DAWSON, Betty, 9, Norwich +
1773 DAWSON, Lionel, 10, Norwich
1774 MIDDLETON, Sybil, 13, Norwich +
1775 MIDDLETON; Pamela, 11, Norwich +
1776 MIDDLETON, Brian, 9, Norwich
1777 TURNER, Pauline, 11, Norwich +
1778 TURNER, Brian, 5, Norwich
1779 MULLINS, Jean, 11, Norwich +
1780 MULLINS (Twins), Daphne, 5,
    Norwich +
1781 MULLINS, Beryl, 5, Norwich
1782 CROPLEY, Marion, 13, Norwich
1783 MINORS, May, 11, Norwich
1784 PORTER, Iris, 13, Norwich +
1785 PORTER, Gerald, 10, Norwich
1786 POTTLE, Vera, 12, Norwich +
1787 POTTLE, Kenneth, 9, Norwich
1788 FRANKLIN, Nancy, 8, Norwich
1789 GREEN, John, 10, Norwich

1790 TURNBULL, Robert, 11, Wallsend-on-Tyne
1791 DENT (Twins), Iris, 12, Newark +
1792 DENT, Joan, 12, Newark
1793 HERMON, James, 11, Willington Quay +
1794 HERMON, Albert, 9, Willington Quay +
1795 HERMON, Brian, 8, Willington Quay
1796 THOMPSON, George, 7, Wallsend-on-Tyne +
1797 THOMPSON, Marian, 13, Wallsend-on-Tyne
1798 SMILES, Edward, 13, Wallsend-on-Tyne +
1799 SMILES, Robert, 10, Wallsend-on-Tyne +
1800 SMILES, Elizabeth, 9, Wallsend-on-Tyne +
1801 SMILES, James, 6, Wallsend-on-Tyne
1802 BATEY, Evelyn, 7, Newcastle-on-Tyne +
1803 BATEY, Joan, 6, Newcastle-on-Tyne
1804 WILSON, Ronald, 5, Newcastle-on-Tyne
1808 MIRLEY, Carmel, 13, Newcastle-on-Tyne +
809 MIRLEY, Basil, 9, Newcastle-on-Tyne
1810 THOMPSON, William, 8, Newcastle-on-Tyne +
1811 THOMPSON, Allen, 7, Newcastle-on-Tyne
1812 MAKER, Theresa, 8, Newcastle-on-Tyne
1814 MOFFATT, Donald, 9, Newcastle-on-Tyne +
1815 MOFFATT, Sheila, 8, Newcastle-on-Tyne +
1816 MOFFATT, Lorna, 6, Newcastle-on-Tyne
1818 OGLE, Margaret, 13, Newcastle-on-Tyne
1819 ROBSON, James, 11, Newcastle-on-Tyne +
1820 ROBSON, Thomas, 9, Newcastle-on-Tyne
1821 YOUNGER, Joyce, 12, Newcastle-on-Tyne +
1822 YOUNGER (Twins), Gerald, 8, Newcastle-on-Tyne +
1823 YOUNGER, John, 8, Newcastle-on-Tyne
1824 HUGHES, John, 11, Newcastle-on-Tyne
1825 MARSH, John, 7, Newcastle-on-Tyne
1828 ANDERSON, George, 5, Newcastle-on-Tyne
1829 DRUMMOND, Michael, 7, Newcastle-on-Tyne +
1830 DRUMMOND, Peter, 5, Newcastle-on-Tyne
1831 STEPHENSON, Ronald, 13, Newcastle-on-Tyne +
1832 STEPHENSON, Norman, 12, Newcastle-on-Tyne
1833 BRODIE, Raymond, 9, North Shields
1834 BURN, Kenneth, 13, North Shields +
1835 BURN, Lillian, 11, North Shields
1836 MAY, Beryl, 14, Whitley Bay +
1837 MAY, Ronald, 10, Whitley Bay +
1838 MAY, Barbara, 9, Whitley Bay
1839 SIMS, Henry, 11, Mansfield +
1840 SIMS, William, 12, Mansfield +
1841 SIMS, Lilian, 15, Mansfield
1842 DAY, José, 14, Mansfield
1843 MOORHOUSE, Albert, 13, Mansfield
1844 ADAMS, Robert, 14, Walsall +
1845 ADAMS, Peter, 11, Walsall
1853 ROTHERY, Margaret, 14, Cottingham
1854 DONNISON, James, 14, Hornsea
1855 PICKARD, Constance, 14, Hull +
1856 PICKARD, John, 11, Hull
1857 HERN, John, 7, Hull
1858 STYAN, Clifford, 14, Beverley
1859 LLOYD, Martin, 11, Collingham +
1860 LLOYD, Heather, 9, Collingham
1861 CLIFFE, John, 14, Hessle
1862 WOODS, Bernard, 14, Hull
1863 HUDSON, Dorothea, 6, Hull
1864 BIMSON, Mavis, 15, Hull
1865 STEPHENSON, Gerald, 8, Hull
1866 VALE, Brian, 10, Hull
1867 SHEPARD, Raymond, 10, Hull
1870 DAVIS, John, 14, York
1871 CUTT, Terence, 8, York +
1872 CUTT, Graeme, 7, York
1873 HARRISON, Desmond, 10, York +
1874 HARRISON, Margaret, 8, York
1875 BELLERBY, John, 15, York +
1876 BELLERBY, Margaret, 14, York +
1877 BELLERBY, Irene, 8, York
1878 FORD, Mary, 14, York
1879 BARKER, Edward, 12, York +
1880 BARKER, Gerald, 9, York
1881 DUNFORD, Dorothy, 13, York +

1882 DUNFORD, Audrey, 11, York +
1883 DUNFORD, Kenneth, 6, York
1886 MAW, Edith, 15, York
1887 KNIGHT, Nesta, 11, York
1888 CAMIDGE, Mary, 12, York
1889 LAMB, Muriel, 14, York +
1890 LAMB, Edward, 13, York +
1891 LAMB, John, 11, York +
1892 LAMB, Eric, 7, York
1893 COLEMAN, Irene, 9, York +
1894 COLEMAN, Audrey, 12, York
1895 LEWCOCK, Cynthia, 13, York
1898 SEALE, Gladys, 9, York +
1899 SEALE, Marguerite, 11, York +
1900 SEALE, Jean, 13, York +
1901 SEALE, Ethel, 15, York
1902 BROWNE, Maureen, 15, York +
1903 BROWNE, Sheila, 5, York
1904 JONES, Barbara, 10, Middlesborough +
1906 JONES, Alfred, 11, Middlesborough
1907 STAMP, Arthur, 10, Middlesborough
1908 HETHERINGTON, Ronald, 11,
      Middlesborough
1912 CONWAY, Joyce, 12, Middlesborough
1913 SHAW, Jean, 14, Brighouse
1914 MOORHOUSE, Joan, 12, Bradford
1915 SIMPSON, Mary, 10, Bradford +
1916 SIMPSON, Margaret, 6, Bradford
1919 JAGGER, Barbara, 11, Bradford
1920 MYERS, Marion, 10, Bradford +
1921 MYERS, Kathleen, 8, Bradford
1922 SKINNER, Audrey, 13, Rotherham
1923 LEWIS, Wendy, 6, Barry
1924 SLEE, Dorothy, 15, Barry +
1925 SLEE, Vera, 14, Barry
1930 NEW, Desmond, 12, Newport, Mon.
1931 JAMES (Twins), Royston, 12,
      Newport, Mon. +
1932 JAMES, Iris, 12, Newport, Mon.
1933 WEBBER, John, 14, Newport
1934 ELLWOOD, Diane, 8, Newport
1936 RICHARDSON, June, 12, Newport
1937 FROST, Ian, 11, Newport
1938 TUDOR, Joyce, 11, Montgomery +
1939 TUDOR, David, 14, Montgomery
1940 JONES, Peter, 12, Leeds +
1941 JONES, Jacqueline, 14, Leeds
1942 HALL, Kathleen, 11, Leeds +
1943 HALL, May, 9, Leeds

1946 INNES, Dorothy, 15, Blyth +
1947 INNES, Charles, 13, Blyth
1948 POTTER, Marion, 7, Plumstead +
1949 POTTER, Raymond, 8, Plumstead
1950 HINDLE, Isabel, 12, Paddington
1951 ROSE, Joan, 6, Fulham
1952 WELLS, Peter, 14, Holloway
1953 CROWHURST, Leonard, 13,
      Tulse Hill +
1954 CROWHURST, David, 10, Tulse Hill
1955 SMITH, John, 10, Goole +
1956 SMITH, Eileen, 13, Goole
1957 CROZIER, Christine, 9, Hackney +
1958 CROZIER, Edward, 12, Hackney
1960 JAMES, Arthur, 14, N16
1961 MARTIN, Victor, 12, Bromley
1962 WILSON, Anne, 10, Streatham
1963 SCOTT, Ernest, 11, Bedford
1964 JARVIS, Paul, 10, Catford
1965 TEMPLE, John, 14, SE22
1967 JEFFERIES, Joan, 12, Hackney +
1968 JEFFERIES, Gloria, 5, Hackney
1969 WILLIAMS, Shirley, 5, SE4
1970 POTTER, John, 6, Weston-super-Mare
1972 FREEDMAN, Marion, 8, Forest Hill +
1973 FREEDMAN, Thelma, 7, Forest Hill
1974 MORTON, Muriel, 14, Dulwich
1975 HILL, Leonard, 13, Brockley
1976 WEST, Brian, 12, Forest Hill
1979 FOWLER, Stanley, 6, Homerton
1980 HARRIOTT, Lennox, 15, Hounslow
1981 HAY, Peter, 8, Brighton
2936 NASH, Edgar, 14, Wintney +
2937 NASH, Kenneth, 10, Wintney
3182 HADDON, Peggy, 14, Bury St Edmunds
3183 ATKINS, Maurice, 14, Beckenham +
3184 ATKINS, Bernard, 12, Beckenham +
3185 ATKINS, Michael, 6, Beckenham
3186 JOHNSTON, Helen, 8, Kenton
3187 SIVERS, Ann, 5, Ashford, Middlesex
3190 NICKELS, Robert, 13, Pinner
3191 RICE, Martyn, 13, Whitton +
3192 RICE, Bernard, 9, Whitton
3193 SMITH, Shirley, 6, Hillingdon
3194 HALL, Sheila, 9, Harrow +
3195 HALL, Harold, 8, Harrow
3196 WATERS, Doreen, 11, Edgeware
3200 JONES, Bryan, 8, Harrow +
3201 JONES, Derek, 6, Harrow

3202 HAMMILL, Peter, 9, Feltham +
3203 HAMMILL, Mary, 6, Feltham
3204 PHILLIPS, Beryl, 13, Warrington
3205 ELLIS, Joyce, 14, Epsom
3206 LUTLEY, Hazel, 10, Woking
3208 ENGLAND, Elizabeth, 13, Wallington +
3209 ENGLAND, Mary, 10, Wallington +
3210 ENGLAND, Margaret, 8, Wallington
3211 STRUDWICK, Jennifer, 11, Banstead
3212 WALLACE, Enid, 14, Purley
3213 POVEY, Yvonne, 11, Mitcham +
3214 POVEY, Pamela, 10, Mitcham
3215 BLURTON, Dennis, 14, Tadworth
3216 JEFFREY, Alan, 8, Tolworth
3219 KELLY, Brian, 8, East Grinstead
3220 NAYLOR, Audrey, 6, Sidcup
3221 McCLUSKEY, Charles, 11, Tadworth
3222 OLIVER, William, 13, Coulsdon
3223 KING, Allan, 10, Cheam
3224 SHAW, Geoffrey, 13, Nottingham
3226 DAVY, Teddie, 14, Great Yarmouth
3227 HULL, Michael, 13, Great Yarmouth
3228 WOODWARD, Reginald, 12, Retford
3231 EDWARDS, Albert, 13, Chelmsford
3232 RISON, Peter, 13, Chelmsford
3233 FINLOW, Joan, 13, Chelmsford +
3234 FINLOW, Charles, 9, Chelmsford
3235 FIGG, Angus, 10, Aylesbury
3236 BALLARD, John, 13, Amersham
3245 LYTTLE, Deirdre, 5, Chelmsford +
3246 LYTTLE, Sheila, 15, Chelmsford
3247 HAIKINGS, John, 12, Scarborough
3249 WHITTINGTON, Arthur, 12, Swansea +
3250 WHITTINGTON, Robert, 10, Swansea
3251 BAILEY, Joan, 10, Sheffield +
3252 BAILEY, Brian, 8, Sheffield
3253 BOYES, Thelma, 8, Middlesborough
3254 SLEIGH, Dorothy, 8, Middlesborough +
3255 SLEIGH, Joan, 12, Middlesborough +
3256 SLEIGH, Regina, 14, Middlesborough +
3257 SLEIGH, Ann, 11, Middlesborough
3258 BROWN, Lieselotte, 12, Middlesborough
3259 WOOD, Raymond, 12, Eastbourne
3264 SILLIS, Marjorie, 15, Norwich +
3265 SILLIS, Dorothy, 12, Norwich
3615 BURROWS, Agnes, 14, Glasgow +
3616 BURROWS, Catherine, 10, Glasgow
3617 CHEYNE, Jean, 9, Glasgow
(See No. 3675)

3618 FARMER, Blythe, 12, Glasgow +
3619 FARMER, Velma, 9, Glasgow
3620 RAE, Mary, 13, Glasgow
3621 REID, Marion, 11, Glasgow +
3622 REID, Verna, 7, Glasgow
(See No. 3684)
3623 RICHMOND, Clara, 9, Strathaven
3624 SCOTT, Hazel, 11, Glasgow +
3625 SCOTT, Violet, 14, Glasgow
3626 THOMSON, Audrey, 6, Glasgow
3627 WEIR, Janette, 8, Glasgow
3628 WILLOX, Maureen, 6, Glasgow
3629 BROWN, Henry, 6, Glasgow +
3630 BROWN, Margaret, 11, Glasgow
3631 BRUCE, Gordon, 5, Glasgow +
3632 BRUCE, Isabella, 10, +
3633 BRUCE, Robert, 8, Glasgow
3634 COWAN, Archibald, ?, Motherwell +
3635 COWAN, Margaret, 12, Motherwell
3636 LEE, William, 6, Glasgow
3637 MACKINNON, Anne, 14, Edinburgh +
3638 MACKINNON, Katherine, 12, Edinburgh
3639 MONTEITH, Doreen, 6, Greenock +
3640 MONTEITH, Margaret, 8, Greenock
3641 NEVILLE, Irene, 12, Glasgow +
3642 NEVILLE, Robin, 8, Glasgow
3643 PATERSON, Moyra, 15, Glasgow
3644 BAIN, Agnes, 10, Glasgow +
3645 BAIN, Dorothy, 13, Glasgow +
3646 BAIN, Douglas, 9, Glasgow +
3647 BAIN, James, 5, Glasgow +
3648 BAIN, Mary, 11, Glasgow
3649 CHAPMAN, Annie, 11, Glasgow +
3650 CHAPMAN, Jean, 13, Glasgow
3651 FANNING, Winifred, 10, Glasgow
3652 KINNEAR, Joan, 15, Edinburgh
3654 McKINNON, John, 7, Glasgow
3655 MACNAB, Emily, 8, Glasgow +
3656 MACNAB, John, 5, Glasgow
3657 ANDERSON, Rona, 14, Edinburgh
3658 ADAM, Elinor, 13, Aberdeen +
3659 ADAM, Sheila, 11, Aberdeen
3698 MACKENZIE, Duncan, 10, Dundee
3660 BROADWOOD, Irene, 14, Edinburgh
3661 BRYCE, Marion, 13, Leith +
3662 BRYCE, Ronald, 6, Leith
3663 HAY, James, 7, Dingswall +
3664 HAY, Jean, 11, Dingswall +
3665 HAY, Morna, 9, Dingswall

3667 MITCHELL, Mary, 10, Brechin
3668 MOYES, Kathleen, 13, Portknockie
3669 ROBERTSON, Anne, 7, Edinburgh
3670 VIRTUE, Denis, 6, Edinburgh
3672 WOOD, Mary, 8, Dundee
3673 BRYCE, Douglas, 8, Leith
    (See Nos. 3661 & 3662) +
3674 BRYCE, Robert, 11, Leith
3675 CHEYNE, George, 12, Glasgow
    (See No. 3617)
3676 FANNING, Richard, 15, Glasgow
3677 KEARNEY, James, 14, Glasgow +
3678 KEARNEY, Frederick, 13, Glasgow
3680 LYONS, Thomas, 13, Glasgow
3682 McMAHON, John, 10, Edinburgh
3683 PRIMROSE, Robert, 9, Glasgow
3684 REID, James, 9, Glasgow
3685 ROBERTSON, Kenneth, 11, Edinburgh
3686 ROBINSON, Douglas, 10,
    N. Queensferry +
3687 ROBINSON, Kenneth, 13,
    N. Queensferry
3688 WELSH, William, 13, Dundee
3689 BELL, Eric, 14, Aberdeen
3691 COWAN, James, 8, Motherwell
3692 CUTHILL, Robert, 11, Glasgow +
3693 CUTHILL, James, 15, Glasgow
3694 DAVISON, George, 10, Lerwick +
3695 DAVISON, Ronald, 13, Lerwick
3696 HOLMAN, Cecil, 15, Dundee
3699 McKIE, David, 9, Edinburgh
3700 SIMPSON, William, 8, Perth
3701 WEIR, Archibald, 11, Glasgow
3702 WILLIAMSON, David, 9, Glasgow
3703 WINCHESTER, Edward, 12,
    (Singapore)
3704 YOUNG, Eric, 11, Inverary
3705 SHIELDS, Robert, 11, Edinburgh
3706 EDMOND, Roberta, 13, Glasgow +
3707 EDMOND, James, 11, Glasgow, +
3708 EDMOND, Margaret, 7, Glasgow
3713 WINTER, William, 12, Glasgow
3714 SCOTT, Gordon, 8, Glasgow
3715 SANSON, Edward, 11, Paisley +
3716 SANSON, Margaret, 7, Paisley
3717 WEBB, David, 12, Glasgow +
3718 WEBB, Mavis, 10, Glasgow
3719 WINTER, James, 6, Glasgow
3820 ANDERSON, Dorothy, 7, Edinburgh +

3821 ANDERSON, Sheila, 9, Edinburgh
3822 BAMFORD, Margaret, 7, Glasgow
3824 COWIE, Margaret, 14, Edinburgh
3825 DALE, Bertha, 9, Glasgow +
3826 DALE, Rosaline, 11, Glasgow +
3827 DALE, Winifred, 14, Glasgow
3828 DUNCAN, Sheila, 9, Burton-on-Trent
3829 KNIGHT, Agnes, 14, Edinburgh +
3830 KNIGHT, Edwina, 9, Edinburgh +
3831 KNIGHT, Janet, 10, Edinburgh
3832 PITKETHLY, Frances, 10, Edinburgh
3833 RITCHIE, Alice, 14, Edinburgh +
3834 RITCHIE, Jean, 11, Edinburgh
3835 ROBERTSON, Isobel, 15, Edinburgh
3836 DOCHERTY, Margaret, ?, Glasgow +
3837 DOCHERTY, Elizabeth, ?, Glasgow
3839 GORMLEY, Virginia, 11, Edinburgh +
3838 GORMLEY, Patricia, 15, Edinburgh
3840 GRANT, Agnes, 14, Glasgow +
3841 GRANT, Jean, 8, Glasgow
3842 HOLLAND, John, 6, Inverness
3843 HUNTER, Norma, 12, Glasgow
3844 HYND, Margaret, 13, Glasgow
3847 REILLY, Margaret, 8, Glasgow +
3848 REILLY, Mary, 12, Glasgow
3849 ADAMS, Catherine, 6, Glasgow
3850 AITCHISON, Doris, 11, Glasgow
3851 CAMPBELL, Doreen, 12, Glasgow +
3852 CAMPBELL, Stephen, 6, Glasgow
3853 DUNCAN, Maureen, 6, Burton-on-Trent
3854 LEISHMAN, Archibald, 6, Glasgow +
3855 LEISHMAN, Christina, 11, Glasgow
3856 McARTHUR, Agnes, 13, Glasgow
3857 McINNES, Grace, 9, Glasgow
3858 SPROULE, Ann, 10, Glasgow +
3859 SPROULE, Elizabeth, 9, Glasgow +
3860 SPROULE, Graham, 6, Glasgow
3861 STEEL, Helen, 8, Glasgow
3862 WILSON, Henry, 7, Glasgow +
3863 WILSON, Marjorie, 9, Glasgow
3864 WOTHERSPOON, Christina, 13, Glasgow
3865 BERKIN, Annie, 9, Glasgow
3867 CHAMBERS, James, 5, Glasgow
3869 DOWIE, Elizabeth, 11, Glasgow
3870 FERGUSON, Fergus, 7, Edinburgh
3871 GALLACHER, Gladys, 13, Glasgow
3872 GRAHAM, Agnes, 10, Glasgow +
3873 GRAHAM, Elsie, 6, Glasgow
3874 MARSHALL, Doris, 12, Glasgow +

3875 MARSHALL, Gordon, 8, Glasgow
3876 NICOLL, William, 5, Portobello
3877 PATERSON, Jean, 12, Glasgow
3878 SMITH, Margaret, 14, Glasgow
3879 ANDERSON, George, 12, Edinburgh
3880 BALDRY, William, 9, Edinburgh +
3881 BALDRY, John, 11, Edinburgh
3883 BRUCE, Robert, 10, Edinburgh
3885 GORMLEY, Edward, 9, Edinburgh
3886 GRAY (Twins), Ian, 10, Edinburgh +
3887 GRAY, Kenneth, 10, Edinburgh +
3888 GRAY, Donald, 15, Edinburgh +
3889 GRAY, Alexander, 13, Edinburgh
3890 HILL, Alan, 12, Edinburgh
3891 McTERNAN, Thomas, 14, Edinburgh
3892 ADAM, Norman, 7, Glasgow
3893 DEANS, Robert, 9, Glasgow
3895 FLEMING, David, 13, Glasgow +
3896 FLEMING, Colin, 9, Glasgow
3897 HOPE, David, 14, Glasgow +
3898 HOPE, Gordon, 12, Glasgow
3899 McINTYRE, Hugh, 15, Glasgow
3900 McKENDRICK, Edward, 11, Glasgow
3901 NOLAN, Christopher, 8, Glasgow
3902 PATERSON, Robert, 7, Glasgow
3903 ROLLAND, William, 14, Glasgow
3904 STEWART, Gordon, 7, Glasgow +
3905 STEWART, Charles, 14, Glasgow
3906 ADAMS, Charles, 11, Glasgow +
3907 ADAMS, Robert, 10, Glasgow
3908 AIRD, William, 14, Glasgow
3909 CHAMBERS, Robert, 11, Glasgow
3910 CORING, William, 13, Glasgow
3911 CRAWFORD, William, 11, Glasgow
3912 DOUGLAS, John, 13, Glasgow
3913 KEATING, Charles, 10, Glasgow
3915 REILLY, Francis, 10, Glasgow
3916 WILLS, William, 14, Glasgow +
3917 WILLS, Hugh, 9, Glasgow
3918 WOTHERSPOON, Andrew, 9, Glasgow +
3919 WOTHERSPOON, John, 11, Glasgow
3920 PARK, James, 6, Glasgow
3924 McKELLAR, Lavinia, 13, Glasgow
3925 GRAHAM, John, 10, Glasgow
3926 McKECHNIE, Frank, 9, Glasgow
3927 WALLIS, Hector, 13, Glasgow
3929 YEOMAN, Bessie, 10, Glasgow
3930 ANGUS, Alastair, 5, Glasgow

3931 BROWN, Robert, 13, Glasgow
3932 BURNETT, Grace, 8, Glasgow
3933 EWINGTON, Crawford, 5, Glasgow
3934 FERGUSON, Jean, 12, Glasgow
3935 FERGUSON, Margaret, 9, Glasgow
3936 FRASER, John, 9, Glasgow
3937 GARDEN, Jean, 9, Glasgow
3938 GREENALL, Andrew, 10, Glasgow
3939 GUNN, John, 12, Glasgow
3940 HARRIS, Daniel, 9, Glasgow
3941 HOUSTON, Stanley, 11, Glasgow
3942 KING, Mollie, 12, Glasgow
3943 McGREGOR, Margaret, 12, Glasgow
3944 NEILL, Annie, 11, Glasgow
3946 PIRRIE, Ian, 15, Glasgow
3947 PRIEST, Josephine, 8, Glasgow
3948 DOCHERTY, John, 7, Glasgow
3949 PURCELL, Frances, 8, Glasgow
3950 ROSS, John, 5, Glasgow
3951 SMITH, Maurice, 11, Glasgow
3952 WHEELANS, Isabella, 6, Glasgow
3953 WHITEHOUSE, Mary, 9, Glasgow
3955 LAPPING, Henry, 10, Glasgow
3956 RENNIE, George, 10, Glasgow
3957 CLARK, Georgina, 14, Glasgow +
3958 CLARK, John, 13, Glasgow +
3959 CLARK, Margaret, 10, Glasgow
3963 McINTOSH, Isabella, 12, Glasgow +
3964 McINTOSH, Jessie, 10, Glasgow +
3965 McINTOSH, Marjory, 8, Glasgow
3966 MASKREY, Kathleen, 9, Glasgow +
3967 MASKREY, Arthur, ?, Glasgow
3968 SCOTT, Margaret, 13, Glasgow +
3969 SCOTT, Agnes, 12, Glasgow
3970 COCHRANE, Margaret, 13, Edinburgh
3971 FENHOULET, Raymond, 11, Edinburgh
5339 WILDE, Douglas, 9, Grantham +
5340 WILDE, Peter, 7, Grantham
5350 THOMAS, Arthur, 15, Finchley
6003 FENN, Elizabeth, 9, Maidstone
6004 BROCK, Christopher, 10, Wrexham +
6005 BROCK, Susan, 6, Wrexham

The CORB Children — New Zealand

2053 NEVILLE, George, 9, Durham
2054 FRANKLIN, Gordon, 13, Bishop Auckland
2055 LONG, Thomas, 13, W. Hartlepool
2056 LAVERTY, Joyce, 14, W. Hartlepool
2057 DENTON, Michael, 11, Romford +
2058 DENTON, Donald, 9, Romford
2063 RAGGETT, John, 12, Alresford +
2064 RAGGETT, Pauline, 11, Alresford
2066 TOWNS, Robert, 11, Brentwood +
2067 TOWNS, Peter, 14, Brentwood
2068 DAVIS, Arthur, 9, Chelmsford +
2069 DAVIS, Bryan, 13, Chelmsford
2070 JOHNS, Hazel, 14, Bristol +
2071 JOHNS, Howard, 10, Bristol
2072 BROWN, Beryl, 13, Colchester
2073 BURCH, Brian, 10, Colchester
2074 HEATH, James, 7, Colchester +
2075 HEATH, Jill, 12, Colchester
2076 DAY, Maureen, 6, Upminster
2077 SIMPSON, Bryan, 12, Newbury
2078 ASH, Rosemary, 7, Boscombe
2081 BULL, Donald, 8, Oldham
2082 MURRAY, Dennis, 12, Bingley
2086 LAYCOCK, Gwendoline, 15, Wakefield
2090 BRADLEY, Ada, 12, Wakefield
2091 SEYMOUR, John, 9, Cosham
2092 SEALEY, Robert, 7, Eastney +
2093 SEALEY, Michael, 6, Eastney
2094 WALDRON, John, 9, Cosham
2095 HESELTINE, Hilary, 13, Portsmouth
2096 CLARK, June, 13, Bristol
2097 BROWNE, Richard, 14, Bristol +
2098 BROWNE, Margaret, 10, Bristol
2099 JAKEMAN, Thomas, 11, Bristol +
2100 JAKEMAN, Margaret, 6, Bristol
2102 FINDLEY, Rex, 13, Bristol
2103 SALKELD, Oliver, 8, Bristol +
2104 SALKELD, Arthur, 10, Bristol +
2105 SALKELD, David, 11, Bristol +
2106 SALKELD, Margaret, 13, Bristol
2107 PORTER, Audrey, 12, Bristol +
2108 PORTER, James, 10, Bristol
2109 LINDSEY, Alan, 8, Welling
2111 HOBDAY, Gwendoline, 13, Ashford
2112 CUSHEON, Eileen, 13, Sidcup
2113 WHITEHORN, Muriel, 13, Orpington
2114 GROOM, Joyce, 14, Slade Green +
2115 GROOM, Rosalie, 11, Slade Green

2116 DAW, Ronald, 6, Welling
2117 HAZELL, Margaret, 14, Bexley +
2118 HAZELL, James, 13, Bexley +
2119 HAZELL, Anthony, 10, Bexley
2120 WRIGHT, Pamela, 6, Swanley
2121 STEPHENS, Mary, 15, Herne Bay
2122 OADES, Viola, 15, Herne Bay
2123 BOYNETT, Daphne, 15, Herne Bay
2124 EDWARDS, Tony, 7, Bexley Heath +
2126 EDWARDS, Doreen, 10, Bexley Heath
2128 ABRAHAMS, Alfred, 9, Sudbury
2131 SYMES, Derek, 6, SW8
2132 THEOBALD, Neville, 13, Putney
2133 LEONARD, Marjorie, 10, W. Moseley +
2134 LEONARD, Shirley, 7, W. Moseley
2135 DOUGLAS, Penelope, 8, Woodbridge +
2136 DOUGLAS, Dorothy, 5, Woodbridge
2137 CRAFER, Colin, 11, Roehampton
2140 KEALEY, Myrna, 5, West Twyford
2141 CLARK, Jean, 10, Greenford
2142 PILBEAM, Audrey, 11, Greenford +
2143 PILBEAM, Alan, 9, Greenford
2144 SMITH, Anthony, 13, Greenford
2145 HAMILTON, Brenda, 8, Greenford +
2146 HAMILTON, Irene, 11, Greenford +
2147 HAMILTON, Frank, 10, Greenford +
2148 HAMILTON, Jack, 12, Greenford
2149 HANNAH, Margaret, 15, W13
2150 WEST, Brian, 9, West Twyford
2151 ROCK, David, 13, Hurley-on-Thames
2152 JOHNSTON, Heather, 6, Harpenden
2155 TELFORD, Gordon, 11, Harrow
2158 EDWARDS, Ursula, 12, Hanwell +
2159 EDWARDS, Adrienne, 15, Hanwell +
2160 EDWARDS, Edith, 10, Hanwell
2161 LOWE, Derek, 13, Bedford Park
2162 GARDINER, Ronald, 11, Sutton
2163 CHITTY, John, 13, Camberley
2164 FIDDES, Vernon, 13, W. Moseley
2165 WALLIS, Peter, 13, Sutton
2166 TAYLOR, Elizabeth, 11, Cheam
2167 ATKINS, Eileen, 13, Walton-on-Thames
2170 CHASE, Edna, 10, Kingsbury
2171 PATON, Margaret, 11, Haslemere +
2172 PATON, John, 7, Haslemere
2470 ASPINALL (Twins), Joel, 14, Padiham +
2471 ASPINALL, Jean, 14, Padiham
2472 FOULKES, Arthur, 13, Stretford

2473 HORSFIELD, Frank, 12, Eccles +
2474 HORSFIELD, Arthur, 9, Eccles
2476 HOLT, Brenda, 9, Hale +
2477 HOLT, Graham, 12, Hale
2478 ROBB, Geraldine, 11, Manchester
2479 HASSALL, Gertrude, 12, Bolton
2482 BEVAN, Kenneth, 8, Southport
2483 PYE, John, 13, Burnley
2485 MILNE, Elizabeth, 10, Manchester +
2486 MILNE, Kenneth, 12, Manchester
2487 FAIRHURST, Joan, 14, St Helens +
2488 FAIRHURST, Bernard, 12, St Helens
2489 LLOYD, Georgina, 6, Warrington
2490 ASHURST, Joan, 12, Wigan
2491 HALLIWELL, Kenneth, 11, Wigan +
2492 HALLIWELL, Bryan, 9, Wigan
2563 ASHLEY, Robert, 11, Patcham
4001 BLACK, Grace, 9, Girvan +
4002 BLACK, Robert, 7, Girvan
4005 CROSS, John, 7, Glasgow
4006 DUNFORD, David, 6, Swindon
4007 LYONS, Allonay, 8, Glasgow
4008 MACKENZIE, Mary, 14, Edinburgh
4009 MALCOLM, Odette, 13, Glasgow
4010 RAE, Jamesine, 12, Glasgow
4011 SHAW, Agnes, 13, Glasgow
4013 STEWART, Davina, 12, Glasgow
   (See No. 4064)
4015 BURDER, Lilian, 13, Greenock +
4016 BURDER, Lorna, 5, Greenock +
4017 BURDER, Margaret, 11, Greenock +
4018 BURDER, Rose, 8, Greenock
4019 CARE, Maureen, 11, Cambuslang
4020 CLARK, William, 6, Motherwell
4022 DRYSDALE, Joyce, 12, Stranraer
4023 HUME, Roy, 6, Leith (See No. 4074)
4028 EMMETT, Marion, 15, Edinburgh
4029 FORBES, Margaret, 12, Edinburgh
4030 FRENCH, Adeline, 12, Edinburgh
   (See No. 4072)
4031 HENDRY, Margaret, 7, Edinburgh
4033 KILPATRICK, Hope, 13, Edinburgh
4034 PETRIE, Louisa, 13, Kirriemuir
4038 STEWART, Christina, 8, Edinburgh
   (See No. 4079)
4039 ANDREWS, John, 11, Hamilton
4040 BRUNTON, William, 12, Portobello
4041 CONNOR, Tom, 13, Shotto
4042 CRUICKSHANK, Michael, 11,
   Glasgow +
4043 CRUICKSHANK, Oliver, 12, Glasgow
4044 FELL, Terence, 13, Edinburgh +
4045 FELL, Donald, 11, Edinburgh
4046 FRAME, James, 11, Alloa
4047 GILMORE, William, 7, Edinburgh
4049 ROSS, Robert, 14, Hawick
4050 SOMMERVILLE, Alexander, 12,
   Coatbridge
4051 YULE, John, 12, Aberdeen +
4052 YULE, Robert, 11, Aberdeen
4053 BEAMS, Anthony, 12, Dudley +
4054 BEAMS, John, 13, Dudley +
4055 BEAMS, Peter, 10, Dudley
4056 BOURNE, David, 12, Aberdeen
4058 CHESNEY, William, 13, Glasgow
4059 CULVER, William, 10, Glasgow
4060 DICKSON, Roy, 14, Glasgow
4061 DUNFORD, Reginald, 11, Sheerness
   (See No. 4006)
4062 HUNTER, Robert, 13, Glasgow
4063 LIVINGSTONE, James, 13, Glasgow
4064 STEWART, Thomas, 10, Glasgow
4065 WARD, David, 9, Glasgow +
4066 WARD, James, 11, Glasgow
4067 ALLAN, Robert, 13, Edinburgh
4068 CAMERON, Violet, 11, Edinburgh
4070 FOOTE, Ronald, 14, Edinburgh
4071 FORBES, Donald, 11, Edinburgh
4072 FRENCH, Norman, 10, Edinburgh
4073 GRAHAM, Ian, 11, Leith
4074 HUME, Thomas, 12, Edinburgh
4075 IRONS, Albert, 10, Edinburgh
4076 KING, James, 14, Edinburgh
4077 MACLEOD, Angus, 14, Edinburgh
4078 SKILLING, Lawrence, 12, Edinburgh
4079 STEWART, Robert, 10, Edinburgh
4081 HOOPER, Betty, 13, Edinburgh
4083 ANDERSON, Robert, 11, Glasgow
4084 BLANCHARD, Margaret, 6, Glasgow
4085 HAIR, Marion, 13, Glasgow +
4086 HAIR, Norman, 11, Glasgow
4087 MITCHELL, Lillian, 12, Glasgow +
4088 MITCHELL, Robert, 8, Glasgow
4089 STUART, Kenneth, 14, Glasgow
4090 FRENCH, David, 10, Glasgow
4091 FORBES, Andrew, 15, Midlothian +
4092 FORBES, Edward, 12, Midlothian
4093 McDOUGALL, William, 14, Edinburgh

The CORB Children — New Zealand

4094 LIGHTBODY, Joan, 11, Edinburgh +
4095 LIGHTBODY, Elizabeth, 6, Edinburgh
4096 LAMONT, William, 6, Edinburgh
4097 WIMBERLEY, Marion, 12,
    Bridge of Allan
4098 STEELE, John, 13, Glasgow
4099 SWORD, James, 14, Glasgow
4101 YOUNG, Lillian, 8, Glasgow
4102 FARRELL, Patrick, 8, Edinburgh +

4103 FARRELL, Derek, 6, Edinburgh
4104 McNAUGHTON, Mary, 12, Edinburgh
4105 LAMB, Allan, 12, Edinburgh +
4106 LAMB, Warren, 5, Edinburgh
4107 PRINGLE, Alexander, 11, Edinburgh
4111 BIRRELL, Isabella, 14, Portobello
6000 ARCHER, Paul, ?, Worcester Park
    (Added when arrived in New Zealand
    with mother during the war)

The CORB Children — South Africa

2173 JOHNSON, John, 13, Gosforth
2176 SADLER, John, 13, Minehead
2177 COLVILLE, John, 13, Swansea
2178 SUTHERLAND, Alison, 8, Cardiff +
2179 SUTHERLAND, Douglas, 10, Cardiff
2180 LILES, Josephine, 11, Cardiff
2181 WILKINSON, Mary, 15, Folkestone
2182 BRAVERY, Ian, 10, Barry Island
2183 BROCKWELL, Patricia, 15, Wakefield
2184 HADFIELD, June, 15, Wakefield
2185 ROBINSON, Audrey, 12, Sheffield +
2186 ROBINSON, Margaret, 15, Sheffield
2187 FURNISS, Audrey, 12, Sheffield
2188 STEVENSON, Ernest, 10, Sheffield +
2189 STEVENSON, Barbara, 8, Sheffield +
2190 STEVENSON, Ronald, 6, Sheffield
2191 OWEN, Margaret, 15, Ossett
2192 LOBLEY, John, 14, Harrogate +
2193 LOBLEY, Henry, 7, Harrogate
2194 PRIESTLEY, Muriel, 12, Harrogate
2196 BORRIE (Twins), Jean, 11,
    Middlesborough +
2197 BORRIE, John, 11, Middlesborough
2198 PLACE, Joan, 10, Stamford Bridge
2199 HOPKINS, Joan, 15, Leamington Spa
2200 ASHDOWN, Pamela, 11, Reigate +
2201 ASHDOWN, Shirley, 13, Reigate
2202 ALEXANDER, Ronald, 13, Catford
2203 SMITH, Barbara, 8, Richmond +
2204 SMITH, Francis, 9, Richmond
2205 WOODVILLE, Stephen, 13, Kingston
2206 HILL, Margaret, 10, Hounslow +
2207 HILL, Peter, 13, Hounslow +
2208 HILL, Robert, 12, Hounslow
2209 PHILLIPS (Twins), Kenneth, 14,
    Isleworth +

2210 PHILLIPS, Robert, 14, Isleworth
2211 CARR, Greta, 15, Morpeth
2212 SHARMAN, William, 13, Gosforth
2213 TWYCROSS, Stephen, 7, Nottingham
2214 BUY, Edwin, 12, Henley-on-Thames
2215 BATES, Sydney, 12, Henley-on-Thames
2216 MARGETTS, John, 9, Oxford +
2217 MARGETTS, Ruth, 13, Oxford
2218 WILSON, Robin, 7, Oxshott
2219 GRAY, Peter, 8, Woodbridge +
2220 GRAY, Jeanne, 6, Woodbridge
2221 PERRETT, Maurice, 13, Rugby
2222 EVANS, Betty, 14, Birmingham +
2223 EVANS, Peter, 12, Birmingham
2224 RYAN, William, 7, Finchley
2227 CUTLER, Olive, 14, Woking
2228 LALE, Dennis, 11, Tolworth
2229 SMITH, Peter, 12, Coulsdon
2230 TURNER, Nellie, 13, Ewell +
2231 TURNER, Ian, 11, Ewell
2235 BOYCE, John, 11, Sutton
2237 CARD, Peter, 12, E. Molesey
2238 HUNTINGTON, Ian, 13, Coulsdon +
2239 HUNTINGTON, Derek, 15, Coulsdon
2240 FERGUSON, Margaret, 8, Coulsdon
2241 GOOLD, Margaret, 13, Epsom
2242 SINDEN, Janet, 14, Epsom
2243 COOK, Elizabeth, 15, New Malden
2244 REED, William, 13, Purley
2245 HUMPHREY, Kenneth, 13, Coulsdon
2248 BIRBECK, Mavis, 12, Coulsdon
2249 NICHOLLS, Elizabeth, 13, Coulsdon +
2250 NICHOLLS, Pamela, 15, Coulsdon
2251 HAGUE, Doreen, 15, Purley
2252 BOTTING, Keith, 12, Coulsdon
2254 WRIGHT, Brian, 13, Purley

2255 BOND, Martin, 11, Ewell
2257 EDWARDS, David, 11, Selsdon
2258 UWINS, Gordon, 12, Sanderstead +
2259 UWINS, Roy, 10, Sanderstead
2260 CHARITY, Anthony, 12, Wallington +
2261 CHARITY, Robert, 11, Wallington
2262 FINCH, Margaret, 14, Epsom
2263 WIMBUSH, Richard, 10, Abingdon +
2264 WIMBUSH, Gillian, 7, Abingdon
2265 ANDREW, Patricia, 14, Abingdon +
2266 ANDREW, Mary, 11, Abingdon +
2267 ANDREW, Margaret, 13, Abingdon
2268 BANKS, Arthur, 13, Crewe +
2269 BANKS, Olive, 11, Crewe
2270 KENNY, Maureen, 9, Manchester
2271 ROOME, John, 10, Wallasey
2275 INGRAM, Pamela, 10, Barking +
2276 INGRAM, Pearl, 13, Barking
2277 MURRAY, Margaret, 6, Hartlepool +
2278 MURRAY, David, 10, Hartlepool
2279 DRAPER, Erica, 6, Gosport
2280 ALLEN, Ian, 6, Portsmouth +
2281 ALLEN, Patricia, 10, Portsmouth
2282 BOND, Gordon, 9, Southsea +
2283 BOND, Eileen, 11, Southsea
2284 DRAPER, John, 10, Rogate
2286 SINDEN, William, 13, W. Hartlepool +
2287 SINDEN, Mildred, 9, W. Hartlepool +
2288 SINDEN, Stephen, 5, W. Hartlepool
2289 DAGGER, Gwendoline, 14, Bristol
2290 McGREGOR, Margaret, 14, Bristol
2291 SUTTON, John, 8, Bristol
2292 CONN, Michael, 12, Bristol
2293 DUNNING, Margaret, 15, Bristol +
2294 DUNNING, June, 14, Bristol
2295 BROOK-SMITH, Thelma, 14, Bristol
2296 COLLETT, Peter, 11, Bristol
2297 PENN, Ruth, 9, Bristol +
2298 PENN, Christopher, 6, Bristol
2299 SERNER, Paul, 12, Evesham
2300 STOCK, Terence, 8, Bristol +
2301 STOCK, Brian, 12, Bristol
2302 MURRAY, Alexander, 11, South Shields
2303 LEADBITTER, Stanley, 13, Sunderland
2304 DOUGHERTY, Arthur, 13, Sunderland
2305 TURNER, Barbara, 15, Maldon +
2306 TURNER, Elizabeth, 14, Maldon
2307 BULLEN, Diana, 12, Loughton +
2308 BULLEN, John, 9, Loughton

2309 CATCHLOVE, Peter, 7, Romford
2310 STIRLING, Bruce, 11, Brentwood +
2311 STIRLING, Ronald, 15, Brentwood
2316 HOAD, Evelyn, 9, Romford
2317 ALLIES, Valmai, 13, Braintree +
2318 ALLIES, Anthony, 11, Braintree
2322 DENNISON, Valerie, 10, Upminster +
2323 DENNISON, David, 5, Upminster
2324 REID, Shirley, 8, Harold Wood
2325 WASMUTH, Peggy, 9, Romford +
2326 WASMUTH, Jean, 7, Romford +
2327 WASMUTH, Frederick, 13, Romford
2328 HULME, Audrey, 9, Romford +
2329 HULME, Patricia, 11, Romford +
2330 HULME, Graham, 6, Romford
2331 WEAL, Stanley, 12, Hornchurch
2332 HALL, Beryl, 15, Brentwood +
2333 HALL (Twins), Jean, 12, Brentwood +
2334 HALL, Pamela, 12, Brentwood
2336 RICHARDSON, Alicon, 10, Brentwood +
2337 RICHARDSON, Mary, 15, Brentwood
2340 SMITH, Barbara, 6, Lincoln +
2341 SMITH, Pamela, 12, Lincoln
2342 SUTTON, Richard, 6, Chiswick +
2343 SUTTON, Geoffrey, 11, Chiswick
2344 GROSE-HODGE, John, 12, Bedford +
2345 GROSE-HODGE, Peter, 10, Bedford
2347 TURNER, John, 9, NW6
2348 BOTTOMLEY, Aileen, 9, Edgeware +
2349 BOTTOMLEY, Barbara, 8, Edgeware
2351 BROOME, Kathleen, 13, Edgeware +
2352 BROOME, Betty, 12, Edgeware +
2353 BROOME, Peter, 5, Edgeware
2354 TRICKEY, Ruth, 12, Burnt Oak
2355 LAMBERT, Alan, 13, Potters Bar
2356 SANGSTER, Frank, 13, Southgate
2357 WHITE, Janet, 8, S. Harrow
2358 CROWFOOT, Brenda, 9, Harrow Weald
2359 MURGATROYD, Norman, 9, Hillingdon
2360 INSKIP, Beryl, 13, Palmers Green
2361 HUCK, Donald, 12, Bedfont, Middlesex
2362 DUVAL, Alan, 10, Hayes +
2363 DUVAL, Malcolm, 9, Hayes
2366 HEDGECOCK, Alec, 10, Southgate
2367 ELDRIDGE, Josephine, 13, Southgate +
2368 ELDRIDGE, Kenneth, 11, Southgate +
2369 ELDRIDGE, Peter, 6, Southgate
2370 MORLEY, Michael, 8, W. Horsley
2371 POTTER, Derek, 10, Potters Bar

2372 LINDSAY, Kenneth, 13, Southall
2373 McGOVERN, William, 10, Ruislip
2374 FIELDING, Richard, 13, Twickenham
2375 FRANKLIN, Doreen, 14, Ruislip
2376 WILKINSON, Edward, 11,
    Lytham St Anne's
2377 CARTER, Amy, 15, Barrow-in-Furness
2378 KERFOOT, John, 13, Chorley
2379 WRIGHT, John, 10, Coalville
2380 DEVEREUX, Eunice, 11, Beaconsfield
2381 DONKIN, Ann, 7, Slough
2382 EDLEY, Evelyn, 14, Landbeach +
2383 EDLEY, Emily, 9, Landbeach
2384 REAY, Dorothy, 14, Wisbech
2386 ROBERTSON, Joan, 5, Cambridge
2387 WEBSTER, Eleanor, 14, Carlisle
2388 SMITH, William, 14, Carlisle +
2389 SMITH, Barbara, 11, Carlisle
2390 ARNOTT, Lilian, 10, Carlisle
2394 DONOGHUE, Derek, 6, Trowbridge +
2395 DONOGHUE, Jean, 15, Trowbridge
2396 PACKMAN, Jillena, 7, Parkstone +
2397 PACKMAN, Jean, 10, Parkstone
2398 BERESFORD, Rosemary, 6,
    Leominster +
2399 BERESFORD, Diana, 9, Leominster +
2400 BERESFORD, David, 8, Leominster
2401 VERDON, Hilary, 12, Mickleover +
2402 VERDON, Dennis, 8, Mickleover
2403 GODFREY, Barbara, 12, Ilkeston
2404 JEPSON, Gerald, 13, Derby
2405 EVANS, John, 10, Duffield
2406 MITCHELL, Frederick, 12,
    Little Eaton +
2407 MITCHELL, Arthur, 10, Little Eaton
2408 AUSTIN, Arthur, 15, Bromley +
2409 AUSTIN, James, 13, Bromley
2410 SAMPSON, Graham, 12, Bromley
2411 RENDELL, Eric, 13, Hayes
2412 HULL, Sheila, 14, Bromley +
2413 HULL, James, 9, Bromley
2414 SCOTT-BROWN, Helen, 7, Bromley
2415 SEMPLE, Kenneth, 11, Northwood +
2416 SEMPLE, William, 13, Northwood
2419 HALTON, Dorothy, 14, Wigan
2420 KING, Anna, 15, Blackburn
2421 MATHER, Katherine, 15, Chorley +
2422 MATHER, Margaret, 12, Chorley
2423 SWINTON, Peter, 13, Liverpool

2424 LESHNICK, Catherine, 13, Manchester
2428 HOLMES, Richard, 11, St Albans
2429 CAMERON, Frances, 13, Dartford +
2430 CAMERON, Patricia, 9, Dartford
2431 NEWING, Patricia, 5, Bristol +
2432 NEWING, Valerie, 10, Bristol
2433 KNEALE, Joan, 13, Liverpool +
2434 KNEALE, Patricia, 6, Liverpool
2435 WILDER, Iris, 9, Sidcup +
2436 WILDER, June, 11, Sidcup +
2437 WILDER, Violet, 13, Sidcup
2438 MEDWAY, Gerald, 13, Sidcup
2439 ELSON, Michael, 6, Sidcup
2440 CLIFTON, Alan, 11, Peckham
2441 CUTLAND, Evelyn, 13, Bromley
2442 CARPENTER, Peter, 13, Orpington +
2443 CARPENTER, Bernard, 11, Orpington
2444 SOER, Francis, 13, Welling
2445 MARTIN, Yvonne, 12,
    Tunbridge Wells +
2446 MARTIN, Anthony, 13, Tunbridge Wells
2449 **BANYARD, Margaret, 11, Beckenham**
2450 FENWICK, Owen, 13, Faversham +
2451 FENWICK, John, 10, Faversham +
2452 FENWICK, Nigel, 6, Faversham
2453 MACLEAN, Ailsa, 13, SE19 +
2454 MACLEAN, Iona, 12, SE19 +
2455 MACLEAN, Jura, 7, SE19
2457 KIRKBY, Diana, 8, Hereford +
2458 KIRKBY, Ruth, 11, Hereford
2459 SMITH, Kathleen, 11, Andover
2462 MOORE, James, 10, Kidderminster +
2463 MOORE, Robert, 7, Kidderminster
2465 PELLOW, Edward, 13, Eastleigh
2466 INGE, Sheila, 14, Eastleigh
2467 SMITH, Mary, 10, Southampton +
2468 SMITH, David, 6, Southampton
2493 FINNIGAN, Kathleen, 13, W12
2494 LINCH, Michael, 13, S21
2495 PARKER, Rhoda, 14, Reading +
2496 PARKER, Michael, 11, Reading
2497 KNIGHT, Arthur, 13, Rosyth
2498 SINGLETON, Ann, 6, Stockport
2499 BESWETHERICK, John, 14, Putney
2502 THIEL, Sheila, 14, Colchester
2503 MARSH, Alan, 15, Birkenhead
2504 MALLOWS, Dennis, 14, Chelmsford +
2505 MALLOWS, Colin, 9, Chelmsford
2506 DAVIES, Margery, 13, Chelmsford

2507 DAVIES, Megan, 12, Loughton +
2508 DAVIES, Gwenda, 11, Loughton
2509 HARRIS, Patience, 12, Chelmsford
2510 GRAHAM, Jean, 9, Chelmsford +
2511 GRAHAM, Christopher, 6, Chelmsford +
2512 GRAHAM, Anthony, 15, Chelmsford
2513 LAMB, Audrey, 14, Wigan
2514 BLACKBURN, Ivan, 14, Colne
2515 RYDER, Mervyn, 10, Liverpool +
2516 RYDER, Rosemary, 12, Liverpool
2517 MAWDSLEY, Irene, 13, Liverpool +
2518 MAWDSLEY, George, 10, Liverpool +
2519 MAWDSLEY, William, 8, Liverpool
2520 KEMP, Jacqueline, 5, Manchester +
2521 KEMP, John, 7, Manchester
2522 HAZELL, Olive, 14, Warrington
2524 LORD, Peter, 14, NW9 +
2525 LORD, Jean, 12, NW9 +
2526 LORD, John, 11, NW9
2527 PEARCE, Joan, 12, Hounslow +
2528 PEARCE, Jean, 13, Hounslow
2529 TUCKER, Alan, 14, Hounslow
2530 ROWE, Shirley, 10, N11
2531 TILBURY, Alan, 14, Banstead
2532 IRELAND, Anthony, 14, Wallington
2533 GOODWIN, Warren, 14, Wallington
2534 WADE, John, 14, Sanderstead
2535 WARBURTON, Alan, 14, Walton-on-Thames
2536 COOK, Peter, 14, Ewell
2537 LYNE, Barbara, 11, Keighley
2538 HOLT, Gladys, 14, Gateshead
2539 HUTCHINSON, John, 14, Leeds
2540 MATTHEWS, Derek, 14, Bradford
2541 FIELD, Richard, 11, Bradford +
2542 FIELD, Peter, 13, Bradford
2543 BARCHI, Peter, 11, Bradford
2544 GIBSON, John, 11, Halifax +
2545 GIBSON, Olwyn, 14, Halifax
2546 RICHARDS, John, 13, Huddersfield
2547 JONES, Donald, 13, Leeds
2548 SMITH, Audrey, 12, Leeds
2549 DONOVAN, Desmond, 13, Leeds
2844 MACKEITH, Donald, 11, Aldershot +
2845 MACKEITH, Marian, 14, Aldershot +
2846 MACKEITH, Robert, 7, Aldershot
2847 BAYLIE, Ernest, 14, Warlingham
2902 VERSTRAETEN, Marinus, 14,
    (Netherlands Red Cross)
2903 KENNEDY, Elizabeth, 15, W2

4112 BROWNING, John, 15, Ayr
4113 GRAY, William, 13, Kilmarnock
4114 HOSSACK, George, 13, Lanark
4115 LITTLEJOHN, Alexander, 15, Hamilton
4116 McLEAN, John, 14, Falkirk
4119 BALFOUR, Thomas, 14, Edinburgh +
4120 BALFOUR, Robert, 11, Edinburgh +
4121 BALFOUR, George, 8, Edinburgh
4122 CLARKE, Drew, 8, Edinburgh (See No. 4148)
4123 DEGNAN, Felix, 10, WC1
4124 DICKSON, William, 15, Edinburgh
4125 GOODALL, Alexander, 11, Auchinloch +
4126 GOODALL, Ian, 12, Auchinloch (See No. 4137)
4128 McARTHUR, Colin, 9, Edinburgh
4129 McPHILLIPS, Alex, 8, Edinburgh +
4130 McPHILLIPS, Alfred, 9, Edinburgh
    (See Nos. 4153 & 4154)
4131 TATTERSALL, Robert, 13, Edinburgh
4132 WATT, Allan, 8, Edinburgh +
4133 WATT, Leslie, 14, Edinburgh
4135 BUCHANAN, Alma, 10, Coatbridge
4136 CUNNINGHAM, Isabelle, 12, Billshill
4137 GOODALL, Sheena, 5, Auchinloch
4138 HOSSACK, Kathleen, 15, Lanark (See No. 4114)
4139 NEILSON, Alexandra, 12, Airdrie
4143 SPENCE, Moira, 10, Ayr +
4144 SPENCE, John, 6, Ayr
4145 ALLAN, Eileen, 13, Edinburgh
4146 BLANE, Marjory, 12, Larbert
4147 CAMPBELL, May, 9, Edinburgh
4148 CLARKE, Fay, 8, Edinburgh
4149 DUNN, Dorothy, 10, Oban
4150 FRASER, Agnes, 15, Glasgow +
4151 FRASER, Christine, 8, Glasgow
4152 LAWSON, Jean, 14, Edinburgh
4153 McPHILLIPS, Mary, 5, Edinburgh +
4154 McPHILLIPS, Pamela, 7, Edinburgh
4155 MAITLAND, Barbara, 13, Larbert
4156 MOIR, Helen, 13, Leith
4157 LEVER, Anthony, ?, ?
4158 YOUNG, Donald, 13, Lanarks
4159 SMITH, Ian, 13, Leith
4160 DOBBIE, Margaret, 14, Rothesay
4161 McNEILL, John, 14, Leith
4162 TURNER, Kenneth, 14, Edinburgh
4163 SELLAR, ?, 13, E. Lothian
6001 McADAM, Jill, 8, Hong Kong
    (Added to CORB list during later war years) +
6002 McADAM, Sheila, 4, Ditto